The SCM

A–Z of Origen

Other books in The SCM Press A–Z series

The SCM Press A–Z of Evangelical Theology
The SCM Press A–Z of Patristic Theology
The SCM Press A–Z of Roman Catholicism

THE SCM PRESS A–Z OF
CHRISTIAN THEOLOGY

The SCM Press
A–Z of Origen

Edited by

JOHN ANTHONY McGUCKIN

scm press

First published in the United States in 2004 by Westminster John Knox
Press, Louisville, Kentucky

Published in 2006 by SCM Press
9–17 St Alban's Place,
London N1 0NX

www.scm-canterburypress.co.uk

British Library Cataloguing in Publication data

A catalogue record for this book is available
from the British Library

0 334 04103 1 /978 0 334 04103 0

Printed and bound in Great Britain by
William Clowes Ltd, Beccles, Suffolk

Contents

Series Introduction

The SCM Press A–Z of Christian Theology series provides a set of resources for the study of historic and contemporary theological movements and Christian theologians. These books are intended to assist scholars and students find concise and accurate treatments of important theological terms. The entries for the handbooks are arranged in alphabetical format to provide easy access to each term. The works are written by scholars with special expertise in these fields.

We hope this series will be of great help as readers explore the riches of Christian theology as it has been expressed in the past and as it will be formulated in the future.

The Publisher

Preface

The essence of Origen is hard to capture. The present *SCM Press A–Z*, it is hoped, will go some way to giving an accurate and detailed picture of a theologian whom Jerome once described as clearly the most important Christian thinker since the generation of the apostles. He is difficult to synopsize, partly because, like many great and seminal thinkers, he changed his mind over details as he progressed, and partly because the canvas on which he painted was so breathtakingly large in scale. Not for Origen the small interests of institutional church life (in so voluminous a body of work we find very little information about such day-to-day matters); we discover rather a grand passion to tell the epic tale of God's first creation (long before the earth was made), when all rational life was gathered in harmony around the Divine Logos (the source of all reasonable intelligence) to comprise the chorus of superangelic spirits; and thence the long story of the decline from primeval bliss to the condition of embodied souls lamenting their separation from God (and one another) in the sorrows of this "vale of tears." Origen was stunned by the high dignity and awesome destiny of even the most humble person he met, for each and every soul on earth was, for him, once a great and preexistent spirit who had (only recently in God's time) fallen into cosmic sorrow because of their lapse from contempla-

tion (see **Fall**). In all the twists and turns of his telling the great tale, the kerygma of the divine salvation of the cosmos, Origen never lost sight of the one single thread that holds it all together: the restless and unswerving love of a God who is determined to bring back the cosmos to the unity of the circle of love that was its original conception and reality.

Origen's life and scholarly obsessions made him, in many instances, a fussy and text-obsessed thinker. He was, after all, the Christian church's first and greatest biblical scholar. He had his magnifying glass poised over every detail of a word's semantic freight, and would not let his reader go until the last detail had been logged and noted. Such was not a training that could normally be expected to flower into the great psychic and poetic panoramas that are clearly his soul's inner vision. But then again, he was far more than a librarian-scholiast; he was also the Christian church's first great mystic, describing the divine Word's quest for the soul through the recesses of time and space, and the soul's fearful search for its lost Lord, in terms drawn from the Song of Songs, where the bride seeks her beloved in the starlit garden. Behind Origen's scholarly and disciplined exterior, there always beat the heart of a poet.

Thomas Merton put his finger on it when he tried to describe Origen's life,

ix

character, and impact in his poem "Origen." "His sin was to speak first among mutes," he said, describing Origen's effect on later ages as akin to that of a "mad lighthouse," emitting incessant pulses of illumination, setting a compass point for the whole West.

In his own lifetime Origen had many passionate defenders, students, and patrons (see *Disciples of Origen*) as well as many hostile critics. No age of the church has seemed to be different in this regard. His influence over monastic asceticism was so powerful three centuries after his death that it brought down on his head a posthumous condemnation, for all the agitation he had caused in the deserts of Egypt and Palestine (see *Origenist Crises*). This would have more or less finished the career of any other theologian. But despite the devastation of the textual tradition of his works, Origen's manuscripts were still copied and circulated (like samizdat literature), and he always kept a body of Christian admirers who were themselves powerful voices in the formation of Christian theology in their own generations.

The modern era saw a remarkable revival of Origenian studies, beginning with Huetius, the bishop of Avranches, who brought out the first scholarly edition of the works in 1688, to be followed later in the mid-eighteenth century by two Benedictines, Charles De La Rue and Charles Vincent De La Rue (uncle and nephew), who brought out the edition that was the basis of Migne's widely circulated *Patrologia Graeca* text of the nineteenth century. Some of the most extensive and dedicated work of scholarship on Origen has been the product of the last half century, beginning with the learned Jesuits Bertrand, Daniélou, De Lubac, and the most indefatigable of them all, Henri Crouzel. The availability of the best critical editions of Origen's works has also steadily progressed, not least in the series of *Sources Chrétiennes*. And in the aftermath of that has come the modern English translations of an increasing number of his works, for a new popular readership.

Several significant patristic theologians of the latter part of the twentieth century have been attracted to Origen (with varying degrees of sympathy), not least R. P. C. Hanson, who was one of the first (with De Lubac) to bring back to center stage the significance of scriptural exegesis for a modern understanding of Origen. The contemporary scholarly disciples of Origen are readily recognized (at least to one another) as the international, albeit sporadic, community that gathers for the four-yearly Origen colloquia, whose papers are published in the *Origeniana* series. "Origenists" they may not all be, but their scholarly enthusiasm has proved them to be "Origenians" in the best sense. Many of them are represented as authors in this present book, and it has been a privilege to work with them in the construction of a volume of reference designed for English-speaking students. They are some of the brightest minds in the world of early church scholarship today. The extent and range of the scholarly work represented by the *Origeniana* series suggest that Origen's influence is far from waning more than seventeen hundred years after his death. The present *SCM Press A–Z* will, it is hoped, take Origen studies into a new dimension among those who approach his work with fresh eyes, as they first come into contact with him through their seminary or university courses. Much of the commonly available picture of Origen has been dependent on inaccurate and outworn reference works; so Westminster John Knox Press is to be warmly congratulated in having had the imagination and foresight to commission such a book as this. Donald McKim, in particular, has been an enthusiastic supporter of the scheme from the very outset.

The book could have been far more detailed than it is, but then it would have been much larger too, and doubtless more expensive. It has been designed to provide the best services of a modestly sized encyclopedia (hence the A–Z registry) as well as to offer a generic introduction (hence the initial chapters of the life of Origen and a short annotated list of his works).

A reader can use the book in two different ways. If a controversy or issue is referred to in general theological sources, a ready reference can be made, in the alphabetical lists, to see here what Origen had to say on the subject. More times than one can tell, his reflection on an issue was massively influential on the later course of Christian theology (although in the West, after the sixth century, Augustine's influence came to predominate). If, however, a reader wants to begin with a general overview of Origen's importance and continue reading to see what Origen's systematic theology amounted to, the A–Z entries will provide a carefully detailed set of synoptic essays that will provide just that. Each essay includes cross-references to other closely related topics in the A–Z registry. If the reader wishes a comprehensive study of Origen's thought, however, I would suggest that a program of study could be drawn up in the following way.

Begin with the introductory chapters on the life and works and then read selectively as follows:

1. *Origen's Metaphysical Foundations*
   A. God, Christology, Logos, Holy Spirit, Trinitarianism, Epinoiai, Providence.
   B. Cosmology, Anthropology, Preexistence, Image of God, Souls, The Fall, Atonement, Divinization, Resurrection, Angels, Demonology, Apokatastasis, Hades, Eschatology, Universalism.
2. *Origen's Theological Foundations*
   A. Scripture, Old Testament, Gospels, Apostles, John the Theologian, Paul the Apostle, Scriptural Interpretation, Allegory, Anagogical Interpretation, Typology, Apocrypha, Hexapla.
   B. Law, Sacraments, Eucharist, Baptism, Faith, Rule of Faith, Tradition, Church, Transfiguration, Glory.
3. *Origen on Ethical and Spiritual Life*
   Repentance, Grace, Number Symbolism, Asceticism, Mysteries, Contemplation, Light, Love, Mystical Thought, Martyrdom, Transfiguration, Glory, Mary, Preaching, Priesthood, Virtue, Worship.
4. *Origen and Philosophy*
   Philosophy, School of Alexandria, School of Caesarea, Gnostics, Law of Nature, Miracles, Clement of Alexandria, Philo of Alexandria, Celsus.
5. *Historical and Controversial Matters*
   Origenist Crises, Roman Empire, Bishops, Disciples of Origen, Judaism, Image-Making, Heresy, Heracleon, Transmigration of Souls.

For each of the entries, notes at the foot of the text will allow a cross-reference to the bibliography that will, in turn, provide the next steps for more detailed personal research. The bibliography is a select one, comprising those works (predominantly in the English language) that the various scholars have referred to in the course of writing their entries. At the end of it, however, there is a short note suggesting next steps in where to take one's reading. The whole business is contagious. Origen had a motto that he taught to his students as the guide to their whole intellectual (and psychic) lives: *Hopou Logos agei*, which translates as "Go wherever the Divine Wisdom leads you." Studying Origen, and being led more and more deeply into his speculations on God and the cosmos, is a highly infectious thing. If you get as far as the further study recommendations in the final bibliography, you are very much in danger of becoming a modern-day Origenian yourself. But, then again—*Hopou Logos agei*.

John A. McGuckin

Contributors

Stamenka Emilova Antonova
Research Scholar
Columbia University
Department of Religion
New York, New York
[*Mysteries, Providence*]

Paul M. Blowers
Emmanuel School of Religion
Johnson City, Tennessee
[*Rule of Faith, School of Caesarea*]

Pamela Bright
Concordia University
Department of Religion
Montreal, Quebec
[*Priesthood*]

Brian E. Daley, S.J.
University of Notre Dame
Department of Theology
Notre Dame, Indiana
[*Eschatology, Resurrection*]

Elizabeth M. Harding
Research Scholar
Union Theological Seminary
New York, New York
[*Origenist Crises*]

Ronald E. Heine
Puget Sound Christian College
Edmonds, Washington
[*Epinoiai, God, Heracleon*]

Hannah Hunt
Research Scholar
University of Leeds
Department of Theology
Leeds, England
[*Love, Repentance, Sacraments*]

Charles Kannengiesser
Concordia University
Department of Religion
Montreal, Quebec
[*Christology*]

Julia Konstantinovsky
Research Scholar
Oriel College
Oxford, England
[*Prayer, Worship*]

Lillian Larsen
Research Scholar
Columbia University
Department of Religion
New York, New York
[*Disciples of Origen, Virtue*]

Elizabeth Dively Lauro
Loyola Marymount University
Department of Religion
Los Angeles, California
[*Fall, Preexistence, Universalism*]

Fred Ledegang
Research Scholar
Vroomshoop, The Netherlands
[*Apostles, Baptism, Eucharist*]

Johan Leemans
Faculty of Theology
Department of Church History
    and Theology
University of Louvain, Belgium
[*Angels, Miracles*]

John Woodrow McCree
Research Scholar
Union Theological Seminary
New York, New York
[*Glory*]

John Anthony McGuckin, Editor
Department of Religion, Columbia
    University
Department of Church History, Union
    Theological Seminary
New York, New York
[*Preface, Life of Origen, Works of Origen,
    Image of God*]

Neil McLynn
Faculty of Law
Keio University
Yokohama, Japan
[*Bishops, Roman Empire*]

Christoph Markschies
Wissenschaftlich-Theologisches
    Seminar
Kisselgasse 1
Heidelberg, Germany
[*Gnostics, Paul the Apostle,
    Trinitarianism*]

Peter Martens
Research Scholar
Scottsdale, Arizona
[*Divinization, Holy Spirit*]

Frederick W. Norris
Emmanuel School of Religion
Johnson City, Tennessee
[*Apokatastasis*]

Richard Norris
Professor of Church History Emeritus
Union Theological Seminary
New York, New York
[*Heresy, School of Alexandria, Typology*]

John J. O'Keefe
Creighton University
Department of Theology
Omaha, Nebraska
[*Allegory, Anagogical Interpretation,
    Apocrypha, Scriptural Interpretation*]

Joseph S. O'Leary
Sophia University
Department of English Literature
Tokyo, Japan
[*Atonement, Grace, Judaism, Logos*]

Alan G. Paddle
Research Scholar
Union Theological Seminary
New York, New York
[*Contemplation, Faith, Mystical Thought,
    Tradition*]

Ken Parry
Department of Ancient History
Macquarie University
Sydney, Australia
[*Image-Making*]

Jeffrey Pettis
Research Scholar
Union Theological Seminary
New York, New York
[*John the Theologian, Light, Number
    Symbolism, Transfiguration*]

Riemer Roukema
University of Strasbourg
Strasbourg, France
[*Law of Nature, Souls, Transmigration
    of Souls*]

David T. Runia
Queens College
Parkville, Australia
[*Philo of Alexandria, Philosophy*]

William G. Rusch
Research Scholar
Faith and Order Commission
National Council of the Churches
    of Christ in the U.S.A.
New York, New York
[*Church, Mary, Preaching*]

Jason M. Scarborough
Research Scholar
Union Theological Seminary
New York, New York
[*Hades*]

Thomas P. Scheck
Research Scholar
Iowa City, Iowa
[*Law*]

Mark Sheridan, O.S.B.
Dean of the Faculty of Theology
Pontifical Athenaeum of San Anselmo
Rome, Italy
[*Old Testament, Scripture*]

Stephen Colquitt Thomas
Fomerly Senior Lecturer in Theology
Christ Church College
Canterbury, England
[*Anthropology, Celsus*]

Fiona Thompson
Trinity and All Saints College
Horsforth, Leeds, England
[*Cosmology, Demonology*]

Frederick W. Weidmann
Department of Education
Riverside Church
New York, New York
[*Gospels, Hexapla, Martyrdom*]

Vincent L. Wimbush
Department of Biblical Studies
Union Theological Seminary
New York, New York
[*Asceticism*]

Abbreviations

THE WORKS OF ORIGEN

1. Origen's Homilies

Homilies on Genesis	HomGn
Homilies on Exodus	HomEx
Homilies on Leviticus	HomLev
Homilies on Numbers	HomNum
Homilies on Joshua	HomJos
Homilies on Judges	HomJd
Homilies on 1 Kings (1 Samuel)	Hom1R (1S)
Homilies on the Psalms	HomPs
Homilies on the Canticle of Canticles	HomCt
Homilies on Isaiah	HomIs
Homilies on Jeremiah	HomJr
Homilies on Ezekiel	HomEz
Homilies on Luke	HomLc
Fragments of the Lukan Homilies	FragmHomLc
Homilies on 1st Corinthians	Hom1Co
Homilies on 2nd Corinthians	Hom2Co

2. Origen's Commentaries, Fragments, Scholia, Excerpta and Selecta on the Old Testament Canon

Commentary on Genesis	ComGn
Selecta on Genesis	SelGn
Commentary on Numbers	ComNum
Commentary on the Psalms	ComPs
Scholia on the Psalms	ScPs
Selecta on the Psalms	SelPs
Fragments on the Psalms	FragmPs
Commentary on Proverbs	ComPr
Commentary on the Canticle of Canticles	ComCt
Commentary on Isaiah	ComIs
Fragments of the Commentary on Isaiah	FragmComIs
Commentary on Ezekiel	ComEz
Selecta on Ezekiel	SelEz

3. Origen's Commentaries and Fragments on the New Testament Canon

Commentary on Matthew	ComMt
Series of Commentaries on Matthew	SerMt
Fragments on Matthew	FragmMt
Commentary on Luke	ComLc
Fragments on Luke	FragmLc
Commentary on John	ComJn
Fragments on John	FragmJn
Fragments of the John Commentary	FragmComJn
Commentary on Romans	ComRm
Fragments on 1 Corinthians	Fragm1Co
Commentary on Galatians	ComGa
Commentary on Ephesians	ComEp
Fragments from the Commentary on Ephesians	FragmComEp
Commentary on Titus	ComTt
Commentary on Philemon	ComPhm
Commentary on Hebrews	ComHe
Fragments on 2nd Epistle of John	Fragm2Jn

4. Treatises and Other Works

Peri archon (De principiis)	PArch
Fragments of the Peri archon	FragmPArch
Exhortation to Martyrdom	ExhMart
On Prayer (Peri Euches)	PEuch
Against Celsus (Contra Celsum)	CCels
The Hexapla	Hexapla
Miscellanies (Stromateis)	Strom
Dialogue with Heracleides	DialHer
On the Resurrection	Resur
The Philocalia	Philoc
Letter to Gregory	EpistGreg
Letter to Julius Africanus	EpistAfr
Autobiographical Letter	EpistAut
Treatise concerning the Demons	DeDaim
That the King Is the Only Creator	KgCreat
On Pascha	PPasch

GENERAL ABBREVIATIONS

ACW   Ancient Christian Writers. U.S. edition, Westminster, Md.: Newman Press. U.K. edition, London: Longman & Green

AER   American Ecclesiastical Review

ANCL   Ante Nicene Christian Library, 25 vols. Edited by A. Roberts and J. Donaldson. Edinburgh: T. & T. Clark, 1864–97

ANF   Ante-Nicene Fathers. Translations of the writings of the Fathers down to A.D. 325. Reprint, Grand Rapids: Eerdmans, 1978–79

AThR   Anglican Theological Review

BETL   Bibliotheca ephemeridum theologicarum lovaniensium

BLE   Bulletin de littérature ecclésiastique

BP   Biblioteca patristica. Firenze

CCL   Corpus Christianorum Latinorum

CH   Church History

CR   Clergy Review

Crouzel   Origen. Translated by A.S. Worrall. Edinburgh: T. & T. Clark, 1989. E.T. of the original French edition of 1985

CWS   Classics of Western Spirituality. (Ramsey) New York, and Toronto: Paulist Press

DCB   Dictionary of Christian Biography. 4 vols. Edited by W. Smith and H. Wace (John Murray). London: 1877–87

DOP   Dumbarton Oaks Papers

EG   Erkenntnis und Glaube

EP   Ekklesiastikos Pharos (Theological Review of the Patriarchate of Alexandria)

E.T.   English translation

ETL   Ephemerides theologicae lovanienses

EvQ   Evangelical Quarterly

FC   Fathers of the Church. Washington

GCS   Die griechischen christlichen Schriftsteller. Berlin

GOTR   Greek Orthodox Theological Review

GTT   Gereformeerd theologisch tijdschrift

H.E.   Historia ecclesiastica (Church history)

HTR   Harvard Theological Review

IKaZ   Internationale katholische Zeitschrift

IPA   Institutum Patristicum Augustinianum. Rome.

JAC   Jahrbuch für Antike und Christentum

JECS   Journal of Early Christian Studies

JEH   Journal of Ecclesiastical History

JSL   Journal of Sacred Literature

JTS   Journal of Theological Studies

LXX   Septuagintal text of the Old Testament

MTZ   Münchener theologische Zeitschrift

NPNF   A Select Library of the Nicene and Post-Nicene Fathers of the Christian Church. 1st and 2nd Series. Edinburgh: T. & T. Clark, and Grand Rapids: Eerdmans

N.S.	New Series	*RSR*	*Recherches de science religieuse*
PBR	*Patristic and Byzantine Review*	SC	Sources chrétiennes
PG	Patrologiae cursus completus. Series graeca. Edited by J. P. Migne. Paris	SCH	Studies in Church History
		SecCent	*Second Century*
		SJT	*Scottish Journal of Theology*
PL	Patrologiae cursus completus. Series latina. Edited by J. P. Migne. Paris	SPM	Studia patristica mediolanensia
		StPatr	Studia patristica
POC	Proche-Orient Chrétien	*TD*	*Theology Digest*
Praef.	Preface (*of an ancient work, often substantial in length—usually listed separately from book 1 and referred to by its internal paragraph sections*)	*TS*	*Theological Studies*
		TSK	*Theologische Studien und Kritiken*
		TU	Texte und Untersuchungen
		U(NRM)	Update: New Religious Movements
ProEccl	*Pro ecclesia*	*USQR*	*Union Seminary Quarterly Review*
RAC	*Reallexicon für Antike und Christentum*	*UUC*	*Unitarian Universalist Christian*
RBI	*Revue biblique internationale*	*VC*	*Vigiliae christianae*
RCCM	*Rivista di cultura classica e medievale*	*VetC*	*Vetera Christianorum.* Bari
		ZAC	*Zeitschrift für Antikes Christentum*
REG	*Revue des études grecques*		
RHPR	*Revue d'histoire et de philosophie religieuses*	*ZKT*	*Zeitschrift für katholische Theologie*
RHT	*Revue d'histoire des textes*		
RSPT	*Revue des sciences philosophiques et théologiques*		

The Life of Origen
(ca. 186–255)

SOURCES

Origen's fame in the Christian world, already notable in his own lifetime, ensured that his personal history was relatively well charted in antiquity, even if the nature of the sources for that life have brought some degree of confusion into the interpretation, or rather the sequencing, of some of the events.[1] His own writings provide important information, though (as usual with ancient authors) far fewer details than one would like to have. Other major sources are a *Letter of Thanksgiving* or *Panegyric* dedicated to Origen by Theodore, one of his students at the School of Caesarea, whom Eusebius the church historian tells us later became a great luminary in the Cappadocian church, none other than Gregory Thaumaturgus.[2] The *Panegyric* gives us priceless information about Origen the scholar and about the curriculum he offered at what was (more or less) the first Christian university, his own foundation and mind-child.[3] The single most important secondary source is that of the fourth-century church historian Eusebius, who dedicated to Origen the large part of the sixth book of his *Ecclesiastical History*.[4] Eusebius demands close attention, even when one disagrees with him, for he was himself (as bishop of Caesarea) the successor of his teacher Pamphilus, one of the

---

1. Cf. Nautin (1977), who made an extensive source-redactional study of the materials and has a healthy (and justified) suspicion of Eusebius's ability, in his *Church History,* to have synthesized correctly all the disparate sources he used for constructing a life of Origen. Not all of Nautin's theories have gained the same degree of hearing among scholars, but he successfully demonstrated the difficulty of taking all the literary evidence "straightforwardly," and this certainly accounts for modern divergences on the details of the sequencing of Origen's *Vita.* There is a clear and cogent presentation of all the historical data collated from all the ancient sources in Crouzel (*Origen,* E.T., Edinburgh, 1989), though the latter proceeds so confidently in his chronological narrative only by virtue of having dismissed many of the source-critical problems (2).

2. So named from the tradition of his many miraculous wonders performed in the course of his preaching ministry. He was a spiritual guide for Basil the Great's grandmother and was highly influential in the shaping of Cappadocian patristic theology (which itself took Origen's work to a wider international audience through the *Philokalia of Origen* collated by Basil and Gregory Nazianzen).

3. Cf. McGuckin (1992a).

4. Henceforth *H.E.*

most dedicated Origen-disciples of his age. As Pamphilus's protégé, Eusebius was the keeper of the library archives at the Caesarean church. So it was that he had unrivaled access to Origen's own books and to notes of his correspondences[5] that are now otherwise lost. Eusebius constructed his small *Life of Origen* from his own readings of the primary text, as well as from a now fragmented treatise composed by his own teacher.

While in prison for his faith, Pamphilus had written a robust defense for his theological hero entitled *Apology for Origen.*[6] Eusebius was his research assistant in the writing of it and so had an early familiarity with the "Origen archives" of the great library he would soon come to direct. In the *Apology* Pamphilus not only explained aspects of the teaching of Origen, but also collated materials designed to offset hostile criticism. He had access to the complete text of an important letter Origen wrote to defend himself against episcopal charges of irregularity soon after he had moved to Caesarea. This otherwise lost text, known as the *Autobiographical Letter,*[7] is embedded now throughout the text of Eusebius, unrecoverable, of course, except through the redactional use made of it in turn by both Pamphilus and Eusebius—both of whom have urgent reason to defend Origen from any charge of unorthodoxy, because in so doing they were also defending their own reputations as church leaders and theologians. Other lists of Origen's writings[8] or notes about his life can be found in various ancient historians and litterateurs, such as Jerome and Rufinus, who both preserved sections of his partly autobiographical *Letter to Friends in Alexandria;*[9] Socrates Scholasticus,[10] a later church historian; the highly unreliable Epiphanius of Salamis;[11] and the late but very important witness, the learned ninth-century patriarch of Constantinople, Photius. The latter is of interest to the historian for his preservation of otherwise lost original sources that he could read from Eusebius and Pamphilus. Photius was head of a scholarly book reader's circle of close friends and published his notes on the various books they studied. This work, entitled *Bibliotheca* (The Library), has a chapter (118) that concerns Origen and his writings.

CHILDHOOD AND YOUTH IN ALEXANDRIA

Eusebius tells us that Origen was "not yet quite seventeen"[12] when the persecution by Emperor Septimius Severus broke out against the church, falling with particular severity in Egypt. Given that this happened in 202, Origen's date of birth can be deduced as 185/186. He was born at Alexandria, then the great center of Hellenistic learning, at the

---

5. Eusebius tells us (*H.E.* 6.36) he had collected more than 100 letters of Origen, now all dispersed.

6. Text in Migne, PG 17.521–616.

7. Cf. Eusebius, *H.E.* 6.19.12–14. This is possibly the same as the letter Origen wrote to Pope Pontianus of Rome to defend himself against charges (by Demetrios of Alexandria) of irregularity of ordination and unorthodoxy in doctrine. It is mentioned by Jerome in *Ep.* 84.9, "To Pammachius and Oceanus."

8. Some now lost, not only because of the ravages of time, but also because there was a concerted campaign to burn his books, especially after his posthumous condemnation by church authorities in the fifth and sixth centuries (see **Origenist Crises**).

9. Rufinus, *De adulteratione librorum Origenis,* 8 (text ed. by M. Simonetti, *Corpus Christianorum* 20.7–17); Jerome, *Apologia contra Rufinum* 2.18–19; also Letters 33 and 84.

10. Socrates, *H.E.* 5.

11. *Panarion* (*Medicine Chest against All Heresies*) c. 64.

12. Eusebius, *H.E.* 6.2.12.

mouth of the Nile in Egypt. It was a city with deep and ancient traditions of philosophy, literary criticism,[13] and speculative theology. At the time of Origen's youth, Clement had served as a noted Christian professor, possibly even a member of the clergy of Alexandria. Origen's father, Leonides, was active as a literary professor in the city and known as a Christian. His very name (a thoroughly Egyptian populist one, derived from the Greek for "Child of Horus")[14] suggests he was the child of a mixed marriage between one of the *honestiores* and a woman from the class of *humiliores*.[15] At that period not everyone in the empire had the right to citizenship, and children of such mixed-class marriages were excluded from the political rights and privileges of their fathers. More significantly, Origen's ability in later life to attend, with impunity, the executions of his disciples who had been delated for their profession of Christianity,[16] to encourage them to persevere to the end, despite the fury of the crowd this raised against him, is an indication that he did not have citizenship rights—for the persecution of Severus was directed solely against citizens who had adopted the Christian religion.[17]

Origen's father, Leonides, a marked man, was first imprisoned, then beheaded.[18] The impact on his family was devastating financially as well as emotionally, for the whole patrimony of those executed was confiscated to the treasury. As Origen was the eldest of seven sons,[19] the support of the family fell onto his shoulders. His first instinct had been to run to join his father in prison and profess his faith, but he was prevented by his mother.[20] Despite his eagerness for the honor of martyrdom, he was denied it by the very law that put his students of the higher classes to death. Even at the end, the witness of martyrdom would elude him. He would be severely tortured in his old age but would also outlive the persecutor Decius; so he was technically a confessor but not a martyr.

The posthumous lack of the title, more than anything else, left his reputation vulnerable to revisionists of later centuries. Eusebius gives the information that Origen died, "having completed seventy years less one,"[21] about the time that Gallus became

---

13. The Great Library was located there where were elaborated the principles of literary exegesis that mark all of Origen's later work; cf. McGuckin (2002).

14. Horus was the child of the goddess Isis by Osiris. The Isis movement was the most powerful of the pagan religions of Egypt in Origen's time.

15. Cf. A. Rousselle, "The Persecution of the Christians at Alexandria in the 3rd century," *Revue historique de Droit français et étranger* 2 (1974):222–51, esp. 231–33. Origen's mother, according to Jerome (*Epist.* 39.22), was either a Jewess or a Christian. He tells us that she taught the young child to recite the psalms from an early age.

16. Eusebius, *H.E.* 6.3.4–5; 6.4.6–5.

17. The *Historia Augusta* (Severus, 17.1) says that this persecution was aimed at those who proselytized for Christianity. Crouzel (*Origen* [1989], 5) takes it as an indication that Leonides might have been an important figure in the catechetical school of the church (into which office Origen seems to have been later inducted). It might be so, but suppositions about the episcopal school of catechesis in Alexandria often elide the important difference between a schola belonging to a private didaskalos-philosopher (such as Origen was) and a teacher of catechesis under the direction of the bishop (as Origen also seems to have been for some time). That Origen was not simply a catechist under Demetrios, but a powerful and famous Didaskalos in his own right, is the source of all the friction between them.

18. Leonides's execution by beheading denotes his class rank.

19. Eusebius, *H.E.* 6.2.12.

20. Eusebius gives the story that she hid all his clothes to stop him volunteering himself for arrest.

21. Eusebius, *H.E.* 7.1.

emperor after Decius's assassination. The two details conflict historically,[22] and preference ought to be given[23] to Eusebius's note of his sixty-ninth year, which reflects local knowledge, whereas the reference to the reign of Gallus is more of a retrospective projection and, like many other dates in Eusebius, relatively loose.[24] So, if Origen was born in 186, he died in the reign of the ill-fated Valerian, in 255, a victim of the anti-Christian persecutions begun under the emperor Decius. His life spans one of the most important periods for the development of the Christian church—both intellectually and organizationally. In almost everything he set his hand to, both as an intellectual and as a church leader, Origen was to be an important trendsetter for generations to come, and this accounts for the enthusiasm as well as the hostility his name commanded in later generations.

Eusebius's account in the *Ecclesiastical History* already characterizes him hagiographically as a saint, marked out by God from his earliest years as a prodigy of grace and intellect. We are told (something of a standard element of such ancient lives of the sophists) that his learned father could hardly answer the biblical questions his young son put to him in the course of his education. A childhood story that Origen must himself have treasured in memory of his father is that often, when he was asleep, Leonides would kiss him on the heart. Eusebius transmutes this tender memory of a murdered father into an awesome testimony from a martyr that here, in Origen, was a veritable and elect tabernacle of the Holy Spirit, whose gifts would soon radiate out to the church.[25]

ECCLESIASTICAL DUTIES AS A CATECHIST

When he was eighteen[26] Origen was appointed to the task of giving catechetical direction for the Alexandrian church. This should not be understood to mean, as it often has been, that he assumed the mantle of Clement of Alexandria as head of some prestigious and official school of theology; rather that he was given care of the preparation for catechumens. Clement was most likely an independent professional philosopher. Origen is basically being inducted by the bishop into the lower orders of the paid ministers of the church, a fitting "relief effort" for the destitute family of a martyr. His private teaching tasks coincided to a certain degree with his church work, because he probably continued in his father's profession as Grammaticus, teaching private pupils, as well as instructing catechumens. But it is premature to envisage Origen at this early stage as heading an official episcopal school of theology. Eusebius gives sufficient information to indicate that Origen fulfilled his church duties courageously in difficult times. Meanwhile he extended his private school and turned more and more to the self-designation of a Rhetor-Philosopher, rather than a Grammaticus. He adopted the characteristic simple style and behavior of the Sophist. Eusebius describes this[27] in a way that highlights its Christian ascetical character, and it became an iconic picture of the sleepless student of the sacred Scriptures who embraced poverty, celibacy, and the disciplines of prayer and fasting, in such a way that it more or less co-opted Origen into the role of founding father of the monks, who were becoming more and more a feature of life in the fourth-century church when Eusebius was writing.

---

22. Making a divergence of two years in the chronology that Eusebius himself has set up for the reader. It is an internal conflict that is by no means uncommon throughout Eusebius's history.
23. As Crouzel notes (*Origen* [1989], 2).
24. Gallus was overthrown in May 253, having ruled for less than two years.
25. Eusebius, *H.E.* 6.2.11.
26. Eusebius, *H.E.* 6.3.3.
27. Eusebius, *H.E.*

Probably sometime in his early twenties, Origen sold his father's grammarian's library[28] for a small pension that allowed him to study philosophy—a sign that already he had found wealthy patrons who were willing to help him in his career.[29] One of these was Ambrose, an adherent of Valentinian gnostic Christianity, who became a lifelong supporter of Origen's work in Alexandria and Caesarea, both commissioning new works (such as the *Treatise on Prayer* and the *Commentary on John*) and supplying stenographers to make multiple copies as Origen discoursed. Another of his unknown supporters was the wealthy woman who took the young Origen into her household as a scholar. She was a *patrona* also of a famous gnostic theologian from Antioch[30] who used her household as a base for his lectures and was highly successful as a teacher in Alexandria. Eusebius is at pains to tell his fourth-century readers that while Origen studied in the same house, he never once "prayed in common" with a gnostic.[31]

ORIGEN'S DEVELOPMENT AS A PHILOSOPHER-DIDASKALOS

So, while Origen served the bishop in some sense as a literate catechist, he was already laying the foundations to develop himself in the career of a philosopher-rhetorician. The way in which he designed his philosophy as fundamentally a religious speculation was to make those twin career tracks come into conflict soon enough. While he was studying at the schools of Alexandria, his own teachers included the famous Platonist Ammonius Saccas, who was also (a few years later) the teacher of Plotinus. The latter, twenty years Origen's junior, is regarded as the founder of the Neoplatonist school. This influential movement of thought marked a new epoch of forging a very close association of the philosophic and religious quests. Origen himself, though technically more of an eclectic in his own philosophic tradition[32] and having close relations with the Middle Platonists whom Ammonius had introduced to him, can also lay claim to having at the heart of his life's work the weaving together of the philosophic and mystical imperatives. Even the conflict between the Plotinian school and the Christian heirs of Origen[33] is a sign of how close were the agendas between the leading Hellenist and Christian intellectuals of the day.

---

28. The one part of the patrimony that seems not to have been confiscated by the state after Leonides' execution; cf. Eusebius, *H.E.* 6.2.13.

29. The amount of money he received (four obols) was less than the regular wage of a poor laborer. It signals, I think, not his inability to command a good price, but his determination to live in voluntary poverty, under the dole of a *patronus* or *patrona.*

30. Paul of Antioch, a teacher of whom nothing else is known. He is typical of the independent Christian Didaskalos of Alexandria in the third century, who attracted the hostility of the Alexandrian bishops, then rising in their power and their control over the whole Christian affairs of the city.

31. Eusebius, *H.E.* 6.2.13–14.

32. He is technically a Christian Middle Platonist, much influenced by Plato, Numenius, Albinus, and others. But equally marked on him is the influence of Aristotle and Pythagoras. Into the rich soup of this kind of eclecticism we cannot forget that he was driven, perhaps above all else, by his close reading of the Scriptures and his faithful adherence to the ecclesial tradition mediated to him in his time, not only through prior theological patterns, but through the liturgy and through his belief in the ongoing inspiration of the preacher/teacher in the church assembly; cf. McGuckin (1985).

33. Porphyry, the leading disciple of Plotinus, attacked Origen for betraying the Neoplatonist cause by his "Christianizing" agenda (cf. *H.E.* 6.19.4–8); much to the outrage of Eusebius. In this passage Eusebius seems to confuse Ammonius Saccas with Ammonius of Thmuis, a Christian author whose works he knows.

Eusebius's statement that Origen had been taught by Clement of Alexandria[34] is probably a later retrospective, dependent on Eusebius's (misguided) presumption that the catechetical school of third-century Alexandria was like that of Caesarea in the fourth. Origen himself shows no signs of having had the Christian philosopher Clement as his personal teacher, though he does apparently refer to Clement's ideas on a few occasions, as much to correct him as to follow him.[35]

His associate in Christian teaching at that time, and possibly also an assistant in his own house-school for philosophy, was Heraclas, brother of his pupil Plutarch, who had recently been martyred.[36] Heraclas was an avid disciple of the Alexandrian philosophers. He was to be ordained a priest at Alexandria and eventually become bishop. In later years when Demetrios of Alexandria was prosecuting him for irregular ordination, Origen ruefully pointed to the manner in which Heraclas still wore the cloak of a philosopher, even as an Alexandrian priest, and wondered why he alone seemed to draw fire because of his philosophical work.[37]

Eusebius tells his readers that the young philosopher lived a most ascetic life, fasting, abstaining from wine, and choosing to live in simple poverty.[38] He also reports that Origen at this time took an extreme step to ensure his reputation and respectability as a private instructor of young men and women. He allegedly attended a doctor and paid to be castrated. Eusebius explains this away as evidence of his immaturity, because he had taken the words of Jesus in Matthew 19:12 (speaking of being a eunuch for the kingdom) in a literal way. Eusebius commends him for his zeal, if not for his wisdom. The *Ecclesiastical History* features the story as the fundamental explanation (along with the implied attribution of personal jealousy) of why Bishop Demetrios of Alexandria wanted to prosecute Origen so doggedly, at the episcopal courts in Rome, as well as in Palestine and in his own diocese of Egypt. Eusebius tells his readers that Demetrios was told of the castration by Origen in secret and approved of it; but Demetrios later publicized it, when he had fallen out with Origen, and used it to attack the validity of his ordination. The story is hardly credible. We have no indication that the motive of castration for respectability was ever regarded as standard by a teacher of mixed-gender classes. Women disciples (of whom Eusebius knows and is sufficiently surprised to list some of them) in Alexandria in Origen's day would certainly have been members of the higher class and would naturally have had several attendants. More to the point, when Origen turns his attention to Matthew 19:12,[39] he himself derides the literalist interpretation of the eunuch, saying it was something only an idiot would consider. His tone suggests quite clearly that he regards the idea as offensive, and Origen's text ought always to be preferred as a historical source over and above Eusebius.

---

34. Eusebius, *H.E.* 6.6.

35. In the *Commentary on Matthew* 14.2. Origen refers to the exegesis of Matthew 18:19–20 that Clement offers in his *Stromateis* 3.10 68.1. (See *Clement of Alexandria*.)

36. Eusebius, *H.E.* 6.3.2; 6.15.

37. Eusebius, *H.E.* 6. 19.12–14.

38. Eusebius, *H.E.* 6.3.9–13. While this is a picture drawn by Eusebius to relate Origen of the third century to the ascetics of the late fourth century for whom he was writing, there is no reason to doubt the accuracy of his remarks. The asceticism he speaks of was commonly seen to be a charism of the philosophic life—Sophrosyne—the sobriety and simplicity that demonstrate the willingness of the teacher to live out the implications of their doctrine. Origen, though not a monk, was in fact influential on the developing patterns of Christian monasticism. (See *Asceticism*.)

39. *ComMt* 15.1–5.

Origen's interest in celibate living, then, did not come to him from Matthew 19:12 but from his preference for Paul (1 Cor. 7:5–9). Like Paul, Origen's celibacy was a directing of his energies dramatically into the service of the Word. Castration from infancy (often practiced in antiquity) was a very different matter from medical castration in maturity. Origen's indefatigable energy and productive drive as a scholar and his physical strength, witnessed in his heroic resistance to several political oppressions, all belie the story of his medical castration. Several patently false stories about Origen—not least the tale that he had offered incense to the gods in time of persecution—were put out about Origen in later times. Such slanders were designed to damage a reputation that was growing, alarmingly so, for many hierarchs of the fourth century. Epiphanius is a prime example of such a gatherer (and creator) of dubious tales in his *Panarion*.[40] If the tale of his offering incense was put out to offset his disciples' claims for his stature as a veritable martyr-theologian, the tale of the castration seems to have been designed by friends of Origen[41] to distract from other reasons why Demetrios the bishop of Alexandria might have wanted to prosecute him in ecclesiastical courts. Those who argue in favor of the tradition of castration have generally not seen through the apologetic agenda in Pamphilus's and Eusebius's Origen stories.[42]

Eusebius, it has been argued, had access to the accusatory letters of Demetrios, where he attacked Origen's ordination as irregular. This is possible, though of course it is also a dubious kind of argument from silence. Though it was certainly the case that Demetrios claimed the ordination for the presbyterate at Caesarea to be irregular, I shall shortly argue that his grounds for objection were not canonical issues of "regular procedure" but actual charges of heterodoxy. By making the issue of Demetrios's objections turn on the issue of whether a eunuch was fit for ordination, Eusebius touches a nerve that would resonate with the monks of his own era. Only recently the Council of Nicaea had made eunuchism a disqualification from orders, with an exception for those who had suffered in persecutions. Any ascetic of the fourth century would have been annoyed by Demetrios's prosecution of such an ascetic confessor, for such a reason, and this is exactly the textual intent of Eusebius, who prioritizes this story. For such reasons, I think that the famous castration story, though much beloved by generations of theology students, is historically a smokescreen of Pamphilus's own invention, canonized by Eusebius.

As Origen in his early twenties turned more and more away from the identity of a Grammarian to that of a Rhetor-Philosopher, it is understandable that he seems to have passed on his duties in church catechism at Alexandria to his younger colleague Heraclas,[43] while he himself began to redraw himself as a master of philosophy—that is, "Our Philosophy," a term which had come to be increasingly used by Christian intellectuals to signify the entire Christian way of life. In emerging as a Christian Professor (Didaskalos), however, he began his collision course with the official church leader, Bishop Demetrios. Demetrios was one of the most energetic church administrators of the third century, and one responsible for elevating the episcopal office into a new institutional primacy. It was not merely an aspect of his personality but also

---

40. *Panarion* c. 64.

41. Probably Pamphilus.

42. Crouzel's argument (1989, 9, n. 32) that Origen writes with an apparent firsthand knowledge of the physiological problems of a eunuch, is entirely explicable by the fact that he is borrowing at such instances from the medical treatise of Galen. Already in the nineteenth century, D. Boehringer (*Kirkengeschichte* [Zurich, 1869] 28) saw through the tale. It has become increasingly suspect in modern historiography.

43. Later to become the successor of Demetrios as archbishop of Alexandria.

shows the pastoral instincts of one who was determined to keep the church under a tight rule through one of the most bitter and bloody persecutions that had ever fallen on a Christian congregation. Up until his day the presbyters of the Alexandrian church seem to have elected one of their number to represent them; after the time of Demetrios the strict separation of presbyteral and episcopal identities is enforced. Origen thus appears as a Didaskalos in the straightforward Hellenistic manner of the schools. Nothing remarkable here, but when this was transferred to a Christian environment, he appeared to revivify an antique Christian argument, for in the previous generation individual Christian teachers at Rome and Alexandria had set up private schools and speculated in a quasi-independent manner from their local church officers, causing much conflict—what has come down to the modern era as the so-called gnostic controversy.[44] The first sign of Origen's new identity as Didaskalos was his traveling to other schools. The second would be his publications, when he first emerged beyond the private select circle of advanced students. He began to compose his first large-scale work, a treatise on *First Principles*. This was a new birth for systematic theology conceived in the manner of an organized manual of philosophic instruction. It demonstrates one of Origen's basic principles, that the pursuit of reason (Logos) is a divine task. The footsteps of the Creator are left abundantly in the cosmos and in the mental capacities of humans; the professor is the high priest of Christian mysteries. It was a far-reaching and ambitious project, the event that, when it was released, provoked the gathering storm to break. In the meantime, however, we are able to see a small record of his travels.

TRAVELS ABROAD AND ORIGEN'S GROWING FAME

Eusebius tells us[45] that Origen visited Rome at the time Zephyrinus was pope.[46] The reason, he suggests, was "to see the most ancient church of the Romans," though we might add a less hagiographical motivation, to see and be seen by leading Sophists of the age. Alexandria, Antioch, and Rome were the three major centers of philosophy in his day. This visit is generally attributed to the year 212. One of the lecture rooms he attended at that time was that of the Logos theologian Hippolytus, who, as Jerome reports,[47] drew the attention of his audience to the distinguished presence of Origen among them.

Other visits, according to Eusebius's chronology of events, took place in this same period and also bear witness to his growing international fame as a teacher. According to Eusebius,[48] the Roman governor of Arabia sent letters to the prefect of Egypt[49] asking him to send on Origen, accompanied by official bodyguards,[50] so that he could hear more of the Christian movement from one of its leading intellectuals. That this military escort was other than an arrest puts the occasion in the reign

---

44. The notion of the independent Didaskalos was denounced by Irenaeus in his anti-gnostic propaganda, for such teachers were customarily free from hierarchical control and often departed radically from what Irenaeus called the "Rule of faith," that is, the simple apostolic tradition as it had hitherto been received in the churches.

45. Eusebius, *H.E.* 6.14.10.

46. Pope between 198 and 217.

47. *De viris illustribus* 61.

48. Eusebius, *H.E.* 6.19.15.

49. As well as courtesy letters to Bishop Demetrios, he says. One wonders if the latter detail is added in by Eusebius for the sake of fourth-century ecclesiastic formalities.

50. Thus at state expense as part of an official cultural exchange delegation.

of Antoninus (Caracalla) rather than Septimius Severus. Eusebius tells his readers that Origen made the trip and quickly returned to Alexandria, just in time to be present for a major riot that determined him to go back east, to Palestine, for his own safety.

The "war breaking out in the city" that Eusebius refers to in this context is probably that of the autumn and winter of 215–16, when Caracalla made a state visit to Alexandria. Infuriated by the student political mockery of him,[51] he ordered his troops to ravage the city, execute the imperial governor, kill protesters, and exile the faculty who were teaching in the schools. If the Caracalla riot took place "some time after"[52] the official visit to Arabia, we can tentatively place the latter in 213. It was a visit to Jordan that must have introduced Origen to the holy places at Jerusalem, where a learned theologian, Alexander, was prominent in the hierarchy and as bishop of the city was soon to become one of Origen's most important sponsors. He found the ecclesiastical environment very pleasant. Alexander had not only studied at Alexandria but was also bent on a project to make the church library of his city a focal point of learning.[53] It was an idea that also gripped Origen,[54] and many of his travels far and wide— to Nicopolis of Actium[55] (a city in the Epirus), to Rome, Athens, and throughout Palestine—were in part motivated by the need to collect books, ancient and new. His eventual transfer to the permanent staff of the church at Caesarea is synonymous with the church of that city establishing its own library archive, with Origen presiding over it as collector-archivist, priest and professor. This work of book collecting was begun in Alexandria in his time there but substantially translated to Caesarea and energetically developed there.

ORIGEN'S INCREASING ALIENATION
FROM THE ALEXANDRIAN CHURCH

If Origen fled from Alexandria after the rough treatment of academics in 216, therefore, it was a natural choice to return to Palestine, where we presume he had already gathered some detailed knowledge of the church, in the course of his visit to the adjacent province of Arabia. In fact the two leading hierarchs of the Palestinian church, Theoctist of Caesarea and Alexander of Jerusalem,[56] soon became his admirers. According to Eusebius's chronology, after the Caracalla riot of 216, Origen decided to take time away from Alexandria and went directly to Palestine. There the bishops asked Origen to give discourses in their respective churches. The distinction between a discourse on the interpretation of the Scriptures and a preached homily in church was a very fine one. Tradition had restricted scriptural interpretation in the churches to the ordained clergy, the bishop himself, or one of his chosen presbyters. To have invited Origen to discourse was a novel thing but not wholly unexpected, given his international stature. It infuriated Demetrios, however, and eventually he sent deacons from the Alexandrian church, carrying letters to the Palestinian hierarchs, demanding the immediate return of "his" theologian, or at least his catechist. He

---

51. They touched a nerve by referring to him as Geticus, that is, emperor by virtue of having murdered his own brother Geta.

52. Eusebius, *H.E.* 6.19.16.

53. Eusebius, *H.E.* 6.20.1.

54. Cf. McGuckin (1992, 2002).

55. Cf. Eusebius *H.E.* 6.16.1–3.

56. Eusebius, *H.E.* 6.27 Another leading hierarch, Firmilian of Cappadocia, was also Origen's staunch defender (*H.E.* 6.26–27).

criticized their uncanonical behavior in allowing a layman to preach at all.[57] It drew
from them a reply that in turn criticized his evident hostility toward a famous man:
"Where one finds a person capable of doing good for the brotherhood they have been
invited by the holy bishops to address the people."[58] It is one of the public manifesta-
tions of the growing tension between Origen and his local bishop. The implied censure composed by the Palestinian bishops is that Demetrios is not open to Origen's
great importance as a theologian who is far more significant than one who holds
merely the status of a basic catechist. To put it in official terms, they were implicitly
criticizing Demetrios for not advancing Origen to the office of presbyter. What
Demetrios's real objections were has not survived in the written record. We can presume, however, that they were more than the niceties of canonical practice and concerned the kind of theological speculation and biblical exegesis that Origen was
advancing. Clement of Alexandria, well before Origen's time, had reason to lament
the anti-intellectualism of the early Alexandrian Christian community. The rise of
Logos theology in the third century and the great flowering of allegorical exegesis
which advanced that rise were, of course, two of the most distinctive marks of the
career of Origen as a thinker; and it might well be that Demetrios had reason to be profoundly suspicious of Origen's claim that Logos theology marked out the future of the
Christian kerygma, just as much as the Roman bishops suspected and resisted the rise
of the Logos school in Rome, as can be evidenced in the career of Hippolytus and his
conflict with the popes of his day.

Origen obeyed Demetrios's summons, and returned to Alexandria. He came home
with two prizes, the first being the highly favorable impression he had made on the
Palestinian church, which clearly wanted him for its own and would soon become his
permanent refuge; the other was an antique scroll he had purchased in Jericho. It was
an ancient text of the Scriptures that he "found in a jar,"[59] and which he added to his
list of versions for the great six-column edition of the Bible he was preparing, known
as the *Hexapla*. It sounds suspiciously like an early exemplar of what was later to
become famous in the twentieth century as the Qumran finds.

While Origen was studying philosophy at Alexandria, he was also advancing his
studies of the Scriptures with leading thinkers. His profound knowledge of the (Septuagint) text of the Old Testament is all the more remarkable when one realizes that
he lived in an age that predated concordances and computer-generated word searches.
He had an encyclopedic grasp in his later years that could come only from assiduous
and constant reading over the course of many decades. His knowledge of the New
Testament betrays a deep preference for Paul and the Gospel of John, but all the literature had been closely studied by him. He was, however, one of the earliest and greatest of the church's Pauline theologians. Paul was more than a mere systematist of the
Christian tradition, as far as Origen was concerned; he was especially that theologian
carried off in rapture to the third heaven,[60] whose special revelation afforded him
a mystical insight into the mystery of Jesus that often escaped the other disciples,
with the exception of the great apostle John. Time after time the source of Origen's

---

57. "It has never been heard of and never happens even in this day that the unordained
should preach in the presence of bishops" (Eusebius, *H.E.* 6.19.16–19).

58. Eusebius, *H.E.* 6.19.18. The canonical letter of Theoctist and Alexander was probably sent
to the Roman Pope Pontianus, to whom Demetrios had appealed to support his censure of
Origen. Their text consistently refers to Demetrios in the third person, even though Eusebius in
his text says it was addressed to Demetrios (*H.E.* 6.19.17).

59. Eusebius, *H.E.* 6.16.3.

60. Cf. 2 Cor. 12:2.

particularly nuanced biblical interpretations of the Old Testament text can be explained on the basis of the Pauline or Johannine text through which he is reading the old narratives.

Origen referred at this time to one of his other influential professors; a note in his *First Principles* mentions a teacher from Alexandria whom Origen calls his "Hebrew master."[61] His personal knowledge of the Hebrew language is affirmed by Eusebius, though denied by most modern scholars, who see no evidence for it in his works.[62] The claim to have had a Hebrew master can probably be best explained as a reference to a teacher who influenced him greatly in describing to him the intricacies of Hebrew semantics in relation to the exegesis of the text, a form of rabbinic word-mysticism that was parallel to the great interest Hellenist text interpreters had in etymologies as keys to the mystical meanings of sacred texts. Origen's Hebrew master seems to have been Judeo-Christian, for the interpretation he gave of the seraphic cry of "Holy, holy, holy" in Isaiah 6:3 is very much in line with early Christian Trinitarian tradition.

In this second decade of the third century, therefore, Origen's studies took him along wide and creative paths. He took as his motto the axiom *"Hopou Logos agei—* Follow wherever Holy Reason leads." He was already growing in fame as a teacher of philosophy and was known to the major intellectual communities of Alexandria— the Christian gnostics, the episcopally-led Catholic community, the Jewish and Hellenistic text interpreters, the private teachers of philosophy and rhetoric. Eusebius suggests that it was at this time that his name came to the ears of Julia Mammaea,[63] the mother of Emperor Alexander Severus, "a most pious woman if there ever was one," according to Eusebius.[64] Julia sent for him to take part in debates on religious themes in Antioch. The visit was under state subsidy and undoubtedly would have provided Origen with a generous payment in gold in its aftermath. It explains his ability to buy books for his library project for years afterward. The empress also seems to have invited other theologians from Alexandria, including some Valentinian gnostic thinkers. If this took place while he was in Alexandria, it falls in the period 222–31. There are reasons, however, to suspect it could have been a visit made soon after his relocation to Caesarea, a visit to Antioch which might be the same as the one where Origen complains[65] that he engaged in disputations with "a certain heretic" who also contradicted him in a disputation in Ephesus on another occasion. We shall touch on this aspect in a moment. If this is the case, the date of the Antioch (and Ephesus) visit ought to be postponed to between 231 and 235.

---

61. Princ. 1.3.4 (*Hebraeus magister*); idem, 4.3.14 (*Hebraeus doctor*).

62. Much of his knowledge of the Hebrew text, apart from specific etymologies for which he seems to have consulted when he was interested, could well have derived from the hyperliteral Greek translation of the Hebrew text provided by Aquila, which Origen set as one of the columns of the hexapla version he edited of the Scripture and its various renditions. When Origen was resident in Palestine, he consulted on several occasions with famous rabbis. He tells us in the preface to his *Commentary on the Psalms* that some of his ideas came from a consultation with the rabbinic patriarch Ioullos. Talmudic texts also have Origen in discussion with the Caesarean Jewish scholar Hoschaia Rabba. For more information see Halperin (1981), Kimelman (1980), De Lange (1976), McGuckin (1989, 1992b).

63. Eusebius, *H.E.* 6.21.3–4.

64. Hippolytus also dedicated a treatise *On the Resurrection* to her. After the fall of the dynasty, she suffered a political "damnatio memoriae." In the Athens archaeological museum a bronze statue of her face, smashed in implosively with a heavy hammer, is a stark reminder of the cataclysmic fall of the young emperor, her son.

65. In his *Letter to Friends in Alexandria.*

At Alexandria the growing fame of the philosopher-Didaskalos attracted many disciples to his school.[66] Through this kind of exposure he came to know a wealthy government official, Ambrose, and his sister Tatiana.[67] They were slightly older than Origen and attached themselves as his pupils, patronizing his school by endowing it financially. Ambrose had formerly belonged to the Valentinian school of Christian thought, and his conversion to the side of Origen and the Catholics of Alexandria helped to focus Origen's mind on the necessary distinctions to be observed between "Orthodox" and gnostic exegesis.[68] Ambrose helped Origen financially when he was in his last years at Alexandria and also continued to help him in setting up at Caesarea. Later in life Ambrose retired to live at Nicomedia and became a deacon in the church. There was at least one visit between Origen and Ambrose in that city while Origen was resident in Caesarea Palestina.[69]

Ambrose commissioned several books from him, and was directly responsible for pressing Origen first to compose, and then to complete,[70] his masterpiece of theological writing: the great *Commentary on John*.[71] Ambrose paid for seven stenographers to take down his orally delivered discourses, as well as copyists and calligraphers, young women of skill and intelligence, who made his school a center of text production and dissemination.[72] One of the texts produced at this period was the *De principiis*, or *First Principles*; another was the beginning of the *Commentary on the Gospel of John*, which for its earliest chapters had Alexandria as its home and was resumed and published in Caesarea after Origen had taken up permanent residence there. Eusebius gives a listing of the main works Origen composed while resident in Alexandria. In addition to the *De principiis*, and the first five books of the *Commentary on John*, Eusebius lists the first eight books of the *Commentary on Genesis*, *Commentary on Psalms 1–25*, the *Commentary on Lamentations*, two books on the resurrection, and ten books of stromata.

---

66. Eusebius, *H.E.* 6.17.2.

67. Ambrose, as a deacon in Nicomedia, was married to Marcella and probably had a family (cf. *ExhMart.* c. 14). Tatiana is called his sister (a term sometimes designating a spouse) in the *Treatise on Prayer* c. 2 and probably was a deaconess colleague. For other information apart from Eusebius, *H.E.* 6.18 and 6.23, see Jerome, *De viris illustribus* c. 54; Epiphanius, *Panarion* 64; *Letter of Origen to Africanus;* and Preface to book 5 of the *Commentary on John*.

68. To prepare his own *Commentary on John* Origen made a close study of the first systematic commentary on Scripture that had been written, the *John Commentary* of the Valentinian gnostic Heracleon. It partly survives in Origen's text, since he refers to it so many times.

69. Eusebius, *H.E.* 6.31.1–3.

70. Origen was losing interest in the idea. Often he began a great work and, when he felt he had said all he wanted to say about the subject, suggested others should follow up the details themselves. Ambrose knew him very well and would not let him set aside the *John Commentary*. He thus kept Origen at the task until more or less the Last Supper narrative. Origen wryly referred to him as "God's taskmaster," who was like the Egyptian overlords who pressed the poor Hebrew to build public monuments. See Jerome, *De viris illustribus*, 61; also in a fragment to the preface to the (now lost) book 5 of the *Commentary on John*. Text in Sources chrétiennes, 120:372. His grumbling against Ambrose is relatively good natured, but nonetheless deeply felt (remarks from his personal correspondence have also been preserved by the Byzantine writer George Kedrenos, PG, 121:485).

71. See McGuckin (1995). Ambrose directly commissioned, paid for, or inspired the *De principiis*, the *Commentary on John*, the *Treatise on Prayer*, the *Exhortation to Martyrdom*, and the *Contra Celsum*, not to mention his unflagging encouragement of the other exegetical works of his favorite theologian.

72. Eusebius, *H.E.* 6.23.2.

The writings brought to a head the growing tension between the philosopher theologian Origen and the local bishop Demetrios. One could suspect that his doctrine of
incorporeal resurrection bodies and the other speculations that must have been contained in the *Stromata*,[73] as well as many of the unusual points of doctrine still extant
in the *De principiis*,[74] would have been enough to give Demetrios grounds for complaint. The latest conflict between Origen and his bishop seems to have been the last
straw and the immediate cause of his abandonment of his home city for pastures new,
where the hierarchs appreciated him.

FROM ALEXANDRIA TO PRIESTHOOD IN PALESTINE

Eusebius gives the chronology of these events[75] in terms of references to the reigns of
the popes, but his dating system is unreliable. A clearer indication is given later in the
Ecclesiastical History,[76] which suggests Origen once more began his travels in the tenth
year of Alexander Severus, which means 231. Eusebius tells us first that Origen was
sent on official church business to Palestine by way of Athens. The visit to the latter
city could be construed as another book-buying trip to build up the collection that
would comprise the Christian library. The question remains, however: the Christian
library of which city church, Alexandria or Caesarea? Here there is still controversy as
to the exact sequence of events. Eusebius implies that Origen left Alexandria on official church business and was ordained in Palestine, and then went on to Athens (presumably still in the service of the bishop of Alexandria), whereupon Demetrios of
Alexandria made the strongest level of protests over Origen's ordination by alien bishops, and the controversy forced Origen to take up permanent residence in the Caesarean church. I do not find this version of events persuasive,[77] but it functions well
enough in Eusebius's strategic agenda to make the uncanonical ordination the chief
cause of Demetrios's complaint—a tactic that well served Pamphilus's and Eusebius's
overarching motive of providing rehabilitation for Origen's reputation.[78]

When Origen went to Palestinian Caesarea to meet up again with bishops Theoctist and Alexander, he was immediately given full authority to preach on the Scriptures and "perform the other duties of ecclesiastical teaching," which is more simply
described in the *Ecclesiastical History* 6.23.4. as his "ordination as presbyter" in the Caesarean church. This ordination is tantamount to a permanent enrollment of Origen
among the officers of the local Caesarean church, and could only have occurred (in my
opinion) as a direct result of Origen having already decided to leave Alexandria per-

---

73. A genre of speculative philosophical miscellanies, such as produced earlier by Clement.

74. Some of the key issues between Origen and the bishop could be construed as the Platonic
schema of soteriology that leaned to the preexistence of *souls* (see also **Anthropology**), and the
concept of **apokatastasis**. But an abiding issue was, probably, the manner in which Demetrios
and Origen conceived very differently the relative importance of the offices of Didaskalos and
Episcopos.

75. *H.E.* 6.23.3–4.

76. *H.E.* 6.26.

77. Although it is possible to see in Origen's request for ordination by foreign hierarchs (see
Bishops) an attempt on his part to make a bid for the succession to the Alexandrian throne in
Demetrios's old age—for which the Alexandrian hierarch censured him severely.

78. Eusebius clearly blurs the exact course of events of the Alexandrian crisis in his *H.E.* and
refers the reader to his *Apology for Origen* (*H.E.* 6.23), where the issue is treated more fully. This
sadly has not survived, though Photius's information (*Bibliotheca*, 118) about Demetrios's
attempts to have Origen deposed by local and international synods probably derives from it.

manently, or at the very least to have been successfully persuaded to remove himself
to Palestine when he was received there. It is not the first, or the last time, that intellectual stars have been lured into new areas, and both Theoctist and Alexander of
Jerusalem were most eager to build up the intellectual resources of their church. So I
think it is improbable that Origen could have received ordination in Palestine and still
expect to return to Egypt. The versions of this major controversy were raked over
again in the later fourth century as Origen's legacy was being reassessed in the light
of his posthumous impact on the Arian crisis. As such, reference is made to it in several sources.[79] It leads me to conclude that the trip to Athens is part of the definitive
leave-taking of Alexandria and occurred in the year 231.

Photius, reproducing Pamphilus's and Eusebius's deliberate attempts to make the
crisis only a matter of uncanonical ordination,[80] certainly not a matter of doctrinal suspicion,[81] tells his readers that Origen had left the city without the bishop's permission,
thereby directly conflicting with Eusebius's own account in the *Church History*, where
he describes the visit to Athens as a matter of "a pressing necessity of ecclesiastical
affairs." The latter is a phrase so vague that it has to be deliberately so. If Origen had
known that he would be received gladly by the Palestinian bishops and honored as
an official part of their presbytery, whereas he was under the grudging suspicion of
the Alexandrian bishop, then indeed his removal to Palestine could legitimately be
called ecclesiastical business. Eusebius has written it in such a way however, that
many readers, then as now, interpret it as "official business in the name of Demetrios."
This is, of course, exactly what Eusebius does not say. The visit to Athens, therefore,
if we are right to see it as a book-buying expedition, was the first occasion where the
priest Origen goes out with "church money" to buy up a collection to inaugurate a
new school—at Caesarea.

After it had become known Origen had been received into the Palestinian church,
Demetrios raised a storm of protest, both to the Palestinian bishops themselves and to
the synod of the church at Rome. His successor, Origen's former colleague Heraclas,
sustained those protests rather than allowing them to dissolve away.[82] Eusebius tells
the reader only that Demetrios ungraciously published abroad the story that Origen
was a eunuch and unfit for ordination. In another passage he says, "Not long after
[Origen's ordination], Demetrios, bishop of the church of Alexandria, died after having held the office for forty-three full years." Eusebius pushes the death notice of
Demetrios into the corner, as it were, and rushes on to announce that "Firmilian of
Caesarea (in Cappadocia) was most conspicuous at that time and was so deeply

---

79. Cf. Eusebius, *H.E.* 6.23.4–5 and 6.8.4–5; Photius, *Bibliotheca,* 118, citing part of
Pamphilus's *Apology for Origen*; Jerome, *Letter 33 to Paula*; Origen's own *Letter to Friends in
Alexandria*, preserved in Jerome's *Apology against Rufinus* 2.18–19. The same text is also partly
preserved in Rufinus's *On the Falsification of the Books of Origen*, par. 6–8; and Origen's Preface to
the *Commentary on John*, book 6.

80. In the fourth century this aspect would have been considered, since canon 16 of the
Council of Nicaea was framed to prevent such events (common enough to merit a special legislation). Photius says Demetrios summoned a synod in Alexandria and censured Origen for
taking holy orders from another bishop, exiling him from Alexandria, but not depriving him of
his priesthood.

81. A charge that by the fourth century would have been fuel for the fire in relation to how
Origen's legacy had been appropriated in the Arian crisis, and which had to be avoided at all
costs.

82. He is said by Photius to have severely censured Bishop Ammonius of Thmuis for continuing to support Origen (Photius, *Ten Questions and Answers*, Qn. 9, in PG 104).

devoted to Origen that he urged him to come to his country."[83] He then goes on to tell how the Palestinian bishops ordained him and appointed him as chief theologian of Caesarea. Again, all this seems to be editorial sleight of hand to distract the reader from the storm of controversy Demetrios is known to have raised against Origen when the latter finally made a permanent break with Alexandria. The charges were more than the canonical niceties of leaving one jurisdiction for another without permission, or of the medical condition of ordinands, and probably related to issues of theological controversy contained in the *De principiis* and *Stromata*.

The telling point of evidence, as usual, comes from the hand of Origen himself. For in his *Letter to Friends in Alexandria* the new priest-theologian is determined to defend not his canonical status but his orthodoxy of doctrine. One of the issues that seems to have been raised against him from the outset was the charge that he had taught a particular form of *apokatastasis*—a doctrine of universal redemptive restoration. The most cartoonlike aspect of this (and ancient debates loved to reduce opponents' subtle positions to lurid cartoons) involved the premise that Origen had claimed the devil himself would be finally saved. Origen, in a passage preserved by Jerome,[84] refers to a debate he had in Athens with an unnamed "heresiarch" (a term that suggests the latter was a well-known gnostic teacher) and goes on to claim that any report he had indeed taught the salvation of the devil was false. If the textual record seemed to support it, he says, it could only be that the heresiarch had interpolated such an idea in the text by going to the stenographers and insisting they add it in. The circulation of the story that a Christian priest had taught so unorthodox a doctrine was the real point of contention that seems to have raised the eyebrows of hierarchs in both Alexandria and Palestine. Origen had to demonstrate his innocence to his Palestinian hierarchs,[85] but probably only because the Alexandrian hierarch had already denounced him to the Palestinians for heterodoxy, using the example of Origen's dialogue with the gnostic teacher as evidence of his unsuitability as a theologian, and their recklessness in ordaining him. Jerome, in a later passage[86] of the same book, gives the reader to know that Origen debated with Candidus, a Valentinian gnostic teacher, on the issue of the salvation of the devil. Candidus supported a fixed predestinarian system. Origen seems to have answered the statement that the devil was beyond salvation by arguing that if he is damned, it is only on account of his freely chosen evil, and thus he can be seen only as morally reprobate, not absolutely reprobate. This was enough, under the terms of any ancient debate, to father the idea onto Origen that he had taught the potential

---

83. Eusebius, *H.E.* 6.26–27.

84. "After a debate I had with a certain heresiarch, in the presence of many witnesses, the proceedings were transcribed. My opponent took the manuscript from the secretaries and added what he wanted to add, altering the version as it seemed fit to him. Then he began circulating it as if it were a work of mine, and rebuking us for what he himself had written. The brethren in Palestine were indignant about this and sent a man to me in Athens to get accurate copies from me. I had not yet had sight of the text, or even corrected it, and could not lay my hands on it. But I finally sent them a copy, and when next I met the man who had falsified my book I took him to task. His reply was that he had made the changes: 'in order to correct and improve the discussion.' All I can say is that he corrected me in the same way Marcion and his disciple Apelles corrected the Gospel and the Apostle" [that is, by mutilating them], *Letter to Friends in Alexandria* (Jerome, *Apology against Rufinus* 2.18–19).

85. The fragment of the *Letter to Friends in Alexandria* that Rufinus preserves (*On the Falsification of the Books of Origen,* par. 6–8) has Origen protesting that the idea of the devil's salvation is a foolish one and he never maintained it.

86. Jerome, *Apology against Rufinus* 2.19.

salvation of Satan. And this charge was used to attempt to damn his reputation by simple association with gnostic heretics.

The *Letter to Friends in Alexandria* speaks of another "heretic" who had also claimed to have bested Origen in debate and written a false record of the occasion. This opponent had heard him speak in Ephesus and then taken the false account of his dialogue with Origen to Antioch. From this we know that Origen had taught in both cities, and had met with some suspicion of his orthodoxy, because of what he claimed were false reports circulating about him. The story of the falsified dialogue sounds very like the Candidus episode, but it is difficult to place the events clearly now. It is not even sure when the visits to Ephesus and Antioch took place. Even if the Antioch visit was the occasion when Origen spoke before Julia Mammaea,[87] it was possibly undertaken when Origen was already in Palestine as priest at Caesarea (between 231 and 235), even though, as we have seen, Eusebius's ordering of this story implies it was during his sojourn in Alexandria, between 222 and 231. Origen speaks of this "heretical" opponent who had falsified accounts of debates with him, first at Ephesus and then again at Antioch, as having sent on to Rome a corrupt account of his work. It is my suspicion that the false account to Rome was part of the canonical charges the Alexandrian church raised against him at the Roman chancery after his departure for Caesarea. The contextualizing of this "gathering of damning evidence" suggests to me that the Antioch and Ephesus visits, despite Eusebius's implied sequence, ought to be understood as early in Origen's Palestinian career, soon after his ordination in 231.

THE FOUNDING OF THE CHRISTIAN SCHOLA

Origen's early duties as presbyter in Caesarea went hand in hand with his other vocational task, which was to establish the church of that city as a major center of intellectual activity. The establishment of a Christian "School of Caesarea" at this period parallels what we know of Caesarea as a center of Hellenistic philosophical activity, and more particularly a center of the rabbinic movement that was to produce the body of Torah philosophy and commentary later known as the Mishnah. Origen's commission was to found a schola that would revolve around him as its leading professor and the president of a major new archive and library. To this task of establishing his school, all his remaining energies were dedicated. The site appears to have been near the city harbor, adjacent to the Augustus temple. Only ruins survive to the present, but his work in his lifetime successfully established an important library, a rival to the archives of the church of Alexandria, and the first exemplar of how the church ought to be vested as a major center of learning, as part of its essential mission to the world.[88] The Caesarean library attracted a series of learned bishops until the fifth century. Even after the seventh-century invasions of the Holy Land, when the importance of Caesarea as a center of Christian learning was only a memory, the achievement of Origen was not lost, for the principle had been established throughout Byzantine Christianity—that the church leadership ought to base its cultural mission around a nexus of higher education services. It is largely to Origen that Christianity owes this insight and its practice for centuries following.

Origen's transition to Palestine was, therefore, a stormy one, a time when he had to engage in some serious self-justification before the ecclesiastical court of Rome, as well as in his native Alexandria (to his friends if not to the bishop), and we might presume to his new patrons in Palestine. The bitterness of what he felt to have been hos-

---

87. *H.E.* 6.21.3–4.
88. See A. Knauber (1968) and McGuckin (1992a).

tile attacks is clearly seen in the first great work he resumed at Caesarea, the preface of the *Sixth Book of the Commentary on John*. Here he compares himself to an Israelite who has escaped the perverse persecution of Egyptians. But he seems soon to have settled down, with the confidence and support of encouraging hierarchs, and his preaching as a priest unfolded hand in hand with the period of his greatest literary activity. He was increasingly used by his hierarchs as a theological expert in several Palestinian and Arabian church synods. Whatever the furious charges raised against him by Alexandria, they more or less failed with the death of Demetrios. As a presbyter, Origen was called on to perform a range of services that involved him in working with a greater range of educational ability than hitherto had been his custom as a professional teacher. The effect of this change is seen in the genre of the preached church homily. Every Wednesday and Friday, as well as the Sunday synaxis, the church gathered for preaching and prayer, sometimes in the context of a eucharistic offering, and sometimes not.[89] Some of his orations on the Scripture were delivered extempore. His *Homily on the Witch of Endor*[90] shows that he did not always know which reading would be required for comment on the day; it begins with a request for Bishop Theoctist to choose which of the four readings he will speak about. Origen then evidently spoke extempore. Eusebius tells us[91] that he refused to allow anyone to transcribe these church sermons until he was over sixty—a moral to all preachers that high inspiration never excuses the task of preparation.

As Crouzel points out,[92] this means that his surviving *Homilies* represent the preaching of his last decade. An exception to this is the series of *Homilies on Luke*, which were delivered early in his time at Caesarea and show signs of having been written down before their delivery. Generally speaking, Origen's surviving *Homilies*, as distinct, for example, from his *Commentaries* or *Treatises*, are simpler and more to the point in highlighting a moral or spiritual message for a general congregation. One of his important works from Caesarea shows the influence of his newly achieved presbyteral status: the *Treatise on Prayer*. It was a work requested by his old friend Ambrose and "his sister" Tatiana, who were now probably clergy at Nicomedia. Origen begins the work with a systematic consideration of forms of prayer and petition as they are listed in the Bible, and considers the question whether or not prayer interrupts the plan of divine providence. So far it is classically Origenian in its systematic intent, but in the middle of the book there is a section devoted to the exegesis of the Lord's Prayer.[93] This seems to have been part of the lecture series he offered to the catechumens, or baptismal candidates, of his own church who were preparing themselves for baptism at the end of Great Lent, in the early thirties of the third century. As such, it is an important and early example of liturgical preaching, with a direct and forceful pastoral style.

Origen was now at the height of his powers as a world-famous Didaskalos and priest in Caesarea, and accordingly the construction of the Christian school has to be seen as a major aspect of the official church's mission. As the learned bishop Alexander was busy building up the library of the church in Jerusalem, so Origen was making a larger collection at his city, which was then the metropolitan cathedral, having a supervisory remit over all the churches of Palestine. His time spent in gathering students and extending the curriculum of his university-school was punctuated by

---

89. Socrates (*H.E.* 5.22) says that Origen preached every Wednesday and Friday.

90. 1 Sam. 28:3–25. It is one of the few *Homilies* to have survived in the original Greek. Select translations of the *Homilies* can be found in Tollinton (1929).

91. Eusebius, *H.E.* 6.36.1.

92. Crouzel (1989), 30.

93. *PEuch* cc. 18–30.

lecture tours and book-buying expeditions near and far. One of the pupils he attracted soon after his arrival in Caesarea was a wealthy young man who was en route with his brother to study law in Beirut. While delivering their sister to the safekeeping of a family member who was in the imperial administration at Caesarea, they stopped to listen to Origen lecturing. They abandoned the idea of going to Beirut and became his dedicated pupils. The student, Theodore,[94] vividly describes the impact Origen made:

> It was like a spark falling in our deepest soul, setting it on fire, making it burst into flame within us. It was, at the same time, a love for the Holy Word, the most beautiful object of all that, by its ineffable beauty, attracts all things to itself with irresistible force, and it was also love for this man, the friend and advocate of the Holy Word. I was thus persuaded to give up all other goals. . . . I had only one remaining object that I valued and longed for—philosophy, and that divine man, who was my master of philosophy.[95]

Theodore published his graduating address, a *Panegyric* in praise of Origen, a revealing glimpse into the curriculum of Origen's school. Studies began with Socratic-style exercises in logic and dialectic.[96] Cosmology and natural history followed.[97] Theodore demonstrates how Origen made the study of the natural order a foundational exercise for the contemplation of God's design for and providence in the world.[98] After that came ethics,[99] and finally theology proper,[100] which Origen taught as the summit of philosophic wisdom, the fourth of his major divisions of Christian philosophy. Theodore was much impressed by Origen's open and eclectic attitude to his teaching.

Unlike many other Sophists of the age, Origen seems to have encouraged a wide curricular reading of different philosophic traditions.[101] Porphyry, the Neoplatonic philosopher who had once gone to hear the greatest teacher of the Christians, raises this against him, accusing Origen of having betrayed the insights of philosophy by subjugating them to the exegesis of the Christian Scriptures.[102] But what for Porphyry stood as a fault was for Origen the glory of the Christian philosophy: that divine revelation as given in the sacred texts should be harmonized with philosophical searching, through the medium of spiritualizing exegesis. Porphyry tells us some of the authors Origen studied, apart from his evident dependence on the writings of Plato, Aristotle, and Pythagoras. They include the main thinkers of his era: Numenius, Chronius, Apollophanes, Longinus, Moderatus, Nichomachus, Chaeremon, and Cornutus—a roll call of major Platonist, Pythagorean, and Stoic intellectuals.

What made Origen's eclecticism specifically focused, of course, was his strong advocacy of the Christian tradition as he had received it. The tradition of the faith was something Origen set himself to maintain and defend. For him, that meant not only a

---

94. He probably assumed the name Gregory at his baptism; it can be presumed also that Origen arranged this at Caesarea. He became known to later Christian tradition as St. Gregory the Wonder Worker (Thaumaturgus), one of the most important theologian-hierarchs of Cappadocia (cf. Eusebius, *H.E.* 7.14). Theodore's brother Athenodorus also became a leader of the Christian communities of his region.

95. Gregory Thaumaturgus, *Panegyric on Origen* 6.

96. *Panegyric on Origen* 7.

97. That is, physics, geometry, and astronomy. A good example of this style of cosmological-theological speculation has been provided by the recent study of A. Scott (1991).

98. *Panegyric for Origen* 8.

99. *Panegyric for Origen* 9–12.

100. *Panegyric for Origen* 13.

101. *Panegyric for Origen* 14.

102. Eusebius, *H.E.* 6.19.1–11.

complete christocentric, or soteriological, focus[103] in all his thought patterns, but more precisely, that the plan of cosmic meaning was given to the inspired commentator primarily in the text and subtext of the sacred books. As the Scriptures of the Old and New Testaments spoke at first level about patterns of historical salvation, so too at a deeper level they drew the pattern of a vast cosmic illumination to which souls were called, and which enlightened souls could recognize as their call to divinization. The exegesis of the Scriptures was all-important for him and made Origen's whole eclectic philosophical stand, however much it might be indebted to the Hellenists, entirely and unarguably a Christian and biblicist enterprise.[104]

POLITICS OF RESISTANCE

Soon after Origen had settled in Palestine, an event took place that was again to rock the foundations of his security. Emperor Alexander Severus, whose court had proved so hospitable to Christian and other religious philosophers, was murdered; his military commander Maximin the Thracian took the throne and instigated a purge of the supporters of the young emperor and the senatorial party who opposed his usurpation. The revolt began in 235 and would last for three years. During this time the pogrom was extended to include well-known Christian leaders. In Rome Pope Pontianus and the theologian Hippolytus were sent into exile in 235, and Origen must have known he was in considerable danger. He seems to have gone into hiding, while continuing to write. His friend and patron Ambrose was arrested in Nicomedia, and the leading priest of Caesarea, Protoctetus, was also arrested. The prospects looked grim, and so Origen composed for them an *Exhortation to Martyrdom*, which has ever since been received as one of the church's major pieces of resistance literature. It is known that Origen traveled extensively through the Holy Land,[105] specially seeking out the places associated with the ministry of Jesus. Perhaps during this period of persecution he literally followed in the footsteps of his master, who himself had advocated flight in time of persecution.[106]

The historian Palladius, when passing through Caesarea in the late fourth century, found a book in the library there with a marginal note written in Origen's own hand: "I found this book at the house of the virgin Juliana, at Caesarea, when I was hiding there. She said she had got it from Symmachus himself, the Jewish commentator."[107] Palladius introduces this scholar's note by reporting that Origen had fled from the "rising of the Greeks" and had taken refuge for three years with "the Virgin Juliana a woman of great wisdom and faith, who lived at Caesarea of Cappadocia." Crouzel

---

103. The concept that all the world's history and all its meaning, longing, and sense of direction were summated in the rescue from the collapse into ignorance and alienation that the Logos of God provided. Chief among the instances of the Logos's determination to recall the wandering souls back to himself was the incarnation of Jesus. This recalling, or cosmic vision of salvation (known as soteriology), is typical of all Origen's thought and serves as an organizing principle for him.

104. Which does not imply, of course, that it was generally recognized or received as such by the church in various ages. For the approach to spiritual exegesis as the highest level of philosophical initiation, cf. Theodore's *Panegyric* 15; see also McGuckin (2002), Torjesen (1986, 1995), R. Heine (1995).

105. Epiphanius tells us how he preached in Jerusalem on Ps. 50:16 and had the congregation in tears. It is a text particularly apposite for a time of persecution (cf. Epiphanius, *Panarion* 64.2). He also went to Jericho (*ComJn* 6.24) and Sidon, where he stayed some time (*HomJos* 16.2).

106. Matt. 10:23.

107. Palladius, *Historia Lausiaca*, 147. PG 34.1250.

notes the perplexities this note raises[108] but, wrongly in my opinion, refers it to the flight from Alexandria after the Caracalla riot of twenty years earlier. It is simpler to believe that Palladius, a Cappadocian by birth, has presumed wrongly that the "Juliana the Virgin of Caesarea," whom Origen speaks of as his protector in flight, had to be a woman of a town different from his own local church. This would spring to Palladius's mind, most naturally, as the great Cappadocian city of Caesarea. In his own comments, then, he offers this as a personal deduction.

Origen does not say this at all, and the most natural reading of the original manuscript note would be that it refers to Juliana's house in Caesarea Palestina. There is no indication in the text of Theodore's *Panegyric* that Origen interrupted his studies so as to leave his school for so long, and this has a greater weight than Palladius's retrospective presumptions. Eusebius also knows of the same marginal note of Origen, but he implies that Juliana was a Palestinian Christian virgin who had known Symmachus, the Ebionite Christian teacher.[109] The hiding of Origen, therefore, was most likely within his own town during the troubles of 235. His sequestering with the virgin Juliana shows his ready acceptance by the Christian intellectuals of Palestine, chief among them his bishop and admirer Theoctist, who also avoided imprisonment during the persecution, for he went on to rule over the church for another twenty-five years. Theoctist, taking Origen with him on numerous synodal occasions, brought him to the attention of another leading theologian of the period, Firmilian, bishop of Caesarea in Cappadocia. Eusebius tells us that Firmilian became a devoted admirer of Origen and "urged him to come to his country [Cappadocia] for the benefit of the churches."[110] On the basis of this, many commentators have presumed a visit of Origen to Cappadocia. The text never says that he went, only that Firmilian tried to induce Origen to move there but in the end had to come to Caesarea Palestina in order to hear Origen.

MORE TRAVELS AND DEBATES

Sometime between 238 and 244[111] Origen journeyed once more to Athens, and his stay lasted some time, as Eusebius tells us he completed in that city the *Commentary on Ezekiel* and started his great *Commentary on the Song of Songs*. Again sometime before 244, according to Eusebius's implied chronology,[112] Origen received a letter from a Christian scholar Julius Africanus,[113] who had gone to study with Heraclas in Alexandria and sent on to Origen critical points of biblical exegesis.[114] Origen replied to this letter, noting that he was in Nicomedia with Ambrose. If, and it is not impossible,[115]

---

108. *Origen* (1989), 16–17.

109. Eusebius, *H.E.* 6.17.1. The Ebionite movement refers to the Judeo Christians of Palestine. Origen knew Symmachus chiefly as one of the famous early translators of the Bible and one of the earliest Christian writers of commentary.

110. Eusebius, *H.E.* 6.27.1.

111. Eusebius, *H.E.* 6.32.2 sets the visit only within the reign of Emperor Gordian III.

112. Eusebius, *H.E.* 6.31.1–3, tells the story of the *Letter to Africanus* before announcing the end of Gordian's reign in 244.

113. Julius, who occupied the post of librarian archivist at the Pantheon in Rome, was one of the most learned textual critics of his age and a Christian.

114. Africanus argued that the Susanna story had clear syntactical evidence within it indicating it did not belong to the book of Daniel as a whole. Origen would not accept his opinion, one that is now universally accepted by modern text critics.

115. Scholarly opinion is still divided. The earlier belief that the Origens were the same as the Christian teacher has of late been considerably qualified.

Origen the philosopher mentioned by Porphyry,[116] is the same as our Origen, then he also made a visit (either to Antioch or to Rome) to see the only philosopher of the age who could rival him in importance, another former student of Ammonius in Alexandria, the greatest of the Neoplatonists, Plotinus.

As a priest-theologian in Caesarea, Origen's fame and importance rose in an unbroken curve, despite any of Rome's or Alexandria's misgivings as to his orthodoxy. The hierarchs of his province trusted him entirely as an arbiter of orthodoxy. While he was resident in Caesarea, he completed his mature works. Eusebius gives a list of them in his church history and then breaks off, complaining that to make a complete record would involve him in a bibliography too extensive for the capacity of his present book.[117] He was also taken with the hierarchs to the local councils of the Palestinian region. Conciliar episcopal conferences had been established even by the second century as a preferred way of establishing an international standard of orthodoxy.

When the news of the famous Bishop Beryllus of Arabian Bostra[118] reached the ears of the Palestinian hierarchs, they knew that sensitive action was required. Beryllus was one of the most energetic and outstanding bishops of Arabia, but his thinking on many aspects of biblical theology was out of harmony with the increasingly international standard of Logos theology. Origen was called in by his hierarchs to convince Beryllus of the error of his ways in a public disputation in Arabia. Beryllus seems to have denied the preexistence of the Lord (presumably indicating that he was not a Logos theologian) and went on to argue that the divinity attributed to Jesus was simply and solely an indwelling of the deity that properly belonged to the Father. In other words, he sounds like a typical old-fashioned monarchian theologian.[119] After his ideas had gained notoriety among the local hierarchs the metropolitan of Caesarea was summoned to adjudicate. He asked Origen to lead a public disputation. According to Eusebius this was so successfully resolved that Beryllus agreed to abide by Origen's interpretations of Logos theology henceforth.[120]

---

116. Porphyry, *Vita Plotini* 14. The issue of identification is conflicted as Porphyry, in his own *Vita Plotini*, speaks of Origen as if he were entirely a Hellenist philosopher with a range of works apparently different to his familiar Christian corpus; whereas the Porphyry of Eusebius's text points unmistakably to the Christian writer, but in a passage in which the Christian historian confuses the identity of Ammonius Saccas. The existence of two famous Origens, both with similar interests to Plotinus and not distinguished by Porphyry, seems to contradict Occam's basic principle of the razor.

117. Eusebius, *H.E.* 6.32.1–3. Explicitly numerating the commentaries on Isaiah, on Ezekiel, on the Song of Songs and then referring the reader for a fuller list to the *Catalogue of the Caesarean Library* prepared by Pamphilus and also to the *Life of Pamphilus* Eusebius also composed. Later in the *H.E.* (6.36) he lists other works from the Caesarean period, namely, the *Contra Celsum*, the *Commentary on Matthew*, the *Commentary on the Twelve Prophets*, and various epistles including those to the Emperor Philip the Arab and his wife Severa, Pope Fabian of Rome, and others, in defense of his orthodoxy.

118. Jerome, not easily impressed, described him as a bishop who "ruled his church most gloriously" (*De viris illustribus* 60). Eusebius tells us that he left behind many elegant treatises but does not detail them (*H.E.* 6.20).

119. Eusebius, *H.E.* 6.33.1.

120. Eusebius, *H.E.* 6.33.2–3. "Origen was invited to discuss and went there for a conference in order to discover his true opinions. When he had understood Beryllus's views, and saw that they were erroneous, he persuaded him by arguments and convinced him by demonstrations, and so brought him back to the profession of true doctrine, and restored him to his former soundness of mind."

Eusebius also tells of another synod in Arabia, which concerned the refutation of local ideas concerning the death of the soul with the perishable body. Origen again was invited to the local church to lead the disputations in a local synod. His arguments on the immortality of the soul were so successful that Eusebius says, again, that "the opinions of those who had formerly fallen were once more changed."[121] The disputation was probably the synodical debate involving Origen a record of which, the *Dialogue with Heracleides*, was discovered in the Toura papyri finds of 1941. Heracleides was an Arabian bishop who maintained an ancient Judeo-Christian attitude that the soul was synonymous with the blood of the living being. According to the rules of ancient debate-summary, he could be designated "a denier of the immortality of the soul." Both synods mentioned above seem to have taken place during the reign of Emperor Philip the Arab (244–49), who, if he was not Christian himself,[122] was certainly a protector of the Christians of Palestine and a patron of Origen as a significant rhetorician.

ARREST AND TORTURE

After the assassination of Philip, those associated with him were in double danger, as the succeeding emperor, Decius, began another pogrom against Christians, during which the leading bishops and theologians of Palestine suffered considerably. Pope Fabian was martyred at Rome, and Origen's old patron, Alexander of Jerusalem, was arrested and thrown into prison in Caesarea, where he died as a confessor. A similar fate befell Babylas, the great martyr bishop of Antioch. Origen was a marked man. He had evaded previous persecutions by hiding in the houses of the faithful. This time he was deliberately sought out as the leading Christian intellectual of the age and was arrested. His treatment was specially designed to bring him to a public recantation of the faith. To this end he was tortured with special care, so that he would not die under the stress of his pain. He was chained, set in the infamous iron collar, and stretched on the rack—four spaces, no less, as Eusebius tells his readers,[123] who knew exactly what degree of pain that involved, and how many dislocations of bones and ripping of sinews it brought with it. He who had encouraged others in his time now received a gracious encouragement himself in the form of an "exhortation to martyrdom" from his admirer Dionysius,[124] who had now risen to episcopal office in Alexandria and had rehabilitated Origen's memory there. Eusebius clearly recognizes the martyr's heroism in Origen's endurance. He was saved time after time, only because the governor of Caesarea had commanded he should not die under the torture before he had publicly denied the faith. This was why he suffered throughout the two years of persecution and was liberated only by the death of the persecutor, Decius, assassinated with his children in 252 after a blessedly short time as emperor. Origen's health had been broken by his ordeals, however. He was by the standards of his age an extremely old man already at sixty-nine, and died from the accumulated sufferings of his impris-

121. Eusebius, *H.E.* 6.37.

122. Eusebius thinks he was; cf. *H.E.* 6.34.

123. Eusebius, *H.E.* 6.39.6. Some translations misstate this as having his legs stretched "four paces," which is ridiculous. The four spaces refers to the ratchet divisions of the Roman torturer's racking machine, and is a near fatal amount that leaves the victim permanently crippled, if not paralyzed.

124. Eusebius, *H.E.* 6.46.2. Eusebius specifically claims Dionysius as Origen's pupil, though the association has been questioned in modern times. Dionysius is, however, the first clear "Origenian" Logos theologian of Alexandria.

onment shortly afterward. That he died as a confessor, not as a martyr under the rack, was one reason for the loss of much of his work in later centuries, when he was censured for unorthodox opinions.

THE DEATH OF ORIGEN

Eusebius gives us to understand that Origen in his last year of life, broken in health, spent his time dictating letters of encouragement to those who had also suffered for the cause of Christ: "After these things Origen left many words of comfort, full of sweetness, to those who needed assistance, as can be seen abundantly and most truly from so many of his epistles."[125] Eusebius says that he died in his sixty-ninth year, soon after Decius's assassination, in the reign of Gallus (251–53),[126] which we have already seen conflicts with his own internal chronology. Accordingly we need to set the date of the death to a year or so after Gallus, which places it early in the reign of Valerian (253–60), probably in the year 254.

Jerome tells us that Origen was buried (and so presumably was also resident at the time of his death) in the Palestinian city of Tyre.[127] This gave rise to an abundance of later medieval tales of his tomb being held in special honor in the Crusader cathedral of Tyre,[128] walled in the back of the high altar.[129] The Crusader stories demonstrate only how his memory remained high in the hearts and minds of Christians of all generations, despite his official censure by subsequent church authorities. It is not a historically meaningful tradition apart from that. Where Jerome got his knowledge about Tyre as the original place of Origen's burial remains unknown. Perhaps it was mentioned in the lost *Apology* that Eusebius wrote. There is no mention at all in the *Ecclesiastical History*, which cuts off the story most abruptly. The likely place of Origen's sufferings, where most of the other confessors underwent their torture and imprisonment, was the Roman administrative center of Caesarea itself. Of course, given that he died some years after his release, when he must have been more or less permanently crippled and in constant pain, Tyre might have been a place where the church authorities sent him for terminal care, perhaps to a Christian community there or to the last of his several unknown wealthy patrons, who throughout his life had recognized his genius and quietly fostered the work of one of the greatest, yet most self-effacing, men of his epoch.

This time, he was held in honor not only for his inspiring theory and his scholarly goal to assimilate himself entirely to the discipleship of Christ. This time he demanded honor even for the broken wreck of his body, which had preached his total loyalty to Christ in the most persuasive form.

So it is that the greatest Christian of his age passes out of our notice quietly and without fuss. Even from his deathbed he was concerned to console those who had been scarred, both psychologically and physically, by the time of torture. His heart's desire, even in this excruciating posttraumatic context, was to offer "sweet words of consolation" to the faithful who were grieving after surviving the latest cruel tyranny against them. It is also a sad irony that the texts have not survived.

John A. McGuckin

---

125. Eusebius, *H.E.* 6.39.5.

126. Eusebius, *H.E.* 7.1.

127. Jerome, *De viris illustribus* 54.

128. Not in existence in Origen's day.

129. For details of the twelfth- and thirteenth-century writers, see B. F. Westcott, *Origenes,* in W. Smith and H. Wace, eds., *Dictionary of Christian Biography,* vol. 4 (London, 1887), 103.

The Scholarly Works of Origen

AN OVERVIEW

Origen's works still occupy a large space on the shelves of those who have a complete set of the Greek and Latin versions of his writings. The collection of the works that have been rendered into English is considerably smaller. What remains, however, is in reality only a smoldering ruin of the monumental body of work this creative writer produced. Time and moth have ravaged many things from Christian antiquity. There is no need to search out a conspiracy theory every time to explain why so much has been lost to the record. The fundamental problem for the historian of Christianity is that succeeding generations in the church habitually did not consider the work of preceding ages all that relevant (despite making a great show of what they did choose to preserve). In 325, the state-sponsored Council of Nicaea, and the concomitant excitement of a church emerging as the heir of empire, made the fourth century a watershed on which was lost many of the earlier "pre-Nicene" writings of the Christian church. Often significant writers of the earliest periods seemed archaic and irrelevant in the light of the post-Nicene imperial ages, and in the fourth century, of course, they lacked that sufficient weight of "antiquity" that might have saved them for posterity.

So it is not surprising that even the works of Origen suffered significant loss. What accelerated the loss in his case, however, was something far more pointed. His speculative mind stretched the boundaries of Christian thought and imagination for his own day and for generations after him. While Origen himself felt he was always working within the tradition of ecclesiastical wisdom, as it had been established by the Scriptures and apostles on the basis of the teachings of Jesus (something he refers to explicitly as a basic axiom for a theologian, in the preface to his book *On First Principles*), his successors were not so sure he had always followed his own advice. On many central points (especially Trinity, Christology, and anthropology) later generations of Christians departed from his teachings, even when they followed his lead in pursuing many of the questions he had first posed. In the fourth and fifth centuries, when the definition of Christian orthodoxy was becoming ever more rigidly established and policed by imperial and synodical laws, Origen became more and more problematic.

Precisely because his legacy lived on, as undoubtedly the greatest genius the early church ever produced, and because his memory and teachings were revered by generations of later Christian thinkers (especially the monks who loved him as one of the first Christian ascetics and mystics), his reputation became something the church had to control and correct. Thus it was that after several "Origenistic controversies" agitating the church from the fourth through the sixth centuries, the Emperor Justinian moved against him with a decree in 543 to proscribe and burn his books. This damning of his memory in the sixth century is largely responsible for the great damage that has occurred to his received canon of works. The hostile judgment of the Fifth Ecumenical Council—even if the canonical condemnation of him by name is not authentic to the acts of that synod—certainly weighed against him overall, as did the Gelasian Decretal in the West, which put his works on a list of banned authors. That even so there remains so much is an extraordinary testimony to the love the church retained for this irrepressible genius, even after an imperial and synodical verdict of posthumous condemnation. Of course, all of the greatest thinkers of the patristic age were in his debt, and even after his condemnation he was too deeply inserted into the fabric of Christian theologizing ever to be dismissed or forgotten. He had been the founding architect (as far as its international reception was concerned) of biblical commentary as a mode of organizing Christian reflection, and no one who took the Bible seriously in the first millennium of the church was able to avoid his groundbreaking writing.

Eusebius of Caesarea was one of the first Origenian scholars to draw up a complete list of works, which he added to the (now lost) biography he made of another Origenian scholar, his own friend and mentor, the martyr Pamphilus (cf. Eusebius, *H.E.* 6.32.3). Jerome knew this list and used it at Caesarea when he visited the library there (Jerome, *Adv. Rufinum* 2.22). Jerome says that Eusebius listed just under 2,000 treatises as the sum of Origen's lifework. Epiphanius (who had no love for Origen at all) made an estimate of Origen's corpus as totaling 6,000 works (Epiphanius, *Adv. haer.* 64.63). In this list Epiphanius explicitly cites "books" (*biblous*), though ancient lists of works can often amplify and distort the total by listing scrolls as separate volumes even though to a commonsense view they were only parts of a single work, and Epiphanius is generally taken to have overestimated the collection. Jerome also drew up his own list mentioning specific works of Origen, which he sent to his correspondent Paula (Jerome, *Epist.* 33). This itemizes 800 titles. It had long been abbreviated by medieval copyists (thus making it useless for the purpose of studying Origen's opera), but a full version was rediscovered in the middle of the nineteenth century. Jerome's list is not complete by any means but is a good indicator on several other levels. The complete text of Jerome's letter is given an English translation in Crouzel (1989), 37–39.

The following list, discussed here, shows how very little, relatively speaking, has survived either more or less complete. More has survived in tiny fragments and accidental citations, and the task of producing a comprehensive modern critical edition of the works of this, the greatest writer of Christian antiquity, is still in progress.

1. CRITICAL TEXTS

(a) *Scholia* (*Advanced Notes*)

Jerome (*Epist.* 33) records that Origen wrote extensive Scholia—or learned commentary notes—on the books of Exodus, Leviticus, Isaiah, Psalms 1–15, Ecclesiastes, and the Gospel of John. Rufinus also included some of Origen's Scholia on the book of Numbers in his Latin translation of Origen's homilies on Numbers. None of the Scholia have survived intact or complete, though several fragments exist in the Catenae (the "chains" of patristic commentary-notes that were collected in antiquity—after the sixth century—to serve as manuals for preachers, illustrating the various verses of the Bible), and others can be found in the *Philocalia* of Origen, a collation of his writings on scriptural interpretation made (probably) by Basil of Caesarea and Gregory of Nazianzus in the fourth century. Other Scholia had been gathered together by Pamphilus in his apology for Origen. Five books were by Pamphilus, and the sixth book was added by Eusebius after his teacher's martyrdom. Only the first book of the apology survives now in Rufinus's Latin translation. Chapter 27 of the *Philocalia* contains excerpts from Origen's Scholia on Exodus. The Scholia are also known (in the Latin use established by Jerome and Rufinus) as Excerpta (Selections). Some later Greek writers also refer to them as Semeioses.

Further Reading:

Junod (1995); Quasten (1975), 46.

(b) *The Hexapla*

Origen began to make a six-column edition of the Bible from his early years in Alexandria. But it was at Caesarea that this lifelong task mainly took shape. He set out the Hebrew text of the Old Testament (in Hebrew characters), and then in an adjoining column wrote down the Hebrew in Greek transliteration (a sign that while he had a smattering of Hebrew he was not particularly fluent in it—and in any case regarded the Septuagintal Greek text as the church's supreme inspired version). Other columns contained the Greek version of Aquila (a Jewish scholar from the time of the Emperor Hadrian, A.D. 117–38); the Greek version of Symmachus (another Jewish scholar from the time of the Emperor Septimius Severus, A.D. 193–211); the Greek Septuagint text (300–200 B.C.); and finally the Greek version of Theodotion (a Jewish scholar from ca. A.D. 180). These were the four standard Greek versions of the Scriptures to which Origen added, in some cases, an additional two (or three) columns. These latter are today called the Quinta, Sexta, and Septima. Quinta and Sexta had been discovered by Origen, and bought for his use, on one of his several book-finding expeditions. The Quinta came from Nicopolis near Actium of Epirus in Greece, and the Sexta was found in a jar from a cave near Jericho (quite possibly part of the Qumran library). Origen was closely inspired by textual critical traditions established at the Great Library of Alexandria and so was the first Christian scholar to introduce critical annotations into the biblical text. He marked the Septuagintal column with a series of signs taken from the Great Library: the obelus in the margin of a Septuagintal passage (÷) indicated a passage in the Septuagint that was not in the Hebrew. An asterisk (*) signified a missing element that he normally inserted from one of the other Greek versions (usually that of Theodotion). *The Hexapla* was a massive and monumental work of research. Origen also produced a smaller Tetrapla version of the four columns most likely to be used by Christians (cf. Eusebius, *H.E.* 6.16.44; Epiphanius, *Weights and Measures* c. 19). In the *Hexapla* section representing the Psalms he added another three Greek versions in columns, where he had them (making it in parts an Enneapla).

The Hexapla was, like many other major research tools, meant to be a cornerstone of the library collection of the new school at Caesarea, marking Caesarea's emergence and significance as a center of serious textual study of the sacred canon, and thus a Christian rival to the powerful rabbinic school of scriptural exegesis that had been established there. It was also meant as a text for use in the appeals to scriptural authenticity that must have been common in the apologetic exchanges between the Christian and Jewish scholars of the respective Caesarean schools (cf. Origen, *ComMt* 15.14). It was copied in a few instances, though not widely or largely disseminated. Its very bulk militated against it. It survived up to the time of Jerome, who records how he had seen and used it in the library at Caesarea (Jerome, *Commentarioli in Ps.*). The Septuagintal column it represented was the basis for the dissemination of the Septuagint as the Christian version of the Old Testament, for Eusebius used it as the master copy for his scribes who prepared (at the command and commission of the Emperor Constantine) fifty new pandects (complete copies of the Bible) which he wanted to be sent to the great churches and new shrines he was building. There are today fragmentary remains of *The Hexapla,* and a more or less complete version exists from a Syriac copy of it made in the seventh century by Paul, bishop of Tella. Epiphanius (*Weights and Measures* c.18) records that Origen finished the work at Tyre, just before his death.

Further Reading:

Dorival (1974, 1987); Guinot (1995); Jellicoe (1974); Munnich (1995); Quasten (1975), 45.

2. HOMILIES (SERMONS OR TRACTATES)

The historian Socrates (*H.E.* 5.22) records that Origen, once he had settled as a priest in the church at Caesarea, preached every Wednesday and Friday at the liturgical gatherings held on those days. He is also known to have preached on several occasions at Jerusalem and at synodical gatherings in Arabia. Origen's first biographer, the martyr Pamphilus, recorded that he preached almost every day, and so his collected sermons must have covered a wide remit of the scriptural text and have been extensive in size. As a respected scholar and leader of the Christian Schola in Caesarea, it is more than probable that his sermons were taken down by scribes as he delivered them. He shows on several occasions, however, that he was nervous about allowing "unproofed" materials to be circulated, and he advocates the recording of sermons only when the preacher has had long experience. Eusebius records that only when Origen passed the age of sixty (regarded as advanced old age in antiquity) did he allow his stenographers to take down in writing his public addresses: "For then he had acquired, by virtue of his extremely long preparation, a very great facility indeed, and he then allowed this to be done, something which he had not hitherto permitted" (Eusebius, *H.E.* 6.36.1). The homilies have been heavily eroded by time and censorship. They generally represent a simpler and more pastoral face of Origen, speaking to his parishioners, most of whom would not have been particularly learned, although this argument ought not to be forced too much, as the students of his Schola would have been in constant attendance on him, even when he served liturgically as a priest. The homilies are a priceless resource insofar as they shed a rare light on liturgical preaching in the third century. All in all, 279 homilies have survived; he probably delivered close to 600 of them originally. Of those that have survived, only 21 have come down in the original Greek. Chief among these are the twenty homilies on Jeremiah (twelve of which Jerome parallels in Latin) and his *Homily on the Witch of Endor* (1 Sam. 28:3–25). Greek fragments of his homilies on Luke (*Hom.* 35) and Matthew have also been discovered. Rufinus translated many of Origen's sermons into Latin, and his version exists for sixteen homilies on Genesis, thirteen homilies on Exodus, sixteen homilies on Leviticus, twenty-eight homilies on Numbers, twenty-six homilies on Joshua (a fragment of the Greek text of the twentieth homily of this series is found in the *Philocalia,* c. 12), nine homilies on Judges, and nine homilies on the Psalms (five on Psalm 36, two on Psalm 37, and two on Psalm 38).

Jerome's Latin translation exists for several other sermons: two homilies on the Song of Songs, nine homilies on Isaiah, fourteen homilies on Jeremiah, fourteen homilies on Ezekiel, and thirty-nine homilies on the Gospel of Luke. Hilary of Poitier's (abbreviating) Latin version exists in fragmentary form for twenty of Origen's homilies on Job. An anonymous Latin translation (perhaps by Rufinus) also exists for the homily on 1 Samuel 1–2, and there are other fragments in Latin for the homilies on Jeremiah, 1–2 Samuel, 1–2 Kings (the latter books collectively known in the Latin manuscript tradition as the Four Books of Kings), 1 Corinthians, and Hebrews.

One of the great losses in this body of literature is the extensive amount he wrote on different individual psalms. Jerome's list in his *Epist.* 33 gives a close idea of how many psalms Origen commented on. Recently V. Peri (*Omelie origeniane sui Psalmi. Studi e Testi 289.* Vatican City, 1980; idem, CCL 78) has restored to Origen a total of seventy-four homilies on the Psalms formerly attributed to Jerome, who was, it now appears, only their translator.

Further Reading:

Quasten (1975), 47–48; Tollinton (1929); Torjesen (1995).

A useful List of Origen's homilies with a digest of their contents was made by B. F. Westcott for *DCB* 4:104–18 (London, 1887).

3. COMMENTARIES (*TOMOI, VOLUMINA, LIBRI*)

The commentaries were designed by Origen as a more systematic and "scientific" analysis of specific books of the canon of Scripture than that represented by his homilies. The commentaries approach the various scriptural books according to the canons of literary criticism established at the Great Library of Alexandria, as well as being specifically Christian appropriations of the "sacred literature" of the Jewish people, and take as their generic theme how the old covenant relates to the Gospels and apostolic writings. None of his commentaries has survived complete. In this genre of literature, of which he is the first major exponent, Origen shows himself to possess an encyclopedic knowledge of the text. He is able to cross-register word appearances from all over the scriptural record, an impressive feat in the days before concordances and reference tools were available. His memory was well trained, and his reading was extensive, making him entirely familiar with the whole corpus of Scripture. He is, of course, most steeped in the Pauline and Johannine literature, for he regards these two apostles as the high points of God's revelatory activity—princes of revelation: one who was caught up to the third heaven, and one who rested on the very bosom of the Logos of God. Origen's elaboration of a hermeneutic using the allegorical method, advanced in these commentaries, both established him as the Christian world's greatest exegete and formed the foundational architecture of Christian interpretation of the Scriptures.

Further Reading:

Heine (1997); McGuckin (2003); Quasten (1975), 48–51.

(a) *Commentary on the Gospel of John*

Origen began this, perhaps his greatest biblical work, at Alexandria between 226 and 229. Having completed the first four books, a storm of controversy rose up against him (probably related to the publication of his treatises *On First Principles* and *On the Resurrection*). With growing hostility against him in the Alexandrian church and a new opening for him with encouraging Palestinian bishops in Caesarea, he made the move to settle there, thus disrupting the writing of a large-scale commentary. The John commentary had been requested of him by his wealthy patron Ambrose, a former gnostic, who had attached himself devotedly to Origen's side. Ambrose paid for several stenographers so that Origen could be induced to embark on this work. Origen himself seems to have balked before the size of such a project, which he knew he could not finish for years. The overriding idea of Ambrose and Origen was that the genre of Gospel commentary must not be left to the gnostic theologians, who seem to have invented it. The commentary on John by the gnostic (Valentinian) teacher Heracleon was well known but treated the Gospel as evidence for the complete transcendence of God from the material cosmos and for the gnostic doctrine that there were two gods— the god of the Israelites, a deceptive demiurge whom Jesus wished to expose, and the true God. Heracleon used allegorical exegesis extensively in his work. Origen intended to rescue both the commentary as genre and the process of allegorical exegesis, which had become deeply tainted with "gnostic" associations by the majority church of the third century. He resumed the commentary on John, possibly writing book 5 on his travels in the east, and taking up the final books (6–32) shortly after arriving in Caesarea. His progress in Caesarea appears to have been slow enough to cause Ambrose to renew his appeals to Origen to complete the work. Origen's comments on the Gospel text end more or less at the account of the Last Supper. It is probably not a question of lost books; it is more likely that Origen originally ended here, having felt he had said all he needed to say on the text. He often left behind a writing project when other work beckoned or he had exhausted his original schematic, suggesting to his readers that others take up the work where he had left off. Today there survive only nine books in Greek (books 1, 2, 6, 10, 13, 19–20, 28, and 32), but they are an extensive remainder.

Further Reading:
McGuckin (1995); Wiles (1960).

(b) *Commentary on the Gospel of Matthew*

Origen in his old age composed a commentary on Matthew in twenty-five volumes. By this monumental work, destined to remain a classic for all later generations (even after he was condemned, the main ideas of his commentary made their way into more or less all other commentators of the Christian tradition), Origen established Matthew as the primary canonical Gospel of the Christian tradition. The Matthean text had already made its way to the fore in liturgical usage, but with this commentary Origen ensured its preeminence as the mainstream representative of the Christian didactic tradition. This is all the more notable (not simply because of the long subsequent history this would have) given Origen's oft-expressed preference for the apostolic witness of John and Paul, the two theologians whose writings he regarded as the pinnacle of Christian wisdom. In establishing the Matthew commentary as his major work of Synoptic commentary, we see Origen approaching the task of commentator as the theologian servicing the priestly, liturgical task of preaching. From his time to the present the genre of Christian scriptural commentary has always sustained this relationship. Of the twenty-five books of the Matthew commentary, eight survive in Greek (books 10–17), which comment on Matthew 13:36–22:33. More of the work survived in an anonymous Latin translation of the late fifth (or early sixth century), which was passed on through the tradition in the form of thirty-five homiletical narratives on Matthew (confusing many readers, since they were not originally homilies of Origen). The Latin version begins at the point of the Greek text that corresponds with Greek book 12, chapter 9 (relating to Matthew 16:13), but as it develops after that there is no way of telling where one is in terms of the original Greek volume structure. The Latin version carries on more or less to the end of Matthew (Matt. 27:66) omitting Matthew 28 altogether. It has been printed from modern times in a twofold way. The first section, which corresponds to the Greek text (covering Matt. 16:13–22:33) is known as the Vetus Interpretatio. The other section, which has no corresponding Greek original (Matt. 22:24–27:66), is called the Commentariorum Series. It is divided into (and thus referenced as) 145 chapters, apparently based simply upon verse divisions.

Further Reading:
Bastit-Kalinowska (1995a, 1995b).

(c) *Commentary on the Epistle to the Romans*

Origen wrote this commentary in Caesarea, probably before the Matthew commentary and thus before 244. It originally extended to fifteen books. Only small fragments remain of the original Greek. Some of these were discovered in the archaeological finds at Toura, near Cairo, in 1941, when a small library of theological texts was discovered in a quarry. Other Greek fragments had been preserved from antiquity in the *Philocalia,* the Origenian compendium of texts collated by Basil the Great and Gregory Nazianzen. Other Greek fragments occur in the patristic Catenae, and new ones have been turning up occasionally since the last century, even extensive sections in hitherto unrecognized manuscripts (especially Athonite Codex 184 B 64). The work is substantially represented by the translation Rufinus made of ten books into Latin at the end of the fourth century. Rufinus's ten books in Latin cover the whole course of the epistle, and thus Origen's fifteen books, suggesting Rufinus was engaged in some abbreviating. Rufinus is generally a reliable translator, but also (as especially in this case) many scholars regard his translations as having been largely "sense related" and, for long works, reductively paraphrastic. Rufinus also substituted the Latin version of the epistle to the Romans for the Greek text that Origen would have used. The historian Socrates (*H.E.* 7.32) tells us that in book 1 of this commentary Origen discussed the title Theotokos as it applied to Mary. This is a section now lost, presumably because Rufinus did not much care for the christological caveats Origen presumably added to the notion of Theotokos, which had been used in his time in a predominantly pagan context (the divine mother Isis) and was only just making its appearance as a Christian term. Fragments of books 5 and 6 in the Greek were found at Toura, covering the text of Romans 3:5 through 5:7.

Further Reading:

Hammond-Bammel (1995); Murphy (1954); Quasten (1975), 50; Roukema (1988); Wratislav (1860).

(d) *Commentary on the Canticle of Canticles*

Origen composed a ten-book commentary on the Canticle of Canticles, conscious of the work of the great Rabbi Akibah and with the explicit intent of showing how the Song was of relevance to the Christian canon of the Bible. He wrote the first five books of commentary while on a visit to the church of Athens sometime between 238 and 244. He completed the remaining five books when he returned to his home base in Caesarea (Eusebius, *H.E.* 6.32.2.). The commentary survives now only in part, in the Latin version Rufinus made in 410, which represents only the first four books. Jerome knew the whole work and himself translated two of Origen's homilies on the Canticle of Canticles into Latin. In his preface to his translation of the homilies (before he turned against the memory of the great Alexandrian) Jerome expressed the following sentiment: "In his other works, Origen habitually excels all others. In this commentary (on the Canticle of Canticles) he excelled himself." Origen continues the exegetical tradition of Akibah, who approached this love song allegorically. For Origen, the covenant love song is not simply a king marrying a bride, or even God speaking to Israel, but more specifically the divine Logos addressing his bride. In Jerome's version the bride is predominantly seen to be the church of Christ. In Rufinus's version the bride is predominantly the soul of the disciple, mystically initiated into the bridal chamber of the Logos. In both interpretations (and doubtless both emanated from Origen himself) a profoundly biblical ecclesiology is advanced, but especially in the tradition that sees the soul as the bride. Origen's work in the commentary can be rightly regarded as the first major Christian text outlining a theory of mystical union with the Bridegroom. Almost all Christian spiritual and ascetic literature, ever since, has been indebted to Origen's foundational architecture of Christian mysticism.

Further Reading:

Crouzel (1989), 122–23; Kimmelman (1980); Quasten (1975), 50; Tollinton (1929); Urbach (1960).

(e) *Lost Commentaries*

The substantial part of Origen's biblical commentaries has been utterly lost or profoundly fragmented. What fragments survive among the ruins of this great work have been preserved in the Catenae and in patristic quotations. Origen is known to have written thirteen books of commentary on Genesis (Jerome, *Epist.* 36, To Damasus), the first eight books of which he wrote at Alexandria); forty-six books on the Psalms; thirty books on Isaiah; at least five books on Lamentations (Eusebius, *H.E.* 6.24.2); twenty-five books on Ezekiel according to Eusebius, and twenty-nine according to Jerome (there is a Greek fragment of book 20 of this in the *Philocalia* c. 11); and at least twenty-five on the minor prophets (Eusebius, *H.E.* 6.32.2) (there is a fragment of his commentary on Hosea in *Philocalia* c. 8). Small fragments of a hitherto lost commentary on the book of Kings was discovered among the Toura papyrus finds in 1941. A commentary on Job (three books in a Latin translation) that was formerly attributed to Origen is no longer regarded as authentic. Origen is also known to have written fifteen books of commentary on Luke, which are now lost. His commentary on Acts has been totally lost except for the one Greek fragment of book 4 that is found in the *Philocalia* 7.2. He also wrote five books of commentary on Galatians; three books on Ephesians, and other commentaries on Philippians, Colossians, Thessalonians, Hebrews, Titus, and Philemon. Jerome admitted that his own commentaries on Galatians, Ephesians, Titus, and Philemon were close copies of those of Origen. Of the originals nothing except a few scattered fragments in the Catenae has survived. Origen is not known to have written anything at all on Mark or the Catholic Epistles. Nor has any work survived on the book of Revelation, though he does seem to have indicated his intention to write on that subject (*SerMt* 49).

Further Reading:
De Boysson (1913); Quasten (1975), 51.

4. APOLOGETIC OR CONTROVERSIAL WORKS

(a) *Against Celsus (Kata Kelsou, Contra Celsum)*

The treatise *Against Celsus* is the only extant work of Origen where he turned his considerable skills as a rhetorical apologist against an "outside" opponent in a sustained work of critical rebuttal. The apologetic element is present in much of Origen's work, but this treatise is sui generis. It is a major work of apologia, a defense of Christianity that simultaneously looks back to the past (when Christian writers before him—"the Apologists"—had produced a considerable body of such literature) but marks a decisive new beginning. It is a curious book on many levels, not least because in it Origen is arguing with a formidable Sophist who profoundly despised Christianity but belonged to a previous century and had written his own work seventy years before Origen. The *Contra Celsum* is a work that simultaneously lies within and without the apologetic tradition because of the peculiar genius Origen demonstrates. Celsus, who wrote *The True Word* attacking the Christians in 178, was one of the most serious intellectual critics the early church ever faced. The general response to his original attacks was a profound silence in the church. Ambrose, Origen's wealthy patron, was determined not to let this matter rest and pressed Origen to answer the charges and mockeries that Celsus had leveled against the Christian religion. Origen's first response was a traditional one, to prefer to let it all lapse into profound obscurity (the church "lost" a great deal of hostile material by refusing to acknowledge or reproduce it over the centuries), and he explicitly argued that this was Jesus' own method of refutation, as when he refused to answer the hostile high priest during his trial. But once Ambrose had brought the issue to his attention, the fundamental claim that Celsus had made (that no self-respecting philosopher of the Platonic tradition and no cultured Hellenist could possibly be so stupid as to enter the ranks of Christians) rankled with him so much that he had to write a refutation. In doing so, he not only addresses the individual points Celsus raised, but he also began to sketch out a Christian interpretation of culture and philosophical religion on a much more profound basis than the earlier apologists ever did. It was the first draft, as it were, of a sustained Christian reflection on the evangelization of Hellenistic culture that was to move at greater pace in the work of the Cappadocian fathers in the fourth century and finally become the intellectual charter of Christian Byzantium—the "Christianization of Hellenism," as Florovsky called it.

Origen also saw, with his usual intellectual honesty, that Celsus had raised some serious problems that needed a reflective answer from Christians. The approach Celsus took was generally that of the urbane and inclusive Hellenist. Christians are accused of pandering to the Hellenistic folk mythology that reduced the sublime divinity to earthly "avatars." The figure of Jesus is assailed in the text of his *True Word* as singularly unsuitable even to sustain this low-level mythology of God-made-man, insofar as Celsus accuses him of being merely a magician advancing his vainglorious cause by deceit and reliance on simplemindedness. Celsus had clearly studied to write his book and gives the reader a unique perspective on the Scriptures—the first record of an outsider's opinion on the Christian canon. He was not impressed and makes many literary charges concerning the evident inconsistencies among the various Gospel accounts over basic historical matters. Overall, Celsus thinks that the Christians could be "tolerated" because they have a reasonable grasp of ethics and a potential for sublime thought in their (flawed) doctrine of the perennial logos of God, but they need "to do better" by leaving aside their misanthropic exclusivism and learning from Hellenistic wisdom.

When Origen embarked upon this book, he was partly predetermined by the agenda of Celsus; and so he follows the points closely enough that a good idea of the original scheme of *The True Word* can be reconstituted from Origen's work. Origen also had an agenda of his own, which he specifically refers to in his preface (par. 6) to the book. This writing, he says, is not a work for Christians, but for waverers—those who are considering entering the ranks of the church but are of "weak faith" and need some encouragement. He was over sixty years of age when he started this work (Eusebius, *H.E.* 6.36.1), thus sometime after 246, and part of his interest in it must be related to the efforts he had expended in Caesarea to establish a Christian Schola. The school, as it was developing and gaining in reputation, had as part of its general intent to serve as a missionary outreach to contemporary Hellenist society. To have a treatise that answered serious critical objections that had been raised against the new religion, suitable to give to inquiring pagan intellectuals who attended the school for their general education in sciences and humanities, but who were also then attracted to the Christian faith, was a pressing need for the mid-third century.

In the time of the Constantinian expansion of the church, Eusebius regarded the book as such a treasure that (for him) it answered all contemporary charges against the Christian religion and all charges that could possibly be raised in the future (Eusebius, *Against Hierocles* 1). The work is a testimony to Origen's serious engagement in honest intellectual debate with Celsus (as much as any ancient apologia was ever such a thing) and set a tone that was not always honored among Christian apologists in times to come. In taking up issues such as why the Gospels were self-contradictory, Origen set the compass-bearing for an inestimable number of Christian intellectual questions for generations to come. One of the leading "lights" of his book, however, is the sense driving him throughout it all, that Celsus, while a very clever man, is far from being a wise man. Origen presses the issue to develop a theology of graceful revelation: the inner spirit of the Gospel, despite its outer shabby dress (its uncouth appearance), contains within it a power and a freshness that attract open and honest minds across the generations. This spirit, for Origen, is the divine power that provides the perennial renewal and refreshment of the Christian religion and offers, for the first time, the genuine possibility that all men and women (not merely the clever or the wealthy) can access the understanding, the mercy, and the very presence of God. The treatise against Celsus, therefore, is far more than a simple Christian apologia in the old style. It opens a window on the mission Origen had established for his school in Caesarea and is a chief witness for the "character of Christianity" that he wanted it to present to the world. The compilers of the *Philocalia* made extensive use of this text as a useful apologetic for the fourth-century church. Almost one-seventh of the text of the *Philocalia* derives from this one treatise.

Further Reading:
Borret (1997); Le Boulluec (1998); Quasten (1975), 56–57.

(b) *Dialogue with Heracleides*

This fascinating text, rediscovered among the Toura papyri in 1941, is a stenographer's record of an actual dialectical debate, or colloquium discussion, between Origen and an Arabian bishop theologian called Heracleides, held in Arabia sometime around 254. The stenographer was probably part of Origen's academic establishment. The text presents Origen as a theological peritus who has been called to assist a synod of bishops who are concerned about the orthodoxy of a member of their episcopal bench—Heracleides. Origen's reputation as a leading international theologian, and heroic confessor (after the recent persecutions in Palestine) made him an ideal candidate to represent the authoritative voice of international Christianity. He also was present at the Arabian synod in the role of a representative of his own Palestinian hierarchs, the bishops of the dominant sees of that region, Caesarea and Jerusalem. The dialogue is lively and has all the marks of a faithful record of the actual discussion. Heracleides seems to have been a representative of quasi-monarchianist thinking, certainly not a devotee of the Logos school of theology that was making its ascendancy in Rome and in Caesarea. One of the results of the rise of the Logos school, of course, was the need to articulate a more precise theology of the divine unity than had hitherto been acceptable in the more poetic scriptural accounts of the relationship of the divine Son and the Father. The issue "how many gods are there" is central to the *Dialogue*. Heracleides insists that there is only one God. Origen questions him as to whether or not he includes the Son in the divine being, in the process defending his own use of the terminology "two gods," which Heracleides found objectionable. The discussion was not a formal trial of Heracleides but an informal theological exchange designed to ensure that all the bishops agreed on common doctrine. The Modalist-Logos theological tension was becoming a point of stress in several places in the third-century church (not least in Rome), and this dialogue shows a lively concern among the bishops and the leading theologians of the day to resolve it in a way that would avoid the controversy the issue had publicly generated at Rome, as for example between Hippolytus and Callistus. The resolution of the "problema" is presented as an affirmation of the best in the two Christian traditions of the Monarchians and the Logos theologians:

> **Origen said:**   Is the Father not God?
> **Heracleides answered:**   Yes.
> **Origen said:**   Is the Son not other (*heteros*) than the Father?
> **Heracleides answered:**   How could he be at one and the same time both Son and Father?

Origen said:	But is this Son, who is other than the Father, not also God himself?
Heracleides answered:	Yes; He is also God himself.
Origen said:	Do not the two gods therefore become one?
Heracleides answered:	Yes.
Origen said:	Therefore we confess two gods?
Heracleides answered:	Yes—but the power is but one (*dynamis mia estin*).

By admitting that the Son was not simply the Father under another title, Heracleides proved himself not to be a Modalist heretic; and by accepting Origen's explanation of the "two gods," and gaining Origen's admission that the affirmation of two was always understood to affirm equally a singleness of the divine "dynamis" or activity, a resolution of all the problems was attained. It is substantially the classic architecture of Trinity that will emerge in later centuries (after the fires of several other controversies) to state that in the Christian understanding of God there is a plurality of divine persons and a singularity of divine essence, power, and will.

The *Dialogue* moved on to consider other "theologoumena" of the Arabian church that were seen to be increasingly out of line with the international confession of Christian faith, nascent orthodoxy, as it were. This latter part of the *Dialogue* concerned the questions raised by two other Arabian bishops, Dionysius and Philip. The first asked whether the soul was the same as the blood. The question rises out of a deeply Semitic mindset, formed by the Scriptures, where the blood was seen as the sacred life of a being infused by God (and one of the reasons for the sacral prohibitions in the old Law regarding the consumption of blood—a thing that early Christian legislation also banned in the church). Origen affirms that the blood truly is the soul, but not in a physical sense (which seems to have been the attitude of Dionysius). The "blood which is the soul" for Origen is the "interior man," the creature as covenant-elect of God, or what Scripture elsewhere calls the "righteous." When physical death occurs, it is this soul-blood that separates from the body and enters the company of the just, in communion with Christ.

This question on blood and soul led on immediately to another query from Bishop Philip as to whether the soul was immortal or not. Platonic thought, of course, had no issue with the understanding of the soul as an inherently immortal reality. But scriptural testimony in the Old Testament did not affirm this at all clearly, and elements of the New Testament seemed on some occasions to suggest that it was immortal and at other times to suggest it was only "conditionally" immortal. Origen's careful consideration of the overall nature of the biblical record did much to establish his opinions as the common view on the soul, which would henceforth be standard among Christians. He answers that the soul is both mortal and immortal, and is such according to its relation to three kinds of death. The first is the "death to sin" (Rom. 6:2), since the one who is dead to sin is made alive to God. The second is the "death towards God" (Ezek. 18:4), since the one who is dead toward God lives only for sin. The third is what is commonly understood as natural death. The soul of the human being is not subject in any sense to this third kind of death. In this regard alone it is naturally immortal. In regard to the other two deaths, however (to sin, and to God), the soul is potentially mortal. If it dies to sin, it finds immortal life anyway, and so its spiritual mortality, in this case, is in fact its true immortality, a sense of immortality central to the Gospel proclamation. If it dies to God, however, this spiritual mortality renders its natural immortality a curse, for the whole purpose of its true life is thereby frustrated. All in all, Origen reconciles the biblical insight that creaturely life (be it physical or psychic) is fragile, conditional, and dependent on the gift of God, with the Hellenistic philosophical insight that the soul is an immortal entity; and he teaches a synthesized view that while the human being is indeed a fragile being poised between life and death (Athanasius of Alexandria would later take him to posit a peculiar me-ontic condition poised between being and nonexistence), the human nevertheless extends its fragile potentiality by having as its existential goal no less than communion with the deity (and humans thus take, as their specific ontological risk, profundities of the perversion of being that no other sentient creature can imagine). It is such an insight that gives all of Origen's writings, whether biblical, dogmatic, or philosophical, a profoundly soteriological cast, concerned with the ascent of creaturely being to transcendent status.

Further Reading:
Capelle (1951); Lee (1967); Quasten (1975), 64.

5. DOCTRINAL AND PRACTICAL TREATISES

(a) *First Principles* (*Peri archon, De principiis*)

In Alexandria, in his time as young and flourishing theologian there, sometime between 220 and 230, Origen wrote the four books of the *On First Principles,* the first ever Christian systematic theology handbook. It was probably the issuing of these volumes that initiated the bitter controversies with Bishop Demetrius of Alexandria, which finally drove him out of the city, to make him take up residence in Caesarea. Only fragments of the original Greek remain of the work, mainly preserved in the *Philocalia,* and in the edicts of the Emperor Justinian. Rufinus, however, set himself the task of making a complete translation of the treatise, and so it survived more or less complete in his Latin version. Modern critical editions of the *First Principles* note where the Greek text is extant, and usually list it alongside in parallel columns, so that readers can take notice of the divergences between the original and the translated versions. Rufinus was well aware, when he began this translation, that Origen's reputation in the fifth-century church was increasingly problematic. He set out from the beginning with the intention of "smoothing over" and "correcting" the elements he found there of dubious orthodoxy (often cutting them altogether). Jerome, whose earlier friendship with Rufinus had by this time turned to a deep hostility, decided to kill two birds with one stone and denounced Origen as an unreliable theologian by showing up Rufinus as a devious apologist and an unreliable translator. In order to show the many times Rufinus had "cut corners" he began his own translation of the *First Principles,* with the intention of producing a completely faithful and accurate Latin version. Sadly, this has not survived.

The treatise begins with a magisterial essay from Origen on the nature and task of theology, in relation to tradition, the scriptural record, and the spiritual capacity of the intellect of the theologian-disciple (it would be resumed in the *Five Theological Orations* of Gregory of Nazianzus, an admiring disciple from the fourth century, and so would have a long-term impact on Christian consciousness).

Here he argues that all Christian understanding proceeds from the teaching of Christ and the first illuminated disciples in an "apostolic tradition" of the sacred kerygma. He notes, however, that many believers already seem to have divergences over substantial matters of Christian belief, and so it was necessary to list and order the sacred kerygma. All his task, however, was to manifest the truth: "And that alone is to be accepted as truth which in no way whatsoever differs from ecclesiastical and apostolical tradition" (*PArch* Praef. 1–2). After his preface, Origen divides his work into four subtreatises, each commanding a whole book: theology, cosmology, anthropology, and teleology.

Book 1 considers the heavenly world: the oneness of God, the nature of divine spirit, and the relations of the three divine persons. It concludes with a discussion of the original nature and fall of the angels. Book 2 considers the material cosmos. Humankind was created in the aftermath of the fall of angels. Humanity is the sum of fallen spirits enclosed in fleshly bodies. The book treats the fall of Adam and humankind's redemption in Christ and ends with the doctrines of resurrection, last judgment, and immortal life. Book 3 develops the destiny and duty of human-kind in terms of a cosmic moral struggle. Demons attempt to make permanent the human falling away from God and frustrate the race's realization of essential wisdom in communion with God. Even so, angels assist humans in their psychic ascent to the vision of the Godhead. Free will is the focus of his moral teleology. The final book sum-mates all his "first principles" of Christian philosophy and teaching, and comes back to the positing of the interpretation of Scripture as the fundamental theolo-gical method—the perfect system of arriving at wisdom. Here Origen outlines his basic understanding of the three senses of Scripture (body, soul, and spirit) (*PArch* 4.1.11). The *First Principles* was a tour de force for Origen, an attempt at no less than a synthesis between the curricula of the schools of philosophy, as they were then represented by leading *Didaskaloi* in Alexandria, and the Christian sys-tem of truth ("our philosophy"), which Origen wished to make available for seekers, based on a profound immersion in "sacred literature," "sacred tradition," and its detailed literary and philosophical analysis. Nothing like it had ever been seen before in Christianity, and although many of its sketched-out avenues for develop-ment caused more alarm than admiration for many later thinkers, it is neverthe-less unarguable that behind all the theological arguments of the next three centuries, it was Origen's agenda in this book (in Trinitarian thought, Christology, anthropology, hermeneutics, eschatology, and ecclesiology) that served as the point of departure.

Further Reading:
Harl (1975); Kannengiesser (1986); Quasten (1975), 61–62.

(b) *Miscellanies (Stromata)*

Private philosophical teachers were expected to take their students systematically through the various subjects fit for the education of the upper classes. In preparing his *Peri archon* Origen had sketched out what was different about his particular form of Platonism compared to all others, and what was significant about the Christian eclec-ticism that was the hallmark of his own Schola. The *Peri archon* is the announcement of an agenda of a whole career's work. It was also customary, however, for an advanced teacher to have a dossier of advanced seminar-type classes. This is what is basically represented by Origen's book of *Stromata*. The word also means "carpets," "tapestries," or simply "bits and pieces" (hence *Miscellanies*). The work would have been a collection of higher level questions to pose and resolve among the group of his advanced students. It is now completely lost, apart from tiny fragments existing in quotations. It had been written at Alexandria before 231; Eusebius knew of it in the fourth century and undoubtedly had the autograph copy of the work before him when he wrote, "This he composed in ten books in the same city [Alexandria] before his removal, as is demonstrated by the annotations in his own handwriting in the front cover of the volumes" (Eusebius, *H.E.* 6.24.3). This book was probably what Jerome had in mind when he said that Origen compared elements of Christian teaching with the doctrines of the various schools of philosophy, particularly as represented by Plato, Aristotle, Numenius, and Cornutus (Jerome, *Epist.* 70.4).

Further Reading:
Berchman (1984); Quasten (1975), 65.

(c) *On Prayer* (*Peri euches, De oratione*)

Origen wrote this short treatise on the nature of prayer—another first, for it was a determinative text for the church considering the nature and practice of prayer—at the request of his patron Ambrose and his sister Tatiana. He composed it shortly after coming to Caesarea, between 233 and 234. The work falls into two parts. The opening section (chaps. 3–17, resuming and concluding in chaps. 31–34) deals with the question of prayer in general, and how it can be reconciled with issues such as free will, the foreknowledge and predestination of God, and inevitability in the natural order (viz., is there any use in praying for particular things to happen if they are already determined in God's ordained plan for the world?). Origen approaches the question of prayer both practically and philosophically. In practical terms he discusses the suitable place of prayer, and the correct postures and orientation. He also covers a range of biblical examples of "good prayer" from which one can learn by studying the Scriptures. He characterizes prayer as falling under four basic types: petition, adoration, supplication, and thanksgiving (cf. 1 Tim. 2:1). Origen is clear in this work that prayer ought to be addressed to God the Father alone. Christ's mediating role precludes his reception of prayer "as to himself," since the Logos's primary function is as mediating "priest" of the Father. In other works on prayer, written later in his life, Origen did not sustain this strict division and often addressed prayers himself directly to Christ as saving divine Lord, but it was a cause of controversy among later spiritual writers, who regarded the christological implications with disapproval.

In his philosophical discussion Origen refines the understanding of God's foreknowledge of all things, distinguishing it from the wrong notion of God as a totalist predeterminer of all things—and here he evokes the sense that the divine plan includes within it the invitation to human beings to share in shaping destiny (the calling down of the kingdom) through prayer and fidelity. His major thrust in this section is to present an apologia for Christian praxis in prayer and spirituality, while making an answer to the gnostics, who were more inclined to theories of predeterminism and fatalism and who generally regarded the biblical instances of people praying to God for interventions and favors as simplistic pieties that were inappropriate for spiritually mature people. Origen was careful to make a direct line of connection between the spiritual experience of God in the old covenant and the providence of God as revealed in the incarnation of the Logos.

The second section of the treatise (chaps. 18–30) is an extended commentary on the Lord's Prayer taken verse by verse. Again, it is the first written commentary on the Our Father that the church produced and served as a model for the commentaries of many later theologians, chief among whom was Origen's ardent disciple from the Byzantine era, Maximus the Confessor. Origen is the first Christian theologian to argue that the conception of God's fatherhood in the church (as given by Jesus) is distinctively different from anything that can be found in earlier religious experience among humans. Origen's general premise in this work (that the soul of the disciple must be purified before there can be any expectation of standing in the divine presence) was of monumental significance in influencing all later ascetical writings on prayer. In his *Commentary on Canticles* and in his *Treatise on Prayer*, Origen can rightly be said to have founded the monumental Christian tradition of spiritual literature that would soon follow. For this reason, although not technically a monastic himself (although he was certainly an ascetic Sophist), Origen has also often been seen as a forerunner and theorist of the Christian monastic movement. The section on the philosophical questions related to prayer stands sufficiently apart from the commentary on the Lord's Prayer to suggest that the latter was the result of his Lenten priestly catechetical lectures to the baptismal candidates of the church of Caesarea in the mid-230s. It was customary for the priests to prepare the candidates by exorcising them and instructing them in ethics, the creed, and the basic prayers of the church. The commentary upon the Lord's Prayer is probably, therefore, one of the earliest examples of Christian prebaptismal catechesis that has survived.

Further Reading:
Bertrand (1992); Perrone (1993); Quasten (1975), 69; Sheerin (1988).

(d) *The Exhortation to Martyrdom (Protreptikos, Peri martyriou, Exhortatio ad martyrium)*

While resident in Caesarea in 235, Origen was informed of the outbreak of a new persecution against the church, which was ordered by Emperor Maximinus Thrax. Origen wrote the *Exhortation to Martyrdom* to encourage those who had been captured (he particularly refers to the priest Protoctetus and the deacon Ambrose), to help them stand fast to their faith and trust in God's providence. Among circles in his church there were sentiments beginning to circulate that it did not matter so very much if one sacrificed to the Roman gods, if one "still held the faith in one's heart" (*ExhMart* 45–46). Origen stands fast to his native Egyptian tradition on martyrdom, which held to a much more rigorous attitude, a tradition he had maintained since his youth (cf. Eusebius, *H.E.* 6.2. 2–6). Any vacillation, he says, is a betrayal of the baptism Christians have received; and so he is concerned that the clergy of the Palestinian church should give a perfect witness and that the evils of apostasy and false worship should not stain the church membership in this time of trial. Chapters 22–33 offer a series of biblical examples of martyrial faithfulness. His work then goes on to consider the Gospel evidence (chaps. 34–44) that tells how Christ will demand fidelity of his disciples and offer the kingdom only to those who did not deny him. The work ends with the rousing cry to stand firm and a reminder that God himself will not look by idly as his righteous saints are murdered, but will demand a reckoning for their blood. In the meantime, the sufferings of the saints will purify them and redeem others too (chap. 50).

Further Reading:
Bright (1988); McGuckin (1993); Quasten (1975), 72–73.

(e) *Concerning Pascha (Peri pascha)*

Fragments of the treatise of Origen dealing with Pascha (Easter) were found in the same manuscript at Toura in 1941 that contained the *Dialogue with Heracleides*. Before this discovery it had been known only from a passing mention of it in the first chapter of the Book of the Reckoning of Easter (*Liber Anatoli de ratione paschali*, PG 10.210). An edition was published in 1979 by P. Nautin, who exercised meticulous skill in attempting to reconstitute the meaning of the text, since it had been recovered in a state of advanced decomposition. In 1992 R. J. Daly produced a most helpful translation and commentary on the surviving fragments. In his references to the Scriptures Origen comments twice on Exodus 12:1–11 and Exodus 12:1–24, without appearing to anticipate or refer back to either of his versions. Partly on this basis the scholar Sgherri has argued recently that there were originally two separate tracts of Origen relating to the Paschal liturgy and that these fragments combine them.

Further Reading:
Halton (1983); Sgherri (2000).

(f) *Treatise on the Resurrection*

Origen wrote two books on his understanding of the resurrection while still resident at Alexandria and before beginning the *First Principles* (*PArch* 2.10.1; Eusebius, *H.E.*

6.24.2). Jerome also refers to two dialogues on the same subject that Origen dedicated to his patron Ambrose. Quoted fragments of these works survive in (generally hostile) apologies against Origen's belief in the spirituality of the resurrection body, written by Methodius of Olympus (*On the Resurrection*) and Jerome (*Against John of Jerusalem* cc. 25–26). When one compares the surviving Greek fragments common to Methodius and Epiphanius, Methodius emerges as a heavy paraphraser, intent on giving the ideas of Origen in digest form, not in a faithful version of the text.

Further Reading:

Chadwick (1948); Crouzel (1973, 1980).

6. LETTERS

A theologian of such eminence as Origen can be expected to have left a vast body of letters. Eusebius of Caesarea appears to have made an edition of them in the fourth century (Eusebius, *H.E.* 6.36.3) totaling nine volumes in all, counting more than a hundred letters then available to him. Of this epistolary canon only two letters of Origen have survived complete, and a few tiny fragments otherwise in citations.

(a) *Letter to Theodore* (*Address to Theodore*)

Origen's *Address to Theodore* is the first of the large surviving letters. Theodore is generally understood to be his disciple, a young man studying with him in Caesarea, who subsequently became a leading missionary of the Cappadocian church under the name of Gregory Thaumaturgus. The text of the letter is preserved in the *Philocalia*, chapter 13. It seems to have been written from Nicomedia between 238 and 243. Origen describes an attitude that was to become constitutive of Christian approaches to Hellenistic culture and learning ever afterward—follow the example of the Hebrews who left Egypt, and despoil the Egyptians of their gold and silver so that it can be reused to decorate the shrine of God. Just so, Christians should take from the Hellenes "the treasures of the mind" and use them in the service of the true God. The letter encourages Theodore to continue his studies day by day, through the assiduous reading of the divine Scriptures.

(b) *Letter to Julius Africanus*

The second letter, again emanating from Nicomedia (for Origen mentions in the prologue that he is staying with Ambrose, who is serving as his scribe), was written circa 240. It is known as Origen's *Reply to Julius Africanus*. Julius was a vastly learned Christian bibliophile, who at one stage in his career was librarian at the Pantheon in Rome. He had written to Origen remarking that he had read his discussion of the elders disputing with Susanna in one of his earlier works; he criticized Origen for not recognizing that this passage could not possibly be regarded as divine Scripture, first because it was not found in the Hebrew text, but second because it was so different both in tone and stylistic character from the rest of the book of Daniel that it was clearly a corrupt interpolation. The letter from Africanus was probably the only time in Origen's life when he had encountered an intelligence as polymathic as his, and it sparked off an interesting reply that was preserved, not only for its inherent interest, but also because it turned on an important matter of principles of establishing the canon of Christian Scriptures. Origen made a strong defense of the canonicity of the story of Susanna and the elders and threw in for good measure a defense of the other comparable "deuterocanonical" texts, such as the story of Bel and the Dragon, the Prayers of Azarias, and the story of the three youths in the fiery furnace—stories in Daniel that exist only in the Septuagintal version of the Bible. In spite of his spirited defense of stories that had already made a great impact on early Christian piety and primitive iconography (the three youths were a favored catacomb fresco subject long before the third century), Origen in the end largely ignores the literary questions Africanus raises, and settles instead for a view of canonicity as established by church tradition. He wags a finger back at Africanus and warns him, "Do not remove the ancient boundary marks which have been set up by your fathers" (Prov. 22:28).

The large remainder of the letters has been lost. Eusebius (*H.E.*, book 6) mentions several of the more significant among them, notably a letter to the Emperor Philip the Arab (possibly the first of the Roman emperors who was Christian) (see **Roman Empire**); a letter to the wife of Philip, the Empress Severa; and several letters to Pope Fabian (236–50). Eusebius, who had the collection of the letters before him as he composed his "Life of Origen" in book 6 of his *Church History*, seems to have made particular use of an "Autobiographical Letter," probably from the time when Origen was busy defending his reputation in Rome, Alexandria, and Palestine against the criticisms that Demetrius of Alexandria had raised against him. At this time he also addressed Pope Fabian, whom Demetrius had involved in his canonical process. The letter Origen wrote at this same time to his "Friends in Alexandria" was an important source for Eusebius in drafting his life of Origen.

Further Reading:

Crouzel (1989), 37–49; Quasten (1975), 74–75.

John A. McGuckin

CRITICAL EDITIONS OF ORIGEN'S WORKS— LATIN AND GREEK

These are the three most commonly used editions of the Greek and Latin works of Origen.

1. Migne–PG

The Migne Patrologia Graeca (PG) version, reproduced by J. P. Migne in the nineteenth century (as PG, vols. 11–17) from the earlier Maurist edition (so called as it was sponsored by the monastery of St. Maur). This was the labor of the learned De La Rue monks who were uncle and nephew. This edition was later emended by Lommatzsch (viz., *Origenis opera omnia quae graece vel latine tantum exstant et ejus nomine circumferuntur. Ed. C. et C. V. Delarue. Denuo recensuit, emendavit et castigavit. C. H. E. Lommatzsch.* I–XXV, Berlin, 1831–48).

2. GCS

The "Berlin-Leipzig" critical edition was the best for its day and is not yet superseded in some volumes, viz., *Die griechischen christlichen Schriftsteller der ersten Jahrhunderte* (*GCS*). The Origen volumes in this series are sometimes cited by the "Origen volume" number rather than the volume number of the *GCS* series as a whole, which also covers many other patristic writers.

P. Koetschau	*Die Schrift vom Martyrium, Buch I–IV gegen Celsus* (Origenes Werke, I). Leipzig, 1899.
P. Koetschau	*Buch V–VIII gegen Celsus, Die Schrift vom Gebet* (Origenes Werke, II). Leipzig, 1899.

E. Klostermann	*Jeremiahomilien, Klageliederkommentar, Erklärung der Samuel- und Königsbücher* (bearbeitet von P. Nautin) (Origenes Werke, III). 2nd ed. Berlin, 1983.
E. Preuschen	*Der Johanneskommentar* (Origenes Werke, IV). Leipzig, 1903.
P. Koetschau	*De Principiis* (Origenes Werke, V). Leipzig, 1913.
W. A. Baehrens	*Homilien zum Hexateuch in Rufins Uebersetzung (Die Homilien zu Genesis, Exodus und Leviticus)* (Origenes Werke, VI). Leipzig, 1920.
W. A. Baehrens	*Homilien zum Hexateuch in Rufins Uebersetzung (Die Homilien zu Numeri, Josua und Judices)* (Origenes Werke, VII). Leipzig, 1921.
W. A. Baehrens	*Homilien zu Samuel I, zum Hohelied und zu den Propheten, Kommentar zum Hohelied in Rufins und Hieronymus' Uebersetzung* (Origenes Werke, VIII). Leipzig, 1925.
M. Rauer	*Die Homilien zu Lukas in der Uebersetzung des Hieronymus und die griechischen Reste der Homilien und des Lukas-Kommentars* (Origenes Werke, IX). Berlin, 1959.
E. Klostermann and E. Benz	*Origenes Matthäuserklärung I. Die griechischerhaltenen Tomoi* (Origenes Werke, X). Leipzig, 1935.
E. Klostermann and E. Benz	*Origenes Matthäuserklärung II. Die lateinische Uebersetzung der Commentariorum Series* (bearbeitet von U. Treu) (Origenes Werke, XI). Berlin, 1976.
E. Klostermann and E. Benz	*Origenes Matthäuserklärung III. Fragmente und Indices* (Origenes Werke, XII/1). Leipzig, 1941.
E. Klostermann and L. Fruchtel	*Origenes Matthäuserklärung III. Fragmente und Indices* (zweite, durchgesehene Auflage besorgt von U. Treu) (Origenes Werke, XII/2). Berlin, 1968.

3. Sources Chrétiennes

The most modern critical edition of the works is in the series Sources chrétiennes (SC).

L. Doutreleau	*Homélies sur la Genèse.* SC 7. Paris, 1976.
M. Borret	*Homélies sur l'Exode.* SC 321. Paris, 1985.
M. Borret	*Homélies sur le Lévitique.* 1. (Hom. 1–7). SC 286. Paris, 1981.
M. Borret	*Homélies sur le Lévitique.* 2. (Hom. 8–16). SC 287. Paris, 1981.
L. Doutreleau	*Homélies sur les Nombres.* 1. (Hom. 1–9). SC 415. Paris, 1996.
L. Doutreleau	*Homélies sur les Nombres.* 2. (Hom. 11–19). SC 442. Paris, 1999.
A. Jaubert	*Homélies sur Josué.* SC 71. Paris, 1960.
P. Messié et al.	*Homélies sur les Juges.* SC 389. Paris, 1993.
P. and M. Nautin	*Homélies sur Samuel.* SC 328. Paris, 1986.
H. Crouzel and L. Brésard	*Homélies sur les Psaumes 36 à 38.* SC 411. Paris, 1995.
M. Harl and G. Dorival	*La chaine palestinienne sur la psaume 118* (Origène et al.) SC 189–90. Paris, 1972.
O. Rousseau	*Homélies sur le Cantique des Cantiques.* SC 37. Paris, 1966.
L. Brésard et al.	*Commentaire sur le Cantique des Cantiques.* Vols. 1–2. SC 375–76. Paris, 1991–92.
P. Nautin et al.	*Homélies sur Jéremie.* 1. (Hom. 1–11). SC 232. Paris, 1976.
———	*Homélies sur Jéremie.* 2. (Hom. 12–20 and *Homélies latines*). SC 238. Paris, 1977.
M. Borret	*Homélies sur Ézéchiel.* SC 352. Paris, 1989.

R. Girod	*Commentaire sur l'Évangile selon Matthieu.* 1. (Livres 10–11). SC 162. Paris, 1970.
H. Crouzel et al.	*Homélies sur S. Luc.* SC 87. Paris, 1962.
C. Blanc	*Commentaire sur S. Jean.* 1. (Livres 1–5). SC 120. Paris, 1966.
——	*Commentaire sur S. Jean.* 2. (Livres 6 and 10). SC 157. Paris, 1970.
——	*Commentaire sur S. Jean.* 3. (Livre 13). SC 222. Paris, 1975.
——	*Commentaire sur S. Jean.* 4. (Livres 19–20). SC 290. Paris, 1982.
——	*Commentaire sur S. Jean.* 5. (Livres 28 and 32). SC 385. Paris, 1992.
M. Borret	*Contre Celse.* 1. (Livres 1–2). SC 132. Paris, 1967.
——	*Contre Celse.* 2. (Livres 3–4). SC 136. Paris, 1968.
——	*Contre Celse.* 3. (Livres 5–6). SC 147. Paris, 1969.
——	*Contre Celse.* 4. (Livres 7–8). SC 150. Paris, 1969.
——	*Contre Celse.* 5. Introduction générale—tables et index. SC 227. Paris, 1976.
H. Crouzel and M. Simonetti	*Traité des Principes.* 1. (Livres 1–2). SC 252. Paris, 1978.
——	*Traité des Principes.* 2. (Livres 1–2—fragments). SC 253. Paris, 1978.
——	*Traité des Principes.* 3. (Livres 3–4). SC 268. Paris, 1980.
——	*Traité des Principes.* 4. (Livres 3–4 fragments). SC 269. Paris, 1980.
——	*Traité des Principes.* 5. (Compléments et index). SC 312. Paris, 1984.
J. Scherer	*Entretien d'Origène avec Héraclide.* SC 67. Paris, 1960.
H. Crouzel	*Remerciement à Origène de Grégoire le Thaumaturge suivi de la lettre d'Origène à Grégoire.* SC 148. Paris, 1969.
M. Harl	*Philocalie. 1–20. Sur Les Écritures. Et le lettre d'Africanus sur l'histoire de Suzanne* (ed. N. De Lange). SC 302. Paris, 1983.
E. Junod	*Philocalie 21–27 sur le libre arbitre.* SC 226. Paris, 1976.

ENGLISH TRANSLATIONS OF THE WORKS OF ORIGEN

1. Series of Translations

ANCL vol. 10 (= vol. 1 of Origen's Works). F. Crombie, trans. Edinburgh, 1869. Containing *On First Principles; Letter to Julius Africanus; Letter to Gregory; Contra Celsum,* book 1. Reprint, Grand Rapids: Eerdmans, 1976.

ANCL vol. 23 (= vol. 2 of Origen's Works) (= *ANF,* vol. 4). Containing *Contra Celsum,* books 2–8. F. Crombie, trans. Edinburgh, 1872. Reprint, Grand Rapids: Eerdmans, 1976.

ANCL "Additional Volume" (= *ANF,* vol. 10). Edinburgh, 1897. Containing *Epistle to Gregory; Commentary on the Gospel of John,* trans. A. Menzies, selections = books 1, 2, 4–6, 10; and *Commentary on Matthew,* trans. J. Patrick, selections = books 1, 2, 10–14. Reprint, Grand Rapids: Eerdmans, 1974.

ACW 19. Containing *On Prayer; Exhortation to Martyrdom.* J. O'Meara, trans. Washington, 1954.

ACW 26. *The Song of Songs: Commentary and Homilies.* R. P. Lawson, trans. Washington, 1957.

ACW 54. *Origen: Treatise on the Passover and Dialogues of Origen with Heraclides and His Fellow Bishops, on the Father, the Son, and the Soul.* R. J. Daly, trans. New York, 1992.

Gregory Thaumaturgus: Origen the Teacher. W. C. Metcalfe, trans. London and New York: SPCK, 1907.

Treatise on Prayer. E. G. Jay, trans. London and New York: SPCK, 1954.

On First Principles. G. W. Butterworth, trans. London: SPCK, 1936. Reprint, New York: Harper Torchbooks, 1966.

FC 71. *Origen of Alexandria: Homilies on Genesis and Exodus.* R. Heine, trans. Washington, 1982.

FC 80. *Origen's Commentary on the Gospel according to John.* Books 1–10. R. E. Heine, trans. Washington, 1989.

FC 89. *Origen's Commentary on the Gospel according to John.* Books 13–32. R. E. Heine, trans. Washington, 1993.

FC 83. *Origen: Homilies on Leviticus 1–16.* G. W. Barkley, trans. Washington, 1990.

CWS. *Origen.* Contains *Exhortation to Martyrdom; On Prayer; First Principles,* book 4; Prologue to the *Commentary on the Song of Songs; Homily 27 on Numbers.* R. A. Greer, trans. New York: 1979.

2. Other Editions

Origen's Homilies on Joshua: An Annotated Translation. B. J. Bruce, trans. Michigan, 1990.

Contra Celsum. H. Chadwick, trans. CUP, 1953, 1980.

J. A. F. Gregg. "The Commentary of Origen upon the Epistle to the Ephesians." *JTS* 3 (1902):233–44; 398–420; 554–76.

C. Jenkins. "Origen on 1 Corinthians." *JTS* 9 (1908): 231–47; 353–72; 500–514; *JTS* 10 (1909):29–51.

The Philocalia of Origen. G. Lewis, trans. Edinburgh: Clark, 1911.

A. Ramsbotham. "The Commentary of Origen on the Epistle to the Romans." *JTS* 13 (1912):209–24; 237–368; *JTS* 14 (1913):10–22.

3. Anthologies

Alexandrian Christianity: Selected Translations of Clement and Origen. Containing selections from *On Prayer; Exhortation to Martyrdom,* and *Dialogue with Heracleides.* J. E. L. Oulton and H. Chadwick, eds. London, 1954.

H. Urs von Balthasar. R. J. Daly, trans. *Origen: Spirit and Fire. A Thematic Anthology of His Writings.* Washington, 1982.

The SCM Press
A–Z of Origen

Articles

48   Articles

Allegory   According to Origen, the interpretation of Scripture takes place at three different levels: that of the letter, that of the soul, and that of the spirit (*PArch* 4.2). The second and third levels in Origen's scheme are similar; both are a species of a practice that many modern scholars would call "figural reading." The concept of figural interpretation in antiquity was expressed by a variety of terms, one of which, *allegoria*, enjoyed a kind of privileged status because of its appearance in the letters of Paul (Gal. 4:24). For Origen and other ancient interpreters the term *allegoria* referred to the exegetical practice of discerning, in the text of the Bible, meanings that were not immediately evident and could not be uncovered without the application of a theologically enhanced exegetical gaze. This interpretive practice of seeing the mystery of the Christian economy hidden beneath the veil of the literal text of the ancient Scriptures allowed Origen, and the vast majority of later patristic interpreters, to retain the **Old Testament** as a living text of the Christian church. However, since the practice of allegorical reading contradicts in important ways some of the basic methodological laws of contemporary historical-critical method, it has been a frequent target of attack. These attacks and the defenses provoked by them have obscured rather than illuminated this ancient practice.

Modern historical method rests upon the assumption that history is the primary locus of revelation and that correct reading of a text depends upon a careful reconstruction of historical context. From this perspective, the ancient practice of allegorical reading appears to be nothing more than subjective eisegesis—a "reading in" of meanings rather than an honest "reading out." Many modern critics have dismissed ancient exegetical practice as unsalvageable. Some commentators, however, recognizing that figural reading in one form or another is a necessary component of Christian faith, have distinguished between "allegorical reading" and "typological reading." The former, it is argued, detaches a text from historical events, while the latter continues to value history by maintaining a connection. For example, the tendency to read the Song of Songs as the story of the soul's relationship to God is classed as illegitimate because the spiritual reading negates and ignores the actual historic sense of the text. On the other hand, reading the story of the exodus and the crossing of the Red Sea as a "type" of the passage of Christ and the Christian from death to new life is classed as legitimate, because such a reading is "event to event" and does not destroy the integrity of the source narrative. While this modern distinction between allegory and *typology* may seem an attractive way to reconcile patristic sensibility with modern exegetical concerns, it must be admitted it does not do much to illuminate ancient principles of exegesis.

Understanding the significance of allegory in Origen is further complicated by the late medieval development of the doctrine of "the four senses of scripture": the literal, the tropological (moral), the allegorical, and the anagogical (eschatological). While the use of these individual terms dates back to the patristic period, they are not systematically or universally employed in that era as a methodological set (see **Anagogical Interpretation**). Origen and other ancient authors did not even consistently distinguish between typology and allegory. Because of this, many modern readers find themselves confused about the meaning of allegory, especially as the practice is encountered in actual patristic sources. Another source of confusion surrounding the term *allegory* is the tendency of the ancient interpreters to avoid it after the outbreak of the late fourth-century **Origenist crisis,** giving the false impression that the practice it describes was then abandoned. As a result of that controversy, the use of "allegoria" was condemned, after the late fourth century, as the source of what anti-Origenists believed to be the theological errors of Origen and his intellectual descendants.

The general exegetical practice, however, survived virtually unchanged under the new designation of "theoria." Indeed, allegorical reading continued to be practiced without serious opposition in most Christian preaching and exegesis until the advent of historical-critical method in the modern era.

Allegorical reading, then, was a basic strategy of early Christian exegesis by which the unity of the Old and New Testaments was preserved and by which the christocentric character of the whole Bible was made manifest. Origen was certainly the most sophisticated practitioner of this method, but it was a common substrate for all patristic exegesis. Like most of his peers Origen believed that the literal meaning of a text was of limited value. At best the literal could provide basic instruction to the spiritual debutant or to the unsophisticated Christian. Those who were advancing in faith must find first the "soulish" (psychic) and then the "spiritual" (pneumatic, noetic) meaning of a text if they were to derive any lasting nourishment from Scripture. Interpretation at the level of the "soul" has sometimes been described as an attempt to discern the moral meaning of a text, but careful studies of Origen's work have demonstrated that such a view is not systemically sustainable (Torjesen 1986). Although Origen describes the psychic level of interpretation (PArch 4.2–3), he does not consistently attempt to tease out meaning at this level, making it difficult for modern readers to understand exactly what he meant. Rather than being simply "moral exegesis," his sense of psychic exegesis is rather an allegorical or figurative reading that does not pertain to the *mysteries* of the Christian faith.

The spiritual meaning was the level of scriptural interpretation that interested Origen the most, and the method he used to reach it was allegory. In his view, all of Scripture was a symbolic account of the mysteries of the Christian faith (see **Sacraments**). The **Holy Spirit** intentionally hid these mysteries in the form of the literal text, both as an accommodation to the simple who could benefit from the literal text and as a goad to the intelligent who would work harder at understanding because of the difficulties associated with spiritual reading (PArch 4.2.7 and 4.2.8). Allegory in Origen was not, as some have characterized it, the reading of the New Testament in the Old Testament. Neither was it a simple attempt to map the events of the old covenant on to the events of the new. Rather, allegory allowed Origen to read the whole Bible as a revelation of the progressive kingdom of Christ. It was a fundamentally eschatological process for Origen. In other words, allegorical method offered the inspired Christian reader a window into the heavenly Jerusalem, which was already invading and transforming the present age. Origen did not, as some have tried to argue, use allegory to destroy history; he used it to describe the fulfillment of God's plan for the world, the details of which are not accessible through the letter alone.

Dawson (1992); Dively-Lauro (2001); Torjesen (1985); Young (1989, 1997).

JOHN J. O'KEEFE

Anagogical Interpretation The English word *anagogical* derives from a Latin transliteration of the Greek *anagoge*. The term literally means "elevation, a lifting up, or a bringing back," but Origen and other patristic authors frequently used the word as a technical exegetical term designating spiritual interpretation (*pneumatike diegesis*). As such, in this more technical sense, it referred to a spiritual interpretation as distinct from a literal reading and was thus the functional synonym of allegory (*allegoria*) and spiritual contemplation (*theoria*). In later medieval usage, the anagogical, together with the literal, the allegorical, and the tropological, comprised the "four senses of the Scripture." In this context, anagogical exegesis meant interpretation specifically oriented toward discerning the eschatological dimension of the Scriptures, while the allegorical dealt with the mysteries of doctrine, and the tropological with the moral life. In the patristic period, however, this tradition of the four senses had not yet stabilized. Predictably then, the term *anagogy* in Origen's exegesis tends to function technically only some of the time, and it is never used to target only eschatological meaning.

A few examples should suffice. Sometimes Origen uses the word in its simplest etymological sense: "Is it not the case, then, that the bodily Israelites *carry back* (*anagoge ekousin*) to the patriarchs . . . " (*PArch* 4.3.7). Here the word is functioning quite basically. However, in the same chapter (*PArch* 4.3.4), the word takes on the more technical meaning of spiritual interpretation: "And again, who would deny that the command which says: 'Honor your father and mother, that it may go well for you,' is useful quite apart from any *spiritual interpretation*" (literally, "apart from any *anagoge*"). In this case, Origen has used the word to help him to distinguish between the simultaneous literal and spiritual meanings of a biblical text. Similarly (*ComJn* 1.8), Origen explains, interpreting Revelation 14.4–5, that "we must not be unaware that the discourse concerning the 144,000 virgins has a spiritual (anagogical) meaning."

Although Origen uses the word "anagogy" frequently, he does not limit usage to designate figurative readings that are eschatological. This does not imply, of course, that Origen did not engage in eschatological interpretation. On the contrary, one could argue that all of Origen's spiritual exegesis was designed, in some way, to point his readers and hearers toward the reality of God's eschatological kingdom (see **Allegory**). For Origen, finding spiritual meaning is not about mapping events in the Old Testament onto events in the New. Rather, finding spiritual meaning is a question of finding the spiritual reality, which is

generally eschatological rather than temporal, to which the text points, however obliquely.

While the relative imprecision of patristic exegetical terminology is often confusing to people who are new to the topic, it is helpful to remember that the refining of a technique can come only after that technique is actually in place. Origen used nonliteral, allegorical techniques of interpretation to show how the entire Bible cohered as a narrative about the economy of the Son of God. In so doing, he pioneered much new exegetical territory for Christians. Later linguistic precision would be the domain of those who followed along the trail he blazed so brilliantly.

Dawson (2002); De Lubac (1998, 2000); Torjesen (1986).

JOHN J. O'KEEFE

Angels

Angels   When Origen is presenting the elements that constitute the basics of ecclesiastical preaching (*PArch Praef.* 10), he mentions the existence of angels: "This also is contained in the ecclesiastical teaching that there are certain angels of God, good powers who serve Him in the cause of effecting the salvation of humankind." His interest in the theme ranges over other questions too, such as the nature of angels, the manner of their creation, and their functions in the cosmic order. Origen did not approach angelology in any systematic manner, but from (sometimes lengthy) passages scattered over his works the main lines of his view on the subject can be sketched.

Angels possess a soul, a "vital and sensible substance" (*substantia sensibilis et mobilis*) (*PArch* 2. 8). They all share this same essence, which is extremely subtle, a mixture of fire and air (*ExhMart* 13; *CCels* 6.70) that is completely sui generis. Essentially, angels are spiritual beings (*CCels* 4.24–25; *PEuch* 27) and do not experience any corporeal needs in the manner of humans. They need food, just as corporeal humanity does, but their food is radically different from ours and consists of their direct participation in divine Wisdom (*ComJn* 13.214–26; *PEuch* 27). Angels are present everywhere, or rather "all things are full of angels" (*omnia angelis sunt plena*) (*HomEz* 1.7). Their role is first and foremost to be God's servants (*CCels* 8.13). They are part of the divine court, God's heavenly entourage (*ComMt* 15.7; *ComRm* 1.4). Angels are also ethical beings: having a free will, they are capable of making ethical decisions and hence of sinning. They are not beyond reproach or blame (*HomNum* 11.4; 20.3). The angelic hierarchy is based on merit (*PArch* 1.8). Angels are our examples in knowledge of God (*CCels* 5.5), though holy Christians, in this respect, can potentially climb even higher than the angels (*CCels* 4.29) and can see what remains hidden for the angels.

For Origen, angels operate as collaborators with divine providence, assisting in implementing God's care for his creation in general, and for humankind in particular. This is the aspect that comes most to the fore in what Origen has to say on the theme, and the general patristic tradition follows this same trend. Origen shares with many of his religious and philosophical contemporaries the idea that the entire creation, including heavenly bodies (*PEuch* 1), stars (*CCels* 4.29) and small insects, is guarded by a divine providence, embodied brilliantly in the presence of angels (*HomJr* 10. 6; *CCels* 8.31; *HomNum* 23.3).

Texts such as Psalm 90:11–12 and the story of Tobit had already popularized the notion of angelic protection for families or elect individuals. Following the LXX version of Deuteronomy 32:8, Origen taught that each nation also has its particular guardian angel (*HomGn* 9.3; *HomJos* 23.3; *CCels* 5.30–32). And showing the influence of parts of the book of Revelation, he also taught that each local church has an angel as her "heavenly episkopos" (*HomNum* 20.3; *HomLc* 13.5). From those biblical roots it was only a

small step to the belief that every single individual also has a guardian angel, assigned to protect and give spiritual guidance. This belief is deeply rooted and probably the most popular and cherished element of Christian angelology in all times. To the general patristic reflection on the role and function of individual guardian angels, Origen made an important contribution. He took Matthew 18:10 ("Take care that you do not despise one of these little ones; for, I tell you, in heaven their angels continually see the face of my Father in heaven.") as his major starting point and biblical authority for his doctrine of the angels' relationship to individual beings. He most notably develops his position in his commentary on this evangelical verse (*ComMt* 13.26–28).

Origen the preacher often encouraged his congregation to believe in the existence of individual guardian angels (*HomNum* 24.3). Probably because he was one of the first Christian thinkers to develop this aspect of angelology, his position is not always coherent. So, to the question exactly who has a guardian angel, his answer is ambiguous, even contradictory. In one passage Origen states explicitly that every person alive, Christian or non-Christian, has a guardian angel sent by God (*ComMt* 13.26). From other passages it would seem that only a Christian has the privilege of a guardian angel (*PArch* 2.10; *HomEz* 1.7). And again, in other places, one reads that only the righteous, the holy, are escorted by a heavenly spirit or angel; either because sinners have shown themselves unworthy of this benefaction (*ComMt* 13.6; 14.21), or simply because it is taken for granted that only the righteous should benefit from this kind of assistance (*CCels* 8.36; *HomNum* 5.3). In the end, he gives his opinion that only the imperfect need a guardian angel, since those gnostically perfected in the spiritual life have Christ himself as their helper (*HomNum* 24.3; *ComMt* 13.26). A similar ambiguity attaches itself to Origen's thought on the question as to when the guardian angel assumes a protective role. In one instance he says that the angelic oversight starts from the moment of a person's conception (*ComJn* 13.325–29), while elsewhere he surmises that it will commence from the time of *baptism* (*ComMt* 13.26).

Origen's generic view of the angelic role in the governance of human life (comparable to the role they will play as stern tutors for recalcitrant souls after life) is that they act as spiritual guides. They try to direct human beings to conversion to the true faith of Christianity when they see that the souls of their protegés are erring (*CCels* 5.57). As spiritual guides in the church their higher goal is to lead Christians toward the perfection of holiness. Thus they lead souls into the divine mystery, where they can become reacquainted with the knowledge of things divine (*HomNum* 14.2). They are fundamentally a support, like a pedagogue, for embodied souls who try to achieve progress in virtue and spiritual insight through the course of their earthly lives. Angels are ambassadors with God on behalf of human beings.

Origen envisaged the angels as mediators between God and humans. In this capacity the angels travel incessantly, up and down as on Jacob's ladder, in order to present to God our wishes, thoughts, intentions, and prayers (*HomLev* 9.8). Moreover, our guardian angel adds to our prayers those of his own in order to render them more efficacious (*PEuch* 11). When the angels return to earth, loaded with divine benefactions, they offer them to us in compensation for our respective merits (*CCels* 5.4).

Origen's doctrine of the angels would have a great effect in bringing devotion to the angels into the mainstream of Christian spiritual practice. Many of the monastic teachers on *prayer* in succeeding centuries would particularly emphasize his concept of the angels assisting the prayers of the saints; and his concept of the individual guardian angel whom God appointed for each Christian soul became a deeply rooted aspect of Christian spirituality.

———

Blanc (1976); Monaci-Castagno (2000), 6–15; Daniélou (1952).

JOHAN LEEMANS

Anthropology   Origen's anthropology can be separated only artificially from his theology of creation, an account of the diversity of beings, including the different grades of angelic beings, good and bad (Col. 1:16; 2:15), and in the human being the diversity of male and female, Christian and pagan, Greek and barbarian, whole and disabled. For Origen, nothing is a matter of fate: God's ordering of the world is rational and merciful. There are reasons for the diversity. First, beings are born, or placed, either in a perfect state or in the state consequent upon the aggregation of their free choices. Our choices dictate what we become. Second, the fall from a better to a lesser state remains within God's merciful economy, because the state of any creature also invites reformation through purgation. The main lines of Origen's anthropology derive from his reformative approach, which has the additional advantage of providing a theodicy: evils such as disease and pain have a purgative function (see *Cosmology*).

The Nature of Soul

In *PArch* 2.8.1, Origen declares humanity as essentially "soul" (see *Souls*), basing his view on Genesis 2, where God places in the man a "living soul" (*psyche*). His definition of soul is plastic. It is, ideally, the purely rational and spiritual in humanity, the body being accidental, so that soul equates, as far as the Latin translations allow, with the Greek *pneuma* or *nous*. However, the soul in practice has fallen into the condition of *psyche*, which Origen derives etymologically from "to cool," to indicate that the soul has to some extent lost its original ardor and attention to God (*PArch* 2.8.3). The soul, being "immortal by participation" (*PArch* 2.4.5), can participate in the Divine Light; the extent of the participation depending upon the degree of the soul's attention to God. Freedom to approach, or regress, from God is an essential characteristic of the soul: "It lies within ourselves and in our own actions to possess either happiness or holiness, or by sloth and negligence to fall from happiness into wickedness and ruin" (*PArch* 1.5.5). The fall from the soul's original created state of beatitude is, then, a result of its choice (see **Fall**). It follows that the soul is capable of sin and is indeed the source of sin. This idea Origen passed on to later schools of monastic asceticism (especially that of Evagrius): sin begins with our thoughts, leading to choices.

It follows that the human soul is not sinful just because it is embodied. The body becomes sinful when the soul goes astray and both become involved in carnality and passions that estrange the human being from God. Body or "matter" (*Soma, hyle*) is a corporal garment united to the human soul by God for a redemptive purpose, according to the needs and circumstances of the soul. Origen defines matter just as plastically as he does the soul. Matter is not an unchanging substance that by its nature presents a sharp repugnance to the spiritual or soul. On the contrary, it is more of an "unfinished reality" (*PArch* 4.4.8). This *hyle* was, as it were, the first level of created matter, unformed and bare of all qualities. This incomplete *hyle* is diversely formed by God's providence. Matter is thus not intrinsically resistant to spirit; indeed the highest destiny of all matter lies in the fact that it may be spiritualized (*PArch* 2.3.2). This is especially so with humanity, who, even at the most spiritual—that is, most restored to participation with God—is still to some extent a "body." Origen finds it hard to imagine that humanity will ever be entirely unembodied, just as he sees even **angels** as having an ethereal kind of material form. In this he was embracing Paul's idea of the redeemed, spiritualized humanity, resurrected in heaven, as a "spiritual body" (*PArch* 2.2.4; 1 Cor. 15:44). Origen primarily defined humanity as soul, but he was sensitive enough to Scripture to amplify this view by also making full use of Paul's concept of the "inner being" (*PArch* 4.4.8; Eph. 3:16), the latter being an idea that does not entail the separation of soul and body for its vision of spiritual realization. For Origen, however, it is always the soul which is that faculty capable of recognizing the image of God in humanity through its intelligence and virtues (see **Image of God**). As he sums it up: "Even if the mind falls through negligence so that it cannot receive God into itself purely and entirely, it nevertheless always retains in itself as it were certain seeds of restoration and of being recalled to a better understanding, when the 'inner self' (Rom. 7:22), which is also called the rational self, is called back to the image and likeness of God (Gen. 1:26), who created him" (*PArch* 4.4.9).

The soul can freely initiate a progress from the "bodily" by rational virtuous activity in harmony with God. This psychic perception has a divine quality that makes it superior to the "bodily," which latter can be holy if directed by the soul to God, but carnal if undirected. The corruptible, "sinful body," then, is used in the Pauline sense, as opposed to the spiritual body. The soul is essentially the free, rational nature of a human being.

On the Making of Humankind

Origen's *Homilies on Genesis* present a clear idea of what it means for humankind to be made "in the image of God." Too much can be made of Origen's two accounts of God's making of humankind (his interpretation of Genesis 1 stressing the "spiritual" and that of Genesis 2 stressing the "literal" or "bodily"), as if Origen establishes a dualism in which the spiritual humanity of Genesis 1, made in God's image, is at odds with the earthly humanity of Genesis 2. This dichotomy is largely the creation of later commentators, who have been too quick to attribute Platonic dualism to Origen. In fact neither exegesis in itself excludes its opposite: Genesis 1 does not exclude the historical or literal creation of the body, and Genesis 2 does not exclude the spiritual. Origen's solution to the difference in styles of Genesis 1 and Genesis 2, is subtle: the inspired biblical writers present complementary accounts, prioritizing the two different aspects of humankind, the psychic and spiritual, on the one hand, and the physical and historical, on the other.

Origen's reasons for two creation accounts (in contrast to Clement of Alexandria) are given in his ninth homily on Genesis, entitled "On the promises made to Abraham a second time." Origen explains that God's promises to Abraham are narrated twice in order to indicate the two levels; first, "according to the flesh," the historical level, and second because Abraham was the "father of those who are of faith" and come to the inheritance through the passion of Christ (Rom. 4:16). The duality here, then, is not anthropological but "revelatory": between Old and New Covenants, the historical Abraham and the Abraham who prophesies Christ.

In his commentary on Genesis 1:26, Origen prioritizes the meaning according to the "inner being" (Eph. 3:16). He does not deny that Genesis 1 is a literal account that involves the creation of male and female. However, the key to the Christian meaning of this verse is "in the image of God," which is Christ. Human beings are made in the image of the Image. The renewal of the inner man is the true potential of humanity (2 Cor. 4:16). Contemplation of the image of Christ within orientates the human person to God's true image (Christ) and this enables the next step, the acquisition of "likeness," by which the whole human being (and all humanity) is transformed. The regular interplay between the singular (human person) and the collective

(humanity) is allowed by Origen's Greek much more readily than its English translation, since *anthropos* stood for both. Thus the indestructible, naturally endowed form defines both what it means to be human, in pointing beyond the fallen state to our inheritance and the opposite, fallenness, which results from contemplation of the devil's image.

Origen interprets the significance of "male and female" in a spiritual sense, but again it is clear that he allegorizes in a way that is not in conflict with the concept of literal sexual difference. He prefaces his spiritual account by the acknowledgment of sexual differentiation and human procreation as an active part of God's creation. His allegory is intended rather as a deepening understanding of this difference, and it presumes his belief in the reality and goodness of the body. Spiritually, male and female represent the harmony between two parts of the soul, the pneuma and the psyche; the spirit (*pneuma, nous*) being the higher power. When this harmony is broken, bodily desires, that is, unclean conceptions or ideas, arise. These desires cause the body to sin. The body as such is not the source of sin, but rather the soul's inner disharmony. Such an account is not accurately called body-soul dualism (in the common gnostic and Oriental sense), though this charge had often been unfairly laid at Origen's door. The vision of the inner disharmony may owe something to the image in Plato's *Phaedrus* of the soul as a chariot drawn by two horses, one with a spiritual tendency, the other wayward through desire. Origen, however, seems to suggest a bodily purity, the result of the soul's harmony, which is more deeply biblical and foreign to Plato. Conversely, Origen's interpretation of the literal creation of humankind (Gen. 2) is not pursued without reference to the soul. Here Origen defines humankind as soul in the sense that the soul is not something owned solely by the human being but has its origin and nature from above. Consequently, when he discusses the text about how "many souls went down into Egypt" with Jacob, the mystical meaning of this he finds in the spiritual fatherhood of the patriarch. These teachings concerning the second creation narrative must be borne in mind when one reads that humankind was made "from the slime of the earth" (*HomGn* 1).

The Purgation of the Soul

One of the key points Origen wishes to make through this dynamic anthropology is that just as a soul can fall through freedom, so it can by freedom turn back to the contemplation of good and be restored. The term that Origen uses for restoration is the critically important notion of *apokatastasis.* When we pray, "Lead us not into temptation," Origen tells us, this does not mean that we pray for the elimination of testing, but that we should not be overcome by it (*PEuch* 19). Indeed Origen might have said, "in order that we may profit by it." The spiritual life is a cosmic psychic struggle to turn the soul to the good and keep it there, against the pulling desires, passions, and thoughts, the contemplation of which sully the soul and can cause it to use the body sinfully. For Origen, this struggle takes place fundamentally at the level of ideas, and it is through ideas, conceptions, and imaginations that the soul is induced to turn away from the real object of its contemplation. Evagrius's understanding of asceticism, accordingly, had as its aim the goal of imageless prayer, which was the sought-after communion with the True Image of God, the Divine Logos, beyond all corporeal fantasy or imagination, those ideas or representations of the external world presented internally to the human psyche. Through this channel Origen had a significant influence over the burgeoning ascetical movement after the late fourth century.

Origen's *Homilies on Exodus* serve as a guide for those who would purify their souls in a journey from the servitude to passions and imaginations toward purity. Origen's "moral interpretation" of the Scripture here was the application of the mystical to the soul in its fallen state, with a view to its restoration. The patriarchs, then, are "fathers of souls," and the multiplication of the sons of Israel signifies the spiritual birth of soul-awareness. It is accomplished in the "body." The two kings, or pharaohs, the one favorable to Israel and the other hostile, stand for the two dominant tendencies operative in the inner life of human beings: the orientation to God or to the devil (*HomEx* 1.5). For Origen, the whole biblical account of the servitude in Egypt stands as a coded narrative for the arena of the human soul's ascetic struggle.

The Metaphysics of Apokatastasis

In the *First Principles* Origen seeks a reason for the "falling away" of the free souls made to contemplate God, which resulted in the phenomenon of embodied souls, for while matter was not evil, neither was it originally conducive to the spiritual development of the soul to which it was attached. He concludes that human embodiment can be explained only if the body is a corrective medium, a soteriological economy. But correction for what sin, since the fall in paradise cannot count as the first fall? His deduction leads him to ponder whether there must not have been an earlier fall by which human beings came to be embodied spirits in a physical world, which in turn served as their penitentiary? Origen appears to have entailed two opinions that would later cause him to be seen as heterodox, although it must be emphasized that Origen saw himself as speculating here, not dogmatizing (*PArch* 2.8.5). First, he at least implies a preexistent state of human souls before their embodiment, and not just a momentary preexistence, but a life such that the free acts of that soul led to a falling away, the consequence of which was God's embodiment of that soul as a punitive purgation, something that was simultanrously a sorrow and an opportunity. Second, Origen's rigorous consistency about the reversibility of any free soul's fall entails the concept of the potential restoration of all the fallen, at least as a possibility (see *Apokatastasis*). He would become embroiled with this latter issue when his opponents debate with him the possibility of the redemption of Satan, something that embarrassed him greatly in his relations with the hierarchs of his time, since the redemption of the fallen angels had never been part of the prior ecclesiastical tradition, which he had claimed to be elucidating in the *PArch*.

Origen's idea of universal salvation arises from an idea of primordial unity of all Being which he shared with his contemporary Plotinus. If the ultimate constitution of everything is spiritual, and (as seemed axiomatic) the spiritual is quintessentially one (diversity being a mark of disharmony), then why do different kinds of souls exist, and what is the reason for matter? Origen explained diversity as the "falling away" of rational creatures. It is as if some of the souls, listening forever to a vast symphony, became inattentive. The image is clearly expressed in a passage some have disputed (*PArch* 1.8, also in *PArch* 1.3–4). In this lack of attention, some fell severely and became demons. The relaxation of their will, albeit in abstract, before utter perfection was achieved, brought about a cosmic fall. This relaxation also introduced into the cosmos a hierarchy of spiritual creatures. This was something Origen could prove readily from Scripture, citing the existence of "Thrones, Dominations, Principalities and Powers" (*PArch* 1:5; Heb. 1:14; Eph. 1:21). Thus drama was introduced into the universe along with diversity. No spiritual being is fixed, because it is still free to move to a smaller or a greater extent back toward God or farther away from God. Human beings are a particular kind of spirit or soul, one that has been endowed with a body that bears with it all the peculiar conditions of psy-

chic life in such a corporeal frame, but like all other spirits within the cosmos human beings stand in the same relation to God within that dynamic of ascent and descent, insofar as movement toward or away from God is the fundamental postulate of their freedom of being. Only the divine Trinity does not participate in this cosmic drama.

Origen conceives of this movement as a salvific possibility for every soul. The diverse situation of every soul is a change in its condition as a result of its falling away, which may be reversed. If, then, the human being is tied to a body while being essentially a spirit, the conclusion that human beings lived a life as "pure souls" before they lived as "souls in bodies" appears to Origen to be inescapable. This vision of the unembodied, preexistent state lacks the metaphysical fixity of Plato's concept of soul perhaps, but it bears more than a superficial resemblance to the myth of Er in book 10 of Plato's *Republic*, when the gods give Er the privilege of descending to Hades and returning to tell the tale with full memory of what he experienced. Er saw souls returning polluted and dusty to be purified in Hades. Other souls, having endured a period of purgation, were allowed to leave for another new life. Some souls, those of tyrants, were condemned to eternal torment in Hades. Plato suggested that souls migrate into a variety of states, men, or animals. Origen's account is similar and different: for example, he envisages no eternal torment, nor the reincarnation of souls as beasts or reptiles (see *Transmigration of Souls*). Moreover, the entire dynamism of Origen's theory is provided from a biblically driven soteriology (the overarching vision of the relentlessly pursuing mercy of God). In view of Origen's conscious and oft-repeated repudiation of pagan philosophers ("The waters of Egypt are the erring and slippery teaching of the philosophers" [*HomEx* 4.6]), it is perhaps safest to say that he reworked a myth substantially older and deeper than Plato (similar to the law of karma in Indian religions), that what one has done in a previous state determines the condition into which one is born. However, in the end he remains closer to biblical metaphysics in the manner he fundamentally asserts that it is no law of necessity that fixes these states, but rather God's providence and mercy in dialogue with human freedom.

Origenism as Anthropological Heresy

However free to speculate about humanity's metaphysical origins he may have felt himself to be, in reality, opposition to Origen's views was never absent. Methodius of Olympus represents decided opposition already focused by the early fourth century, and it was doubtless many of the anthropological views that fanned the wrath of his own Alexandrian bishop Demetrius even in the third century. As Origen's ascetical anthropology was widely popularized through Evagrius and the late fourth-century monastic movement, the course was set for a collision, and two particular aspects of his anthropology, the idea of the preexistence of the human soul and the concept of apokatastasis, were singled out for special condemnation at the Fifth Ecumenical Council of 553 (see *Origenist Crises*).

Review

If these two central pillars of his metaphysical structure, the preexistence of the soul and *Apokatastasis*, called down condemnation on his head, it remains necessary to state that Origen's most valuable contribution to Christian anthropology remains perennially significant: his dynamic and cosmically large vision that the Christian life is a ceaseless struggle of the soul with itself, a battle for attention toward God by banishing the thoughts and phantasms from which sin is derived; a progressive journeying of the soul toward God in ascending degrees of spiritual illumination, fundamentally inspired by insight into the sacred Scriptures. This is ultimately the heart of Origen's philosophy: the wise reading of God's oracles, which point the soul back to its true nature and point it forward in free repentance to the ascent to God.

Bianchi (1981); Burke (1950); Castagno Monaci (1980); Crouzel (1989), 87–98, 205–18; Edwards (1998); Sfameni-Gasparro (1980); Pierre (1984).

STEPHEN THOMAS

Apocrypha   The term *apocrypha*, the Greek word for "hidden things," is used to designate two different sets of literature relevant to the Christian biblical canon. Most commonly, the term refers to books that are included in old Greek copies of the *Old Testament* but that are not found in the Hebrew Bible. These books are the Epistle of Jeremiah, 1 Esdras, Tobit, Judith, Additions to Esther, the Wisdom of Solomon, Ecclesiasticus (or Ben Sira/Sirach), Baruch, the Prayer of Azariah and the Song of the Three Young Men, The History of Susanna, Bel and the Dragon, and 1 and 2 Maccabees. These texts were generally received by the early church as the word of God and considered to be canonical. The books of Wisdom, Sirach, and Tobit are the most frequently cited in early Christian literature.

Although all of these texts were the authentic products of ancient Judaic spirituality, later rabbinic Judaism (perhaps as a reaction against the Christian use of the Greek Septuagint Bible) rejected the apocryphal books in favor of the more restricted list of the Hebrew canon. The Council of Jamnia (ca. A.D. 100) is often cited as the event that fixed the Jewish canon, but many scholars doubt that such a council actually took place and argue that considerable canonical fluidity remained within the Jewish community well beyond the turn of the second century. The reception of the apocryphal books in the Christian

West was complicated by Jerome's decision to leave them out of his Latin Vulgate translation of the Bible. Because of the authority of the Septuagint, however, they were added to later editions of the Vulgate. During the Protestant Reformation, Martin Luther, unaware of the role these texts had played in the early church, advocated a "return" to the Hebrew list, which he considered to be more authentic. Roman Catholic and Orthodox Christians have always accepted these texts as part of the body of sacred revelation, though some Roman Catholic scholars have applied the word *deuterocanonical* (or second-order canon) to describe them.

In addition to the Old Testament, the word *apocrypha* also refers to a body of extracanonical texts dealing with the life and significance of Jesus. These texts, usually called "the New Testament Apocrypha," are much more numerous and varied than the Old Testament Apocrypha. They include Gospels, such as the *Gospel of the Hebrews;* treatises, such as the *Gospel of Truth;* apocalypses; acts, such as *the Acts of Paul and Thecla;* letters; and liturgical pieces. Generally, the early Christian community never received these texts as canonical and often labeled them as heretical.

Because of his work on the *Hexapla,* Origen was aware of many different textual traditions and canon lists. As a member of the church, however, he accepted the overarching authority of the Septuagint. A list of the Old Testament books that Origen considered to be canonical appears in Eusebius's *H.E.* 6.25, and it is possible to find references in Origen's surviving corpus to all of the Old Testament Apocrypha mentioned above. In Origen's day the term *New Testament* was still a novelty and the list of canonical texts had not yet been fixed. Origen, however, recognizes the four canonical Gospels and specifically rejects a number of others (*HomLc* 1). This does not prevent him from quoting from noncanonical texts, such as the *Gospel of Peter,* the *Book of James,* or the *Gospel according to the Hebrews (ComMt* 10.17; 17.31; *ComJn* 2.87; *HomJr* 15.4). He knows the full Pauline corpus, in which he includes the Epistle to the Hebrews. He frequently cites the book of Acts and accepted 1 Peter, 1 John, Jude, and Revelation as canonical. It appears that Origen's list of canonical texts, or at least the range of those sacred books that demanded his attention, contracted as he grew older.

Charlesworth (1992); Van den Hoek (1995); McDonald (1988); Metzger (1987).
JOHN J. O'KEEFE

Apokatastasis   Within the history of Christian theology the term *apokatastasis* (restitution, reinstatement) often stands in treatises that develop the sense of God's absolute power expressed in the saving of all creation. Origen is one of the earliest proponents of the idea of universal salvation (see *Universalism*), and he was condemned for this proposition three centuries after his death. Gregory Nyssa, one of the leading Cappadocian fathers, also supported the idea and was not censured. In Origen's corpus *apokatastasis* usually means the eternal return of creation to God (see *Cosmology, Anthropology*). Nevertheless, the positions that he takes on the issue of universal salvation have often seemed to be contradictory. In scattered places Origen says quite clearly that he thinks all created intelligence will be restored to God at the end of time. In other places he says, equally clearly, that only souls who make the choice for God and practice the virtues God demands will come to rest in heaven. Those who do not live for God shall suffer eternally in hell or perhaps be annihilated there.

If in coming years Origen's treatise on the resurrection is rediscovered, this apparent contradiction may be settled. No clear understanding of Origen's teachings about the resurrection appears in Methodius of Olympus's attack on his teaching of that theme. Methodius obviously misunderstood him, and most subsequent attempts to understand Origen exactly on this issue have relied on the badly flawed methodology of "mirror reading" from the summaries of what Origen supposedly said, which opponents (or, for that matter, friends) have volunteered in the heat of controversy. Until further original fragments come to light, scholars will probably continue to interpret the Origenian idea of apokatastasis either from the basis of a strong preference for one of Origen's two stated positions or from the basis of a synthetic attempt to blend them together.

From the twentieth-century manuscript find at Toura, scholarship learned of hitherto unknown views of Origen, but with the fragile and fragmentary character of his present corpus, it is still hardly possible to construct a single systematic view without aspects that oppose each other. Moreover, it is not beyond the bounds of possibility that even if we possessed all his documents, we still might find Origen insisting on different doctrines within contrasting contexts, for on several other occasions he demonstrates a comparable indifference to strict consistency. In his commentaries, Origen follows the practice of offering various interpretations of biblical verses for his readers, often versions that are not in agreement but which he thinks are important to state together, for his readers to consider and decide for themselves. Origen is a constructive, pastoral theologian, rather than a systematic one in our strict sense of that term.

His understanding of the theologian's task makes that aspect of his work attractive. For him every faithful Christian teacher should insist upon the **rule of faith** (*regula fidei*) that has neither ambiguity nor contradiction. Yet that rule does not include developed lines of argument for the Christian doctrines it states, and it leaves open speculative questions about other themes. In those places where third-century teachers either offered a defense of points within the rule or speculated about questions raised outside the rule, large areas of ambiguity and some senses of apparent dispute must necessarily be accepted. For Origen, it was centrally important that nothing should threaten the faith; no gracious means of bringing simple folk or intellectuals back to the truth should be excluded out of hand (*PArch* Praef.). This "economy" makes his thought flexible.

Both ancient and modern readers of Origen have felt uncomfortable with such a view of his theological system. A theologian with such a formidable reputation, it is thought, should at least be consistent. Augustine passed the test on this aspect of his theology by serially changing his mind and then offering us the *Retractions* to indicate which points he finally decided were correct and which were ill conceived. We have no such retrospective treatise from Origen. For those who approach Origen working back from the condemnatory Council of 553, Origen is expected to teach heretical doctrines. If universal salvation is unorthodox, that is probably what Origen taught. Justinian's council, however, was most concerned with the so-called Origenists who developed positions cantilevered far beyond the views held by the one whose name they honored (see **Origenist Crises**). It is they who were obviously rejected at the council, and not necessarily Origen himself. The extant documents from the council, therefore, are far from being clear sources about his teaching.

This view of Origen through a Justinianic lens had many implications. In the creation of the first modern critical text of Origen's *Peri Archon* (*GCS*, Leipzig, 1913), Paul Koetschau assumed that the Council of 553 had condemned Origen. Moreover he held a deeply skeptical attitude toward Rufinus's fifth-century translation of the book, on the grounds that the translation admitted it was not literal, but had massaged the original in order not to trouble Latin Christian readers with irrelevant "difficulties." Thus, for further illumination, Koetschau felt obliged not only to read Justinian's *Letter to Menas* and Leontius of Byzantium's sketch of the condemned teacher, both written in the sixth century, but also to prefer their various readings of Origen's text to those of Rufinus, even setting them into his construction of the "actual" words that Origen wrote. Because Jerome (d. 420) had viciously attacked Rufinus's translation as an attempt to clean up Origen's theological views and hide the dirty linen, Koetschau also consistently preferred what passages we have surviving from Jerome's lost translation and regarded them also as "true readings" of Origen's *Peri archon,* in contradistinction to Rufinus.

Two recent sets of Origen editors have made very different textual decisions. Neither Herwig Görgemanns and Heinrich Karpp (Darmstadt, 1976), nor Henri Crouzel and Manlio Simonetti (SC, Paris, 1978–84) have thought it right to ask Origen's sworn enemies to provide the true text of the *Peri archon.* Both recent critical editions view Rufinus as a much more trustworthy translator. Thus here the strong case for Origen teaching the most heretical doctrines has been laid aside on historical-critical textual grounds.

That important decision aside, the two positions on apokatastasis remain. *PArch* 3.5.7 explains 1 Corinthians 15:24–28 as involving "the salvation of those subjected and the restoration of those that have been lost." Similar views appear in *PArch* 2.3.7 (but their inclusion in *PArch* 3.6.5–9 in Koetschau's edition depends on Origen's later opponents and is rejected by the Görgemanns/Karpp and Crouzel/Simonetti editions). However, poetic passages elsewhere in Origen's commentaries and homilies (*HomJos* 1.16.91; *ComRm* 8.9) make the same point and render the issue peripheral. Even so, commenting on 1 Corinthians 15:24–28 later in the *Peri archon* (*PArch* 3.6.1–2), Origen insists on humans' free will and the necessity of

their "earnest efforts to imitate God." Even when God is all in all, the divine must not dwell in evil vessels. In a strange but revealing conjunction between Jerome and Rufinus, the warring interpreters of Origen, both agreed that in his letter contesting interpolations that had been put into the manuscript of one of his debates, Origen had explicitly insisted that the devil would not be saved. This we should take as strong evidence that Origen did not teach the strongest form of the doctrine of universal salvation, which would include the final restoration of the devil himself.

As far as we can tell, therefore, Origen never decided to stress exclusive salvation or universal salvation, to the strict exclusion of either case. His treatment of the doctrine of apokatastasis, nonetheless, may make good sense if we remember his deep pastoral concern both for speculative intellectuals and for simple folk. Both audiences within and outside the church can be served by stressing the apparently opposing views in quite different contexts. The return of all God's creatures, except the devil, to fellowship with God invokes the concept of a good and powerful deity, where love conquers all. But the threat of hell, either forever or to the point of total annihilation, does have motivating force toward embodying the life of virtue. In the *CCels* he certainly thinks the idea of hell has a special significance for instructing the ignorant (see **Hades**). Perhaps Origen felt both carrot and stick were always necessary to move humans toward lives of faith and virtue. He admits (*ComJn* 28.8 [7] 61–66) that he does not know whether the fires of hell will last forever or not. He thinks that they might be a temporary and remedial punishment for souls (*ComMt* 17.24; *SerMt* 69; *GCS* 11). One could not know in advance which audience would be most likely to accept the gospel, because of the hope engendered by God's overpowering love or because of the fear stimulated by God's threat of hell coupled with God's demand for ethical living. Most audiences of hearers or readers include both groups; knowing this, Origen the pastoral preacher probably kept his view of salvation economically "open" for a greater effectiveness.

Daley (1991), 47–64; Kelly (2000); Muller (1958); Norris (1992); Vogt (1980).

FREDERICK W. NORRIS

Apostles, Apostolic Writings

The Christian apostolate (*apostolatus*) is the mandate to preach the good news. Apostle was indeed one of the titles of Christ himself (Heb. 3:1), defining Jesus as a messenger of the Father sent to announce the gospel to the poor (Luke 4:18). Origen does not fail to notice this (*ComRm* 1.7). Basing himself on 2 Corinthians 13:3, Origen concludes that the apostles (those "sent out" by Jesus) derive their apostolic status from the fact that Christ speaks through them (*ComRm* 6.9; *PArch* 1. Praef. 1.21–24). That is why the apostles preach the gospel with authority. Their writings are also divinely inspired (*PArch* 1.3.1.11–18; 4.2.6 [13].209 [256]) and for that reason profoundly authoritative (*SerMt* 47). For Origen, the fact that they can deviate from the Hebrew text or from the Greek translation of the Old Testament when calling on the authority of Scripture is part and parcel of their "apostolic authority," for he had clearly noticed in his readings that they often did not cite literally, but "according to the spirit" (*ComRm* 3.2; 8.7, 11). He concluded that in their inspired "reading" of the intentionality of sacred Scripture they were guided, because they were apostles of Christ, directly by the Holy Spirit. Through the Spirit they did not see just the physical Jesus but, after his resurrection, also even the divine Word (*HomLc* 1.4; 24.1; *PArch* 1.3.2.38–40; 7.216–20; 2.7.3.76–81; *SerMt* 40; *ComJn* 28.15.127–28; 32.32.399), no less than God who was made human (*FragmMt* 288; *ComJn* 13.25.153). By the Spirit their words are filled with persuasive power (*CCels* 3.68; 8.47). The close relation of the apostle and the Savior even involves them at the heart of the redemptive economy. Origen teaches that "Christ and his sons," that is, the apostles and martyrs, "take away the sin of the world" (*HomNum* 10.2.1).

Origen takes this tradition of following in the pattern of the apostles to be paradigmatic. It is at once an "apostolic tradition" and a process or manner in which God reveals wisdom to the disciple. Origen says explicitly, "Only that is to be believed as the truth, which in no way conflicts with the tradition of the Church and the apostles" (*PArch* 1. Praef. 2.41–43; 4.2.2[9].55–56[68–69]). The "apostolic tradition," however, is not clearly defined by Origen. In the preface of the *PArch* he gives a list of the most important articles of faith, almost a summary of the *regula fidei* in the manner of Irenaeus (*PArch* 1. Praef. 4.58–10.187; see also *ComJn* 20.30.269–72; 32.16.187–93; *HomJr* 5.13.14–31; *SerMt* 33), but he also writes that the apostles took certain doctrines they believed to be necessary and communicated them in the plainest terms to all believers; the consequences of their statements, however, they left to be investigated further and more deeply by those who, in their own generation, had merited the higher gifts of the Holy Spirit (*PArch* 1. Praef. 3.44–57; *HomGn* 12. 5.64–71). In this company he undoubtedly includes himself and thus implicitly sees all his role as theologian and biblical interpreter as a fulfillment of his own apostolic charism. For Origen, the apostles were master builders who laid the foundation on which others may build further (1 Cor. 3:10–15). In a polemic passage Origen turns against those who attribute an exclusive position to Peter, arguing that upon him alone the whole church was built (*ComMt* 12.11). For Origen, the "power of keys" does not exclusively rest with Peter (*ComMt* 12.14). He notes that Jesus speaks to him about "binding and loosing in the heavens" (plural) (Matt. 16:19), but elsewhere (Matt. 18:18), where the circle of addressees is wider, about "binding in heaven" (singular). And he concludes from this that the disciple who is "more perfect" is able to bind or loose in more expansive heavens (*ComMt* 13.31). The example of Judas is a warning to the church that shows even apostles can lose their apostolicity (*ComRm* 1.2; *HomEx* 6.2.8–15; *HomLev* 16.7.41–48; *SerMt* 78; *ComJn* 32.13.149–50; 14.168; 18.232). Such a personalist view (related to his concept of the **priesthood** of believers) clearly brought him into conflict with those (especially the **bishops**) who envisaged a more institutional understanding of apostolic authority, as something almost synonymous with episcopal office. In a significant question Origen asked, Who are those that followed the apostles in the unbroken succession of faith? (*HomGn* 2.6.56). He himself was skeptical of the view that the bishops were de facto the successors of the apostles. For him the apostolic succession ran mainly through the series of Christian teachers (Didaskaloi) who authentically taught the apostolic doctrine, but even then not exclusively through them. He thus represents one of the key stages in the third-century church of the long-running tension between Christian Didaskaloi and Episcopoi, as to who guarded the tradition of Christian teaching.

With reference to John 13:20 Origen maintains that any disciple could be an apostle of Jesus Christ in the service of the salvation of humanity (*ComJn* 32.17.204). He points, for example, to the Samaritan woman (John 4:1–42), whom he calls a female apostle (*ComJn* 13.28.169; 30.179). For Origen the decisive factor in being an apostle was the degree of a person's perfection and their relation to Christ (*HomJr* 11.3.16–46). The position of the apostles is one of foundational priority. Subsequently, those who belong to the perfect, charismatically and harmoniously build upon that foundation laid by the apostles and prophets (Eph. 2:20), namely, Jesus Christ. And those who instruct in the church hand over this foundation (*FragmHomJr* 12).

Thus the apostles support those who lean on them, and those who lean on them in turn support the weaker faithful (*ComJn* 10.34. 268). There is a taxonomy of perfection as Origen sees it, in which the chief criterion is who has remained closest to the foundation. That may either be the foundation of the apostolic doctrine as such or Christ himself as the living foundation (*HomJos* 9.1).

For Origen, the life of the apostles is something deserving of imitation, since doctrine and life are inextricably bound together (*HomLc* 37.4; *ComMt* 15.24). The words of Paul (who together with John, who "reclined on Jesus' bosom," is the "chief of the apostles" in Origen's estimation) when he said, "Follow my example as I follow Christ's" (1 Cor. 11:1; 4:16) implies that in the end it is always the imitation of Christ (or God) that really matters in the issue of apostolic faithfulness (*HomPs* 38.2.1.39–44; *ComEp* 19.50–53; *HomJd* 1.3.27–47; *ComMt* 16.1; *SerMt* 73; *FragmComLam* 116; *ComJn* 28.4.25). Origen believes that the lives of those who have imitated Christ can be made into an exemplary standard, insofar as they have been canonized by the Scriptures. This is the chief merit he sees in the Acts of the Apostles (*HomEz* 7.3.65–68), an account of the apostolic preachers who inspired people to believe and to live perfectly according to the words of Jesus (*ComMt* 15.15).

His own key intent is to advocate Christian discipleship as a matter of imitating the life of the apostles and of aspiring to be a messenger of God's truth (*HomJr* 8.4.16–22). The difference between the original apostles and those who, as messengers of the gospel, become their imitators is that the former were sent to the Gentiles or to the circumcised (Gal. 2:9), that is, "to many," whereas the apostles of the present day are sent sometimes only to one person (*ComJn* 32.17. 204–13). If the "extension" of the apostolic office seems to have diminished somewhat in Origen's day, his sense that fidelity to its vocation will involve suffering remains a lively one.

Suffering will be the mark of those who are ambassadors of the word. Their fidelity brought **martyrdom** to the original apostles and may also do the same for their imitators (*HomJr* 14.14.1–69; *ExhMart* 34; *PEuch* 29.4).

Since they were all the authentic apostles of Jesus, there is a certain unanimity among the apostolic body and in the corpus of their teachings (*SerMt* 35; *HomLev* 4.4.11–38; *HomEx* 9.3.62–64). Even so, this unanimity is not a simple uniformity of doctrine. There were clearly several different ways of thinking present among the apostles and within their writings. Origen sees this as related to the fact that although Jesus is one, he has manifold aspects (see **Epinoiai**) wherein he reveals himself; and those who saw him did not see him all in the same way but had the gift of vision, depending on their ability to comprehend and upon the depth of their relationship with Jesus. Thus there is a marked difference between Peter, James, and **John** (who saw Jesus' glory on the mountain) and the other apostles (*CCels* 2.64.1–14; *HomGn* 1.7.57–60; 4.5.35–43). And Peter has a different approach to the cross from that of **Paul**. For Peter, Christ was a model to be studied (1 Pet. 2.21), whereas for Paul, Christ on the cross was the victor who had defeated the devil (Gal. 6.14). Origen thinks that both interpretations are legitimate (*HomJos* 8.3; *HomNum* 2.2.2–3), though clearly one is more profound than the other.

Origen's conceptualization of the apostolic office is critical to his theory of the inspiration of the Bible and the ongoing manner in which God reveals truth to the church as it progresses through the ages. In this he clearly emerges as a major theoretician of Christian *paradosis*, the sacred tradition of revelation, advancing considerably on Irenaeus's theological foundations (his treatment of apostolicity and the *regula fidei*) in the previous generation.

Eno (1973); Frank (1979).

F. LEDEGANG

Asceticism   Origen could not be a more profoundly influential—if not sometimes enigmatic—figure when considered in conjunction with the controversial and puzzling historical phenomenon that is now called "asceticism," the English term that is the usual (all too flat) translation of the astonishingly multivalent Greek term *askesis*. Within Christian circles of the late ancient Mediterranean and European medieval worlds, most especially within monastic traditions, Origen was a pivotal, complicated, and complicating figure, both as an early exemplar of ascetic piety and as an ascetic theologian. A part of what has made Origen so challenging was his determination to understand asceticism not as a reference to an independent reality, a particular set of practices, a particular religious doctrine, or even a particular aspect or dimension of a life, but as a profound abbreviation for the whole of a particular type of orientation (*bios*) to what he and many other Christians of his time referred to as the "true life," participation in Christ, otherworldly existence. How to model the different orientation in personal comportment, how to think about it, and how to be articulate about the profound goal and the necessary steps to be taken to reach it and sustain it—these were among the challenges that Origen took upon himself to address. They were challenges of such magnitude and complexity as to bring upon Origen, during and beyond his lifetime, mixed reviews and misunderstandings about his substantive arguments and intentions.

According to Origen, the single most important challenge to be addressed by those who would participate in Christ's life was how to think about, and what to do with, the "tent" (*skene*) that was the body; that is, how to relate the challenges of embodiment to otherworldly visions and aspirations. A related primary and practical challenge had to do with the source(s) of revelation and authority for clarification regarding such matters. It was obvious to Origen and to his contemporaries in the faith that the *Scripture* was the chief source of authority in these matters. Yet it was apparent to Origen that there remained the challenge about how to read the Bible so that the truths and mandates regarding participation in the life of Christ might be made evident. He felt that a particular type of reading of the Bible (intellectualist, with emphasis upon spiritualizing) was needed, especially for the mature. As much as he was the consummate and prolific biblical exegete, Origen was also the philosopher-theologian much influenced by Middle-Platonic teachings and discourses (see *Philosophy*). Origen's writings and teachings represent a profound confusion of these two discursive worlds. Such confusion in turn had great impact upon the teachings and modeling and institutionalization of Christian piety after him.

Drawing upon his philosophic and rhetorical training, Origen creatively and selectively engaged Platonic teachings about the philosophic life as a type of otherworldly existence and as a conceptual and language bridge in order to engage and translate the more ancient truths of the Bible about participation in the life of Christ. Understood in terms of the (quest for the) resurrected life and as superior existence, it was the life in which the believer could claim to "see God in the heart . . . and know [God] with the mind" (*PArch* 1.1.8), in contrast to the experience of dullness and death of earthly corporeal existence (*PArch* 3.4.2). So bodily existence was framed by and subsumed under the governance of the spiritual and was, therefore, rendered problematic. It was not altogether rejected or denied; it was valued in limited terms as the needed locus of the soul's preparation for participation in the spiritual realm. Yet was also seen as the stumbling block in the way of flight to the other realm. In this situation the believer's body provoked complex thinking and negotiation so that it might always be properly oriented toward the otherworldly (see *Anthropology*).

Here then is where the ascetic life is made compelling. The life oriented toward the otherworldly can be realized only to the degree that a larger perspective (informed and focused by the Bible and philosophical traditions) about the origins and destiny of the world and about the mixed constitution of human beings is recognized. Origen understood the visible world to be the result of the fall of soulness into an embodiment of materiality that is destined for corruption (see *Fall, Souls*). Human beings are constituted as spirit, soul, and body (the first two often synonymous for him). Such a constitution sets in motion the struggles between the original spiritual realm and the belated material realm. These struggles are played out in the soul housed in the body (*ComRm* 1.18). Yet Origen also argued that the body is not intrinsically evil and that the soul is not merely a neutral entity housed by, or clothed in, the body. The problem is that the interests and needs of the body and those things associated with it distract the soul from a primary focus upon the spiritual realm (*PArch* 3.4.4). This is why the body is sometimes characterized as "death" or "corruption," and the soul (*nous*) as that which can produce the virtues of otherworldly existence, namely righteousness, self-control, courage, wisdom (*PArch* 4.4.10).

Whether or not we now accept Eusebius's report (*H.E.* 6.8.1–5) about Origen's supposedly radical act of ascetical self-castration in his youth (for Origen himself denounces such a literalist interpretation of the Gospel text [Matt. 19:12] as "an outrage") [*ComMt* 15.1–5]), it is clear that Eusebius reported the tradition for the edification of his fourth-century readers and is at some pains to describe Origen's dedicated scholarly life in terms that would be easily identified as protomonastic (Eusebius, *H.E.* 6.3). Origen's mature exegesis always shows a layered, albeit complex, reading of the Scriptures and of the human constitution itself.

Just as human beings are complex organisms constituted by spirit, soul, and body, so the truths of the Scriptures, especially regarding Christian practice in the world, must be seen as layered and engaged by different "senses" or types of readings (see *Allegory, Typology*), the superior reading being the allegorical or spiritual. It is this system of reading which, for Origen, helps the mature believer understand the complexity of the fundamental truth of the ascetical imperative: that the body is not intrinsically polluted, that no human being is naturally or fatalistically oriented toward life or death (but must choose), that the believer can be made perfect only by God's will, but must nevertheless freely choose to discipline the body in order to cooperate with the process of being made perfect (*PArch* 1.5.5–7) (see *Grace, Virtue*).

Chadwick (1962); Crouzel (1989), 135–49; Gould (1995); McGuckin (1985a); Rubensen (1999); Wimbush and Valantasis (1995).

VINCENT L. WIMBUSH

Atonement Both Harnack (1895–1903) and De Faye (1928) claimed that the traditional Christian lore about the redemption as being centered in the cross, though richly expounded in Origen, remained subordinate or merely an annex to his personal vision of redemption as the restoration of rational creatures to their original state, guided by the enlightening presence of the Logos. The tension between these two pictures can be allayed somewhat if we note a certain chronological sequence in the development of Origen's thought. A Platonizing perspective on the incarnational economy prevails in the early Alexandrian masterpieces (*PArch* and *ComJn* 1–5). Here Origen describes it as follows: "On earth he is not as he is in heaven, for he has become flesh and speaks through shadow, types and images," thus offering a shadow of the Logos to simple believers who cannot progress to the vision of the true Logos

(*ComJn* 2.49–50). The perfect have gone beyond faith in Christ crucified (Christ according to the flesh) to knowledge of Christ as Wisdom (*ComJn* 2.29; 33; cf. 1 Cor. 1:23–24; 2:6; 2 Cor. 5:16). However, the incarnation acquires more centrality as Origen the theologian progressively steeps himself in scriptural thought, even though he occasionally still reaffirms the need to graduate from "Christ crucified" to "Christ the Wisdom of God" (*HomEx* 12.4).

The tension between the two pictures of salvation is also allayed by a spiritualizing interpretation of the biblical and ecclesiastical traditions about the atonement, which Origen seeks to reground in his vision of the work of the Logos. This is particularly clear in the result of the incarnational economy. For Origen, the glory of Christ's death for humanity is due not to the impassible Logos but to the man, who is rewarded by being made identical with the Logos (*ComJn* 32.322–26). The humanity of Christ, though originally (almost anticipating Nestorian Christology) an independent hypostasis from the Logos (*ComJn* 1.195–97; 32.192–93), is now "fused" with the Logos (almost as if in monophysite style) (*ComMt* 15.24) and by sharing in its divinity is transformed into God, Christ's body acquiring an ethereal and divine quality (*CCels* 3.41). This ascent to a maximally spiritualized mode of being is something that Origen envisages as a destiny for other humans, too, insofar as they are fallen spirits in the process of return to God (see *Anthropology*).

The redemptive role of the Logos centers on the image of his coming (*epidemia*) into the world, in particular his dwelling in the souls of saints and prophets (Wis. 9; *CCels* 4.3.7). Early texts in the Origenian corpus describe the invisible mission of the Logos to the Old Testament saints almost as equal to the coming of the Logos to the apostles (*ComJn* 1.37; 6.15–16; 28). In later writings Origen is of the opinion that the incarnational economy brings a fuller presence of the Logos (*ComMt* 17.36;

ComJn 13.315–19). Its climactic indwelling in the soul of Jesus is a central nexus in Origen's metaphysical and salvation-historical vision (*CCels* 7.17). Universal participation in the Logos is enriched by the special coming of Christ to the saints, who may thereby be said to be the only truly Logos-filled people (*logikoi*) (*PArch* 1.3.7). Curiously, an early text (*ComJn* 1. 273–75) associates this universal presence with the incarnational economy, whereas the special coming of Christ to the soul is linked to the nonincarnate or "naked" Logos (cf. *ComJn* 6.179). Even so, Origen considers that the universal presence of the Logos in the cosmos was insufficient to save the human race and so had to be sent to the world of humankind as incarnate (*ComJn* 2.83). Origen believes that humans are defective until the Logos is perfected within them, but this occurs not in the incarnational economy but in a surpassing or bypassing of it. Origen's unease about the singularity of the incarnation is connected with his theory of pre-existence, his vision of salvation as restoration to a status quo ante, which differs from the sense of a radically new future found in the earlier soteriologies of Irenaeus and Clement. The process of atonement in Origen is thus "largely" figured as a Platonic *regressus*. The Logos returns to the state in which he was at the beginning with God; his incarnate state is something of a pedagogical detour. However, Origen has read his Scripture carefully. The Logos in heaven still carries the marks of the passion, and when we contemplate him we will not forget, he says, that he came to us in a human body (*ComJn* 2.61). But for all practical purposes, in his vision of the transcendent fulfillment of salvation into which the Logos inducts restored souls, the world of bodies will be little more than a memory.

Even in later texts, Christ's healing work in his incarnation, death, and physical resurrection, though proclaimed necessary for salvation (*HomJos* 4.5; *HomLev* 8.10) and though foregrounded in his apologia against Celsus, may still have a somewhat secondary status beside or within the total salvation process, which concerns the relation of the Logos to rational souls, whether angelic or human. The Logos comes as a physician to sinners, but as a teacher of divine mysteries to those who no longer sin (*CCels* 3.62; *ComJn* 1.124). The commingling of divinity and flesh is more warmly celebrated in his later work, therefore, but the emphasis is on the friendship and communion with God, or divinization, that it allows (*CCels* 3.28). The Logos appears in many shapes or forms (*epinoiai*) (*ComJn* 1.119; *CCels* 3.21; *ComMt* 12.29–30; 36–37), depending on one's degree of spiritual progress (*CCels* 4.16; *SerMt* 100); he appears as a human to humans, as an angel to angels (*ComJn* 1.217; *ComMt* 12.30; *HomGen* 8.8) for the respective needs of each. In linking himself to human nature he uses all its aspects as pedagogic expedients (*ComMt* 10.14; *HomIs* 7.1) and though impassible suffers in his body on the cross (*ComPs* 21:2), suffers in compassion for the multitude (*ComMt* 10.23), and grieves even now when we sin, his work unfinished until we are made perfect (*HomLev* 7.2).

Origen provided the soteriological ideas of the church with a broad and secure biblical basis and at the same time fashioned them into an integrated whole. He fleshed out a biblically resonant atonement language in his allegorical reading of Leviticus and sought to place it within a comprehensively overarching philosophical and theological framework. As is always the mark of Origenian thought, this he did in a profoundly spiritualizing key and, accordingly, he is always ready to say that it profits us nothing that Christ once came in the flesh or once lived in Paul, unless he comes to our minds daily (*HomLc* 22.3; *HomJr* 9.1).

Origen carries through systematically the interpretation of Christ's death as a propitiatory sacrifice made necessary by sin. In a style that would be fateful for later theology, he figuratively describes this sacrifice as a complicated "transaction": Jesus, or the Logos, offers his body to God, his soul to the devil; or he commends his spirit to the Father, whereas his soul descends to Hades, so that his soul, even more than his blood (but not his spirit), is the price of our redemption (our "buying-back"). The theme of sacrifice offers the center of gravity uniting many aspects of common church teaching, which Origen often orchestrates in a popular homiletic style: Christ takes on sin for our sakes (*HomLc* 14.4; *HomLev* 3.1), gives his soul in ransom for ours (*ComJn* 6.274–75), thereby deceiving Satan (*ComMt* 16.8; 13.8–9), a theme that will become very popular with later patristic preachers. The devil bought us into slavery with sins as the money, and Christ buys us back to freedom with his blood as the price (*HomEx* 6.9). Origen also teaches that the Logos comes to correct the poor governance of the world by angels and to teach them the power of obedience by his death (*PArch* 3.5.6). Visibly the Son is crucified, while all the while invisibly it is the devil and his angels who are bound to the cross (*HomJos* 7.3; 8.3–4).

For Origen the scope of redemption is universal: Christ is even sacrificed in the heavenly world (*PArch* 4.3.13; Jerome, *Epist.* 124.12) or at least for it, as suggested by Colossians 1:20, and for all rational beings, including the stars (*HomLev* 1.3; *HomNum* 24.1; *ComJn* 1.255–57; *ComMt* 13.8; *CCels* 7.17; *HomLc* 10.3). The Lamb of God is a healing remedy (*pharmakon*) (*ComJn* 1.233; *ExhMart* 30) and a scapegoat: "One just man voluntarily dying for the community wards off the evil demons who cause plagues, infertilities, risks and other incommodities" (*CCels* 1.31; *ComJn* 28.162–70). The efficacy of his death is correlated with the powerful impact of martyrdom (*ComJn* 6.276–87). Origen's rich discourse on the cross does not interconnect very closely with his discourse on resurrection. Some distracting speculations may account for such a failure to articulate the unity of the paschal mystery; for instance his supposition that the soul of Christ left his body quickly to preserve

it, and in order that the legs not be broken (*CCels* 2.16; 3.32).

In short, the triumph of the cross is not in contradiction with the background macrostructure of Origen's vision of salvation, but it is not the core of that vision. It is the exoteric aspect of salvation, needful to be preached in this present age, but only as a necessary step toward the final state in which the Logos will have subdued all rational spirits (*logikoi*) to himself and to the Father. Perhaps Origen's discourse *On the Resurrection*, though less nourished by biblical sources and traditions of piety, is closer to the center of his soteriology.

Beck (1966); De Faye (1928); Rabinowitz (1984); Simonetti (1993).

JOSEPH S. O'LEARY

Baptism   When Origen comments on the central command "to baptize and teach," in Matthew 28:18–20 (*ComRm* 5.2; 8.4; *HomGn* 13.3.4–13; *HomNum* 12.2.5.242–51), it is clear that he places a far greater emphasis on the "teaching" than on the baptizing. The command to baptize (Matt. 28:19) does not play an important part in his works. He pays more attention, however, to Romans 6:3–4, where the apostle speaks of being buried with Christ by baptism into his death in order to rise into a new life (*ComRm* 5.8; 10; 6.6–7; 13; 7.12; 8.2; 9.39 et al.). It is the "regenerative" theology of baptism that captures his attention (*ComRm* 5.2; *ComMt* 15.23). For Origen, first one has to have "died to sin" and to have come to the regeneration of moral improvement (*HomLev* 6.2.41–78). This is liturgically expressed in the "renunciations" which preceded the liturgical ritual (*HomEx* 8.4.8–15; *HomNum* 12.4.5; *HomPs* 38 2.5.1–23; *HomJos* 26.2), in which he is known to have participated regularly as a priest in Palestinian Caesarea (see **Sacraments**). Origen teaches that in baptism the believer receives the remission of sins (*ComCt* 4.1.17; *ComRm* 5.9) (see **Repentance**). A mystical union between Christ and the soul takes place (*HomGn* 10.5). By baptism the believer comes to participate in the divine nature (*ComRm* 4.9; *ComJn* 20.37.340; cf. 2 Pet. 1:4.). Delivered from the demons, one enters the kingdom of Christ (*HomEx* 5.1.20–34) and is incorporated in the body of the church; one sets foot in paradise (*ComCt* 3.8.9; *ComGn* 2.15). One who is baptized is anointed priest (*HomLev* 6.5.18–34; 9.9.27–37). Jesus himself is exalted, when believers are baptized into his death (*HomJos* 4.2).

The main sources of such a doctrine are clearly Paul and the ancient baptismal liturgy of his time. Chief among the Old Testament readings for the paschal liturgy, when baptisms would have been administered, was the account of the passage of the children of Israel through the waters, and it is no surprise, therefore, to see that these texts also contribute greatly to Origen's understanding of the Christian sacrament. Origen's exegesis of the typology of baptism stands indebted to his typological treatment of two narratives in particular: the passage through the Red Sea, and the crossing of the Jordan by Joshua (Jesus in the LXX text). Both the exodus through the sea (*HomEx* 5.2.45–50; 5.23–47; *HomJos* 26.2) and Jesus' "passing" through the river Jordan into the promised land are taken by Origen as prefigurations of the mystery of baptismal regeneration in Christ Jesus. Origen here underscores the "difference" between Moses and Joshua/Jesus. He considers the passage through the Red Sea under the leadership of Moses as symbolic of the "leaving" of Egypt (the separation from "the world") and as representative of the beginning of the catechumenate. The passage of the River Jordan under the leadership of Jesus is like the entering of the promised land, the veritable completion of the catechumenate by the mystery of baptism (*ComJn* 6.44.227–33; *HomJos* 1.4; 4.1; 5.5). The original context of his remarks is clearly the catechumenal lectures he must have delivered as priest in Caesarea

during the prepaschal Lent. Always, however, he returns from the mystical symbol of baptism, to the point he really wishes to underscore as preacher: baptism is not an indelible gift; rather it is the beginning of a continuous struggle to maintain moral purity and thereby truly transcend (*ComJn* 10.29.182; *HomJos* 4.2; 5.3; 5.6; *HomJr* 16.5.25–33).

Origen distinguishes the baptism of John and that of Christ. That of the Baptist is a "baptism by water" that is designed to exhort to penance and conversion whereas the baptism Jesus brings is "by water and Spirit": it effects the remission of sins (*ComJn* 6.30.154; 6.32.162; 6.33.166–67; *HomLc* 24.1; *FragmHomLc* 51[84]). He also makes a distinction between the administration of baptism in public and that baptism "which is in secret" (*ComRm* 5.8), a sign that already the church was having doubts over the motives of many of its candidates for baptismal initiation. The latter absolutely requires a "right disposition" (*HomLc* 22.6; *ComJn* 6.33.165); otherwise one is washed with water, but does not receive the grace of the Holy Spirit. Origen takes the case of Simon Magus as his evidence at hand (*ComJn* 1.7.40–43; *HomEz* 6.5.1–26).

Origen refers to the established practice of administering baptism with the Trinitarian formula, though he does not amplify much on it (*ComRm* 5.8; *HomJd* 9.2.46–51; *HomLev* 7.4.70–95). There is also a fragment of his *Commentary on John* that seems to speak of the peculiarly sacred character of baptismal water, which is not "simple water" but rather "mystically consecrated" and almost identified with the presence of the Holy Spirit that it contains (*FragmJn* 36; also cf. *PArch* 1.3.2.43–51; *ComJn* 6.33.166). His concluding point is that immoral conduct subsequent to baptism is a great sacrilege (*Fragm1Cor* 32.5–9). He acknowledges the legitimacy of infant baptism (*HomLev* 8.3; *HomJos* 9.4; *ComMt* 15.36; *HomLc* 14.5; *ComRm* 5.9) but all the tenor of his thought turns around baptism as a process of the moral conversion of intelligent souls. For this reason (as well as for the purposes of *encomia* to his church in difficult times) he asserts that "baptism by blood" (see **Martyrdom**) can make a man more pure than baptism by water (*HomJd* 7.2.64–113; *ComMt* 16.6; *ComJn* 6.43.223–24).

Blanc (1972); Ledegang (2001), 684–86; Waldram (1981), 41–95.

F. LEDEGANG

Bishops Origen provides some notably severe criticisms of the contemporary episcopate. He deplores those prelates whose excessive pride in their priesthood provoked indignant cries of "Look, what a bishop!" (*HomNum* 2.1.14) or who passed on their sees, like property, to relatives (*HomNum* 22.4.1). Our problem is to contextualize such outbursts, between the interpretative poles represented on the one hand by Eusebius's testimonials of the high regard bishops had for Origen (*H.E.* 6.27), and on the other by Jerome's insistence that Origen aimed his vehemence at "the bishops and clergy of the whole world" (*Apol. adv. libros Rufini* 2.18).

Origen was already established as a teacher and author when he collided with episcopal authority. Having grown up in an Alexandria where ecclesiastical authority was sufficiently diffused to leave adequate space for independent Christian initiative (we can witness the lightness with which Clement wore his office as Christian Didaskalos and possibly presbyter there), Origen struggled to adjust to the increasingly strident assertion of episcopal claims that the newly competitive ecclesiastical environment of the third century produced. While much remains uncertain about his forty-year tenure, Demetrius of Alexandria, Origen's original sponsor and eventual antagonist, did much both to establish the bishop's predominance within the Alexandrian church and to develop that see's authority over Egypt as a whole. Given the context of state oppressions,

this was probably more "survival strategy" than self-aggrandizing ambition on Demetrius's part, and it also reflected the pressures operative upon bishops increasingly defined by their mutual relationships. This was an environment where Origen's cultivation of an international reputation could easily provoke; hence the careful justifications supplied for each of his early journeys abroad. The decisive clash with Demetrius was deferred until the very end of the latter's long life, implying some connection with the succession arrangements. Origen's behavior does not suggest a passive victim of envy. Nor is Eusebius's version of an ordination at Caesarea en route to Athens (apparently without any commitment, that is, to a specific church) an impossible one; in which case the "new presbyter" might have been signaling a bid to Alexandria. By responding with an appeal against Origen, to Pontianus of Rome, Demetrius internationalized the dispute still further. While finalizing the rupture with his former theologian, he thus helped forge what became a decisive episcopal axis during the next two centuries.

The vivid language of Origen's only direct response to the breach—a "storm" in Alexandria, an "escape" from Egypt, the enemy's bitter "pursuit" by "new letters" (*ComJn* 6.8–9)—requires interpretation in its literary context, as the introduction of an installment of an ongoing project of justification intended for Alexandrian readers. Ostentatiously consigning the storm to the past, Origen presents himself as a model of tranquil self-mastery (*ComJn* 6.10), continuing his exegetic labors despite the tempests conjured by hostile bishops. Origen here creates a persona that could survive formal episcopal condemnation.

The *Letter to friends in Alexandria* relates to a second round of controversy with Alexandria, against Demetrius's successor Heraclas. The occasion is problematical: the debate at Ephesus that triggered Heraclas's initiatives occurred during Origen's return from either his first Athenian visit, or perhaps a second (cf. Nautin [1977], 161–72, 436–38). In the latter case a connection can be supposed with his separately attested doctrinal apology to Fabianus of Rome. In either case, however, Heraclas should be seen as responding to a specific, isolated accusation, not pursuing a vendetta. Origen's Letter (like his prologue to the *ComJn*) seems intended as a final word. The church of Alexandria and its prodigal son otherwise succeeded in ignoring one another.

These circumstances preclude any reading of Origen's generic comments on delinquent bishops as coded attacks on Heraclas and Demetrius. Rather, from the early 230s, his ecclesiastical horizons became essentially those of the church of Caesarea. His voluminous writings make no explicit references to his bishop, Theoctistus, who intrudes into the homilies merely to provide the cue for Origen's virtuosity (*Hom1R (1S)* 5.1). No quarrels are recorded; one surmises that as an outsider Origen neither threatened his bishop's authority as he had Demetrius's, nor felt its weight as oppressively. Nor is the Caesarean congregation likely to have taken Origen's homiletic strictures against episcopal malpractice ad hominem. His charge-sheet usually includes the whole priestly caste, with himself explicitly included (*HomJr* 11.3, 12.3, etc.). Some barbs have also been sharpened by his later translators and his textual transmission, notably the famous denunciation of tyrannical churchmen who oppress the poor: "especially in the larger cities" (*ComMt* 16.8), where the only explicit reference to "bishops" comes from the Latin translation, not the Greek original; and whose dominant key is an inclusive first person plural.

While Origen certainly deplores any Christian replication of a Levitical hierarchy, the episcopate in fact seems almost incidental to his ecclesiology. Of the two "bishops" supervising every church (*HomLc* 13.5–6), the invisible angel is infinitely the more important in his schema.

The paternal authority of the human bishop creates genuine bonds (*HomLc* 20.5), but these pale before the spiritual ties between teacher and disciples; and his main prerogative, the imposition of discipline, becomes curiously inconsequential (*HomLev* 11.2, 14.3).

A central problem for contemporary bishops, meanwhile, was the lack of an agreed mechanism for disciplining one another, and here Origen performed an important practical service. The *Dialogue with Heracleides* shows him intervening in a synod: having first guided the suspect bishop, by respectful cross-examination, to a shockingly paradoxical theological declaration, Origen then persuades the assembled bishops of its acceptability; then he takes questions from individual bishops, transforming a trial into a theological master class but without compromising his interlocutors' authority. The bishops thus had good reason to help promote his reputation as an honest theological broker. Nearer home, too, Origen perhaps provided a bridge between Caesarea and Jerusalem, two sees that would later become bitter rivals. Alexander of Jerusalem, like Origen a genuinely international figure, played a still imperfectly understood role as his patron, guarantor, and arbiter (cf. Nautin [1961], chap. 4). Origen had earned a warm tribute from Alexander (*Hom1R (1S)* 1.1). Once again, here Origen seems to overlap different episcopal jurisdictions, blurring a boundary to the mutual benefit of both bishops concerned.

Origen's Palestinian heyday, however, arguably reflected a temporary stage of ecclesiastical evolution, just like his Alexandrian debacle. Already in 268, the synod that examined Paul of Samosata had moved beyond such mediation as he had practiced; although a presbyter again conducted the proceedings, he acted as a prosecutor (Eusebius, *H.E.* 7.29). A century later, Jerome would discover just how difficult it was to reproduce an Origenian authority within a church where the bishops had consolidated their mastery over their own sees and established an exclusive right to police each other's.

Ferguson (1974); Griggs (1990); Lim (1995); Lyman (1999); Trigg (1981, 1992); Vilela (1971).

NEIL McLYNN

Celsus   The one sure fact about Celsus is that, by the mid-third century A.D., there was attributed to him a treatise against Christianity entitled *The True Word*, or *The True Discourse*. Origen, writing about seventy years after Celsus, called him an "Epicurean" philosopher (*CCels* 1.8; Eusebius, *H.E.* 6.36), referring to some treatises he had written in that style. It is, however, not as an Epicurean (that is, as an atheist and a materialist) that Origen joins argument with him, but rather as the exponent of a vision of salvation that he claims is far loftier than that offered by Christianity. This, Origen presents as evidence of Celsus's insincerity and inconsistency, but it is equal evidence that Celsus was not an Epicurean at all. Most modern commentators see him rather as holding to mainly Platonizing opinions and having, accordingly, a Platonist's dislike for common Christianity. This of itself does not mean Celsus was a Platonic philosopher per se, but rather that he was a rhetorician who knew something of Plato, who chiefly represented to him the sense of "immemorial tradition" which he wanted to defend in his native Hellenistic culture. Celsus refers four times to Numenius, a philosopher of the late second century, and associated with a revival of Pythagoreanism (*CCels* 1.15; 4.51; 5.38; 5.57). This reference suggests a date for Celsus himself in the late second or early third century.

The appellation "Platonist" for this era denotes a philosophy in which tenets of Plato are but one of the ingredients, coexisting with elements from Aristotle, Pythagoreanism, and Stoicism. It is often suggested that Celsus's work belongs specifically to the reign of Marcus Aurelius (161–80). If so, it is possible that Celsus's anti-Christian polemic had some connection with the emperor's persecution of Christians. However, Celsus's intellectual arguments show little affinity with that emperor's Stoicism, except for his eighth and final book of apology, when Celsus enjoins duty toward the state, both in war and worship, ideas akin to Marcus Aurelius's scheme of the rational order and providence of all things.

If Celsus is no genius as a philosopher, however, he remains of abiding interest and importance as the first Greek opponent of Christianity to have a detailed knowledge of its writings and an awareness of the Old Testament Scriptures. In fact he seems to have used an otherwise unknown Jewish anti-Christian polemical tract as one of his sources. Origen refers to it as the "Jew of Celsus" (*CCels* 1. Praef. 6). The detail with which Celsus attacks Christianity does not derive from the antipathy of a lapsed believer but emanates from the informed critique of an educated pagan of the time. Its impact is strangely attested by Origen's almost word-by-word refutations of it more than a generation after it was originally issued, when it still remained something of a handbook of anti-Christian objections. Origen cites so much of his opponent's text that it is almost possible to reconstruct the original. And yet no other Christian writer had referred to its existence. Origen says that he had decided to refute the book as a direct response to the request of his literary patron Ambrose (*CCels* 6.8). Eusebius (*H.E.* 6.34–36) places the composition of the *Contra Celsum* during the reign of Philip the Arab (244–49), a time of relaxation from oppression and of Christian missionary expansion. Eusebius describes Origen, then in his sixties and active in Caesarea in Palestine, as at the height of his powers (*CCels* 6.36).

If we take Origen's response as a guide, the broad outline of Celsus's work is as follows. His attack upon Christianity begins with an account of what were probably standard Jewish objections deriving from his Jewish source. Jesus the natural son of Mary and Joseph, Celsus argues, could not have been divine because of his poverty and obscurity, inconsistent with a divine status. The incarnation is a mythic absurdity. Christ's miracles are folk fables for the ill educated. The doctrine of the resurrection is a corruption of the purer Greek idea of the immortality of the soul. Christian teaching has no power to convert the educated. In regard to incarnation and resurrection, in which he shows contempt for matter, Celsus largely argues as a Hellene and departs (presumably) from his Jewish source. Celsus allows that Christianity has some value in instructing morality among the uneducated but laments its decline from the higher standards of Hellenistic universalism. He concludes by urging Christians to join the majority religion, that is, live good lives in conformity with the state, for only such religion can be synonymous with good citizenship.

Origen's response in the *Contra Celsum* is not, however, the masterly synthesis that one might expect from Eusebius's laudatory remarks about it. Origen's method is, by his own admission, contradictory. He tells us that he originally intended to refute Celsus point by point, by close reference to the very words of the treatise. But once he had launched out on this laborious method, it occurred to him that he should have adopted a more systematic approach based upon general principles (*CCels* 1. Praef. 6). So it seems that Origen conflated the two approaches, with the result that his refutations of Celsus's particular points become longer and longer as Origen, in turn, begins to elaborate his own principles. The lasting value of the work remains largely its character as a rich thesaurus for Christian apologetics, more than as a reasoned apologetic in itself.

The essential difference between Origen and Celsus, in terms of their theories of wisdom or philosophies or salvation, is often obscured by the abundant detail, although the difference is ever present and often emerges in a striking manner at particular moments. It is not until late in his treatise that Celsus substantially attacks Christianity in philosophical terms, praising Plato as far superior to the Scriptures. Origen's counterargument is that there is a qualitative difference between the "wisdom of philosophers" and the "historical revelation" made by God in the Scriptures. While Celsus finds it natural to "pass on" (*CCels* 8.42) to the wisdom of the Persians, Origen sees their religious practices as idolatrous: "they worship the sun and the other works of God" (*CCels* 8.45), which makes a mockery of their claims to wisdom. While Celsus sees all the different philosophies and religions as in some way expressions of general truths that are essentially immanent to human nature, Origen contrasts the particulars of Christian teaching with everything that differs from them, underscoring the truth that he sees as fundamental to Christian revelation: that all truth derives from the direct, historical, initiative of a personal God, who has elected a people. The wisdom of God is, for Origen, often taken as foolishness by humanity.

Andresen (1957); Le Boulluec (1998); Chadwick (1966); Hoffmann (1987).
STEPHEN THOMAS

Christology The figure of Jesus depicted in the canonical Gospels stands at the core of Origen's theological vision. Even though conditioned by philosophical culture, more precisely by the kind of Christian Platonism that *Clement of Alexandria* had popularized a generation earlier, Origen never failed to keep the message of the Gospels central in his doctrine about Christ; though some aspects of his Christology, with a highly imaginative dimension soaring to the highest of heavens and admitting a dualistic status for human beings, may well bear overtones of Valentinian myth (see *Gnostics*). One must only keep in mind that, when he first conceived his Christology, in the first half of the third century, Origen ventured into a conceptual no-man's-land. The time was hardly ripe for a systematic treatise on Christ. However, in his whole written legacy the Alexandrian pioneer exhibits a consistent Gospel-based Christology, whose richness still amazes many historians of Christian thought.

The Heavenly Mystery of Christ

Anticipating by a century the reaction against Arius of his greatest episcopal admirer, Athanasius of Alexandria (299–373), Origen categorically states that Christ is Son of God by being equal in eternity and divinity with the Father (*PArch* 1.2) (see *God*). He venerates him as the eternal Logos in whom God creates the universe, and he concludes that there was never "a time when the Logos was not" (*ComHe* 1.8). Being the very Logos of God and his perfect image, Christ is the proper origin of all things (*HomGn* 1.1; *PArch* 1.2). As God's Wisdom he initiates all transcendent ways for divine creativity to exercise her almighty power (*ComJn* 1.22; *PArch* 1.2.2–4). As divine Truth (*SerMt* 33), he is the key for all knowledge, enlightening believers and giving them access to supernatural mysteries (*ComJn* 1.39; 6.3). Last, but not least, as uncreated Life, Christ leads believers to their ultimate resurrection (*ComJn* 1.11). Thus the Alexandrian theologian enumerates divine titles of Jesus for his fellow Christians at ease with a Platonist otherworld in which supreme values of spirituality are ideally personified; yet he rests his own vision on a firmly Trinitarian perspective: "First we must know this, that in Christ there is one nature, his deity, because he is the only-begotten Son of the Father (and another nature . . .)" (*PArch* 1.2.1).

In his Christology Origen constantly presupposes a Trinitarian theory. He sees Christ as God's Word, his Logos, involved in the whole economy of creation and salvation moderated by divine Trinity. Due to his heavenly supremacy as the Father's Logos, "the very Word of the Father and the very Wisdom of God" (*PArch* 2.6.2), Origen's Christ is present everywhere in the scriptural record on the economy. Hence Scripture deserves to be called "the one body of Truth" (*ComJn* 13.46) and identified as Christ. In its own way Scripture materializes a mysteriously anticipated incarnation of the divine Logos (*ComJn* 1.42; *FragmMt*). By his active presence in the very letter of Scripture, the Logos delivers a salvific revelation. Jesus, riding a white horse in the book of Revelation (*ComJn* 2.4) or entering Jerusalem seated on an ass in the Fourth Gospel (*ComJn* 10.18), symbolizes Christ's activity omnipresent in the Gospel narratives. In fact, Origen's christological view embraces the full content of Scripture, for "the whole Law is spiritual" (*PArch* 1. Praef. 8).

Therefore it is extremely risky "to pretend crossing such a vast ocean of mysteries, as one may find oneself quickly overwhelmed by mysteries, as if one were in a storm on the high seas" (*HomGn* 9.1).

The Scriptural Mystery of Christ

For a proper understanding of Origen's Christology a foremost imperative is to catch the decisive significance of the christological focus in his exegesis. As a first priority for Origen in a lifelong agenda, interpreting Scripture meant finding Christ. The same Logos who created the universe also created Scripture, so that one needs to scrutinize both creations at once (*ComPs* 1.3). Veiled by the letter, but at work throughout Scripture as its living inspiration, the Logos inculcates into the writing of the whole Bible a prophetic anticipation of his coming in the flesh. Origen never tires of discovering symbols and signs in the *Old Testament* by which long in advance, Gospel events received a prophetic prefiguration. Hence his spiritual commentary on Scripture was based on significant "types," characters whose significance to be fully perceived called on New Testament references: for instance, Isaac, ready to be immolated by his father, calling on Jesus in the story of his passion; or Moses, saving his exiled compatriots by a safe crossing of the Red Sea, being a distant announcement of Jesus saving believers through the baptismal rite of passage; or the prince of Tyre, profiling a figure of Satan as fully revealed in the Gospels (see *Typology*). Fascinated by the literal content of narrated episodes, of which the very letter carried on for him a divine inspiration, Origen enriched his immediate paraphrases with views of his own, dictated by the christological orientation of his exegesis. The very popular device of *allegory*, a traditional feature of Alexandrian commentators in secular culture, gave him the capacity to verify on the scale of the whole Scripture Paul's observation about Sarah and Hagar in Galatians 4:24, where he explicitly averred, "This is an allegory," and in so doing gave an authoritative pattern to Christian interpreters after him. Origen used the literary device of allegory as a hermeneutical procedure quite significantly: all Old Testament data could signify something comparable in the New Testament, if only the data were considered in the light of Christ's revelation. In other words, Origen's allegorism was thoroughly christocentric. It allowed him to enrich the language of Christian piety for centuries to come with a profusion of biblical images, and it established a standard format for Christian exegesis still valid in Western churches after the exegetical revolution of the past two centuries.

Even de Lubac's monumental survey of the influence exercised by Origen's allegorism (2000) fails to give a clear account of the extension and exuberance of that versatile structuring of biblical exegesis in Origen's christological discourse. Mainly in his many homilies, but also in his major biblical commentaries, the Alexandrian interpreter attempted, for the benefit of his congregation, a pastoral appropriation of the Old Testament by claiming again and again to recognize in it a consistent prefiguration of Christ. In *HomGn* Noah is a figure of Christ. In *HomEx* the text of Exodus 1:6–7 calls on "the death of 'our' Joseph, whom Judas, one of his brothers, sold for thirty pennies" (*HomEx* 1.4). In *HomNum* 3, Christ is visualized as the "lion of the tribe of Judah" (*HomNum* 3.16.8; 3.17.5; 3.18.4), as the "river of paradise," as the "well" (*HomNum* 3.12.2), namely, "a well that surpasses all others, an extraordinary well"; and even as the unicorn (*HomNum* 3.16.6; 3.17.5: "for there, like everywhere, it represents Christ." Joshua, the son of Nave, becomes a double of Jesus Christ. In the same *Homily on Numbers* in which elsewhere Moses and Aaron are declared "disciples of the gospel more than the Law" (*HomNum* 9.3). Christ is not only the "bridegroom"; he is also magnified as the "Sun of Justice" (*ComCt* 2.2; see also *ComJn* 3.1, frg. 34; *HomLev* 9.10; and *CCels* 2.2). In *ComCt* 2.4 Origen finds the "door" (NRSV, "gate") of John 10:7 and 10:9, and the "good shepherd" of John 10:11. In *ComCt* 3.15 he recognizes the "caring physician" of John 12:6 and 13:29. In the *ComJn* Christ is "the perfect high priest," as in *PEuch* 11 and 15 and in *ComMt* 12.39 (see *Epinoiai*).

The Incarnate Mystery of Christ

Prefigured in Old Testament types or announced by the prophets and anticipated in countless circumstances of the biblical narratives, as Origen interpreted them, the mystery of God's incarnation called on the fullness of this theologian's intellectual capacity. Not only had Origen to produce a rich paraphrase, emphasizing the significance of the mystery covered by the Gospel stories, but he was also to invest the more speculative resources of his cultural identity when trying to uncover the transcendent reality of the mystery. An inner dynamic of faith pushed him to the edge of his rational self, as may be common in theological ventures, so that he ended by projecting the incarnational mystery on the screen of a metaphysical imagination characteristic of a genuinely Alexandrian mind-set.

For about a millennium before his time, Greek religious thought had linked thoughts on deity with a cosmic substratum. Hence a preconceived logic oriented Origen's approach of the mystery of God's incarnation toward a cosmological frame. From childhood he knew that divine Wisdom was carrying the whole universe before all times, as in a womb (cf. *PArch* 1.2). In that mysterious preexistence of God's creation a terrible drama had occurred, clearly mentioned by sacred writers (Isa. 14:12; Luke 10:18). Enough for Origen's inquisitive commitment to the Bible, the sparse confidences of inspired authors set his mind on fire, allowing him to assert that in a supracosmic catastrophe of a purely spiritual nature, Lucifer and his legions of angels had also compromised the fate of human souls included in the "noetic cosmos." He saw in the wake of the massive expulsion of the angels from heaven (the episode John Milton magnified in *Paradise Lost*) how the tarnished human souls were also doomed to fall. Satan and the demonized angels were precipitated to the bottom of the heavenly realm, the rock solid "firmament," as already taught by a popular Jewish-Christian apocryphal book called the *Ascension of Isaiah* not too long before Origen's time. A more benign providence let human souls, in waiting for their descent into the earthly condition (where, imprisoned in bodies, they would undergo an experiment of a kind of reeducation), exercise their free will and finally reach salvation, or perish (if not for "ever") (see *Angels, Anthropology, Apokatastasis, Fall, Souls*).

Origen's vision takes on a decidedly mythical proportion when it leads him to ponder the ultimate destination of each angel or each human being according to the various categories of fallen creatures that he thinks need to be so distinguished. However, his whole gigantic projection had its center of gravity in the pivotal mystery of God's incarnation. His construct intended to offer a plausible representation of what happened to the Son of God in the process of becoming human; such a divine mystery engaged for him, as an Alexandrian theologian, a "theological" issue in need of being thought out in Alexandrian terms.

The same metaphysical framework that inspired Origen's vision of a double cosmology—terrestrial and supraterrestrial, material and spiritual—appears within his christological construct. Among the global mass of souls expecting one day to take part in that tragicomedy of repentant ascent back to a wholly pure spiritual life, which was to be acted out on earth, Origen saw only one soul that remained untouched by the fatal consequences of the angelic upheaval, and this because it was destined to become the very soul of Jesus. It was this soul, Jesus, preexistently chosen by the divine Logos for his own descent to earth at the decisive moment of the universal need for salvation. According to Philippians 2:7–8, the Son of God volunteered to deny himself in such a rescue mission. Deprived of his divine titles, he assumed the nature and the condition of a slave. Bearing human likeness, he revealed himself in a human shape. He humbled himself and, obedient to the Father, even accepted death, death on a cross. Origen magnified the Pauline intuition of Philippians 2:7–8 with an ingenious visualization.

First of all, in order to become credible, the notion of God's incarnation needed to overcome the cosmic dualism deeply engraved in the Alexandrian mind. Origen hoped to offer a solution for such a seemingly insurmountable difficulty. The immaculate soul chosen by divine decision for belonging one day to the humanly born Jesus provided the Logos with the smooth transition required for him to pass directly from one cosmic realm to another. Using that soul like a space suit (in the present case one should rather call it an "earth suit"), the uncreated Logos of God encapsulated himself inside a created spiritual nature, a unique case of intimacy in which the creature instantly gave itself away to its Creator, engulfed in the burning abyss of divine love that changed and exalted its condition. Only the divine Logos, utterly transcendent by nature, could join, without compromising his identity, with the Logos-like transcendence of a Soul unharmed by the fall. Origen concludes: "It is therefore right that this soul, either because it was wholly in the Son of God, or because it received the Son of God wholly into itself, should be called, along with the flesh which it had taken, the Son of God, and the Power of God, Christ, and the Wisdom of God" (*PArch* 2.63). In short, "the Soul with the Word of God is made Christ," according to Colossians 2:9 (*PArch* 2.64).

At this point it is important to note that nowhere does Origen speak about the human soul of Jesus being eliminated by the Logos, either before or after the divine incarnation. He one-sidedly stresses the sovereign initiative of the Logos in the process, as he is always eager to state the integral divinity of the Logos during the incarnational metamorphosis. A century later Athanasius would state more explicitly that only a Savior integrally divine could perform the sort of salvation that would be equal to a new creation of humanity. Far from eliminating the soul of Jesus in its pristine perfection, before or after the incarnation, Origen's theory gives it a pivotal significance in the universal saving mission of the Logos. Now immanent in the incarnate Logos, that human soul allows the Logos to act as its subject, though it continues to react like any human soul to what happens to the embodied Jesus. The gospel eloquently illustrates the humble odyssey of the divinized soul of Jesus through a very human life and death, and it discloses the overpowering charisma of the Logos at work in Jesus each single time the divine Logos

decides to make in him a statement proving the hidden, but actively revelatory, presence of God "incarnate."

The very nature of that "incarnation" as conceived by Origen may look problematic for believers no longer conditioned by the cultural prejudice of cosmic dualism omnipresent in antiquity. But in Origen's case we are dealing with an incarnation of the divine Logos specifically into the human soul (as such, more technically a "soul communion" than an "enfleshment"). Such a miracle was possible only because the soul, though bound to a body, by definition preserves an element of divine transcendence in its inner structure, thereby remaining somehow kindred on earth with the Logos himself. A similar incarnation straight into the flesh of bodily existence was for Origen a nonsense, as he explicitly argues in the *First Principles*.

Hence the whole salvific work of the incarnate Logos in Origen's understanding shapes up as a pedagogical undertaking. The Soul-joined-with-the-Logos operates in the flesh by addressing other souls. His exemplary action calls for imitation. His message dissipates ignorance. He rekindles the spark of noetic transcendence that enables human souls to become again irradiated with the divine Logos, in order to recover their original integrity as images of the image of God who is the Logos himself. With its intellectualist overtones and its still dualistic spirituality (despite the smart twist of a soul-centered "incarnation"), the gnostic-type explanation of the salvific incarnation of God proposed by Origen marked Christian thought through the millennia. In particular it favored Christian *asceticism,* starting with Origen himself, and spreading over the ancient world through subsequent waves of monastic tradition. A highly needed rectification of it was secured by the incarnational theology of Athanasius, bishop of Alexandria from 328 to 373. Athanasius devotedly emphasized much of Origen's teaching in his essay *On the Incarnation of the Logos,* but now he precisely focused on a divine incarnation "in the flesh," no more "in the soul" as such. Origen underlined the point, "The Son of God . . . assumed not only, as some think, a human body, but also a soul, in its nature indeed like our souls, but in will and virtue like himself, and of such a kind that it could unswervingly carry into effect all the wishes and plans of the Word and Wisdom" (*PArch* 4.4.4). His successor Athanasius argued in the opposite direction: "For he did not simply will to become embodied, or will merely to appear. For if he willed merely to appear, he was able to effect his divine appearance by some other and higher means as well. But rather he took on a body of our kind" (*De incarnatione* c. 8).

Without a single note of explicit criticism, the disciple corrected the master: Not by assuming the soul with a bodily appearance, but by properly assuming flesh itself and becoming a body on earth, did the divine Logos save human beings in their real condition, which is at once physical and spiritual. Hence Athanasian exegesis would sound so different from Origen's magisterial achievement as an interpreter of Scripture. It would be only a circumstantial exegesis, directly resulting from Athanasius's physical involvement in church affairs and pastoral care. It would also secure an effective response to Arius, whose biased, schoolbook Origenism (at least as Athanasius demonstrated it loud and relentlessly) resulted in unacceptable contradictions: a divine Logos changed into a human soul, hence a body of Jesus without a human soul, and this body showing unmistakably all through the Gospel stories that the divine Logos should by no means be called God in proper terms.

As a pioneering venture of systematic Christology in the dogmatic vacuum of a Christianity barely emerging from its Judeo-Christian infancy, Origen's hypothetical notion of God's incarnation would overshadow the centuries-long controversies around the notion of the "two natures" of Christ. His christological legacy would prove foundational for a faith in Christ bound to the Gospel affirmation of divine Trinity, and would focus that faith on the issue of the true subject in Jesus Christ. Origen's Christology traces a luminous path of faithful creativity through all Greek-speaking generations of believers to the time of Maximus Confessor in the seventh century and indeed beyond.

Coman (1968); Crouzel (1956); Grillmeier (1971); De Lubac (2000), 83–125; Lyman (1993); Rowe (1987).

CHARLES KANNENGIESSER

Church   For   Origen's   life   and thought the church as both institution and concept is of extreme importance. He saw himself as a person of the church (*HomLc* 16). His career was framed by commitments to the church (*PArch* 1. Praef. 2; *SerMt* 39, 46), as his earlier and later writings disclose. Yet he never provided a systematic treatment of ecclesiology, and only recently has a systematic survey of his ecclesiological images been undertaken (Ledegang 2001). Origen's understanding of the church must be discerned in occasional references, abundant images, allusions, and in incidents he described. His ecclesiology is also intimately intertwined with his teachings about *Christology*, the *Holy Spirit*, and *Eschatology*, which makes it difficult to treat his views of church in isolation from these topics.

Origen is a valuable source for the condition of the church of the third century. He sees the church as an assembly scattered throughout the world (*ComCt* 1; *HomEz* 1.2; *ComMt* 16.22 and 17.24). It is a concrete reality, where the believer may pray (*PEuch* 20.1). The church is a global republic with its own legal system; it is the "city of God" (*ComCt* 2; *CCels* 4.22; *HomJr* 9.2; and *HomJos* 8.17). It is the body of Christ, for this concrete church is animated by Christ in the same way that the ordinary human body is animated by the soul (*CCels* 6.48 and *ComMt*

14, 17). This empirical church is always a combination of good and evil (*HomJos* 21.1 and *ComMt* 10.13). Origen is also critical of the church of his day. Members of congregations are not attentive during homilies (*HomGn* 10.1 and 11.3). Gifts for the poor have been misused, and there is even evidence of fraud (*ComMt* 16.22 and *HomLev* 7.7). Some leaders in the Christian communities are arrogant and ambitious (*HomNum* 12.4; *ComMt* 16.8 and *SerMt* 12). Some of the faithful have been unjustly excluded from the community (*HomLev* 14.3 and *ComMt* 15.15). Origen sees a diminishing of the church, in his own day, and he is nostalgic for earlier, "purer" times (*CCels* 8.8 and *HomJr* 4.3).

The writings of Origen give witness to the threefold structure of the church's ministerial offices. He often mentions together bishops, presbyters, and deacons (*ComMt* 15.26 and *HomJr* 14.16). Despite his voiced criticisms of unworthy leaders (see **Bishops**) Origen nevertheless holds these ministers in high regard (*CCels* 8.75). The bishops are meant to speak directly against sin in the church (*HomJos* 7.6). Bishops also stand in the place of Christ, presbyters in the place of the patriarchs and apostles, and deacons in the place of the seven angels (*SerMt* 10). But Origen is also aware of the distinction in the ecclesiastical structure between the bishop and the office of teacher (*didaskalos*) in the church. For him, it is the teachers who come to the secrets of the faith (*HomLev* 5.3 and 12.7), and for Origen they seem to have a higher intrinsic value than the formal offices of the ecclesiastical structure. Although in Origen's day the offices of bishop and teacher were coming together, it is not clear that the teacher's function was totally identified with that of the bishop and presbyter (*HomEx* 13.4). Origen's writings reflect the continuing tension (*Fragm1Co* 74).

The empirical reality that he knows and sees around him does not exhaust Origen's comprehension of the church. His thinking reflects a sharp tension between this empirical, or earthly, church and the heavenly church. Rooted in his Alexandrian context, Origen seeks to discover beyond the visible and transcendent things of this world the mystery of invisible and eternal realities (*HomNum* 3.3). Origen develops the idea of two churches, two hierarchies (*HomLc* 13). The empirical church includes many who are not truly members of the church, but the heavenly church is comprised only of the perfect believers, those who are truly united with the Logos (*PEuch* 20.1; *ComCt* 2). The heavenly church is "without spot or wrinkle"; it is holy and without blame (*ComMt* 12.12; *SerMt* 139). This is because the heavenly church is joined to Christ (*SerMt* 8; *ComCt* 1.4). According to Origen, the body of Christ is not merely a type of the church, rather it is (animated by the Son of God), the very church itself (*CCels* 6.48). This church has existed since before creation (*ComCt* 2.8): a perfect communion of souls. Origen identified the elect portion of the earthly church with the heavenly church. For him there is "no salvation outside of the Church" (*HomJos* 3.5). Although Origen sees the earthly church with all its defects as a shadow or image of the heavenly church, he also maintains that the two churches do coincide in some way (*ComCt* 2).

One of Origen's most frequent images for the heavenly church is the bride of Christ (*ComCt* 1 and 2). Origen identifies the bride with the church or the soul. In this way he links an ecclesiological dimension to spiritual life. Christ seeks the bride, and the bride awaits and desires Christ. For Origen, all of history from Adam onward is a preparation for this encounter of Christ with his bride. He makes the distinction between the first call to the wedding, to Israel and the synagogue, which was refused (*ComMt* 14.7; *PEuch* 20.1), and the wedding of Christ and the church (*ComMt* 17). This framework allows Origen to affirm both God's unitary purpose in history and also its discontinuity. The coming of Christ was not recognized by most of Israel; thus the calling of the Gentiles to faith. The church becomes the community to the nations. It is based on God's call after the refusal of the call to Israel (*FragmPs* 118.126–27). The passage from the one call to the other is viewed as a passage from one generation to the other (*SerMt* 54). In the context of this second call, the church adheres to Christ in simple faith (*HomLev* 12.5). Thus Origen develops a theology of two peoples (*PArch* 4.1.4; *ComMt* 12.4; *HomJr* 11.6).

Closely connected with this insight is Origen's stress on the unity of the church. The church is not merely an organization, a body that imitates Jesus, but is itself the risen body of Christ, and thus it is one. For Origen, this is the meaning of "being in Christ" (*ComJn* 10.35; *ComMt* 12.25 and 14.47; *CCels* 6.79). Members of Christ are thus in unity with each other because they are in unity with their Lord (*FragmPs* 122.3; *ComMt* 24.21). For Origen on the final day, all persons who will be saved will belong to the church (*ComJn* 10.35).

Bardy (1947), 128–65; Camelot (1970), 7–10; Chenevert (1969); Ledegang (2001); McGuckin (1985b); Vogt (1974).

WILLIAM G. RUSCH

Clement of Alexandria

Clement came to Alexandria (ca. 175) after traveling around the eastern Mediterranean world from Italy to Syria in his quest for knowledge. Here he found his greatest teacher in Pantaenus, a Stoic who had converted to Christianity, and here he remained, learning and teaching until the persecution of 202, when he left for Palestine, where he remained until his death in ca. 215. Alexandria was the definitive environment of Clement's thought, a treasury of classical learning, all of which he saw fulfilled (like the **Old Testament**) in Christ. His genius was to see that some problems of Hellenistic philosophy ran parallel alongside Christian theology: the one and the one-many alongside the Christian concept of God and the Logos; or the idea of the rule of truth and the practice of argument alongside the Christian notions of faith and knowledge. Clement also possessed a great versatility of style and thought, writing to different readers in different ways. As he said in his treatise *To the Newly Baptized* (par. 222): "It is necessary to adapt your utterance to the needs of the hearers." His extraordinary knowledge of Scripture can still bewilder the modern reader.

His main works, *Protrepticus* (Exhortation), *Paedagogus* (Instructor), *Stromateis* (Miscellanies), follow a series that some scholars dispute. In the *Protrepticus* he speaks to pagan Greeks, inviting them to turn from the absurdities of their colorful heritage to the sovereign Logos, the Word of God. In the *Paedagogus* he gives instruction to Christians on all the details of daily life: eating, drinking, sleeping, walking, dressing; at the same time he includes passages of great theological penetration. The *Stromateis* are marked by studied disorder, so that, as his revered Heraclitus required, they who seek for gold must dig much earth to find a little gold. There is, however, a sequence in the work, which is the chief source for his theology. Someone new to Clement's thought should go to his treatise *On the Rich Man's Salvation* (Quis dives salvetur?), where the central ideas of Clement's thought can be found expressed in simple Greek and lucid concepts. There is also a surviving sermon on patience, addressed, it seems, to the newly baptized. Fragments of his *Hypotyposeis* (Exegetical notes) exhibit Clement's concern for historical detail, which confounds those who class him as a pure allegorist. Remarkably a copy of the *Hypotyposeis* was rediscovered two hundred years ago in Egypt, but it has not been traced since that report of it.

Clement saw the Christian Bible as the true philosophy, which brought together the fragments of truth found in classical thought and literature. It should be handled with logic and piety.

Most false interpretations were due to logical errors. At the same time, Scripture was studded with metaphor and allegory, Clement drew on Philo for some of his allegory, and indeed his whole philosophical treatment of Scripture followed that of Philo. Marked differences from Philo occur, nevertheless, because Clement's chief concern was for biblical writings outside the Pentateuch, namely, prophets, Psalms, Gospels, and epistles. There is greater vitality in Clement but Philo must not be despised, for his joining of philosophy and Scripture was a monumental achievement. Clement, with a central interest in Christ, was playing with more pieces on his board, so that his virtuosity is more apparent.

Like Irenaeus, Clement took the shape of his theology from the primitive Christian kerygma: God, the divine economy in creation, prophets and history, recapitulation in Christ, and salvation for all who believe. Clement developed this structure in different ways. The plan of salvation included the Greeks, to whom God gave philosophy, just as he had given the Law to the Jews. Clement's central theological understanding came from John and Paul. He took from John 1:18 (No one has ever seen God. It is God the only Son, who is close to the Father's heart, who has made him known) the theme of Christ as the "known center" of the unknown *God*. Above all, he accepted the opening claim that the Word was with God and was God, the ultimate reciprocity in God.

While Clement's "negative theology" has drawn much attention, his understanding of Johannine reciprocity (the Father in the Son, and the Son in the Father) is really the final key to his thought. From the mystery of love between Father and Son flows the saving love of God for humankind and the love of humans for each other. Following John 17, Clement put no limit on the potential unity of the believer with God. His *Stromateis* reach their peak in book 7, where he describes the true man of

knowledge, who lives a life of continual prayer and moves toward the vision of God "face to face." Such a person, he says, is worthy of the respect, not the enmity, of philosophers. Clement's use of Paul ("God's apostle") begins with the centrality of faith and ends with the dominance of love and the vision of 1 Corinthians 13. Clement's attitude to heretical gnostics is open on some questions, as is evident in the *Excerpts from Theodotus*, but strongly hostile on the gnostic denigration of faith and the immorality of certain gnostic sects described in *Stromateis* book 3.

Clement's relation to Origen remains a puzzle. While the latter is Clement's intellectual successor, he does not mention Clement explicitly. The dates of their activity is one explanation. Clement left Alexandria during the persecution in which Origen's father was martyred. Origen's enthusiasm for martyrdom would also limit his appreciation for Clement, who fled, while Origen's father received the ultimate prize. Nevertheless almost every element in Clement's theological architecture and attitudinal stance finds a clear echo in the later Origenian system, though that system obviously developed along more biblico-exegetical lines.

Bigg (1981); Lilla (1971); Osborn (1957); Runia (1995).

ERIC OSBORN

Contemplation

In Origen's thought contemplative activity consists of two stages: the active life of moral, spiritual, and intellectual preparation (*praxis*) and true contemplation (*theoria*). In the process of spiritual growth, the active life is necessary and valuable, but is only preparatory to contemplation itself. Origen illustrates these stages with pairs of biblical figures. Mary and Martha (*FragmHomLc* 13) represent the contemplative and active lives respectively. Origen contrasts John, the beloved disciple, and Peter in a similar way (*ComJn* 32.20).

In the prologue to his *Commentary on the Song of Songs*, Origen divides the contemplative process further into three parts: moral, natural, and inspective contemplation (*ComCt* 40); the first two represent the beginning and the more advanced parts of the active life, while the last is *theoria*, no less than the contemplation of heavenly realities.

This schematic division reflects Origen's belief that the ability to contemplate divine mysteries is not a given but is attained only by an elect few, after a long prior period of *prayer*, study, and the struggle to master human passions through ascetic discipline (see *Asceticism*). These elect are aided by the *Holy Spirit*, who gives a special grace to "those who by God's foreknowledge have been previously determined, because they would live lives worthy of Him after He was made known to them" (*CCels* 7.44). This final, perfect apprehension of contemplation is for Origen an evocation of that perfect union with the Logos that souls enjoyed before the *Fall*, when they enjoyed the vision of God mediated to them directly through the divine Logos (see *Anthropology, Cosmology, Preexistence*).

The first level, that of moral contemplation, "inculcates a seemly manner of life and gives a grounding in habits that incline to virtue" (*ComCt* 41). It involves the keeping of the Law in faith, in accordance with study and understanding of the literal meaning of Scripture, as the beginning of purification of the soul. Origen illustrates the three stages of contemplation with the figures of Abraham, Isaac, and Jacob, whereby "Abraham sets forth moral philosophy through obedience" (*ComCt* 45).

The second level, natural contemplation, discerns the deeper purposes of creation. Here, "the nature of every single thing is considered; so that nothing in life may be done which is contrary to nature, but everything assigned to the uses for which the Creator brought it into being" (*ComCt* 41). This phase of contemplation strives for the final purification from physical desires, the mastery of the passions, and the perfection of Christian love that enables true contemplation. A major component of natural contemplation is intensive focus on the mystical sense, as opposed to the literal sense, of Scripture, as a means to discern the hidden "nature of every single thing." The ability and willingness to engage in deep study marks out the contemplative at the natural level, since God "desires us believe in the [deeper] significance, rather than in the intention of the letter" (*CmJn* 1.23). The prototype of the natural contemplative is Isaac, who is "an exponent of natural philosophy, when he digs wells and searches out the roots of things" (*ComCt* 45).

Even after purification of soul and body, prayer, intensive study, and the attainment of Christian love, Origen thinks the disciple can achieve contemplation only through a special gift of God. He teaches that "human nature is not sufficient in any way to seek for God and to find Him in His pure nature, unless it is helped by the God who is the object of the search" (*CCels* 7.42). This divine help is variously described as a special gift of love of the Spirit, an illuminative breakthrough granted by God, and as an indwelling by the Logos itself in the soul of the believer.

Through this divine illumination we are enabled to engage in "the study which is called inspective (*theoria*) . . . by which we go beyond things seen and contemplate to a degree things heavenly and divine, beholding them with the mind alone" (*ComCt* 41). It is Jacob who "practices the science of *theoria*, in that he earned his name of Israel from his contemplation of the things of God, and saw the camps of heaven, and beheld the House of God, and the angels' paths—the ladders reaching up from earth to heaven" (*ComCt* 45). Jacob is not the only biblical figure that serves as a contemplative model. Moses, who sees the burning bush and enters the cloud of darkness; Paul, who is carried up to the third heaven; and John, who reclines on the bosom of the Logos—all typify the contemplative ideal. It is not just in the figures of the patriarch or apostles that Origen finds models of contemplation in the Bible. The departure from Egypt and the sojourn in the desert are also seen as stages of contemplation (*HomNum*), as a gradual purification from vices through ascetic discipline, which culminates in possession of the promised land and more spiritual relationship to God. Indeed, the very structure of the varied parts of the Bible reflects this spiritual journey and serves as a manual of instruction for contemplation. Origen sees the three books attributed to Solomon (Proverbs, Ecclesiastes, and the Song of Songs) as models of the three stages of contemplation (*HomNum* 27). The various canticles of the Hebrew Scriptures, culminating in the Song of Songs, are also vehicles for progressive spiritual contemplation (*ComCt* 46–50).

For Origen, the end result of this spiritual journey is the ascent to the contemplation of "intelligible and invisible things" (*CCels* 3.56), the final goal being the perfection of spiritual knowledge in apprehension of the Trinity itself (*HomNum* 10.3). The eye of the spirit can now perceive divine light because it has been purified from distorting passions. The image of God in humankind is cleansed and restored, so that "like is drawn to like" in a participation in the divine Logos, and the presence of the Logos is perfected in the human soul. In contrast to the gnostics, Origen thinks that the attainment of the highest contemplation does not denigrate active life in the physical world, but rather completes and perfects it. Origen is careful to emphasize the holistic quality of true contemplation: "For, perhaps, even if in some way we attain the most sublime and highest contemplation of the Word and of the truth, we shall not forget completely that we were introduced to him by his coming in our body" (*ComJn* 2.61). As long as a disciple remains in this earthly life, however, contemplation must remain

imperfect, although one can rise to contemplate God even as the angels do (*ComMt* 17.19). In heaven "the soul whose only desire is to be united to the Word of God and to be in fellowship with Him, [will] enter into the mysteries of His wisdom and knowledge as into the chambers of her heavenly Bridegroom" (*ComCt* 60). True contemplation is thus a spiritual marriage consecrated by the faith and ascetic effort of the believer, and sanctified by the grace of God. In this impressive structure of his teachings about the spiritual process of contemplation, Origen served as the master architect for all subsequent Christian tradition. His work had immediate and determinative influence on monastic understandings of contemplative ascesis, especially through major disciples such as Gregory of Nazianzus and Evagrius. It thereby entered into the very bloodstream of the Eastern church's conception of the goal of theology. The contemplative doctrine was taken even further through the medium of his *Commentary on the Song of Songs* and determined the "mystical theology" of the later Western church too.

Bertrand (1951); Crouzel (1961), (1989), 118–133; Rahner (1979), 82–103.

ALAN G. PADDLE

Cosmology

Cosmology   It is open to debate whether Origen intended to develop a systematic theory of cosmos, but he does present a well-thought-out and structured cosmology that integrates classical philosophical thought and contemporary philosophy with his own perception of orthodox Christian belief. The whole scheme is then presented with a thorough underpinning of Scripture. However, Origen is aware that his thoughts may be considered contentious: "Now we ourselves speak on these subjects with great fear and caution, discussing and investigating rather than laying down fixed and certain conclusions. . . . We are dealing, as well as we can, with subjects that call for discussion rather than for definition" (*PArch* 1.6.1). And contentious they were, as is evident from the anathemas against Origen presented at the Fifth Ecumenical Council in 553, which provide, ironically, a comprehensive summary of what was taken to be "Origenistic" thought on cosmology (see *Origenist Crises*). Two of Origen's works focus particular attention on cosmological theory: his *First Principles*, written in his early years at Alexandria, and then that work of his old age, the *Contra Celsum*, written in Caesarea. Although there are numerous textual problems with the evidence of the first (relating to the degree his translator Rufinus "improved" and "corrected" his source), the original Greek version of the latter is extant.

Origen's primary starting point is the text: "In the beginning God created the heavens and the earth" (Gen. 1:1). He supports this absolutely but says that to understand why God created, and what he created, requires an understanding of God's creative role prior to the making of the material world. God is incorporeal and invisible, and the same is to be said of the three hypostases of the Trinity. The only begotten Son of God (see *Christology*) was made by the Father and, in turn, the *Holy Spirit* was also made. As this creative act was prior to the creation of cosmic time, it can be argued that the Father was "never without the Son or Holy Spirit." The Son is further described as "the invisible image of the invisible God" (*PArch* 1.2.6.) and is the divine agent of creation. A finite number of rational, immortal souls were then created within the agency of the Logos's mediation of the divine creativity. These souls were engaged in *contemplation* of God, entirely through the Son, but through exercise of free will they began to fall away through a cooling of their ardor. Because they chose to move away from God, as an economy of pedagogical reform, the world (all that is visible and invisible) was created by God as a place for these cooled souls to abide in a corporeal state (incorporeality being the state of the sinless) so that there they might undergo a process of rehabilitation (see *Anthropology*). The souls were placed in "bodies" to inhabit this world, and the diversity of the created world was caused by the various degrees to which the souls had cooled, their final place in the cosmic order being determined, therefore, purely by merit. The first soul to cool, and thus the one to fall the farthest, became the devil in the created world. He was followed by those souls that became demons, then human beings, followed by the "gods" (whose existence, Origen notes, was mentioned in the Psalms), then the sun, moon, and stars (whom Origen sees as exalted, sentient, and philanthropic beings), and finally the angels and archangels. One soul remained so devoted to the image of God that "what formerly depended upon the will was eventually, by the influence of long custom, changed into nature" (*PArch* 2.6.5). This supremely exalted soul, being perfected to the point of sinlessness, thus became the soul of Jesus Christ. The soul of Jesus would play a considerable role in Origen's *Christology*.

As human beings were weaker than all other rational creatures, they needed assistance in the rehabilitation process. While the incarnation was the pinnacle of God's providence in presenting to humans the correct path to follow, all other higher rational creatures had a pedagogic role to play. The stars and planets were there for those human souls who were at the stage where they could be moved only through the perceptions of their senses; thus they could gaze upon the heavenly bodies and "stand contentedly in these and not fall to idols or demons" (*ComJn* 2.26). The archangels and *angels* had duties to perform in aiding fallen souls to return to God, these duties again apportioned by God on the grounds of merit. Satan and his demons test rational souls through divine appointment, "either for the conversion of men when they drift towards the flood of evil, or with the object of training the race of rational beings" (*CCels* 8.31). The world is a dynamic arena of pedagogic soteriology as souls may, through the exercise of their free choice, advance spiritually or fall farther away. Origen did not elaborate this thought to its extreme, but others did later, wondering whether angels could become humans or demons, or vice versa. Taken to its logical conclusion, it was legitimate to wonder if even the devil could be rehabilitated (Origen eventually responded it was not possible). This conflict rose up even in his own lifetime and caused him problems within the church.

His cosmological vision was indeed spacious: "By the world we now mean all that is above the heavens, or in them, or on the earth, or in what are called the lower regions, or any places that exist anywhere; together with the beings who are said to dwell in them" (*PArch* 2.9.3). While souls are immortal, created bodies are not, and when it fell into mortal dissolution the body was refashioned (resurrected) according to merit. It could be reconstituted as a spiritual body, which was appropriate for those who can now dwell in the heavens or for those who needed to survive the experience of hell (see *Hades*). Hell is not so much a place of eternal, irremediable punishment, but a place where an individual's soul is confronted by its own sins, and where punishment is purgative. Accordingly, for Origen, heaven or paradise becomes a place of learning where those of sufficient merit can "quickly ascend to the region of the air, until they reach the kingdom of the heavens" (*PArch* 2.11.6) and then move beyond, through learning and understanding, back to the right relationship with God. Ultimately, God will restore all things to himself as they were before the world needed to be created (see *Apokatastasis*). Souls will once again contemplate the divine but, even so (he muses in the *First Principles*), may they not cool again and thus new worlds will perhaps be needed in the ongoing process of God's enlightenment of the creation?

Cornélis (1959); Crouzel (1990); Scott (1991); Tzamalikos (1993).

FIONA THOMPSON

Creation See *Cosmology, Anthropology, Souls.*

Demonology
Origen's cosmology posits a precreation state in which rational souls, created by God with free will, are engaged in devout *contemplation* of the "invisible image of the invisible God" (*PArch* 1.2.6). These souls fall away from this state through a cooling of their passion, and thus the world is created to supply material "bodies" for these fallen souls and provide a place for the soul's rehabilitation (see *Fall*). The first soul to cool became that of Satan (*CCels* 6.44). This soul was clothed in an astral body and was at first counted among the stars, but he fell even farther: "Even Satan was once light, before he went astray and fell to this place . . . and so he is called the 'prince of this world.'" (*PArch* 1.5.5). The antichrist is the son of Satan. Origen argues that just as Jesus is called Son of God, "the one diametrically opposed to him should be called son of the evil daemon, who is Satan and the devil" (*CCels* 6.45). Finally, some souls were placed in astral bodies and became Satan's angels, the demons. The position or body that souls held in the created world reflected the degree to which their soul had cooled from its original devotion and love. Some were angels, others humans, and some demons, but there was always the possibility of moving between bodies either upward through the appropriate exercise of free will or downward through greater sin (at least in Origen's earliest thinking, though he seems to have departed from the speculation in later years, as it roused controversy among church circles).

Satan and his demons had a significant function to play in the cosmic rehabilitative process, which Origen saw as the struggle of the souls to ascend back to the contemplation of God. Their role, ordained by God, was to test human beings and thus offer the rational souls housed within human bodies the opportunity to choose of their own volition to move back toward God or farther away. Wherever a human soul may find itself, there would be the possibility of demonic presence, particularly in the manifold forms they were rendered present by heathen cults and oracles. Indeed, they were also the causes of natural disasters by which humans were tested. For Origen, the incarnation destroys the whole conspiracy of demons (*CCels* 3.29), and through the soteriological grace it mediates, demonic power became ultimately ineffectual for those who had turned toward God.

The thought that even the souls of demons could, through the correct exercise of free will, rise once more to a higher union with God was something Origen could not leave aside, so fundamental was it to his overarching vision of a world motivated by God's pedagogical care for his creatures. Origen stood fast to his belief that God will, in due course, restore all souls to himself in a recapitulation of all (see *Apokatastasis*). The corollary to this fundamental axiom haunted him: could demons also leave aside their demonic bodies and rise to become embodied as humans or angels? The logical conclusion of this speculation was whether even Satan could be saved: "The end of the world ... will come when every soul shall be visited with the penalties due for its sins ... the goodness of God ... will restore his entire creation to one end, even his enemies being conquered and subdued" (*PArch* 1.6.1). This caused considerable controversy, even in his lifetime, and both Rufinus and Jerome made reference to a letter in which Origen distanced himself from the possibility of Satan's restoration (Jerome, *Apologia adv. libros Rufini* 2.18). If this (now lost) letter represents a subsequent retraction on Origen's part of his more consistently expressed theories of universal salvation in his early writing, nevertheless the overall thrust of his vision of God's economy of salvation, repeated even in the writings of his old age, stands as a remarkably universalist one: "For Divine Providence will never abandon the universe. And even if some part of it becomes very bad because the rational being sins, God arranges to purify it, and after a time to turn the whole world back to himself" (*CCels* 4.99).

Bettencourt (1945); Monaci Castagno (1996); Crouzel (1994).

FIONA THOMPSON

Disciples of Origen

Disciples of Origen   Origen has never failed to have a succession of disciples. Even those who kept their distance after the later ecclesiastical condemnations of his thought (such as Jerome and Cyril of Alexandria) demonstrate time after time, especially in their exegesis, that they were lifelong dedicated readers of his works. His "discipleship" includes some of the greatest minds of the Eastern church and many, perhaps less intellectual figures, who nonetheless were held in the highest honor for their qualities of discipleship, either as martyrs or leading ascetics.

Origen's First Followers

The most comprehensive listing of the first disciples of Origen is found in the *Ecclesiastical History* of Eusebius of Caesarea (*H.E.* 6). Eusebius records that Origen's first pupils were Plutarch and Heraclas, two brothers who had studied philosophy for five years with Ammonius Saccas (Eusebius, *H.E.* 6.3.1–2). They approached Origen "to hear the word of God" while he was still working as a grammatical instructor in order to support his mother and six younger siblings after his father's martyrdom. At this time, on account of the persecutions, "there was no one at Alexandria set aside for catechetical training" (Eusebius, *H.E.*

6.3.3). In succeeding years, ongoing persecution did little to quell the interest of protégés seeking out Origen as their teacher. Eusebius reports that "soldiers were placed in groups . . . round the house where [Origen] abode, because of the number of those who were receiving instruction from him in the sacred faith" (Eusebius, *H.E.* 6.3.5). He then gives us (*H.E.* 6.3.13) a list of seven who were "arrested and perfected by martyrdom." That little martyrology affords the earliest explicit record of Origen's disciples. The first of those martyrs was Origen's earliest catechumen, Plutarch. Eusebius notes that Origen was "present with him until the very end of his life" (*H.E.* 6.4.1). In the aftermath, Origen himself was almost killed by fellow citizens who held him responsible for his student's death.

Eusebius's list of his martyr-disciples includes six others: Serenus, who "through fire gave proof of the faith he had received" (*H.E.* 6.4.2–3); Heraclides and Hero, who were both beheaded, the former while still a catechumen, the latter only newly baptized; a second Serenus, who was also beheaded after enduring great torture (*H.E.* 6.4); and two women, Herais, who was still under instruction for baptism, and Potaimiaena, who is described as being "in the full bloom of youthful beauty in body as well as in mind" (*H.E.* 6.5.1).

Plutarch's brother, Heraclas, survived the persecutions and went on to become Origen's assistant in his school. When "the instruction of those who were coming to him . . . did not give him time to breathe (for one batch of pupils after another kept frequenting from morn to night his lecture room)" (Eusebius, *H.E.* 6.15), Origen gave Heraclas "a share in the task of instruction, assigning to him the preliminary studies of those who were just learning their elements, and reserving for himself the teaching of the experienced pupils." In his own right, Heraclas was noted for being "greatly distinguished in philosophy and other Greek learning" (Eusebius, *H.E.* 6.31.2). He eventually took Origen's

place in directing the Alexandrian church's "school" (see *School of Alexandria*) when Origen was removed to Caesarea. Heraclas in time also succeeded Demetrius as bishop of the Alexandrian church. However, in this position of authority, despite now long-standing ties, he did little to clear his teacher and colleague's name (see *Bishops*).

It was to be Dionysius of Alexandria, also a student of Origen, and Heraclas's successor as both catechist and bishop (Eusebius, *H.E.* 7), who took up Origen's cause. Dionysius had an illustrious career leading the church of Alexandria. Drawing Origen's Alexandrian involvement full circle, eighteen years after Origen had left Alexandria for Caesarea, he sent to Origen *An Exhortation to Martyrdom* during the Decian persecutions, in the course of which Origen had been arrested and tortured, sufferings that hastened his death (Eusebius, *H.E.* 6.46.2).

Early Patrons and Supporters

Standing just beyond Origen's immediate circle of students was a group of patron-disciples who not only benefited from Origen's great erudition but also significantly aided and abetted his work. The most prominent among these were a wealthy former Valentinian, Ambrose, and his sister (or wife), Tatiana. As disciples and benefactors, they offered Origen financial support during his final years in Alexandria, then helped him to begin again in Caesarea. Eusebius reports that Ambrose "not only plied Origen with innumerable verbal exhortations and encouragements, but also provided him unstintingly with what was necessary. For as he dictated there were ready at hand more than seven short-hand writers, who relieved each other at fixed times, and as many copyists, as well as girls skilled in penmanship; for all of whom Ambrose supplied without stint the necessary means" (Eusebius, *H.E.* 6.23.1–2). Ambrose commissioned several books from Origen and was directly responsible for pressing him first to compose, and then to complete them. In his *Commentary on John* Origen refers to Ambrose as "God's overseer" (*ComJn* 5.1). In time, Ambrose himself retired to live at Nicomedia and became a deacon in the church there. A letter of Jerome to his friend Marcella holds up the friendship between these two men as a source of inspiration. Describing the common life that Origen shared with Ambrose and his other students, Jerome writes: "They never took a meal together without something being read, and never went to bed until some portion of Scripture had been brought home to them by a brother's voice. Night and day were so ordered that prayer only gave place to reading and reading to prayer" (Jerome, *Ep. to Marcella* 43).

Two Palestinian hierarchs were also significant to Origen's career as a teacher. The first was Bishop Alexander, who presided over the church of Jerusalem and is credited with equipping a library at Jerusalem that Eusebius later used in his historical work (Eusebius, *H.E.* 6.20.1). The second was Bishop Theoctistus, who presided over the church at Caesarea. In a doubtlessly idealized picture Eusebius tells us that these two colleague-disciples "continued their attendance on Origen the whole time, as their only teacher, and used to concede to him the task of expounding the divine Scriptures, and the other parts of the Church's instruction" (Eusebius, *H.E.* 6.27.1). It was Theoctistus who welcomed Origen to Caesarea and afforded him complete freedom to teach (Photius, *Bibliotheca* 118). Despite the storms of protest raised against Origen by his Alexandrian opponents, there is no hint that either of these bishops did anything other than stand by Origen, advancing him as a leading theological *peritus* of the Palestinian church, as can be seen from the synods he attended as official *scrutinor*.

Students in Caesarea

It is from Origen's Caesarean period that the most intimate portrayal of his relationship with his students and disciples is presented, in a *Panegyric* written by his student Theodore, known in later history by his Christian name, Gregory Thaumaturgus. Gregory was one of two brothers who sought out Origen's instruction. The pair, while passing through the city, en route to study law in Beirut, chanced to hear a lecture of Origen. Abandoning their previous itinerary, they remained in Caesarea for five years as Origen's pupils. In his *Panegyric* (or *Address of Thanks*), offered to Origen at the end of his studies, Theodore describes Origen as, for "those who are able to contemplate the greatness of his intellectual caliber, endowed with powers well-nigh divine" (*Panegyric* 2). Gregory counted his somewhat serendipitous encounter with Origen as the work of a guardian *angel* "who in addition to all . . . other benefits, had brought me into connection with this man" (*Panegyric* 4). In Gregory's estimation Origen was "possessed of a rare combination of a certain sweet grace and persuasiveness, along with a strange power of constraint" (*Panegyric* 6). His impact was "like some spark lighting upon our inmost soul" (*Panegyric* 6), kindling love and bursting into flame within us. Having been mightily smitten, Gregory "was persuaded to give up all those objects or purposes which had seemed appropriate" and to pursue "but one object dear and worthy of desire, namely philosophy, and that master of philosophy, this inspired man" (*Panegyric* 6). Gregory reports that the pursuit of philosophy under Origen's tutelage was founded on the premise that "those only live a life truly worthy of reasonable creatures who aim at living an upright life, and who seek to know first of all themselves, what manner of persons they are, and then the things that are truly good, which man ought to strive for, and then the things that are evil, from which man ought to flee" (*Panegyric* 6). Studies began with Socratic-style exercises in logic and dialectic (*Panegyric* 7), moving from there to natural philosophy, geometry, and astronomy (*Panegyric* 8). So configured, an understanding of the natural world served as the point of entry into contemplation of God's greater design and providence. Similarly, ethical training not only treated the philosophical consideration of virtue but was aimed at inciting its practice as modeled by Origen's own lived example (*Panegyric* 8–9). At the apex of this training stood the study of theology, read in the context of all discourse about divinity. This reading list was not exclusively Christian. Naming theology as the summit of philosophic wisdom, Origen's "syllabus" dictated a wide curricular reading in a variety of philosophical traditions (*Panegyric* 14). Gregory reports that "he deemed it right for us to study philosophy in such wise, that we should read with utmost diligence all that has been written, both by the philosophers and by the poets of old, rejecting nothing, and repudiating nothing, except the productions of the atheists, who deny that there is either a God or providence" (*Panegyric* 13). As a skilled expert, Origen then helped his students to select what was useful and true and to put aside what was false (*Panegyric* 14).

In a later letter that Origen himself addressed to Gregory, he encourages his student to exercise this intellectual freedom with discretion. Using allegory to elucidate his premise, Origen suggests that even as the Jews took the vessels of gold and silver from the Egyptians for the decoration of the Holy of Holies, so Christians should take over the treasures of the mind from the Greeks and use them in the service of the true God (*Epist-Greg* 2). Origen, however, warns that this process can be dangerous, "having learned by experience that such a one is rare who takes the useful things of Egypt, and comes out of it and fashions the things for the worship of God," for there are many "who from some Greek liaison beget heretical notions" (*Epist-Greg* 3). After remaining with Origen five years (233–38), Gregory and his brother were recalled to Berytus by their

parents (Eusebius, *H.E.* 4.27). In time, both became leaders in the church there. Gregory was consecrated as the first bishop of his native city and later venerated by the Cappadocians as the father of the church of Cappadocia. After his death, his legendary healing power procured for him the title Thaumaturgus (Wonder-worker). Socrates, the historian, reports that even while still a layperson "he performed many miracles, healing the sick, and casting out devils even by his letters, insomuch that the pagans were no less attracted to the faith by his acts, than by his discourses" (Socrates, *H.E.* 4.27).

Other Patrons and Colleagues

Two lesser-known Caesarean patrons of Origen's were Firmilian, bishop of Cappadocian Caesarea, and the virgin, Juliana. Firmilian, a contemporary of Gregory the Thaumaturg, shared his high regard for Origen. Although details of Origen's interactions with Firmilian are sparse, Eusebius reports that Firmilian displayed such esteem for Origen "that at one time he would summon him to his own parts for the benefit of the churches; at another, journey himself to Judaea, and spend some time with him for his own betterment in divine things" (Eusebius, *H.E.* 6.27.1). Equally sparse is the record concerning Juliana, a virgin of Caesarea (which city one wonders) who gave Origen shelter "when he fled from the insurrection of the pagans . . . [keeping] him at her own expense for two years" (Palladius, *Historia Lausiaca* 64).

Later Disciples of Origen

Admiration for Origen did not cease with his death. In relation to his leading "disciples" after his death, mention must be made first of Pamphilus of Berytus, who studied theology in the catechetical school in Alexandria under Pierius (a lector there who had been nicknamed "The Little Origen" on account of having "taught the people with great success and attained such elegance of language and published so many treatises on all sorts of subjects"; Jerome, *De viris illustribus* 76). Returning to his own country, Pamphilus settled in Palestinian Caesarea. Here he was ordained priest and taught in the *School of Caesarea*. Investing his energy in enlarging the library that Origen had founded, he brought together the works of Origen and other ecclesiastical writers, so that "from this collection anyone who pleased could gather the fullest knowledge of the works of Origen that have reached us" (Eusebius, *H.E.* 6.32.3). Many of Origen's writings would have been lost without the care Pamphilus took in listing and collecting them, and it is to this library and to this teacher that Eusebius owes his large knowledge of earlier Christian literature and his own love for Origen as a theologian. Here Pamphilus trained Eusebius in transcribing, cataloguing, and editing texts, introducing him to issues of literary criticism and historiography. In 307, during the persecution of Maximin Daia, Pamphilus was tortured and thrown into prison. He was executed in 309 or 310. During his relatively lengthy imprisonment, he began a defense of Origen in five books (only one of which now survives, in Rufinus's version). It was left to Eusebius to complete the work after his death. Both sought to refute the accusations made against their hero, defending his views with passages quoted from his own works.

Both Jerome and the Cappadocian father Gregory Nazianzen came under the influence of Alexandrian theology in the library at Caesarea. While Jerome later rejected Origen's most "offensive" doctrines, he and Rufinus, by the translations they made, spread Origen's name and fame in the West. In his panegyric (*On Illustrious Men* 54) Jerome declared Origen to be "an immortal genius." In the preface to his *Book of Hebrew Names,* he acclaimed him as "the man whom no one but an ignoramus could fail to admit to have been the greatest teacher of the church since the

Apostles." And in a letter of 384, Jerome suggested that Origen's expulsion from Alexandria at the hand of Demetrius had not transpired on account of the "novelty or heterodoxy of his doctrines, but because men could not tolerate the incomparable eloquence and knowledge which, when once he opened his lips, made others seem dumb" (Jerome, *Epist.* 33). Jerome's contemporary Rufinus must be included in even an abbreviated list of the generations of disciples of Origen. In addition to being a major translator (and preservationist) of Origen's work, unlike Jerome he remained a dedicated Origenian all his life. His monastery, with Melania on the Mount of Olives, was known as a center of Origenian studies. It was there that Evagrius of Pontus, a disciple of both Gregory of Nazianzus and Gregory of Nyssa, who had inducted him into Origen studies, fled after his disgrace in the capital at Constantinople. Melania assisted Evagrius's transferal to desert life, and through Evagrius, Origen's thought world entered the bloodstream of Christian *asceticism.* Evagrius and the "Tall Brothers" were among the most ardent early "Origenists," but many other monastics absorbed principles of ascetical and spiritual theory from Origen and were indebted to his conception of theology as the soul's search for mystical union with the Logos. Also worthy of note as a disciple of Origen was John Cassian, who stood as a conduit for the transmission of Origenian ideas to monasticism in the West. He muted aspects of Evagrian Origenism for the consumption of the Latins (just as Gregory of Nazianzus muted and sanitized Origen for the East). In the Byzantine era Origen proved deeply informative for the two greatest of Byzantine spiritual theologians, Dionysius the Areopagite and Maximus the Confessor. Maximus particularly took his point of departure from Gregory Nazianzen's example of rendering many of the insights of the great Alexandrian teacher so that they could be happily synthesized with later standards of orthodoxy. Origen's buoyant following, despite the controversy it roused (see *Origenist Crises*) was sufficient in the sixth century to cause anxiety at the highest levels of the church, drawing down censures from the emperor, Justinian, and from the Second Council of Constantinople in 553. Even after his posthumous condemnation, Origen's works continued to live on, especially in the patristic exegetical tradition and in ascetical writings on prayer, though it was often an influence either not named or not suspected.

One of the early revivals of Origen studies came in the Renaissance, for he was taken to heart by many humanists as an example of a learned Christian willing to dialogue with secular philosophy and culture. Many of the Reformers looked on him aghast for his theology of *grace*, but for other aspects of his thinking (such as his Eucharistic remarks or his profound biblicism) he seemed a hero to some Reformers, sending the Catholic Counter-Reformation theologians running back to his texts to garner counterarguments to claim him to their side once more, as an example of early Catholicism. As Erasmus famously said, "A single page of Origen teaches more Christian philosophy than ten of Augustine."

Clark (1991); Crouzel (1989); Godin (1982); Kannengiesser and Petersen (1988).

LILLIAN LARSEN

Divinization
Divinization or deification (the terms are synonymous) are the usual translations of the Greek nouns *theopoiesis* and *theosis*: "making divine." Whereas these nouns do not occur in Origen's extant corpus, there are several references in his writings to the verb *theopoieo* ("to make into god") along with other similar expressions (becoming gods, making divine). Explicit terminological precedent in Scripture for the Christian concept of divinization (as distinct from the Hellenistic concept) Origen finds in John 10:34 (citing LXX Ps. 81:6) (*HomEx* 6.5). He does not make much (etymologically) of the occurrence of the idea in 2 Peter 1:4, although the ideas represented there are the substrate of all his *Anthropology* and *Cosmology*.

Divinization is a powerful, all-encompassing image in Origen's theology: it refers to God the Father's bestowal of divinity on the Son and Spirit, as well as on the cosmos; that is, it describes God's gracious relationship to everything in the cosmos. For this same reason it is also a plastic image in Origen's theology, since it describes different realities, becoming or being divine in diverse ways, after God the Father, who alone is properly called "God" (and is therefore not divinized). This includes the divinization of his Son and the *Holy Spirit*, and then the ranks of all the rational creatures. The potential for divinization thus embraces the celestial beings (*PArch* 1.7.5; 4.4.9; *ComJn* 1.288), the angels (*PArch* 1.6.2), human souls (see below), including the soul of Jesus (*PArch* 2.6.6; 4.4.4), and possibly demons (*PArch* 1.6.1; 3.6.5–6; *CCels* 8.72). Scripture is also seen as something to be "divinized" (*PArch* 4.1.1; 4.2.9) and perhaps, he speculates, even "bodies" (*PArch* 2.3.2; 2.10.1–3) for he imagines that resurrected spiritual bodies might even take on the divine attributes of immortality and incorruptibility (see *Resurrection*). In light of the ambiguity of Origen's use of "divinization" and of other terms commonly used to explain it (such as "participation"), a critical problem for the interpreter is to decipher how these different realities are variously understood to be and become "divine," that is, how loosely or concretely Origen understands his image to apply.

Origen famously comments (*ComJn* 2.12–33) on the second and third clauses of John 1:1: "And the Word was with God (*ho theos*), and the Word was God (*theos*)." Noticing a discrepancy in the use of the Greek article, Origen distinguishes between "The God" (*ho theos*), God the Father, and God (*theos*), or God's Son, the

Wisdom and Word of God. God (with the article) is the "uncreated cause of the universe" (*ComJn* 2.14), and as such, the "only true God" (*ComJn* 2.17). The Uncreated Cause is his supreme vision of deity and from this it follows that "everything besides the Very God (*ho theos*), because it is divinized by participation in his divinity, should more properly be called *theos*, not *ho theos*" (*ComJn* 2.17). God the Father does not participate in divinity, but rather is participated in as the source; he alone is the ultimate source of Wisdom, Truth, Life, Sanctification, Immortality, and all other divine characteristics (*ComJn* 2.20; 19.6; *CCels* 6.64). The Word, on the other hand, is the "second God" (*deuteros theos*) (*CCels* 5.39) and always remains so, due to the unique character of his essential participation in God. The profound and inscrutable union of the Logos with the divine Father is sustained by the Son's perennial contemplation of God (which is why **contemplation** is the ultimate salvation of the cosmos too). As Origen says, "The Son continues in the unceasing contemplation of the depth of the Father" (*ComJn* 2.18). Furthermore, by this Word's ministry the subordinate ranks of rational creatures "became gods, for he drew from God that they in turn might be deified" (*ComJn* 2.17). This seems to include even the **Holy Spirit** who, Origen postulates, "seems to have need of the Son ministering to his hypostasis, not only for him to exist, but also for him to be Wise, and Rational, and Just, and whatever other thing we ought to understand him to be by participation in the various aspects of Christ" (*ComJn* 2.76) (see **Trinitarianism**).

Divinization is also one of several images in Origen's writings that describes the salvation of the world and its inhabitants (though here he has a diverse soteriological vocabulary, including the foundational ideas of restoration, transformation, and harmonization). All these images emphasize different aspects of God's one work of salvation and the accent with diviniza-

tion lies in its bold expression of the overall aim (*telos*) of salvation, to restore rational souls to divine communion. For Origen, the human soul "becomes divine" through its gradual acquisition of (participation in) divine attributes, preeminently sanctification, wisdom, and knowledge. The term *divinization* thus predominantly means for Origen (and the later Christian tradition following him) the restoration of deepening fellowship with God, the Word, and the Spirit. This was why it was a term of such importance and centrality for the ascetical tradition that followed Origen. However, by stressing the aim of salvation, this particular image frequently becomes his inclusive term, since any other image (or account of salvation) usually describes a specific stage in the journey toward "becoming divine." Accordingly, when Origen explicates the divinization of the human soul, the specifics of his soteriology (with its recurring twofold emphasis on the meritorious life of the believer and the gracious mediations of the Word and the Holy Spirit) immediately surface.

Many features of the above synopsis can be seen in the following passage: "Christians see that with Jesus human and divine nature began to be woven together, so that by fellowship with divinity, human nature might become divine; not only in Jesus, but also in all those who believe and go on to undertake the life which Jesus taught, that life which leads everyone who lives according to Jesus' commandments to friendship with God and fellowship with Jesus" (*CCels* 3.28; see also *SerMt* 33). Here Origen focuses on the divinizing incarnation of the Word, though he elsewhere stresses the Word's (as well as God's and the Holy Spirit's) illumining and purifying works, which divinize rational creatures both before and after the incarnation (*PArch* Praef. 3; 1.3.4; 1.3.8; 2.3.1; *CCels* 6.13; 7.44; *ComJn* 2.129; 32.338). Furthermore, in practice Origen consistently distinguishes neither between the gifts given by the Spirit and those given by the Word, nor the order in which these gifts are given (see the somewhat obscure discussion in *PArch* 1.3.5–8). Both the Spirit and Word have received the divine gifts from the Father, and all in turn furnish these abundantly to those who prove themselves worthy and in need of these gifts (*ComJn* 2.77; *PArch* 4.4.5).

Lives worthy of divinization are characterized by faith in, and discipleship of, Jesus (see *PArch* 4.4.4–5), which involves prayer (*PEuch* 27.13), love (*HomJr* 5.2.5), in fact all the virtues (*PArch* 4.4.10), as well as purity of life (*PArch* 3.3.3; *CCels* 7.33), a sustained intellectual longing for God (*PArch* 2.11.4–7; *ComJn* 19.12f.), and a searching out of the spiritual meaning of the Scriptures (*PArch* 4.2.7). For Origen, divinization is a gradual process (*PArch* 1.3.8; 3.6.6; 4.4.9; *EpistGreg* 4; *PEuch* 25.2), the ongoing purification and instruction of the soul that culminates in the eschatological bestowal of the divine characteristic of immortality. Then the soul will be unceasingly "with" this God who will then be "all in all" (1 Cor. 15:28) and the soul, in the image of God, will at last be fully divinized, perfected in the likeness of God:

> For He will be all things in each person, in such a way that everything which the rational mind, when purified from all the dregs of its vices and utterly cleared from every cloud of wickedness, can feel or understand or think will be all God and that the mind will no longer be conscious of anything besides or other than God, but will think God and see God and hold God, and God will be the mode and measure of its every movement; and in this way God will be all to it. (*PArch* 3.6.3)

This divinization is "that condition restored which rational nature once enjoyed," before the fall (*PArch* 3.6.3). In this blessed condition Origen envisages the souls as rejoining their archetype, the Word, so as to be ceaselessly engaged in the contemplation of God (*ComJn* 1.92), the activity that once they fell from, and to which God's mercy has now recalled them in their ultimate homecoming.

Balas (1975); Lot-Borodine (1970); Rius-Camps (1970).

PETER MARTENS

Epinoiai

Epinoiai Christou is a Greek phrase that is translated either "aspects of Christ" or "concepts of Christ" and refers, in Origen's thought, to the many things that Christ becomes within his ministry to the created order (see **Christology, Holy Spirit**). The concept conveyed by the phrase is a significant feature of Origen's doctrine of Christ and of his teaching on the formation of Christ in the individual Christian. The phrase is not peculiar to Origen, but it plays a much more prominent role in his works than in any other Christian writings. While the doctrine appears in many of Origen's works, the most sustained discussion of the subject is found in the first book of his *Commentary on John* and in the second chapter of the first book of *On First Principles*.

The *epinoiai* doctrine is built from the many different titles applied to Christ in the Old and New Testaments (*ComJn* 1.125–36). Its foundation, however, rests on Origen's understanding of the function of Christ as the mediator between God and creation, within an overarching Alexandrian scheme of the distinction between the One, and the Many. This demands that while God remains one and simple, the divine mediator needs to become many things because of the manifold needs of multivaried creation (*ComJn* 1.119). The multiplicity of the *epinoiai*, however, does not affect the divine essence of Christ (*ComJn* 1.200; *ComRm* 5.6; *CCels* 2.64) as the eternally begotten Son of God the Father (*ComJn* 1.204; 32.324–26; *PArch* 1.2.2, 6, 8). The necessity for multiplicity in Christ in the context of divine unity constitutes the philosophical foundation of the concept.

Origen perceives an order among some of the *epinoiai*, at least, but it is only at the highest level that this order is rigid. Wisdom always stands as the first of the *epinoiai* (*ComJn* 1.118). Origen bases his understanding of Christ as Wisdom on Proverbs 8:22f. Wisdom has existed eternally with God, being eternally begotten by him and sharing his incorporeal substance (*PArch* 1.2.2). As such, Wisdom is both the repository, so to speak, of the blueprint of the entire creation, and its cause (*PArch* 1.2.2–3; *ComJn* 1.111, 113–15, 244).

The Divine Word, or Logos, stands next to Wisdom at the top of the list of *epinoiai*. The two are basically equivalent in Origen's mind. Wisdom opens the mysteries of God to the creation, and the Logos interprets them. Both have been eternally with God, for God has always begotten the Logos and has always possessed Wisdom (*PArch* 1.2.3). Origen's understanding of Wisdom and Logos here is very similar to the earlier Greek apologists who, following the Stoics, had distinguished between the "internal" (*endiathetos*) Logos, which was eternally a part of God, and the "external" expression of this Logos (*prophorikos*), which carried out God's work (cf. Theophilus, *Ad Autolycum* 2.22). Life and Truth come after Wisdom and Logos at the top of the scale of Origen's *epinoiai* (*PArch* 1.2.4). Origen asserts that Christ would have possessed these four *epinoiai* irrespective of the needs of creation, even though they all, in addition, serve creation's needs (*ComJn* 1.123, 248, 251; 2.125–26; 32.387).

There is no essential order to the remaining *epinoiai* after Wisdom, Logos, Life, and Truth. All of the other *epinoiai* are what Christ becomes solely for the sake of the creation. Origen understands an ascending order among these *epinoiai*, like the steps leading up into the temple. On this model, one begins with the humanity of Jesus and sets out on him as the "way." One then proceeds through him as the "door," after which one experiences him as "shepherd," then as "king," and finally one hears Jesus' words in John 8:19: "If you know me,

you would know my Father also" (*ComJn* 19.38–39). The upward movement toward the divine expressed in this model is typical of Origen's understanding of the function of the *epinoiai* in the life of the Christian, but the individual *epinoiai* that constitute the specific stages vary greatly in different contexts.

The doctrine of the *epinoiai* allows Christ to be accommodated to the specific needs and spiritual capacities of the different persons calling on him (*CCels* 2.64). Origen notes that Paul refers to Christ as a "stone of stumbling" and argues that Christ must be a "stone of stumbling" to those rushing down the broad road of destruction, so that he may block their way, even as he did to Paul himself on the road to Damascus (*ComRm* 7.19). Origen applies the terms "rod" and "flower" (from the LXX version of Isaiah 11:1) to Christ and says that Christ visits iniquities as a punishing rod in order that the flower of mercy may follow. He adds, however, that not everyone must experience Christ as rod in order to enjoy the flower (*ComJn* 1.263–64). Origen sometimes compares Christ to the manna that, according to some Jewish traditions, took on the taste that the individual eating it most earnestly desired (*HomEx* 7.8; *SerMt* 100).

While not all the *epinoiai* can be classified as virtues, Origen does appear to have considered all the virtues to be *epinoiai*. And since all the *epinoiai* are identified with Christ, Christ is considered to "be" all the virtues (*ComJn* 32.127). To "put on Christ," therefore, is to put on the virtues (*ComRm* 9.34; cf. 9.2; *ComEp* 3:12, on Eph. 2:14a). To "learn Christ" is the same as "learning virtue" (*ComEp* on Eph. 4:20–22). To honor the virtues is the same as honoring Christ (*ComRm* 2.5). To "be strong in the Lord" is to be strong in "all the *epinoiai* of Christ". (*ComEp* on Eph. 6:10). The formation of Christ in an individual, therefore, is effected by the individual's growth in the virtues. The disciple cannot have Christ, who is righteousness, dwelling within the soul while he or she continues to live in unrighteousness. Faith, consequently, cannot be "reckoned as righteousness" to those who continue in the unrighteous deeds of the old life (*ComRm* 4.7).

We might draw a comparison between Origen's doctrine of the *epinoiai* of Christ and a person standing in light passing through a prism. Christ would be analogous to the prism through which the light of God is refracted and the person standing in the light would be the individual Christian. While the prism is more than the different hues of light, nevertheless one cannot see it without seeing the hues. Likewise, the person standing in its presence is necessarily bathed in its colors. All in all, the Origenian doctrine of *epinoiai* is a fascinating and rich aspect of Origen's overarching sense of the divine pedagogy of salvation (see **Anthropology**) that the Logos effects within the cosmos.

Crouzel (1989), 189–92; Daniélou (1955), 251–62; McGuckin (1986); Orbe (1955).
RONALD E. HEINE

Eschatology   As in most areas of his theology, Origen's thought about the "last things" represents a remarkable synthesis between an imaginative, scholarly exegesis of the Christian Scriptures and a set of convictions about God and the human person shaped by the church's rule of faith, interpreted with the help of Middle Platonic philosophy. Explicitly committed to traditional Christian hope for the end of the present world, for everlasting life and the resurrection of the body, and for divine judgment and recompense for both human sin and human virtue (*PArch* Praef. 5–7), Origen remains concerned to oppose both the thoroughgoing "realized eschatology" of the Valentinians—the assumption that resurrection and eternal life essentially refer to present gnostic enlightenment—and the more materialistic expectations of many Christians who take the biblical promises literally.

In commenting on Matthew 24:3–44, for instance (*SerMt* 32–60), Origen connects Jesus' dire portrait of the end time with the fears and sufferings of his contemporaries: persecution, the "false prophets" of Christian sects, the sense that the world's resources were running out. Such straightforward explanations, however, he suggests, are most suited to the "little ones in Christ"; for "more advanced" hearers of the passage, he proposes also a figural or spiritual interpretation, in which Christ's second coming is taken to be his presence in the souls of perfected disciples; the "end of the world" is spiritual maturity, the "abomination of desolation" is false interpretation of Scripture, and the antichrist any spurious version of Christian faith or practice. Although God already "reigns" in those who obey him (*PEuch* 25.1) and have begun to "put on incorruption" in holy and virtuous living, this reign will reach its climax only when all are subject to Christ and Christ "delivers up the kingdom to God the Father, that God may be all in all" (*PEuch* 25.2, citing 1 Cor. 15:24, 28, 53f.).

Although the final future form of the redeemed lies beyond our imagining, Origen clearly asserts that it will include some spiritualized form of body—an "exceedingly refined and pure and splendid body" (*PArch* 3.6.4)—perfectly suited to the environment of a spiritual world in which all inequality and negative diversity will have vanished (see **Resurrection**). He is also convinced that the progress of individuals toward that final state will not be immediate but will take place "gradually and by degrees, during the lapse of infinite and immeasurable age" (*PArch* 6.9), as each one is purified from sin and united to God in friendship.

Origen's conception of the beatitude of the saved is both relational and highly cognitive: it is to come to know the inner life of God by assimilation to God the Son. "And when one will gaze on the Father and all that surrounds the Father as now the Son sees the Father, one will be an eyewitness of the Father and of what belongs to him, even as the Son is—no longer understanding his attributes, of which his image [i.e., the Son] is formed, simply from the image. And I think that this is the end" (*ComJn* 20.7; ibid. 1.16). This knowledge of God will also include a thorough understanding of "the reasons for all things that happen on earth," an understanding of God's motives for creation and of the benign working of providence in history (*PArch* 2.11.5). This intellectual character of creatures' final fulfillment is one of the main reasons Origen believes it must be prepared for gradually, in a process of enlightenment or education matched to the degree of darkness and alienation from God in each individual. So he speaks of a "school for souls," located in some part of creation removed from this present world, "which the divine scripture calls Paradise," where they will undergo purification and instruction after death, until they reach moral and intellectual perfection that will prepare them for union with God (*PArch* 2.11.6–7; 3.6.8–9).

Origen recognizes that the prospect of judgment and of the punishment of sinners in "eternal fire" is part of both biblical tradition and church teaching (*PArch* Praef. 5. 2. 10.1). In some of his biblical homilies, he argues that hardened sinners will bear the weight of their sins with them, even after the purifying punishments of this life and of death (*HomLev* 14.4), and so will justly undergo eternal suffering for the sake of universal order (*HomJr* 12.5–6; 19.15) (see *Hades*). In the more constructive context of his *First Principles*, however, Origen interprets the biblical images associated with hell ("fire," "outer darkness," "prison") as metaphors for the spiritual misery we bring on ourselves by our sins, and suggests that the purpose of all the punishments God inflicts upon intellectual creatures is to heal them by painful remedies (*PArch* 2.10.4–6; cf. *HomEz* 1.3).

So Origen raises the question, in a number of passages, whether the punishment of any sinners will actually be unending and suggests, at least as a hope compatible with the church's faith, that ultimately all intellectual creatures will be restored to their original blessed order and unity with God. Drawing on Paul's vision of the reign of God in 1 Corinthians 15:24–28, Origen insists that the end of created history will be a return to its beginning (*PArch* 1.6.2; 3.6.1.3), in which every rational being "will think God and see God and hold God, . . . and in this way God will be all to it" (*PArch* 3.6.3). Origen also seems to believe this state will ultimately be permanent, free from the possibility of future falls (*ComJn* 10.42 [26]; *Hom1R(1S)* 1.4; *DialHer* 27), although he is willing to consider a limited succession of future material worlds to allow for the fulfillment of God's saving purposes (*PArch* 2.4–5). This suggestion of a possible "restoration of all things" (*apokatastasis panton*) remained one of the most controversial theories of Origen and his theological successors (see **Apokatastasis**). Origen makes clear, however, that this hope for restoration is a suggestion rather than a doctrine, on which his informed reader must judge (*PArch* 1.6.3; cf. *ComJn* 28.8 [7]), and he denies ever teaching the future salvation of the evil spirits (*Letter to Friends in Alexandria* [PG 17:624–25]).

Cornelis (1959); Crouzel (1990); Daley (1991); Horn (1969).

BRIAN E. DALEY, S.J.

Ethics   See *Law of Nature*, *Philosophy*, *Virtue*.

Eucharist   In his writings Origen makes several historically important remarks on the celebration of the Eucharist. His approach has the character of conservatism, notably when he argues that the conventions of the church must be carefully observed (*DialHer* 4.28). He often notes the sense of awe with which the Eucharist was approached in the church of his day

(*HomLev* 13.5.52–65; *HomPs* 37 2.6.37–
51; *HomJr* 19.13.46–61; *ComEz* 7.22;
Fragm1Cor 34; *ComMt* 10.25) and the
respectful diligence with which the body
of the Lord was consumed, in case anything of the consecrated gift should be
lost (*HomEx* 13.3.68–72). He speaks also
about the Prosphora (loaves of offering)
and emphasizes that the oblation is
made to God Almighty through Jesus
Christ by reason of his communication
in divinity with the Father, thus underscoring the liturgical principle of the
eucharistic offering: "to God through
God" (*DialHer* 4.24–27). In the *Contra
Celsum* (8.33.21–27) Origen seems to
refer to both the eucharistic Anaphora
(or great prayer of thanksgiving) and the
Epiclesis (the invocation of the Spirit to
consecrate the elements) when he gives
this general description of the eucharistic rite: "We give thanks to the Creator of
the universe and eat the loaves that are
presented with thanksgiving and prayer
over the gifts, so that by the prayer they
become a certain holy body which sanc-
tifies those who partake of it with a pure
intention" (see also *Fragm1Cor* 34;
ComMt 11.14). Elsewhere (*ComRm* 10.33
and *ComCt* 1.1.13) he mentions the "holy
kiss" (or kiss of peace) that is a regular
part of the eucharistic celebration.

To partake of the Eucharist, for Origen, is also to partake of the body of
Christ, the church (*HomPs* 37 2.6.46–48).
Therefore it is unbecoming that those
who shared the table of the Lord should
ever menace each other (*SerMt* 82), thus
revealing some of the social fractures in
his third-century congregation. Origen
is aware of Christians who seem to have
abolished the practice of baptism and
Eucharist, because they feel they have
transcended all sensory perception. He
emphatically rejects their views as erroneous and pernicious (*PEuch* 5.1).
Although not everybody understands
the meaning of the ceremonies of the
Eucharist and of other church rites, Origen argues, nevertheless the rites ought
to be observed faithfully and reverently,
since they have been handed down from

Christ and the enlightened apostles
(*HomNum* 5.1.4).

Even so, Origen as a theologian does
not seem to want to dwell greatly upon
the "common" view of the Eucharist as
communion in the body and blood of
Jesus. He tends to look on this as a mystery intended for more simple souls, and
he himself wishes to penetrate to the
"nourishing word of truth" that is
the higher mystery contained within the
Eucharist (*ComJn* 32.34.310). This is the
motive behind his comments that Christians should not only drink the blood of
Christ in a sacramental way (*HomNum*
16.9.2) or dwell upon "the typical and
symbolical body" (*ComMt* 11.14) but
should rather press on to ascend to the
true Logos in the highest level of spiritual comprehensions.

Origen approaches the theological
significance of Eucharist chiefly in two
ways: an exegetical analysis of the Last
Supper narratives and a reflection on the
significance of spiritual "food." In his
exegesis of the words by which Jesus
founded the Eucharist (*SerMt* 85) he first
states that the visible bread does not refer
to the body of Christ, nor the visible
drink to his blood, but rather signifies the
word that originates from God the Word
and that feeds and drenches souls. The
bread refers to the word of justice but
may also be associated with the grain of
corn that falls into the earth to bear a rich
harvest (John 12:24), while "the blood of
the new covenant" (cf. 1 Cor. 12:25)
points to the word by which we learn of
Christ's birth and suffering. Or, as he
writes elsewhere, the bread points to the
ethical teachings of Jesus, and the wine
signifies his mystically communicated
revelations (*ComJn* 1.30.208).

According to Origen, all the disciples
have within themselves food that they
must share with others, and if they are
pure they distribute this pure food to
others. Since Jesus is entirely pure, his
flesh and blood are purely and completely food and drink, because his
every deed is holy and his every word is
true. Following after Jesus, his apostles

distribute this food once more, and after them come their disciples in turn (*HomLev* 5.5.18–46). By the wood of the cross, Christ's bread (that is his word) even gained strength, and his teachings extended to the ends of the earth (*HomJr* 10.2). Thus, as a regular part of his teaching, Origen associates the Eucharist with the apostolic tradition of the preaching of the word (*HomNum* 16.9.2). Both the Eucharist and the preaching of the word should be approached in the same humble and reverential way (*HomEx* 13.3.66–84). If the Eucharist is approached with scruplous reverence in its reception, he demands nothing less for the manner in which his congregation (whom elsewhere he has told us are not always attentive to him) should approach their "reception" of the preached word (*HomLev* 13.3).

Following his exegesis of the eucharistic words of Jesus (*SerMt* 86), Origen goes on to say that by referring to his body Christ intended to show that he himself is the Word humanity needs, as much as it needs bread. We cannot eat this bread without him. Christ is both host and nourishment: at once the bread and the one who eats it with us; the fruit of the vine and the one who drinks it with us. Origen connects the biblical texts on how the "The Word became flesh" (John 1:14) with the Johannine sections where Christ presents himself as true bread that is real food (John 6:55), which if anyone eats, shall communicate immortality (John 6:51). The heavenly bread, the Word of God, gives to whoever will eat of it a share in its own immortality (*PEuch* 27.9), and thus souls are ontologically nourished by the divine Word that "was in the beginning with God" (John 1:2), so that they may receive no less than *divinization* (*PEuch* 27.13). For Origen, therefore, no worthless person is able to eat it (*ComMt* 11.14; *HomLev* 16.5.36–46; *HomNum* 7.2.2) (which may reveal his anxieties that many of the apparently "worthless" are indeed consuming the eucharistic gifts in his church).

This is why (following Paul in 1 Corinthians) he stresses also that the Eucharist does not always lead to sanctification, but sometimes to punishment. To the simple souls Origen explains that the bread does not automatically sanctify the participant, even though it is hallowed by God's own word and by prayer (1 Tim. 4:5). It is of crucial importance, Origen argues (thus becoming a darling of the Reformation-era eucharistic disputes), that one should receive it in faith and with a pure conscience. In this case the sanctified bread, being matter, goes the way of all bread, but the word that is said over it keeps its strength (*ComMt* 11.14). Origen points out that according to John 13:21–30 Judas received the bread at the Last Supper but did not eat it. For the other apostles it served toward salvation; whereas for the traitor it worked toward his condemnation, for immediately afterward the devil entered him (*ComJn* 32.34.300–312).

Origen opposes the Eucharist, as a symbol of Christian gratitude toward God, against the sacrifices of the heathens to their gods (*CCels* 8.57.18–20; cf. 8.33.21–27). He speaks about "the loaves of blessing" (*ComMt* 10.25; 10.15; *HomJr* 19.14.56–59), in terms that show he has taken the word "blessing" (*eulogia*) as a revealed synonym for "Eucharist" (*eucharistia*). In this, his exegetical motive is to point out that after the Last Supper, when the disciples had already received the bread of blessing, had eaten the body of the word, and had drunk the cup of thanksgiving, only then was it that Jesus taught them to rise and initiate a hymn to God (*SerMt* 86).

Consistently, therefore, Origen appears to wish to make the point that the Eucharist is a prelude to the higher realities of spiritual communion with the Logos. As such the "Bread of the Word" (be it the Scripture or the apostolic preaching) commands a comparable (if not higher) place in his schema. A closer look at his overall doctrine, however, requires some caution in regard to reaching too stark a summation. The context of his eucharistic remarks is very important. His several cultic or liturgical observations show that already by the third century the common Christian sense of reverence for the Eucharist was high indeed, and from this he does not demur. Origen, as a reformatory preacher, is making a specific claim: that preaching "ought to be afforded" equal reverence to the Eucharist. This, although it is entirely in line with his overall doctrine that souls ascend by transcending bodily matters in a cosmic spiritual ascent to pure spiritual communion, is by no means the same as evidence for a common third-century Christian attitude to the eucharistic celebration; of which Origen remains a most interesting, if tantalizing, witness.

Lies (1978); De Lubac (1950), 355–73; Van Winden (1974).

F. LEDEGANG

Faith

Faith   In the writings of Origen there are two main aspects to the concept of faith: faith as the act of belief of the individual Christian and faith as the content of the Scriptures, the gospel proclamation (see *Rule of Faith*), and the teaching tradition handed down by the *apostles,* that is, the faith of the *church.*

For Origen, the initial act of faith of the individual is "the rational assent of a free spirit" (*FragmPs* 115.2) to the content of the Christian tradition, especially as it is experienced in the preaching of the church. Faith that "comes from what is heard" (Rom. 10:17) is necessary for salvation, but it represents only the first and most basic step. Beyond this begins the deepening of faith through the development of intellectual and spiritual abilities, prayer, *asceticism,* and the intensive study of *Scripture*; that is, the development of a spiritual vision that is superior to faith based upon hearing alone. Initial faith is based upon the literal interpretation of Scripture, while the advanced faith, which for Origen is "true and perfect faith," uses allegorical interpretation

as a tool in the contemplation of spiritual *mysteries.* The two types of articles of faith are set out in the preface of the *First Principles.* Here Origen distinguishes the most clear and necessary articles, set forth plainly by the apostles, from those whose theological explanation is left for "those who train themselves to become worthy and capable of receiving wisdom" (*PArch* Praef. 3).

The two stages of faith imply two types of Christian believers: those who are content to believe at the most basic and literal level, whom Origen refers to as simple believers (*simpliciores*), and those who, like Origen himself, strive to understand the deeper mysteries of God and seek to perfect themselves in Christian knowledge. Origen considers the faith of the simple believer to be sufficient for salvation, but it occupies a very subordinate position, its description often accompanied by terms such as "mere" or "irrational." Because of their intellectual deficiency and the spiritual laziness and disinterest in biblical study of some, Origen complains that the simple do not often develop knowledge or spiritual understanding. Their faith has no intellectual anchor and is easily led into apostasy. Their interpretation is entirely literal, so that they are prone to anthropomorphism. They lack an understanding of Trinitarian theology (see *Trinitarianism*) and so fall into modalism, confusing the Father and the Son. They know "nothing except Christ and him crucified, having supposed that the Word that became flesh was the totality of the Word" (*ComJn* 2.29). This seems to imply that such believers were simply uneducated, but we ought not to dismiss the possibility that the *simpliciores* sometimes refers, rhetorically, to theological opponents of Origen, people who opposed his *allegory*-based exegesis and speculations. Origen writes of "friends of the letter [who] will stir up malicious charges against me and will lie in ambush for me" (*HomGn* 13.3). There may, therefore, have been polemical reasons as well as theological ones for his negative characterization of simple believers.

The ambiguity that Origen felt toward the faith of the simple is also expressed in his *Contra Celsum*. *Celsus* attacks Christian faith as being "mere opinion" or "superstition," incapable of intellectual examination, expressed in such commonly heard phrases among the Christians as "Do not question, only believe" (*CCels* 1.9). Origen counters this dismissive charge by stating that the truth of Christian faith is shown by its rapid spread to all nations and classes. The effect of Christian teaching upon the morals of the lower classes of Christians, compared to their pagan counterparts, also provides proof. At the same time, Origen finds the simple Christians an intellectual embarrassment and seeks to distance himself from them. He criticizes Celsus for generalizing all Christian belief and thought from the words of the least educated: "[Celsus was not] able to judge that it is not right to think that the meaning of those wise men is represented by people who do not profess to have any more than mere faith in regard to Christian doctrine" (*CCels* 5.20). Origen's ambiguity is not unusual for those Christian apologists caught between, on the one hand, simple believers and, on the other, the pagan philosophical tradition to which they have attempted to prove the intellectual validity of Christian religion.

Ultimately, Origen argues, a full and perfect Christian faith involved using all of one's talents completely in order to progress in spiritual knowledge. Anything less, including remaining at a beginner's level of faith, was tantamount to burying one's talents in the ground. Origen, like Paul, refused to content himself with the "milk" of spiritual children, but strove for the "solid food" to be given to those who have embraced their destiny to return to communion with God.

Bammel (1996); Hallstrom (1984); Heither (1991); Outler (1984); Van Winden (1970).
                    ALAN G. PADDLE

Fall, The   In Origen's *cosmology,* all spiritual intelligences (*noes*), **souls** (*psychai*), or rational minds existed prior to the creation of the material, bodily world (see **Anthropology, Preexistence**). Each intelligence exercised its individual free choice to contemplate God lovingly and in unbroken unity with one another, through the mediation of the Logos. Eventually, almost all employed their freedom of choice to move away from contemplative communion with God and some fell into the material world to incur the consequences of rejecting God. Because the fall resulted from the divergent choices of each intelligence, each declined from God in a different degree. The resulting hierarchy of positions before God after the fall established diversity or variety among the intelligences (see **Demonology**), which reflected God's judgment and punishment of each according to its own degree of rejecting God (*PArch* 1–3).

The main premise underlying Origen's explanation of the fall is that spiritual intelligences, by their nature, functioned before, during, and after the fall predominantly by free choice. Souls move themselves, rather than being moved by reflex or the force of another (*PArch* 3.1), and accordingly are recognized as rational beings. The life of the soul is one of perpetual motion, which means the soul either chooses to ascend toward God or rejects God and declines farther from the divine communion (*PArch* 2.9; 2.11.1). Origen's overarching stress on the free choice of intelligences stems from his insistence, against the opposing contexts of Hellenistic determinism (particularly astrology) and gnostic and Marcionite views, that God is absolutely good and does not cause evil (*CCels* 6.55). Rather, evil results from the free choices of rational creatures (*PArch* 1.4; 1.5; and 3.1), particularly, the choice to separate from God.

Before falling, each intelligence had chosen to contemplate and acknowledge God. Origen seems to posit that intelligences initially were innocent, although they maintained an immature knowledge of God, and thus their love for God was not fixed but led to their decline (their "cooling off"). Origen describes the souls as becoming "satiated" with God (*PArch* 1.3.8; 1.4.1) or "weary" from their divine contemplation (*PArch* 2.8.3). In this instance the translator's Latin word for satiety probably derives from the original Greek word for "boredom" (*koros*), suggesting that Origen's point was that the spiritual intelligences became disinterested in the singularity of their initial activity. This was why they moved from the warmth of the divine love and from being pure Nous became "souls" (*psychai*), or cooled-off intelligences. In fact, Origen speculates, in typical Alexandrian etymological style, that the word for soul (*psyche*) originated from some ancient understanding that primary intelligences (*noes*) "cooled off" or "froze" (*psychesthai, psychizomai*) (*PArch* 2.8.3).

Origen sees the fall as a long progressive decline. Intelligences continuously fell away from God, and as they neglected divine realities, they became "careless" or "indifferent" to the original object of their attention, and thus the meaning and goal of their existence (*PArch* 1.6.2). Origen compares the fallen soul to a doctor who loses interest in and neglects his work, causing his technical knowledge and skills gradually and progressively to fade from his memory (*PArch* 1.4.1). They acted against their own rationality by succumbing to multiple passions instead of loving the natural object of their attention, which was God (*PArch* 1.8). Decline can be reversed, however, and it is this constant call to ascent and restoration of communion with God that drives all of Origen's vision of the salvific pedagogy of the Logos in the created world.

Although intelligences initially contemplated God in a unity free of ranks, the "weight" of rejecting God pushed each intelligence downward away from God (*HomEx* 6.4) at a distance that corresponded to its individual degree of cooling (*HomJr* 12.2–6; 28.1). As a result, the once equal souls were distinguished in a diversity of ranks and orders before God (*PArch* 3.6.4). According to God's individually apportioned judgment and punishment (*PArch* 1.4; 1.5; 2.1; 2.9), intelligences fell into a hierarchy of angels, astronomical bodies, humans, and demons (*PArch* 1.8). Those who mildly rejected God fell the shortest distance and became angels. Those who fell a little farther became benign and rational astronomical entities such as the sun, moon, and stars. Those who fell still farther took on human bodies, some incurring more burdensome bodies than others so as to reflect the varying distances by which they fell into the material realm (*PArch* 2.9.3). Those who fell the farthest became demons (*PArch* 1.5.2), the most egregious being the devil himself. Origen stresses that Satan was the first intelligence to fall from God (*CCels* 6.44 and *PArch* 1.5.4, citing Ezek. 28 and Isa. 14), providing a bad example to the others (see *Demonology*).

While in some passages Origen arguably expresses uncertainty about whether the fall was universal (*PArch* 1.5.5; 1.6.2; 1.8.4; 2.9.6; and 4.2.7), most scholars understand Origen to include all intelligences as involved in its implications, except for the soul of Jesus, which would later serve the eternal Word of God as the vehicle of incarnation (see *Christology, Souls*) (*PArch* 2.6.3; 4.4.8).

———————

Crouzel (1989), 205–18; Greer (1979); Harl (1966); Simonetti (1962).

ELIZABETH A. DIVELY LAURO

Freedom   See *Grace.*

Glory   Origen consistently associated the Sinai revelation and Moses' radiant descent with themes from 2 Corinthians 3 and the Gospel stories of the transfiguration of Jesus (*ComJn* 32.17; *ComRm* 2:5). For example, in *Homilies on Exodus* 12.3, he cites 2 Corinthians 3:7–8 noting that while "only Moses' face was glorified" after the revelation of the law, "in the

Gospels the whole Moses is glorified anew." By this he means first of all that the true meaning and beauty of the law and the prophets only come to light in the encounter with the Son of God (*PArch* 4.1.7–8) (see **Old Testament**). Even so, in view of the church's battle with Marcion and certain Valentinian gnostics who sharply distinguished the God of the Old Testament from the Father of Jesus, the theology of being transformed (as Paul says) from "glory to glory" also implies that there is one single God who inspired both covenants. Origen wishes to use the concept of "glory" to stress the ideas of the harmony and continuity that remain between law and gospel (even if the glory of the law is eclipsed by the glory of the Gospel). The key to harmonizing Moses and Elijah with Jesus is found in spiritual or allegorical exegesis, since "the letter kills, but the Spirit gives life" (2 Cor. 3:6; *ComRm* 2.5) (see **Allegorical Interpretation**).

For Origen, the capacity for the vision of Christ's glory and the accompanying understanding of the "hidden splendor" of Holy Scripture are reserved for the spiritually mature who have transcended material things. He typically uses the image of the three disciples who are called away from the valleys and plains to see the glory of the transfiguration on the mountaintop (*CCels* 2.64–65; 4.16; 6.68; *HomGn* 1.7; *ComMt* 12.36–43). Such a notion is in keeping with Origen's ubiquitous teaching that Christ appears in many aspects (see **Christology, Epinoiai**) to human beings on account of their varied capacities to receive him. Even when he reveals himself, God remains utterly transcendent for Origen, and all experience of divine glory in the fallen cosmos is partial and according to gradation insofar as only "things hoped for" are eternal, while "what can be seen is temporary" (2 Cor. 4:18), and even "the glory as of a father's only son" (which John 1:14 had proclaimed as "seen") is temporary and destined to pass away; destined to be transcended by the Father's eternal glory, just as

Moses' glory faded before the presence of Christ. For Origen, the Son of God is himself the "reflection of God's glory" (Heb. 1:3); that is, the radiance of the light, not the full glory in itself (*ComRm* 4.8; *PArch* 1.2).

Overall there are four distinctions Origen wishes to make in his theology of glory. First, he notes that there is the incomprehensible glory of God-in-himself; second, the glory of God authentically imaged in the Logos; third, the glory conveyed in all majesty by the Logos to the spiritual hierarchy in communion with him (the angelic orders and restored humanity in the mystery of the resurrection); and last, the glory of God as dramatically curtailed for the sake of humankind in the earthly economy. This hierarchically graded revelation of glory is partly rooted in what Origen describes as "continuous meditation" on the *merkava* (heavenly chariot) described in Ezekiel 1:26–28, a mystical theme Origen seems to have had in common with the rabbis of his day (*ComRm* 4.8.10). Human beings, even prophets, can experience only the "appearance of the likeness of the glory of the Lord" in this age. Late in life, when Origen commented on Ezekiel 1 in response to Marcionites who claimed that the "blazing" God was an evil and destructive demiurge, he took care to note that even when God is "fiery" toward us in loving acts of discipline, such "splendor of glory" is always purgative and never simply punitive. God burns up our sinful works "so that we too may be glorified" (*HomEz* 1).

Origen's theology of glory has had a long afterlife. It still provides an entry point to understanding significantly different emphases between Eastern and Western Christian thought. Western atonement theory tended to focus on the propitiatory nature of Christ's death, while Greek theology, following many of Origen's leads, focused more on God's plan to share the divine glory with humanity, by way of Christ's incarnation, transfiguration, and paschal mystery. Where Romans 3–4, with its emphasis on "justification by faith and not works of law" has often served as a primary hermeneutic guide for biblical interpretation in the later Western church, Origen led Eastern Christian theologians to give priority to 2 Corinthians 3–4 as a hermeneutical key, a foundational text with its emphasis on being "transformed . . . from one degree of glory to another" (2 Cor. 3:18). Under Origen's influence this almost became, for the East, a paraphrastic canon within the canon.

McGuckin (1987, 1989); Munoz Léon (1977).

J. WOODROW McCREE

Gnostics   The relation of Origen and his theology to the "gnostics" is probably one of the most disputed topics in the history of modern research on the Alexandrian theologian. While there is no question that an apologetic against Gnosticism is one of Origen's main interests in his tractates, as well as in some of his homilies, there is still considerable scholarly debate over the extent to which Origen was deeply influenced by a "Gnostic structure of thinking" (Hans Jonas) or whether he developed an alternative model of "Christian" or "Ecclesiastical Gnosticism" (Harnack) or of "Biblical Gnosticism" (Lietzmann). In the opinion of Jonas, who restricted his analysis to *PArch*, Origen was, in the manner of a Plotinus or Mani, the founder of an outstanding gnostic system. For others, such as Crouzel, while Origen often argued against gnostics, and used common terms, his own views were in no way deeply influenced by such groups. Recent scholarly research has made it clear enough that such variant positions are determined by specifically different conceptions of what constitutes the phenomenon "Gnosticism." To avoid these problems it is better first to describe Origen's use of the common Greek term *gnosis* ("knowledge") and then to trace

his struggle against some theologians and groups of Christians whom the church fathers traditionally called "gnostics." After this, we can conclude by returning to the question whether Origen adopted elements of gnostic thought from his opponents, either unconsciously or deliberately.

The term *gnosis* was used in antiquity to describe one of the main ideals of a good life. To reach "knowledge" was, in the reason-focused culture of the Greeks, a fundamental presupposition for right and adequate action. Many ancient religious and philosophical movements of antiquity were concerned, apart from presenting the foundations of knowledge, with instructing their followers on the strategies necessary to arrive at it. Philosophy "promised knowledge of existing things" (Alexander of Aphrodisias, *Commentaria in Aristotelis Metaphysica* 1). Religion also offered "cognition and knowledge of being" (Plutarch, *De Iside et Osiride* 2.352 A). For the Old Testament Wisdom tradition, "The LORD gives wisdom, and from his mouth come knowledge and understanding" (Prov. 2:6). Origen lived and thought in this culture obsessed with reason (*logos*) and knowledge (*gnosis*). His use of the Greek term *gnosis* is a sign of these connections, and it is significant that the word appears more than a thousand times in his corpus. In Origen's understanding, from Christ comes "knowledge (*gnosis*) connected with wisdom" (*CCels* 3.33). His wisdom is, as described by Paul, a paradoxical one: "foolishness to Gentiles" (1 Cor. 1:23), but this is so precisely because it is a transcendent wisdom, which earthly minds cannot grasp (*HomJr* 8.5; cf. *Fragm1Co* 47). In his *Homilies on 1 Corinthians* (now preserved only in fragments) Origen closely connects "knowledge" with the church's doctrine (*Fragm1Co* 2). Wisdom is thus a divine gift (*Fragm1Co* 19; 22); prophecy is "knowledge of invisible things" (*Fragm1Co* 53).

Origen was evidently well informed on the precise teachings of some, but certainly not all, gnostic teachers. In

HomJd 1.1, Origen discusses Marcion's separation between a good and a just god (see *PArch* 2.5.4). But the only gnostic teacher whom Origen cited in any detail, and with whom he disputed systematically, was **Heracleon**. Forced by his patron Ambrose, perhaps himself a former gnostic (Eusebius, *H.E.* 6.18.1; cf. *ComJn* 5.8), Origen began his voluminous *Commentary on the Gospel of John* while he was still in Alexandria and continued it for many years afterward. According to the surviving prologue to the fifth book, Origen intended to write this work against "the heterodox," who are now "rising up against the holy Church of Christ, bringing forward compositions in many books, announcing an interpretation of the texts both of the Gospels and of the apostles." The duty of the biblical commentator, as he saw it, then, was to "reprove those who pursue the knowledge (*gnosis*) falsely so-called" (*ComJn* 5.8; cf. 1 Tim. 6:20). To achieve his aim, Origen heavily referenced the *Commentary on John* by the Valentinian gnostic teacher Heracleon, who lived in the second half of the second century. Some of Heracleon's exegetical explanations Origen cited with respect, acknowledging Heracleon's obvious philological education (e.g., *ComJn* 6.39.197; *ComJn* 13.10.62); others he rejected with sharp critique (e.g., *ComJn* 1.14.100).

But if he shows close textual engagement with Heracleon (so much so that much of the lost gnostic work can be reconstituted by reference to Origen's *ComJn*), this is not so with other gnostic theologians. In many passages in his works, the figures of Valentinus, Marcion, and Basilides appear only as a kind of "standard opponent" without any specific profile attached to them (*HomEx* 3.2; *HomLev* 8.9; *HomJos* 7.7; 12.3; *SelPs* 11; *HomEz* 2.5; 8.2; *HomJr* 10.5; 17.2; *ComMt* 12.12; 12.23; *SerMt* 38; *ComRm* 4.12; *CCels* 2.27; 6.35; *PArch* 2.9.5). His list of gnostic heterodox (already traditional by his day) is complemented by Apelles and the Ophites (cf. also *Fragm1Cor* 47

and *SerMt* 33). In some passages they have even lost their name, so as to become a collective of "unfortunate heretics" (*HomJr* 1.16).

Yet there can be no doubt that Origen developed much of his theological thinking in a continuous debate with gnostics. He rejected a great number of their doctrines sharply. First, there is no place for the concept of an emanation (*probole*) in his cosmological thinking, or in his Trinitarian theology (see **Trinitarianism**). In his dispute with the Valentinian thinker Candidus, at Athens, Origen sharply rejected the concept that Christ was an emanation or emission of the Father (*probole*; Jerome, *Contra Rufinum* 2.19).

Second, in Origen there are no equivalents to the basic gnostic notion of "eternities" (*aiones*). In gnostic systems of thought, especially among the Valentinians, these "eternities" were personal hypostases of the divine thoughts (Irenaeus, *Adversus haereses* 1.1–3) something that is reminiscent of other Middle Platonic thinkers, where the Platonic ideas were redesignated as divine thoughts (cf. Tertullian, *Adversus Valentinianos* 4.2). Origen, however, in no way enriched divine qualities with a mythological personal existence (see **Epinoiai**). Again and again Origen emphasized the fundamental issue of the divine unity, and the deity's intimate soteriological connection with the cosmos, over and against the gnostics and Marcion (e.g., *CCels* 4.29; 8.4; *DialHer* 3; *Fragm1Cor* 34; *Philoc* 8.3). Origen consistently denied Marcion's claim that the God of the Old Testament was not the same God as the Father of Jesus, and he equally attacked the Valentinian view that the creator is not the supreme God (*HomLuc* 20.1; *HomPs* 36.2).

Third, there is a strong tendency toward determinism in most of the gnostic systems, which the church fathers criticized, using the very polemic argument of *physei sozomenos* (i.e., the gnostic schemes implied that we were saved as a natural course of events).

Although not all of the gnostic anthropologies really did imply such a strong determinism (probably it was borrowed from a radical interpretation of Paul's passages on election), nevertheless it is clear that Origen's whole approach is utterly different. In his work there is an immensely strong emphasis on the concept of free will. It is absolutely central for his theology (*PArch* Praef. 5; 3.1.1–24; *Philoc* 1–27) and is something that is clearly directed immediately against the gnostics (cf. *FragmRm* 1 Ramsbotham = *Philoc* 25; *ComRm* 8.11; *ComMt* 10.11; *HomJr* 21.12 and *PArch* 2.9.5).

Fourth, most of the gnostic groups developed a Christology with more or less expressly docetic tendencies. Valentinus himself (though not yet a classical "Valentinian") had expressed his opinion that Jesus did not eat or drink in the normal way during his lifetime (cf. Clement of Alexandria, *Stromata* 3.59.3 = Fragm. 3. Markschies). While Origen does speculate on the idea of Jesus' changing forms, as far as observers could see during his lifetime, he is adamant that Jesus' body was real and had human needs. After he had fasted for forty days, Origen agrees with the Scripture that he was very hungry (Matt. 4:2), and he argues that his body had exactly the same needs as our own (*ComGa* 1; Pamphilus, *Apology* 5).

On the other hand, he shared with the gnostic theologians some presuppositions that were in fact common elements of a Platonizing worldview. First among these was the separation of all things into a material or immaterial world (*PArch* 1.1.1; 1.1.4). The material world was depreciated in comparison to the immaterial world; but for the gnostics this devaluation of the created world was much sharper than it was for Platonic philosophers and for Origen himself. Heracleon had explained the symbol of Mount Gerizim (John 4:21) as being the devil or his world: "The world, however, is the whole mountain of evil, a deserted dwelling of beasts" (*ComJn* 13.16.95). Origen, on the contrary, took the mountain to be a symbol for the mislocated "piety expressed by the heterodox in their fantasy of Gnostic and supposedly lofty doctrines" (13.16.98). For him, creation was fundamentally good, a necessary part of salvation history, and a providential gift of mercy meant to lead rational creatures back to God (*CCels* 7.44; *ComJn* 19.20.132).

Second (and it is something that can be overlooked in our often oversimplified pictures of ancient Platonism), there is the central position of an originally immaterial element in the material world. This has to be liberated from the "prison" of the body (cf. Plato, *Gorgias* 493 A). For disciples of Plato, as well as for disciples of Valentinus and for Origen himself, the *soul* is such an element in the overarching cosmological system. Like his Platonic and gnostic predecessors, when he considers the soul, his immediate instinct is to envisage its escape.

Third, Origen used the common scientific method of literary analysis to interpret Scripture, the allegorical technique related to the Great Library. This was a common approach among the gnostic thinkers, often associated with them in the minds of earlier Christian fathers, and used by them to justify their speculative systems (cf. *Fragm1Cor* 81 and *ComJn* 20.20.166). But, and this in contrast to most of the gnostics, Origen differed from them as interpreters because he was so well trained in the method and so systematic in his intent to apply it. Of all gnostic theologians, only Heracleon could be compared to him in this sense.

Finally, Origen also shared with some gnostics, especially the Valentinians, several ideas that were rejected by most contemporary Platonic philosophers. He was convinced, for example, that there was a creation from nothing (*creatio ex nihilo*) based on no preexisting material substrate (*ComGn* 1, as preserved in Eusebius, *Praeparatio evangelica* 7.19.8–20.9). He explained the current situation of humanity by a *fall* of rational creatures, which can be compared to the gnostic myth of a downfall of one of the "eternities" (cf. Irenaeus, *Adversus haereses* 2.1–4). But this detail of Origen's theology should not be explained as "demythologisation" of a gnostic myth (Strutwolf), but rather as an independent attempt to understand the first chapters of the Bible within the framework of a Platonic cosmology; as such, it ought to be rather compared with Philo than with the Christian gnostics of the second and third centuries.

Plato and his followers in antiquity were convinced (like the gnostics) that teaching through the medium of a myth was a very suitable form of philosophical instruction about the first principles of the universe (Plato, *Epistula* 7.344 d; cf. also Aristotle, *Metaphysica* 1.9 982 b 18f.: "The friend of myths is in some sense a philosopher"). Origen, on the other hand, clearly has little sympathy for such artificial philosophical myths, and he derides the gnostics for their fairy tales and fabulous inventions (*SerMt* 38; 46; *ComMt* 17.33; *HomEz* 2.2; *Hom1R* 1.13; *ComRm* 5.1). In this he probably represents the more scientific evolution of the Platonic system in the third century, because near-contemporary Platonists such as Albinous and Maximos of Tyre also avoided the construction of such myths and turned their scientific activity to commentaries, just as Origen did. This may be one reason why Origen compared the gnostic claim to be a valid form of Christian theology with the Epicurean claim to be an authentic philosophy, and rejected both claims out of hand.

During recent decades of scholarly debate, the question whether Origen adopted elements of gnostic thought from his opponents, unconsciously or deliberately, was a passionately controverted subject. A careful look through his texts shows that the influence on him of specific gnostic teaching has often been overestimated by modern researchers. Origen's concern as a theologian-philosopher ought to be contextualized more in the tradition of Jewish-Hellenistic biblical exegesis (modeled on Philo's attempt). His goal is to interpret the Hebrew Bible within the matrix of a Platonic cosmology and to expound the Christian doctrinal system in the framework of a critical debate with contemporary Platonic philosophers. To be sure, to imagine that Origen was simply one more of a long line of Christian apologists struggling against heterodox Gnostics, using the canons of the rule of faith and the ancient preaching of the church (*PArch* Praef. 2; cf. *SerMt* 46) as his primary weapons, is a position that is far too simple, but the same charge of oversimplification can be leveled also at those who have claimed to see in Origen's corpus of writings a systemic "gnostic structure" of thought.

Le Boulluec (1985); Crouzel (1989); Von Harnack (1895–1903); Jonas (1992); Lietzmann (1960); McGuckin (1986); Markschies (2000, 2003); Poffet (1985); Scott (1992); Strutwolf (1993).

CHRISTOPH MARKSCHIES

God   In his commentary on Psalm 1 Origen says that it is "dangerous to speak of God," even when one tells the truth about him (*SelPs* 1.2). This important piece of wisdom certainly proved true of Origen's own writing about the Deity, for many points of his doctrine came under attack in his lifetime and in the later ages of the church. Origen's doctrine of God has sometimes been criticized for its dependence on Greek philosophy. It is obvious that Origen interpreted the Bible within a framework provided largely by the Platonism of his day. When he did this, he was standing squarely in the Alexandrian tradition represented before him by Philo the Jew and (to some extent, at least) by Valentinus the gnostic, and especially by his earlier contemporary, **Clement of Alexandria.** Origen was conscious of his use of philosophy to interpret the Bible. He advised his student Gregory to take everything possible from the current philosophy and make it a "handmaid" to theology (*EpistGreg*

1–2). This at least indicates Origen's intention and desire to keep philosophy subordinate to the Bible. After that point, Origen did what every Christian theologian does in making use of the best conceptual tools available at the time to interpret and communicate the message of the Bible.

The fundamental point in Origen's doctrine of God is that God is incorporeal. This point controls Origen's hermeneutic as well as his understanding of the divine nature. The attempt to avoid interpretations of Scripture that are "unworthy of God" is a major factor controlling his hermeneutic. Origen believes that any idea God is corporeal (in any sense) is profoundly unworthy of God, for the concept of corporeality includes many assumptions that cannot be true of the divine reality, as will be shown in what follows. This, his primary axiom, is a major distinction Origen wishes to draw between Christian understandings of God and those common in Hellenistic religious practice and the religious philosophy of his day. His apologia is also directed against fellow believers.

When Origen begins his discussion of God in the *Peri Archon*, the first thing he considers it necessary to establish is this fundamental truth of the incorporeality of God (*PArch* 1.1.1–4; 3.6.1ff.). Here he speaks out against those many Christians whom he considered to hold ideas of God that were "unworthy." He never mentions specific persons in the *Peri Archon*, but he notes that many Christians conceived of God in material terms. In his *Commentary on Genesis* 1.26, however, he does single out a specific target and names the earlier writer Melito, bishop of Sardis, as one who held this view and who had even left behind a treatise entitled *On God Being Corporeal* (*SelGn* 73). Those who think God is corporeal, Origen says in the commentary, collect the references in the Old Testament to the members of God, such as his eyes, ears, and mouth, and argue that these describe God's form. They also think that the theophanies in the Old Testament demand that God had a human form. Others, while not necessarily believing God to have a human form, nevertheless considered him to be corporeal. Following a Stoic view of spirit as extended and refined matter (*CCels* 1.21; 3.75; 8.49), they foolishly took the statement "God is spirit" (John 4:24), or the similar statement "Our God is a consuming fire" (Heb 12:29), to indicate his corporeity (*PArch* 1.1.1–4; *ComJn* 13.123–53; *CCels* 6.70–72). It is over and against these materialistic concepts of God, some simple and some philosophically more sophisticated, that Origen basically constructs his argument that God is incorporeal.

Colossians 1:15 and John 1:18 are key texts for Origen's doctrine of God's incorporeity (*PArch* 1.1.8; *ComJn* 13.151–52; *CCels* 6.64; 7.27). Both texts affirm that God is unseen. This does not mean, Origen argues, that he is invisible only to human eyes, but that God "by nature cannot be seen" (*PArch* 1.1.8; *FragmJn* 13; cf. Philo, *Moses* 1.158). For Clement of Alexandria, the fact that Moses allowed no image of God to be worshiped indicates that God is invisible and that he cannot be circumscribed (*Stromateis* 5.11.74.4). Origen, in the same tradition, argues that God does not occupy a place. He is not in any space whatsoever. Heaven is in no sense the locality where God dwells. When he discusses Matthew 6:9 in his treatise *On Prayer*, Origen argues that it is a thought unworthy of God to presume that he is located in a place, for if heaven contained God, then God would be less than heaven. But all things, on the contrary, are contained within God. Furthermore, to conceive that God is in a place would necessitate that God be a circumscribable body. All bodies, however, are divisible, material, and corruptible, and none of these qualities can be legitimately attributed to God (*PEuch* 23.1,3; cf. *ComEp* on Eph. 1:20–23). Thus, when God is said to walk in the garden (Gen. 3:8) one must not think that he actually walked in a literal garden on this earth (*PEuch* 23.3–4). Instead, God's walking in the garden must be understood in the same sense that Scripture says God "dwells" and "walks" in the saints (2 Cor. 6:16). In a similar manner, when the Bible refers to God "coming down" to humans, it does not refer to spatial movement on God's part. He does not leave one place, so that it then lacks his presence, and move to another, so that the latter, which formerly lacked God's presence, is now filled with it (*CCels* 4.5). One may think, instead, of God as "coming down" to humans in his providence (*CCels* 5.12). Similarly when the prophets speak of God "coming down," they are referring symbolically to the descent from his loftiness to the level of human affairs, in the same sense that teachers or advanced students may be said to "come down" to the level of novices (*CCels* 4.12).

The human mind serves as the model Origen uses to conceptualize God's incorporeity (*PArch* 1.1.6–7; *CCels* 7.38; *ExhMart* 47; cf. Philo, *Creation* 23.69–70). Mind needs no physical place for its movement and workings. It needs no perceptible dimension or discernible color or shape or anything else related to material existence. Its working is without any of the delays or hindrances related to material existence. God is raw intellectual (noetic) power, unhindered by any constraints of materiality. And so, because God has no bodily nature, he cannot be perceived by any of our physical senses (*PArch* 1.1.8; 2.4.3; *ComJn* 19.146). This led Origen to the controversial conclusion, later attacked by his enemies as a christological aberration, that not even the Son himself can see the Father. This, of course, is a necessary conclusion given the previous argument. Origen supported this conclusion from Scripture on the basis of the use of the verb "knows" rather than "sees" in Matthew 11:27, where Jesus says that "no one knows the Father except the Son." Perception of God, therefore, can only be intellectual (*ComEp* on Eph. 1:3). Origen

recognizes that Scripture sometimes speaks of "seeing" God, as, for example, Matthew 5:8, but he argues that such passages are not to be understood literally and that the names of physical organs are often applied metaphorically to the soul in Scripture.

Clement of Alexandria had earlier blended Plato (*Timaeus* 28C) with Moses (Exod. 20:21) to argue that God is incomprehensible to humans and inexpressible in human language (Clement, *Stromateis* 5.12.78.1–3; cf. Philo, *Moses* 1.158). Clement had concluded that it is only by God's revelation of himself in grace that he can be known to humans, and this occurs through the Logos (*Stromateis* 5.12.82.4; cf. 5.11.71.3, 5). Origen in turn draws on statements in Exodus 20:21 and Psalm 18:11 about God being hidden in "thick darkness" to assert that knowledge concerning God is "incomprehensible" to humans and to higher creatures as well and that none of our speech can be "worthy of him" (*ComJn* 2.172; *CCels* 6.17). Human knowledge of God depends, in the final analysis, on God's self-revelation in the Son. Following what appears to be the Platonist "way of ascent" for attaining knowledge of the divine (Plato, *Symposium* 210a–212a; Albinus, *Epitome* 10.5–6), in which one begins by contemplating physically beautiful objects and ascends, by the contemplation of ever more abstract concepts, to beauty itself and the good, Origen himself asserts that one "ascends from knowledge of the Son to knowledge of the Father" (*ComJn* 19.35–39). The ascent begins, as Origen envisions it, with the Son's humanity, in which we set forth upon him as the "Way" in order to arrive at the "Door" or, changing the metaphor, we know him first as the "Lamb" who removes our sins so that we may, consequently, eat of his flesh, "the True Food." By following the various aspects of Christ (see **Christology, Epinoiai**) represented in the different titles applied to him in Scripture, especially those higher and more abstract aspects such as Life, Light, Wisdom, and

Word, one eventually arrives at the point that one hears Jesus' words in John 8:19: "If you knew me, you would know my Father also" (*ComJn* 19.39). The inability of human nature to know God by its own efforts without the mediation of the Son-Logos is reaffirmed in the *Contra Celsum* where Origen asserts that God himself must of necessity give aid in the quest for knowledge of himself. Such knowledge is a result of God's kindness and an act of his grace. Furthermore, knowledge of God depends on knowing the Son, for it is possible only through beholding "the image of the invisible God" (Col. 1:15; *CCels* 7.42–44; 6.17.69; *HomLc* 3.1).

The concept of the indivisible oneness of God was also an important aspect of Origen's theology. When he lists the basic Christian doctrines in the Preface (4) to his *First Principles,* he begins with the statement that "God is one" (cf. *ComJn* 32.187). It was the same God who created the universe, gave the law, and was the Father of Jesus Christ. When Origen speaks of the oneness of God in this way, he is formulating his theology in opposition to the teachings of Marcion and his followers, who dissected the Deity by separating the God of the Old Testament from the Father of Jesus (*ComEph* on Eph. 2:19–22; cf. ibid. on Eph. 1:3; *ComRm* 2.14; 3.10; 4.7). Origen also emphasized the oneness of God against the Valentinians, who separated the highest Deity from the creator God, or demiurge, of the Old Testament (*ComJn* 10.216–20). Origen often does not make clear distinctions between Marcionites and Valentinians and refers more usually to the doctrine of the "heterodox" who divide the Godhead (*ComJn* 19.12. 29–32; 20.50. 271–72) (see *Gnostics*).

Origen also employs the concept of God's oneness in a philosophical sense derived from the Platonism of his day. God is distinguished from the Son because he is absolutely "one and simple" (*haplous*) while the Son became multiple in his activity as Savior (*ComJn* 1.119; cf. *CCels* 7.38). In *Contra Celsum* 7.38, God is described as "simple, invisible, and incorporeal." In the *Peri Archon* 1.1.6, when Origen is discussing God's incorporeity, he describes God as a "simple intellectual nature." Then, to underline that God admits no additions or subtractions, he describes him with the philosophical terms "monad" (*monas*) and "oneness" (*henas*). When Origen speaks of God's oneness in this way, he is thinking of God as the ultimate source of all being. This necessitated that God be "simple" (that is, not composite), for otherwise the elements from which he was compounded might precede him as ultimate cause (*PArch* 1.1.6).

Origen sometimes joined statements about God's goodness with statements about his oneness (*ComMt* 15.11). This doctrine, too, seems to have been employed against the teachings of Marcion, who had identified the God of the Old Testament as just, whereas the God of Jesus alone was good. Origen often points out that Marcion's dichotomy cannot be supported by Scripture and that the God revealed in the Old Testament is shown to be good as well as just (*PArch* 2.5.1–4; *ComJn* 1.252–54; *ComRm* 2.4; *ComEp* on Eph. 5:9).

God's goodness has a profound philosophical significance for Origen. God is absolute goodness. The Son, he argues, using Wisdom 7:26 as his base text, is "the image of" the very goodness of God. The Son is good, to be sure, but he is not "goodness itself" (*autoagathos*), nor is he good "in precisely the same sense as the Father is good" (*PArch* 1.2.13; cf. *ComJn* 13.151–53.234). The idea of the "Goodness itself" was a Platonic expression. Plotinus connected it with the "nature of good," which makes it possible for other things to be good incidentally (*Enn.* 6.6.10). Plato had argued that God is good in reality; because "the good" can in no sense be the cause of evil, neither can God (because he is good) be the cause of "all things," but only of whatever is good (Plato, *Republic* 379B–C). Origen appears to have gone beyond Plato, however, for even Plato does not seem to have identified God with "the good itself." Origen, on the other hand, understands God to be "the very goodness itself" and consequently the source of good in all other beings, including the Son. Origen grounds this conclusion in Scripture on Jesus' remark to the rich young ruler: "No one is good but God alone" (Mark 10:18; *PArch* 1.2.13). He goes into more detail in his discussion of the parallel text in Matthew 19:17 in his *Commentary on Matthew*. There he says that "the good, in its proper sense, is referred to no one except God" (cf. *ComJn* 1.254). It is applied, however, "inexactly" to other beings and other things (*ComMt* 15.10). The Son and the Holy Spirit exceed all other beings, but, even so, the Father exceeds them in a degree even greater than they exceed all other beings (*ComJn* 13.151).

In a central passage in the *Commentary on John* 2.95–96, Origen uses Matthew 19:17 to interpret Exodus 3:14, where God identifies himself to Moses as "He who is." This, Origen says, is the same God of whom Jesus says, "No one is good except one, God the Father." As "He who is," God is the source of all other being. But because God is also absolute goodness, this raises the crucial philosophical problem for Origen: can a good God be the source of the many evils in the world? (cf. Plato, *Republic* 379B–C). And if he is not, how can the doctrine of God as the source of all being be sustained by the church? Origen approaches this problem from two perspectives. One relates to evil as an entity, and the other relates to the evil things that happen to people. His answer to the first particularly turns on the concept of God as "being" and is worked out in relation to the meaning of John 1:3. Origen's text of this verse specifically read: "All things were made through him, and without him *nothing* [rather than "not one thing"] was made." By combining Exodus 3:14 with Matthew 19:17 Origen identifies "being" with the concept of

"the good," since God is said to be both things in the respective texts. "Nothing," on the other hand, is identified with "not being." Origen then uses an argument involving opposites. On the basis of his exegetically driven identification of "the good" with "being," Origen goes on to argue that since the opposite of good is evil or wickedness, and the opposite of being is not being, "evil" must therefore be equivalent to "not being." Origen alludes to the philosophical understanding of evil as "insubstantial" and then anchors the idea in Scripture with his interpretation of Romans 4:17, where Paul uses the terms "The things which are not" in contrast to the "things which are." Origen takes the phrase "the things which are not" to refer to wicked things rather than to nonexisting things. This, then, makes John 1:3 mean that "nothing"—that is, evil—was made without the Word, that is, apart from the agency of God.

Origen also noted, however, that Scriptures such as the following speak of God doing things that appear contrary to his goodness: "There is no god besides me. I kill and I make alive; I wound and I heal" (Deut. 32:39). Plato had attempted to justify similar statements in the Greek poets by suggesting that they might mean that the apparent evil served as chastisement and worked to the actual benefit of the people who experienced it, so that God was actually doing good in what appeared to be evil (Plato, *Republic* 380B). Origen developed a similar approach by interpreting such Scriptures to refer to the disciplinary action of God to improve the persons involved. Hebrews 12:7–11, which refers to God disciplining his children, is a key text for this doctrine of Origen (*ComMt* 15.11; *HomJr* 1.15–16; *ComJn* 1.261–64). As far as Origen was concerned, God's punishments were always remedial in intention (*CCels* 6.56).

So far, our analysis of Origen's fundamental understanding of the nature of God in terms of incorporeity, oneness, goodness, and being gives the impression of a very abstract concept of God. Origen's God, however, was not the uncaring God of the Epicureans or the distant Deity of the English deists. On the contrary, for Origen God was both caring and present, but not in an immediate or direct presence. God works in the world in two ways: through his Logos or Son and through his providence. These are not unrelated and often, no doubt, overlap, but we can understand his point best by treating them separately.

God's first action in relation to the world was that of creation. Origen accepted the second-century doctrine of Hermas, that God created all things from what did not exist (*PArch* 1.3.3; Praef. 4; *ComJn* 1.103; 32.187). He argued that Scripture in its entirety proves that all substance received its being from God. He did not think, however, that God was the direct creator of the universe. This was the work of the Logos or Son. God, on the other hand, who gave the command to create, was the creator in the first sense of that term (*CCels* 6.60; 2.9). Origen conceived of creation in two distinct forms (*PArch* 3.6.7; cf. Philo, *De opificio* 16–37; Plato, *Phaedrus* 79A–B). In the first instance, God creates a universe of rational beings before the existence of the material universe (*PArch* 1.4.3–5; 2.1.1). Origen sees this indicated in the Genesis story in the repetition between Genesis 1:1, when God creates "the heavens and the earth" on the first day, and Genesis 1:6–10, where, on the second day, God creates the firmament and names it "sky" and creates the dry land and names it "Earth" on the third day. Genesis 1:6–10 represents, for Origen, the creation of the material universe subsequent to the creation of the rational or spiritual universe of Genesis 1:1 (*CCels* 6.50–51; *ComGn* 1.2) (see *Cosmology, Anthropology*). Origen enumerates the beings in the first rational creation as gods, thrones, principalities, and, in those in the lowest rank of rational beings, humans, meaning not physical bodies but souls (*ComJn* 1.216). (His *demonology* admits lower beings

yet, though he frequently excludes the demons from the ranks of those in the process of ascent to enlightenment, which is his chief meaning of the "rational" creation.) Origen appears to have considered even these first rational beings to have been created by God through the agency of the Logos, for he cites Colossians 1:16, where some of the same heavenly rankings are listed, as proof that "All things" were made through Christ (*PArch* 9.4; cf. *FragmJn* 1). As the consequence of the falling of this rational creation from God (see *Fall*), the material universe was then created, including human physical bodies. Origen sees this creation referred to in Ephesians 1:4, where Paul refers to "the casting down (*katabole*) of the world" (*PArch* 3.5.4; cf. *ComJn* 19.149–50). This creation, too, has its source in God but was accomplished through the Logos or Son.

Origen considered everything in the world to be governed by God's overarching providence (*PArch* 3.3.5). This present world has been established by God as the consequence of his foresight from the beginning, through which he knew in advance the thoughts of all beings (*PArch* 3.5.5). Everything has been arranged to provide salvation for the entire creation. All things have been planned to work together as a single harmonious world, with those needing help receiving it from those capable of giving it, and those requiring difficulties (to convert or discipline them) likewise receiving them from those provided for this task (*PArch* 2.1.1–3; 2.9.6). Providence matches individuals against opposing powers as team coaches match boys of the same size and age against one another in games. This guarantees fairness in the struggle, but not necessarily victory, so that place is left for praise or blame for the competitors (*PArch* 3.2.3). God's providence, even when it causes difficulties, always has the good of humanity in view, for God is ultimately "kind" (*philanthropos*) and "good" (*PEuch* 29.13–14).

The incarnation represents the joining of the Logos or Son with the soul and body of Jesus (see *Christology*). The Son is for Origen the crucial link making knowledge of God possible for humanity. In this respect he is the "image of the invisible God" (Col. 1:15) and "the reflection of God's glory" (Heb. 1:3; *PArch* 1.2.7–8; *ComJn* 13.153). It was the Son's love for the myriad of fallen souls that occasioned the incarnation (*ComMt* 14.17; *HomEz* 6.6; *ComCt* 2.8.6–7). The incarnation in turn made possible the reconciliation to "the God of the universe" of anyone who received its teaching (*CCels* 7.17).

The joining of the Logos with a human body meant, especially, the assumption of mortality (*ComJn* 6.177; 2.123). It seems, however, that Origen did not think that the Logos experienced death, but rather that Jesus, the Great Soul who elected to be the medium of the Logos's advent to history by himself assuming a body as a materialized soul, was the one who properly "died" (*ComJn* 10.23; 20.85). When Jesus descended to death for the ungodly, however, he was in perfect communion with the Logos-Son, who was himself thus accomplishing the Father's will, "since the Father is good, and the Savior is an image of his goodness" (*ComJn* 6.294–95). Origen saw the passion of Jesus, especially, as the place where God's glory was reflected in Christ. Discussing Jesus' words on the night of his betrayal (John 13:31), Origen says, "The Son was about to reveal the Father through the economy of suffering," which is why Jesus said, "And God has been glorified in him." This is further interpreted by comparison with Jesus' statement "Whoever has seen me has seen the Father" (John 14:9), to mean that the one who sees the "image of the invisible God" is also able to see the Father, "the prototype of the image" (*ComJn* 32.359). Origen shared the uneasiness of the current philosophy with attributing suffering to Deity. But he was also a devout Christian and knew well the centrality of the passion of

Christ in the church's Gospels and in the church's doctrine. Celsus had attacked exactly this point in the Christian message, pillorying it as a foolishness, and Origen answered it with a carefully worded defense in which he argued that what happened to the divine in Jesus was not contrary to a refined concept of God, and that the death of the human Jesus on behalf of all humanity could not be considered objectionable (*CCels* 7.17).

For Origen, the incarnation was not a revelation of God's power and wisdom. On the contrary, it was a mysterious act of God's foolishness. It is through this "foolishness" that humanity can be led up to the "wisdom and power of God" that is Christ Jesus (*HomJr* 8.9). Using the imagery of Exodus 33:22–23, where Moses asks to see God and is told only that he may stand on a rock near God, where he will be placed in a "hole [NRSV, "cleft"] of the rock" while God's glory passes by and then he will see God's back, Origen says that "the rock was Christ." Then he adds that if one looks at Jesus' sojourn on earth, one will see during this sojourn the hole through which one may contemplate "the things after God," which is the meaning of God's "back parts" (*HomJr* 16.2). In a similar exegesis of the Exodus passage in his *Homilies on the Psalms* 36.4.1, Origen again identifies Christ as the "rock" on which Moses was placed so that through a "very small hole" he might see God's back. God's "back" is here said to be "those things which will be accomplished in the last times through the assumption of flesh." For Origen, this means that what Moses was allowed to see was a glimpse of the later redemptive work of the incarnate Christ, or the mystery of God's foolishness (*HomEx* 12.3; *ComCt* 4.2.12). Origen takes the imagery of Christ's incarnation as the hole through which God can be known one step further in his *Homilies on Jeremiah* 16.3. Here he suggests that not only was the incarnate Christ the rock and the hole through which God's back was revealed, but that all those who are "imitators of

Christ" become rocks and provide holes, which are the diverse ways for God to be known in and through Christ.

Crouzel (1989), 181–91; McClelland (1976); Widdicombe (1994).

RONALD E. HEINE

Gospels Within an extended discussion of Origen's literary output, Eusebius turns more particularly to the matter of sacred Scripture, and quotes his predecessor at Caesarea as numbering the "covenantal books" of the Hebrew Scriptures at twenty-two. Moving to a consideration of what would generally come to be called New Testament, Eusebius includes a quotation from Origen's *Commentary on Matthew*, where he speaks, "Concerning the four Gospels, which are alone, unarguably, in the Church of God under heaven" (Eusebius, *H.E.* 6.25.1–3). Origen goes on, as Eusebius thus presents him, to consider Matthew, Mark, Luke, and John, that is, the four canonical Gospels in their traditional canonical order. This strategy of Eusebius adducing Origen as a primary witness to the canon of the four Gospels might distract us from the important observation that there was actually no "canon" of New Testament in Origen's own lifetime, such as the church would later come to conceive of one; and it is equally significant to note that Origen does not use the term in discussing the Gospel, or other literature associated with the New Testament. Irenaeus had sketched out a theory of the fourfold Gospel, which Origen knows and to which he seems indebted; but it is Eusebius who is more to the fore here in emphasizing the idea of canon, introducing the quotation cited above with his phrase, "Thus guarding the ecclesiastical canon, and bearing witness."

Was it the case that Origen did see himself as such a guardian? His very process of making learned commentaries and scholia on the biblical books he chooses, not simply the established

Old Testament literature, but more pointedly the Gospels and epistles, bears in itself the character of the Alexandrian Library's long-established process of "canon-making," in the sense of identifying an undisputed collection of authoritative literature, which would demand the allegiance of the scholarly class who would subsequently draw from it and comment upon it. He is also certainly consistent in naming and engaging the canonical four Gospels as we know them. In *HomLc* 29, he again lists the four Gospels in the order that would become traditionally "canonical," while at the outset of *HomLc* 1 he distinguishes the Gospel of Luke, listing it last (perhaps for the particular emphasis of his subject in hand), while presenting the other three in the order Matthew, Mark, and John. Later in that same homily he states: "The Church of God chose these four alone" (*HomLc* 1). These four are the only ones (among the many apocryphal gospels still commonly available in his time) to which he devotes his skill as a biblical interpreter, with substantial commentaries (or at least homilies) on each of them extant.

Besides this intentional grouping of "the four," Origen can also refer at times to "the three Gospels" (*ExhMart* 29). Such categorization may suggest, or even intentionally convey, a sensitivity to the distinctness of (what would later come to be called) the Synoptic Gospels, Matthew, Mark, and Luke, for he certainly sees the Fourth Gospel as a "book apart" ("the first fruits of the first fruits," as he describes it in the prelude to the *ComJn*) though more likely in this particular instance it stands here as a reference to those three Gospels from which he has been most recently quoting. Several lines earlier Origen can conceive of the Gospels as a "unit," meaning a summation of the whole economy of the preaching of Christ and the apostles: "Martyrdom is customarily called 'the cup of salvation' as we find in the Gospel" (*ExhMart* 28).

Yet Origen is well aware of "other Gospels." In his first homily on Luke he specifically mentions: *The Gospel of the Egyptians, The Gospel Written by the Twelve, The Gospel according to Basilides, The Gospel according to Thomas,* and *The Gospel according to Matthias.* How many other apocryphal gospels he knowingly waves off by his passing reference to "and even others besides" can now only be a matter of speculation. He rests, or claims to rest, content with "the four alone"; but his firm exclusivity can stand some scrutiny, for within a discussion regarding Jesus' brothers, Origen is clearly interested in the "tradition" that speaks of a prior marriage of Joseph from which the other siblings derive. After a short presentation and discussion, Origen notes the two written sources of which he is aware that supply this basic information: *The Gospel according to Peter,* and *The Book of James.* (*ComMt* 10.17). Is the latter an apocryphal gospel too? It cannot be the Epistle of James found in the New Testament. No other *Book of James* is known to modern scholarship. The *Protoevangelium of James,* however, the apocryphal Gospel of the Infancy, does contain just such a story. Another work named by Origen is *The Gospel according to the Hebrews* (*ComJn* 2.12). By way of launching into discussion of a fascinating variant on the temptation story, wherein Jesus speaks to the Holy Spirit, saying: "Take me, O my Mother," Origen writes: "And should someone accept the *Gospel according to the Hebrews,* then it is seen that the Savior himself says . . ." A recent analysis of his use of the gospels has called this practice—setting apocrypha aside, as if excluded from the canon, but then also being able to quote from them whenever he values the material—an example of how Origen liked "having it both ways" (Wiles, 456).

On the whole, and not surprisingly, Origen relies heavily on the Gospels for providing him and his readers sure and profound guidance of, and for, divine pursuits. In a significant passage he says, "If we come to the Gospels, the accurate interpretation even of these, since it is an interpretation of the mind of Christ, demands that same grace that was given to him who said: We have the mind of Christ" (1 Cor. 2:16) (*PArch* 4.2.3). For Origen, the sense of the Gospels was simply synonymous with the "mind," or the correct understanding of the intentionality, of the *Logos* incarnate in Jesus (see *Scripture, Scriptural Interpretation, Christology, Apostles*). Such noetic or perhaps even mystical pursuits as this text suggests are also spelled out in the *ComMt* 14.22. Here, following a sustained discussion of both Jesus' manner of teaching and its content, as Matthew portrays it, Origen makes a basic distinction among Christians to which he often returns in his work: "Therefore, among those who come to the name of Jesus, those who know the mysteries of the kingdom of heaven can be reckoned as 'disciples'; those to whom such is not given are 'the crowds,' who might thus be counted as something less than the disciples." The Gospels are a fundamental part of Origen's overarching theology of the return of fallen souls to the light of communion with God in the Logos, a primary aspect of his Christology. In being the first major Christian thinker to devote such extensive attention to their exposition, their right-reading, their harmonization, and their theological significance, however, Origen immeasurably advanced the church of the late third and fourth centuries toward a global theory of the "canon" of a "New Testament," in which the Gospels, as primary witnesses to the apostolic revelation, occupied a privileged and preeminent status.

Bammel (1992); Hanson (1954), 127–56; Van den Hoek (1995); Spada (1987); Wiles (1963).

FREDERICK W. WEIDMANN

Grace   Discussion of Origen's treatment of grace (*charis*) has always turned on the question whether he allows too much autonomy to freedom, underplaying the necessity of grace. As far as

Jerome was concerned, Origen was the "father" of Pelagianism; in the Lutheran perspective he was a preacher of justification by works; while for Jansenius he is in the dock as the worst enemy of divine grace. However, being cautious about introducing later Augustinian criteria to bear upon his writings, we should recognize that though he does not formulate strong theses about grace, Origen's writings are, in fact, suffused with a multifaceted sense of divine grace, which might even serve to correct a certain narrowness of focus in the Augustinian tradition on the issue. If Origen stresses freedom somewhat at the expense of grace, it might equally be claimed that Augustinianism defends grace at the expense of freedom.

In constant dialogue with Scripture, Origen orchestrates the biblical sense of grace, allowing it to correct and overturn the "Pelagian" or rationalistic elements in his initial outlook, which had been constructed under the overwhelming stimulus of his desire to oppose the various "fatalisms" of late antique religion. In fighting the Valentinian doctrine of "natures" predestined to salvation or damnation (*ComMt* 10.11), which denies both freedom and grace, Origen is a staunch champion of both. He also explicitly defends freedom against Epicurean chance, Stoic necessity (*PArch* 3.5.5), and determinism based on astrology or divine omniscience (*Philoc* 23).

For Origen, freedom has the principal role both in the *fall* and the conversion of rational creatures (*CCels* 3.66–69). Salvation depends on how well we use our free will, in synergy with the assistance of divine grace, or perhaps even independently of grace: God gives us the capacity to conquer temptation, not the conquest itself, for then there would be no struggle and no merit (*PArch* 3.2.3). As he says, "To destroy the voluntariness of virtue is to destroy its essence" (*CCels* 4.3). The soul of Jesus is seen (almost in "Nestorian" style) as exemplar of the conjoint triumph of freedom and grace, meriting by its loving fidelity

to become inseparably united with the Logos in a supreme participation (*PArch* 2.6.3–7; *CCels* 6.47–48; *ComJn* 32.325–26) (see **Christology**). For Origen, it depends on our own choice of virtue or vice whether we know God as kind or as severe (*HomJr* 4.4). We all have freedom of choice by which we can be converted to the good, and all souls are made good or bad by the power of free choice (*PArch* 3. 1.1; *ComRm* 8.11).

In his early writings, especially in the *First Principles*, Origen tends to intellectualize sin and grace. Anxious to give a rational explanation for biblical examples of disparity of divine favor, such as that between Esau and Jacob, he sees them as determined by choices in a previous existence; originally God created all spirits equal and alike, and their diversity results from good and bad uses of free will (*PArch* 2.9.6–8). Here predestination is systematically subordinated to divine prescience (see also *ComRm* 8.7). God's hardening of Pharaoh's heart (Exod. 4:21), cited as an "objection" to free will, is explained by Origen as meaning that God's command provoked Pharaoh's own willful reaction of disobedience to it, even though it was meant for the universal good (*PArch* 3. 1.10). Like a good and kind master who looks upon a spoiled and reckless servant and sadly concludes, "It is I who made you wicked," so does God appropriate, as it were, the sin itself. Such texts do not mean God caused the hardening into wickedness, rather that God's prescience had foreseen it, and that God grieves over it, still seeking the conversion of the soul to the good (*PArch* 3.1.11).

Origen largely echoes Philo's sense of radical dependence on grace for our basic activities of perception and thought (*PArch* 3.1.12) but qualifies his total acceptance of this by adding that it "is in our power whether we use [our God-given faculties] for good or for bad" (*ComRm* 9.26). He carefully notes biblical statements that our victory comes not from our own strength but from God's grace (*HomEx* 6.1) and that God lifts up the fallen sinner (*HomPs* 37.2.1), but on other occasions speaks as if sinners lift themselves up by their own efforts (*HomPs* 36.4.2). In his response to Scripture, particularly the Psalms, he often "misses chances" of stressing the sinner's total dependence on God for the grace of conversion. Athletic imagery, reminiscent of Philo, is a noticeable way Origen emphasizes human effort and energy in the moral struggle (*HomPs* 36.4.1; *ComMt* 15.22).

Origen has a strong rhetoric of original sin, but it is skewed by his theory of the fall of preexistent spirits into matter (see **Fall, Anthropology, Cosmology**). Human birth is itself a result of sin in a previous existence and adds to that sinfulness the "shameful" contamination of sexuality and materiality (*HomLev* 8.3; 12.4; *HomLc* 14; *HomPs* 37.1.6; *ComRm* 5.9 [PG 14.1046–47]; ibid. 6.12 [PG 14.1094–95]). It is conceivably possible that these texts may be a source for the later Augustine's thinking on original sin. However, for Origen sin is transmitted less by generation than by bad teaching and example; hence Christ's regeneration comes with good teaching (*ComRm* 5.2 [PG 14.1024]). Sin reigns only with the consent of free will (*ComRm* 5.3 [10260]), and not all who commit sins, but only "many" (Rom. 5:19), are "sinners" in the full sense (*ComRm* 5.5). The Pauline vision of universal sinfulness is further diluted by Origen's talk of degrees of sinfulness and of justification (*ComRm* 3.3–5). Paul's stark cry, "No one shows kindness" (Rom. 3:12), is taken by Origen to mean that no one completely succeeds in accomplishing the good (*ComRm* 3.3) or that we perform only a "shadow of good" in obeying the Law, which is itself a shadow of future goods (*ComPs* 52:2; cf. Heb. 8:5; 10:1; *ComRm* 5.1 [PG 14.1020]).

Origen regularly associates the power of grace with the saving presence of the Logos. Dead through sin, we are miraculously restored to life by the command and *synergeia* of the Logos (*ComJn* 28.49–50; 72). Grace is abundant, for the

Logos has been revealing himself since the beginning of time and, for those sharing his sonship, the power of his Spirit is a constant energy of conversion and sanctification (*HomJr* 9.4). He sees the healing potency of the Logos as so great that in the end all souls will be perfected by using their free will to choose what the Logos requires (*CCels* 8.72).

Just as in Philo the indwelling Logos controls our passions, so with Origen the indwelling Good Shepherd subdues our souls to himself (*HomJr* 5.6). The Logos is present in the words of Scripture, provided as medicaments against our weakness and as educational discipline (*HomPs* 37.1.1). The most vital experience of grace is the breakthrough of spiritual reading of Scripture, in which the veil of the letter is lifted and one encounters the Logos, Christ, speaking in the pages of the Old Testament. Successful reading of Scripture, therefore, is itself a grace. Thus Origen prays, and asks the people's prayers, calling on Christ to "unseal" the text (*ComPs* Praef. [PG 12.1080]; *HomGen* 9.5; *HomEx* 12.4; *HomLev* 1.1; 6.1; 12.4; 13.1–2; 15.4; *HomNum* 26.3; *HomJos* 26.2; *Hom1R* (*1S*) 1.3; *HomIs* 9; *HomPs* 36.4.3; *ComCt* 2 [PG 13.135]; *ComRm* 1.18 [PG 14.865–66]).

As a careful exegete of *Romans*, Origen upholds the notion of justification by faith alone, to which the works of the Law make no contribution (*ComRm* 3.9). (This text, incidentally, was quoted by Cervini at the Council of Trent and by Ursinus in expounding the Heidelberg Catechism.) For Origen, the root of righteousness acquired by faith in God who justifies the sinner is acceptable to God even without the works that normally spring from it (*ComRm* 4.1), another passage approved by no less than Melanchthon. The good thief's confession of faith (without works) associates him with the communion of Christ, the tree of life, embodying all righteousness and virtue (*ComRm* 5.9). However, this is not a forensic righteousness that is clearly differentiated from the sanctification that follows on it. Justification and sanctification are conflated in

Origen's understanding, so that justification is truly complete only when moral perfection is attained, and is never "completed" in this life alone (*ComRm* 3.2 [PG 14.932–33]). Origen insists that one must make "much progress in virtue" before one begins to be known by God (*HomJr* 1.10; *FragmJn* 71). It is the deeds of virtue that make the soul healthy or great (*HomLev* 12.2). If some (such as Jeremiah or John the Baptist) are sanctified in the womb or even earlier (*HomJr* 1.11), even this grace may be due to preexistent merit.

Origen invokes 2 Corinthians 6:14 to stress that justifying faith cannot coexist with sin (*ComRm* 4.1.961; 4.1.7.986) and also teaches that only when purged of sin can we receive the Word (*HomJr* 1.16). The radical opposition of good and evil, life and death, excludes any dynamic of the soul being "simultaneously just and sinful" (*simul iustus ac peccator*) (*HomLev* 12.3); instead, there is a rather unsatisfactory concession on his part that most people are "neither just nor sinful" (*nec iustus nec peccator*) (*HomEx* 2.3) but something in between (*HomGen* 5.1; 3; *HomLev* 8.11). In the *Commentary on Romans*, however, Origen tries to focus more precisely on the situation of the justified, arguing that they can already be called saints if they do not waste the grace of justification by unholy lives, and that grace is not lost by the commission of minor sins. For Origen, the meritorious value of deeds is not in rivalry with faith, but rather is rooted in the grace of justification that it brings to fruition. Yet works are not outweighed by faith: the works of pagans are rewarded, even if they are condemned for their lack of faith, while the bad deeds of believers are punished (*ComRm* 2.7). Works express faith, and without them faith cannot be real. Faith itself is sometimes seen as a work, and sanctification as the practice of virtues.

At one point, Origen refers Paul's phrase "no longer on the basis of works" (Rom. 11:6) to the ceremonial Jewish law, implicitly clinging to the idea of salvation by moral works, and he adds that those who adorn the gift of grace with works of virtue are saved not only "by grace" but "by the election of grace," suggesting a two-tier process of salvation, with freedom playing a greater role in the salvation of the spiritual elite (*ComRm* 8.7). Origen's habitual concerns sometimes distract him from the thread of Pauline argument: he interprets "the flesh" (Rom. 8:3) as a reference to literalist interpretation of the Scripture (*ComRm* 6.12) (much to the annoyance of Melanchthon), and his quest for the interior *sensus* of Romans 3:25 (*ComRm* 3.8.946) takes a spiritualizing turn that is ill-suited to the text.

Even so, whatever the defects in his grasp of Paul's original sense, and whatever further loss of contour occurs in the Latin translation of the commentary that Rufinus prepared, Origen nonetheless engaged the Pauline problematic on grace more closely than any Christian thinker before him and did it with such dynamic interest that his views, as relayed by Rufinus, became an unavoidable reference point, either in praise or in blame, on both sides of the Pelagian controversy and its later sequels. Even when the Christian church, after the fifth century, followed a deeply beaten Augustinian track on the issue of grace, Origen's voice continued to be heard, sounding in a slightly different modality. It was a form of approach not as scholastically watertight as the Augustinian version that predominated, and one that more heavily influenced the approach to the problematic of freedom in salvation in the Eastern Christian world (where Augustine's influence was never strong). In many senses it played out its most active role in underpinning a developing theology of asceticism. It may still have much to offer today.

Bammel (1981, 1992, 1996); Drewery (1960); Holdcroft (1973); Jackson (1966); Roukema (1989); Scheck (2003); Smith (1919).

JOSEPH S. O'LEARY

Hades   Origen's use of the term *Hades* is extensive. A large number of the citations are found in his Gospel commentaries, some in his fragments on the Psalms, and many others scattered throughout the extensive corpus of his writings. Many of these references are set to highly contentious and polemical purposes. In his *Commentary on Matthew*, for example, Origen explicitly explains the creation of the "gates of Hades" as the promotion of heterodox beliefs, among other sins. Thus, Marcion is responsible for building one gate, Basilides another, and Valentinus yet another (*ComMt* 12.12.54). Other references cluster around Jesus' descent into Hades, a point Origen clearly wishes to elucidate in terms of received Christian tradition (*CCels* 2.56.1), and around Origen's descriptions of the purgative fires that await unregenerate souls after death (*PArch* 2.10.4.5).

Origen was a highly organic and thoroughly comprehensive thinker. His use of the term *Hades*, therefore, needs to be situated within the larger ebb and flow of his theology. He was an heir to a highly fluid eschatological tradition. Many of the ways in which he employs the cognate terms *Hades, Gehenna*, and *eternal fire* (*pyr aionion*) bear the stamp of the as yet "open nature" of early Christian **eschatology**, though taken together they give poignant description to a mind unflinchingly set on the logical and biblical pursuit of truth. As with other aspects of his theology, Origen's view of Hades departs from his contemporaries and his predecessors in some significant ways.

The term's etymology is of an unclear origin. It occurs in the writings of Homer as the proper name of the God of the underworld, in the form *Aides* (*Odyssey* 4.834). In Greek myth, the underworld was a grim place, filled with malevolent spirits and apparitions. In later Hellenistic popular religiosity, the idea of the underworld would eventually develop a connection between reward of the good and punishment of the evil, though this connection was originally absent, or at most peripheral. The same, however, cannot be said of the Jewish biblical tradition. The term appears over a hundred times in the Septuagintal Old Testament, in nearly all of those cases as a translation of the Hebrew *Sheol*, the underworld. Initially, it is a dark world in which all the dead are received. In Psalm 89, for example, *Sheol* appears as the inescapable lot and destiny of all humanity, regardless of their success or failure, their virtue or wickedness. Following the exile, the term would undergo a series of subtle and important developments. Among the most important, as seen in Isaiah 26:19, was the introduction of a belief in resurrection (*anastasis*). Historically, the eschatological view of a general resurrection, though not universally held in the Jewish tradition, introduced a finite dimension to the underworld. Eschatological expectation was also responsible, in part, for the view that some souls (of the elect righteous) proceed directly to eternal bliss as they await the consummation of the divine judgment and the events of the resurrection. Hades, therefore, came to be understood predominantly as a realm of punishment in the later biblical consciousness, losing its earlier connotation as an intermediate resting place of all souls, and becoming associated with Gehenna. Most English translations of the Bible simply render both terms as "hell," though in apocalyptic thought, Gehenna was first and foremost a sign of divine judgment.

Literally, the term refers to Valley of Hinnom, an ignominious place associated with child sacrifice in the time of King Ahaz (2 Kgs. 16:3), the symbolic place over which Jeremiah prophesied that God's calamitous judgment would fall (Jer. 19:6, cf. Josh. 15:8). In later Jewish thought, as in the New Testament, the term came to be read apocalyptically. It is the fiery abyss of Matthew 13:42 and the lake of fire in Revelation 20:10. It was the place of punishment after the last judgment. The canonical authors, however, were far from systematic in their use of the term. Luke 16:23, for example, suggests that all souls proceed to the underworld, while Hades is exclusively the place of punishment. Other passages, such as 1 Peter 3:19, suggest that only the souls of the ungodly reside in the underworld, while the larger apocalyptic tradition retained the view of Hades as an intermediate stage, destined eschatologically to be followed by the fires of Gehenna. For the canonical authors, Gehenna was preexistent (that fire "prepared from the beginning of the world"). Origen inherited this tradition, subtly adding to and extending it. With him, as with most early Christian writers, the existence of the underworld was seldom questioned; rather, it was a question of the duration, purpose, and cause of humanity's stay in such a place.

In regard to his doctrine of Hades, clear teleology runs through the writings of Origen, gaining perhaps its clearest expression in his *First Principles*. As he is careful to suggest, his views in that work are to be read in the manner of speculative disputation rather than definition based on clear elements of the apostolic tradition (*PArch* 1.6.1), and indeed much of what he says on the subject should be read in the context of this caveat. Origen begins by working backward, describing the consummation of all things through their beginning. An end, for Origen, is suggestive of a perfection or culmination of things. Once again it is clear that the importance of human free will cannot be overestimated in his scheme of thought. The creation and ordering of the world correspond to a hierarchy of merit (see *Cosmology, Anthropology*). Thus, the created order and its multiplicity represent a falling away, to varying degrees, from an original state of perfection (see *Souls, Fall*).

Origen's overarching insistence upon the freedom of the will (see *Grace*) meant that he could not see how Hades could be eternal. Such a view inevitably implied both that it was possible for humanity to eternally frustrate God's will and that God's judgment was more

interested in eternal retribution than philanthropic rehabilitation. To offset the commonly held view that damnation would be an eternal matter (of the *aion*), Origen draws attention to the finiteness of the term *aion*; to insist that what is meant by such references in Scripture, especially the references to fire eternal (*pyr aionion*) or "fire of the ages," is a long and indefinite, though not necessarily "endless," period of time, as the word had mistakenly come to be understood (*ComRm* 6.5). Origen speaks of this as a process, or a progress, in training; the ascent of souls moving through successive orders to a better condition of communion with God (*PArch* 1.6.3). For Origen, the worst judgment had already been registered in the falling away of rational natures from their original perfection. What remained was God's overwhelming desire to restore fallen souls to their original beatitude. All manner of things would serve this pedagogic end. Ultimately, Origen believed, nothing could withstand God's purposes, the root meaning of the existence and goal of all rational beings (see *Apokatastasis, Universalism*).

Unlike Tertullian, who suggested that the body and the soul suffered in Hades (*On the Resurrection of the Flesh* 16), Origen's view of punishment is corrective rather than castigatory, remedial rather than vengeful. Origen clearly defines the purpose of the fires: they are intended for the purification of souls (*CCels* 6.25). Here, as elsewhere, he grounds the process biblically by referring to Malachi 3:3. Several of his theological contemporaries, for example, Tertullian, tended to be more deterministic. Origen contrasted the fires of 1 Corinthians 3:12–15 with the eternal fires of Matthew 25. Indeed, he argues, all souls must pass through the purifying fires described by the apostle, because every soul has been placed in the flesh. The duration depended on the condition of the soul in question and how responsive it was to its divine pedagogy. However, Origen did not deny that even the most sinful of souls could eventually be cleansed and purified. Ultimately, this was the divine will (*PArch* 3.6.5). His view of the *apokatastasis* represents the logical end of this line of thinking. Hell, for Origen, would eventually serve its purpose. This was his deepest opinion, even though he was probably forced by the controversy roused by some debates over this issue to retract his speculation that even Satan might one day be saved (see *Demonology*). In holding to this, Origen was among the first theologians to allow for purification after death, extending infinitely beyond the visible order through higher and higher stages of perfection. The idea was taken to a higher pitch in his later disciple, Gregory of Nyssa, and the latter's concept of the endless progress of the soul (*prokope*) in the mystery of God. Origen's view of the possibility of postdeath purification and progress contributed to the development of the concept of purgatory, an idea that was so fraught with conflicting traditions that it was advanced predominantly in the Western church, while the Eastern Christian traditions continued to be "open-ended" about the judgment of the soul after death, and the utility of prayers and liturgies of intercession. His grand and generous theme of universal salvation would, of course, contribute in no small degree to his condemnation at the Fifth General Council in 553.

Crouzel (1978), (1989), 242–46, (1990); Horn (1969); Keith (1999); Tsirpanlis 1990.

JASON M. SCARBOROUGH

Heracleon   Heracleon was a Valentinian *gnostic* Christian thinker who taught in Rome in the mid-second century. He had been a pupil of Valentinus (Clement of Alexandria, *Stromateis* 4.9.71.1; Origen, *ComJn* 2.100) and an associate of the gnostic theologian Ptolemy (Irenaeus, *Haer.* 2.4.1). Tertullian asserts that Ptolemy had made some adjustments to the doctrine of Valentinus and says that Heracleon had taken simi-

lar liberties with the master's teachings (*Val.* 4.2; cf. Ps.-Tertullian, *Haer.* 4). Hippolytus associates Ptolemy and Heracleon with the Italian branch of the school of Valentinus (*Refutation* 6.35.6).

Heracleon appears to have written "commentaries" (*hypomnemata*) on some of the Gospels (*ComJn* 6.92). Forty-eight fragments of his work on the *Gospel of John* are preserved in books 2, 6, 10, 13, 19, and 20 of Origen's *Commentary on John*. Origen is, therefore, the major single source of our knowledge of his work. Apart from this, Clement of Alexandria attributes an excerpt explaining Luke 12:11–12 to Heracleon (*Stromateis* 4.9.71.1–73.1), along with another on Matthew 3:11–12 (*Excerpta Theodoti.* 25). The ninth-century author Photius also alludes to a comment of Heracleon on John 1:17 (Photius, *Ep.* 134). In addition to his now scattered commentaries on the Gospels, there may be some connection between Heracleon and the document discovered at Nag Hammadi entitled the *Tripartite Tractate*. Some of the teachings in the latter parallel views found in the extant fragments of Heracleon. The *Tripartite Tractate* provides a sort of systematic presentation of Valentinian theology. Heracleon could have been the author of the treatise, or he and the author may have simply shared similar understandings of Valentinianism. Lacking any specific attribution of the treatise to Heracleon, his direct connection with the *Tripartite Tractate* must remain speculative.

Heracleon uses allegory to read the Gospels within the conceptual framework of Valentinian theology. He understands John 1:3 to mean that the Logos was the cause of the creation of the physical world but that the work of creation was done by the Demiurge (Origen, *ComJn* 2.102–3; cf. *Nag Hammadi Corpus* I.5 100.19ff.). The "all things" in John 1:3 are taken to refer to the creation of only the physical world, since the higher beings constituting the "aeon" existed before the Logos (*ComJn* 2.100). The distinction between the Demiurge of the Old Testament and the gnostic God underlies Heracleon's assertion that John the Baptist, who represents the Demiurge, did not speak the words reported in John 1:18. These are the words of the disciple of Jesus, since he takes them to refer to the higher gnostic deity (*ComJn* 6.13).

Many of the Heracleon fragments speak of the graded division of humanity into the pneumatic, psychic, and sarkic natures. These divisions are linked respectively with the gnostic God (*ComJn* 13.96, 147–48), the Demiurge (*ComJn* 13.95–97), and the devil (*ComJn* 20.168; 170; 198; 211). As in Origen's own exegesis of John's Gospel, places and events are given symbolic meanings. Capernaum and the mountain of Samaria represent the alien material realm of the devil (*ComJn* 10.48; 13.95). Jerusalem and the temple are identified as the realm where the Demiurge is worshiped (*ComJn* 10.210; 13.95). The sacrifice of the paschal lamb signifies the passion of the Savior, while the eating of the lamb points to the "rest" the pneumatics will attain in the heavenly wedding (*ComJn* 10.117–18).

Heracleon is significant as perhaps the first ever Christian exegete of the Gospels who set out to write systematically conceived commentaries. Origen clearly was influenced by Heracleon's invention of the genre of Gospel commentary, even as he determined to offset the fundamental aspects of his gnostic interpretation of the scriptural texts. On several occasions in the *Commentary on John*, Origen specifically rebukes Heracleon for foolish or inappropriate remarks. On as many other occasions, however, he refers in laudatory fashion to unnamed exegetical authorities for "higher understandings" that he agrees with, leaving us to wonder (if this is indeed a veiled form of reference to Heracleon) whether he has preserved even more of the latter's work than that to which he specifically refers.

Foerster (1972), 162–83; Pagels (1973); Quispel (1974).

RONALD E. HEINE

Heresy   Unlike Irenaeus and Justin Martyr before him, Origen cannot be counted a proper heresiologist, for he did not collect heresies or reports of them, and he had, as far as one can tell, no historical account to give of their origin or dissemination. Thus he seems to have had no interest in the notion that the Simon Magus of Acts 8:9–24 was the fount of all heresy, nor did he make much of Irenaeus's notion of successions of bishops in the churches to correspond with successions of heretical teachers. He had, however, inherited from his predecessors the crucial term *heresy* itself, which, when employed of groups within the church, implicitly likened them to the established philosophical "sects" or schools, whose emergence Justin had long since portrayed as a process of degeneration (*Dial.* 2.1ff.). This analogy, however, when applied to the Christian movement, raised an issue about the relation of heresies to the church: the question whether they were, as the sects were in philosophy, native developments within it (a conclusion that might suggest that the orthodox represented simply another such sect) or alien intrusions into its life. To this question Origen paid a great deal of attention.

What made the question both prominent and difficult to answer was the fact that by Origen's day the denotation of "heresy" was essentially a matter of established tradition, so that the teaching of the church was already formulated to exclude it. However much Origen may have differed from earlier thinkers, he took over from them an agenda in which the heresies or heretics had already been named: to echo his own not infrequent and somewhat ritual summation, they could be symbolized as Marcion, Valentinus, and Basilides. Furthermore, Origen regularly spoke of these heretics not as rival teachers but simply as embodiments of particular errors, and not least the error (which Irenaeus had identified as the "first and most important issue" [*Haer.* 1.1.1]) of contrasting the "Artisan" God of the

Mosaic dispensation with the "good God" attested and revealed by Christ, an error that of course entailed, and was closely associated with, a segregation of the Old Testament from the New. Still further, these errors clearly lurk in the background of the ecclesiastical "rule" that Origen outlined in the Preface to book 1 of the *Peri Archon*; which is to say, by his time the Alexandrian church's basic catechesis tacitly defined the reference of "heresy" by embodying what were understood to be teachings contrary to the errors of the heretics (for example, on the subjects of God, human free will, and the Scriptures) and so, in effect, presupposing the falsehood of doctrines associated with Marcion and the Christian **gnostics**. Even when he criticizes, in his *Commentary on John*, the exegesis of the gnostic Heracleon, he does not engage the content of the latter's teaching, either often or at length. The issues had already been settled.

Any inquiry, then, into Origen's understanding of heresy must be clear to begin with the fact that he did not characteristically engage in direct rebuttal of heretical teaching, but concerned himself primarily with the relation of heresy to the church and to its traditional, established teaching, an issue regarding which his views seem to have varied, at least in emphasis, from occasion to occasion. Thus in his *CCels*, a late work in which he takes up an apologetic task, Origen puts what might be called a "liberal" interpretation on Paul's suggestion that heresies are inevitable in the church (1 Cor. 11:19). Heresies, or at any rate "disagreements among believers about the interpretation of the books regarded as divine," had existed from the beginning (*CCels* 3.11), he says, and indeed marked Christianity out as the sort of teaching which, like that of philosophical sects, was significant, useful, and serious enough to make such disagreements inescapable. They came into existence because certain "learned men" (*philologoi*) sought a deeper understand-

ing of the faith (*CCels*. 3.12). Moreover, the person who examines the views of the various groups objectively and "chooses the best" becomes, he says, "a very wise Christian." There are, then, indirect benefits stemming from the existence of heresy.

On the other hand, Origen can insist that there are some points of view (that of the Ophites, for example, who had "abandoned Jesus") that are simply "not Christian" at all (*CCels* 3.13); and while there is no reason to think that his "liberal" view about differences of opinion in the church had no beneficiaries, there is good reason to think that in his own mind he included the established "heresies" in the category of teachings that failed to qualify as Christian in the first place. Thus in another place he appears to qualify, if not to repudiate, his analogy between Christianity and the philosophical tradition. The apostles (not to mention Jesus himself) spoke so that faith rested not "on human wisdom but on the power of God" (1 Cor. 2:5), Origen insists, and they had none of the philosopher's dialectical and rhetorical arts (*CCels* 1.62). Moreover he speaks of sects as being outside the church. Having mentioned "Marcionites and Valentinians" as people who play games with the text of the Gospels, he goes on to say that the criticism of this behavior which **Celsus** raises is not "a criticism of genuine Christianity," any more than criticism of Epicureans and Aristotelians (who were understood to deny divine providence) can be taken as a criticism of "real philosophy." Marcionites and Valentinians, then, do not belong to Christianity proper. They "introduce" (*epeisagein*) into the church teachings that are foreign to that of Jesus (*CCels* 2.27); and what he means by "foreign" is suggested plainly by his comments on the "golden tongue" (Josh. 7:21, LXX) that Achan stole from among the spoils of Jericho. It represents the "beauty" that resides in the speech of philosophers and rhetors, "men of this world," who clothe "perverse teachings" in attractive discourse. Origen says that to introduce them into one's tent is to pollute the church, which is exactly what Valentinus and Basilides, and Marcion too, have done (*HomJos* 7.7). Like the Gentiles, heretics attack the church "from outside" (*HomGn* 2.4). Yet commenting on Matthew 26:23, where Jesus describes his betrayer as one who "has dipped his hand in the bowl with me," Origen portrays heresy as betrayal of friendship and fellowship (*SerMt* 82): in other words, here he sees heresy as arising from within the church itself.

Maybe the best elucidation of such apparently inconsistent pronouncements is to be found in Origen's well-known *Letter to Gregory*. For Origen the "outside" threat to Christianity came primarily from Hellenic philosophy, of which he was himself at once an adept and a severe critic. In that letter he commends study of the philosophical tradition as a propaedeutic to that of the Christian Scriptures, even as philosophers see the liberal arts as a propaedeutic to their discipline. Taking in this instance a leaf from Irenaeus's book, Origen describes this undertaking as spoiling the Egyptians of "their jewelry of silver and gold and clothing" (cf. Exod. 11:2; 12:35) in order to employ it in the worship and service of God. But he acknowledges that people who go down to Egypt and settle there may, if they return thence to Israel, do it harm: they may, Origen says, "beget heretical ideas" from their foreign learning, and corrupt the Scriptures, "the House of God," with their self-made idols. Origen thinks, then, that some heresy is indeed derived from a wrong use of Greek philosophy and is to that extent of "foreign origin"; but its importation into the church is ultimately the work of (deviant) Christians. On this view, heresy is foreign to the church in at least some of its content, but native to the church in the persons of its (original) teachers.

Le Boulluec (1985); Norris (1998).

R. A. NORRIS

Hermeneutics   See **Old Testament, Allegory, Mysteries, Scriptural Interpretation.**

Hexapla   In an extended discussion of the effort that Origen brought to the study of "the divine books," Eusebius first notes his teacher's affinity for the Hebrew language and possession of Scriptures in their Hebrew "original." He then notes Origen's pains in "investigating" not only the widely used Septuagint version (common, that is, at least among Greek-speaking Jews and Christians), but several other Greek translations and editions as well, including those of Aquila, Symmachus, and Theodotion. Almost as an aside, Eusebius also notes some of the more obscure Greek versions that were available to Origen and could still in his day be noted in a perusal of the "Hexapla of the Psalms." He then goes on: "Gathering all these together, dividing them into phrases and setting them parallel to one another, alongside the Hebrew text itself, he has left behind for us copies of the so-called 'Six columns'" (Eusebius, *H.E.* 6.16.1–4).

Hexapla is a Latinized form of the Greek term that Eusebius employs as a plural substantive: the "six columns" or, perhaps, "the six-columned thing." It contains, as Eusebius indicates, a running text of the given books of the *Old Testament*, first in the Hebrew and then in other Greek versions (beginning with a Greek transliteration of the Hebrew), along with attending textual notes.

Had Origen accomplished nothing else, his career would be notable in the history of the transmission and study of the Bible (see *Scriptural Interpretation*). As it is, the *Hexapla*, and such work as went into conceiving and forming it, are intimately intertwined with the broad array of accomplishments of which it is a part: For Origen the whole dynamic of his work as a writer and thinker was based around the task of interpreting the sacred Scripture. Accordingly, establishing the text of the fundamental canon (understood at this period at least as the core curriculum of an ancient school (*schola*) if not yet a coherent canon of Bible such as would emerge in the later fourth century, was a major aspect of Origen's intentionality, and in this he was acting out of precedents established by the learned scholars of the Great Library, who had done much to establish the "critical text" of the classics of the larger Hellenistic literary and philosophical canon.

If this was his larger motive for preparing the *Hexapla*, we need not neglect a more immediate motive too: namely, the extent to which Origen was concerned with numerous inconsistencies among the various manuscripts of the Septuagint that were at his disposal. As he says : "When I was uncertain of the Septuagint reading, because the various copies did not tally, I settled the issue by consulting the other versions and retaining what was in agreement with them." This was a suitable solution, as far as it went. However: "Some passages did not appear in the Hebrew; these I marked with an obelus as I did not dare to leave them out altogether. Other passages I marked with an asterisk to show that they were not in the Septuagint but that I had added them from the other versions in agreement with the Hebrew text" (*ComMt* 15.14). Origen's actions and explanations are fascinating on the face of it, and also in light of his broader output. There is the immediate and presumed awareness of, and respect for, the Hebrew text; something that few of his contemporary Christian writers shared. At the same time, of course, he witnesses an overarching respect for the Septuagint text (and, more broadly, the "Greek" text supporting it).

It is not merely engagement of the Hebrew text, but also with **Judaism** as practiced, that drives such philological pursuits as the *Hexapla* represents. The monumental labor was a permanent treasure in the research library of the Christian Schola at Caesarea, both in Origen's time and that of his successors several centuries later. It is no accident that Caesarea was also a major center of rabbinical textual study of the Old Testament. In this context the *Hexapla* has to be considered as an important missionary "prospectus" of the Christians in Palestine (see **School of Caesarea**). The background context of Christian-Jewish apologetic is something Origen explicitly mentions in his *Letter to Julius Africanus*:

> I make it my endeavor . . . not to be ignorant of their various readings, so that in my controversies with the Jews I may avoid quoting to them what is not found in their copies, and also may be able to make positive use of what is found there, even when it is not to be found in our scriptures. If we are prepared . . . in this way, they will no longer be able, as so often happens, to laugh scornfully at Gentile believers for their ignorance of the true reading, which they have.

In a fragment of the recently rediscovered work *Peri Pascha*, Origen seems to take up where this statement leaves off, and provides a concrete example of the sort of lesson the *Hexapla* might have taught a reader: "The majority of the brothers, perhaps all of them, believe that the Pasch is so called on account of the passion of the Savior (*pathos*, from the Greek verb *paschein*). Nonetheless, the actual word for the festival in question is not, in Hebrew, Pascha, but the word Phas. The letters of Phas, plus the roughly aspirated breathing, which is much stronger in their language (than in Greek), constitute the correct word for the festival; which means, in translation, a passage" (*PPasch*, cf. Trigg [1988], 24). All of this information, which he communicates so readily to the edification of his readers and listeners alike, would be readily available in the *Hexapla*, from a comparison of the Hebrew word as found in the first column to the Greek of the third through the sixth columns, in light of the Hebrew pronunciation available in the transliteration provided by the second column. We can also note how, even without knowledge of

Hebrew, the concerned Greek reader could have easily ciphered all that Origen presents here. The great labor involved in the production of the *Hexapla* was thus undertaken for precise and practical purposes. The size of the whole opus, however, was always a major disadvantage in an era when each copy of a book had to be made, equally laboriously, by hand. And so, by Eusebius's day, the continued existence of the *Hexapla* in the Caesarean library endowed it with a significance and importance, perhaps, not so much as a basic research tool, but more an awe-inspiring witness to the indefatigable labors of the great founder of the School.

Simonetti (1994); Trigg (1988); Wiles (1963).

FREDERICK W. WEIDMANN

Holy Spirit Origen refers to the "Holy Spirit," also to the "Spirit of God," the "Spirit of Christ," the "divine Spirit," simply the "Spirit," the "divine Power," and the "Paraclete." While there are many names, Origen will chiefly insist, against those who attempt to sever God's plan of salvation (namely, Marcion and the *gnostics*), that there is only one Spirit and that the Spirit guarantees the unity of the biblical revelation: "Now just as it is the same God himself and the same Christ himself, so also it is the same Holy Spirit himself who was in the prophets and the apostles" (*PArch* 2.7.1). The same point is made in the third article of the rule of faith that he sets out in the *Peri archon* (*PArch* Praef. 4). It is from the Old and New Testaments alone that the knowledge of the Holy Spirit is gathered. While the knowledge of God, and even of the Son of God, is available without recourse to Scripture: "No one except those who are familiar with the Law and the Prophets, or those who profess their belief in Christ, could have even a suspicion of the personal existence of the Holy Spirit (*de subsistentia vero spiritus sancti*)" (*PArch* 1.3.1).

In the *Commentary on John* Origen had been clearly insistent that only the Father (*ho theos*) is "Very God" (*autotheos*): "And everything besides this Very God, because it is divinized by participation in His divinity should more properly be called divine (god) but not Very God (*theos* not *ho theos*)" (*ComJn* 2.17). This includes the Word who is divinized by his "unceasing contemplation of the depth of the Father" (*ComJn* 2.18). The Word, who has drawn his divinity from God, in turn deifies the Holy Spirit, who, Origen postulates "seems to have need of the Son ministering to his hypostasis, not only for him to exist, but also for him to be Wise, and Rational, and Just, and whatever other thing we ought to understand him to be by participation in the aspects (see *Epinoiai*) of Christ (*ComJn* 2.76). It follows then that in Origen's estimation, the Holy Spirit is divine because he has drawn the divine attributes directly from the Son. In turn this Spirit, "in whom is every manner of gift" (*PArch* 2.7.3), supplies these divine attributes or gifts that come ultimately from God, by Christ, to those who are deemed worthy to participate in him, and they, as a result, become divinized through him (*ComJn* 2.77; *PArch* 1.3.4–8) (see **Trinitarianism, Divinization**).

The Spirit's presence and distribution of these gifts is patterned in Origen's systematic as follows: First, the ascension of Christ is a pivotal point in the ministry of the Holy Spirit:

> The special coming of the Holy Spirit to men is declared to have happened after Christ's ascension into heaven rather than before his coming into the world. Before that time the gift of the Holy Spirit was bestowed on prophets only, and on a few others among the people who happened to have proved worthy of it; but after the coming of the Savior it is written that, "It shall come to pass in the last days, that I will pour out my Spirit upon all flesh." (Acts 2:17; Joel 2:28) (*PArch* 2.7.2)

Origen can also note the miracles which accompanied this special coming of the

Holy Spirit, both during Jesus' ministry (for example, in relation to the virgin birth, see *PArch* Praef. 4) and thereafter (*CCels* 7.8).

Second, the gift given depends on the worthiness and need of the recipient. Only the worthy can receive the Holy Spirit (*HomJr* 14.5.1; *PArch* 1.1.3), that is, those who are faithful (*PArch* 2.11.5), who are disciples of Jesus (*PArch* 1.3.5), who are purified from sin (*HomNum* 6.3), and who assiduously practice all the virtues (*HomLev* 6.2). The Spirit, conversely, is removed from the unworthy (*PArch* 1.3.7; 2.10.7; *HomGn* 15.3; *HomNum* 6.3; 7.2), which helps clarify why **baptism** for Origen does not guarantee the continued reception of the Spirit's gifts, since unworthiness before or after baptism can quench the Spirit's presence (*PArch* 2.10.7; *HomLev* 6.2; *HomNum* 3.1; *HomJr* 2.3; *HomEz* 6.5; *ComJn* 6.162–69; *PEuch* 28.3). Moreover, different recipients have different needs. "For to some is granted by the Spirit the word of wisdom, to others the word of knowledge, to others faith; and thus to each individual man who is able to receive him, the same Spirit becomes, and is apprehended as, the very thing of which he who has been deemed worthy to partake of him, stands in need" (*PArch* 2.7.3). The Spirit, therefore, just like Christ, has many attributes or "aspects" (see **Epinoiai**), which are variously perceived and received by different recipients. Here we encounter a prevalent feature in Origen's theology, a distinct and regular overlapping of pneumatology and **Christology**. In this same passage Origen notes that both the Savior and Spirit can be called "Paraclete." Nevertheless, he finds two different senses for this same title and proposes that the Spirit is titled Paraclete because he consoles those to whom he reveals the unspeakable truths of God. This passage is also an important one because it is one of the few where Origen offers a manifold (and anonymous) critique of the Montanist pneumatology (see also *ComTt* [PG 14.1306]).

Third, there is alongside this particular distribution of the Spirit a more universal ministry. As he says: "Now we are of the opinion that every rational creature receives without any difference a share in the Holy Spirit, just as in the Wisdom of God and the Word of God" (*PArch* 2.7.2; 1.3.4). This is a controversial passage, since it contradicts other statements where Origen appears to insist emphatically on the Spirit's particular ministry. This he does, for example, in another passage of the *Peri archon*: "The working of the power of God the Father and God the Son is spread indiscriminately over all created beings, but a share in the Holy Spirit is possessed, we find, by the saints alone" (*PArch* 1.3.7). One possible reconciling approach to this problem is to consider these statements about the ministries of the Spirit that are specific (to the saints alone) and general (to all rational creatures) as ultimately complementary and not mutually exclusive. Just as the Father and Son have general and specific ministries, as he has developed earlier in his text (*PArch* 1.3.5–8), so too, perhaps, is the Spirit assigned a general ministry (*PArch* 2.7.2) that intends to correct and complement the exclusively specific ministry as Origen knows he has sufficiently discussed earlier in *PArch* 1.3.7–8. It is also important to note that in *PArch* 2.7.2 the universal ministry of the Holy Spirit is not clearly differentiated from the general distribution of the "Wisdom of God and the Word of God" and this typical convergence of pneumatology and Christology might also explain the apparently conflicting statements about the scope of the Spirit's ministry in Origen's thought.

However, it is clear enough that Origen directs most of his attention to the specific salvific ministry of the Spirit. The key aspect of it is that the Holy Spirit graciously distributes the gifts of divinity (see **Divinization**) in such a way as never to interfere with the soul's own will and judgment (*PArch* 3.3.4). This principle is integral to Origen's debate with the gnostics, since he insists that rational souls are not determined, whether to good or to evil (see **Grace**). The most frequently emphasized gifts of the Spirit are those that purify (especially sanctification) and those that illumine, inspire, or teach (especially wisdom and knowledge). This sanctifying and illumining work of the Holy Spirit is part of the Father's and Son's "ceaseless work on our behalf" to help believers attain the holy and blessed life (*PArch* 1.3.8).

When he considers the Spirit's role in the purification of souls, he stresses the principle of participation (*methexis*). The "grace of the Holy Spirit" is, fundamentally, that "those beings who are not holy in essence may be made holy by participating in this grace" and so they receive "their holiness from the Holy Spirit" (*PArch* 1.3.8; cf. also 4.4.5). This grace can be available through baptism (*ComJn* 6.166; *PArch* 1.3.7; *HomLev* 6.2). The Spirit produces "fruits" (*HomLev* 2.2.7; 8.11.14–15; *HomLc* 22.1.10; *ComRm* 4.6.9) and chastens Christians for their sins (*ComJn* 32.189). The Spirit accompanies believers on their spiritual journey (*CCels* 6.70; 7.51), ushers the worthy into a new relationship with Christ (*PArch* 1.3.8), and intercedes with God for them in their earnest prayers (*PEuch* 2.3–4).

When he considers the Illuminatory role of the Spirit, Origen's thought turns to the issue of inspiration. In the third article of the rule of faith, he sets out in his preface to the *Peri archon,* Origen writes: "It is, however, certainly taught with the utmost clearness in the Church, that this Spirit inspired each one of the saints, both the prophets and the apostles" (*PArch* Praef. 4; 1.3.1; 4.2.2; 4.2.7; 4.3.14; *CCels* 3.3; 5.60; *HomLev* 13.4.2; *HomNum* 26.3.2, passim). Scripture is "composed by the aid of heavenly grace" (*PArch* 4.1.6); Origen generally tends to attribute inspiration to the Holy Spirit, though sometimes the "angels and God" are credited with it (*PArch* 3.3.4), and sometimes he alternates between the Spirit and the Word (*PArch*

4.2.8–9). In two passages he even refers to the Trinity's involvement in inspiration (*PArch* 4.2.2; 4.2.7). For him, the purpose of inspiration, and purification too, is to bring about the salvation of Scripture's readers, the fallen souls who need to be brought back to divine communion. Scripture "has been prepared by God to be given for man's salvation" (*PArch* 4.2.4). How the Scriptures are a vehicle for salvation is conceived of in at least two ways in *PArch* 4.1–2. First, Scripture prevails (in the sense that it wins new followers of Christ) because of its divine character. Despite its lowly style, the scarcity of its preachers, the threat of death to converts, its words have been uttered "with authority and power" and so, "it is clear that 'the word and the preaching' have prevailed among the multitude, not in persuasive words of wisdom, but in demonstration of the Spirit and of power" (1 Cor. 2:4) (*PArch* 4.1.7). Inspired Scripture is also a vehicle of salvation because a spiritual meaning is woven throughout its whole fabric (*PArch* 4.1.7), and whether evident or concealed (*PArch* 4.2.7–8), this meaning consists of Christian teachings, such as "the doctrines concerning God and His only-begotten Son; of what nature the Son is, and in what manner he can be the Son of God, and so on" (*PArch* 4.2.7). Since souls "cannot otherwise reach perfection except through the rich and wise truth about God" (ibid.), the elaboration of these teachings becomes a hallmark of Origen's biblical scholarship.

This ministry of inspiration or illumination extends not only to Scripture's authors, but also to Scripture's interpreters: "The inspired meaning is not recognized by all, but only by those who are gifted with the grace of the Holy Spirit in the word of wisdom and knowledge" (*PArch* Praef. 8). This is a basic and oft-repeated feature in Origen's hermeneutics: "The grounds of these statements, the Apostles left to be investigated by such as should merit the higher gifts of the Spirit, and in particular by such as should afterwards receive, through the

Holy Spirit himself, the graces of language, wisdom and knowledge" (*PArch* Praef. 3; 2.2.2; 2.7.2; 4.2.3; 4.3.14; *CCels* 6.17; *HomGn* 9.1; *HomLev* 6.6; 13.1.1; 13.6; *HomEz* 11.3; *ComJn* 1.89; 2.6; 10.172–73; *ComRm* Praef. 2, passim). In addition to helping believers interpret the deeper meaning of Scripture, the Spirit also helps in interpreting the deeper meaning (the hows and whys) of natural phenomena (*PArch* 1.7.3; 2.7.4; 2.11.5; 4.1.7). Ultimately, the Spirit leads believers to a knowledge of God (*CCels* 6.17; *PArch* 1.3.4), and not least, communion with the Holy Spirit is a source of unfailing joy, since the Spirit consoles, gladdens, and comforts the hearts of those whom he has illumined (*PArch* 2.7.4).

At once it is clear that Origen has a rich and complex pneumatology, one that resumes most of the themes of the classical Christian tradition before him, though in Origen's hands it is given a profoundly sophic and pedagogical character; although it is a pneumatological schema that also shows the marks of transition, for it belonged to the succeeding Christian generation to elaborate the doctrine more fully and coherently, drawing out the correlations with the christological mystery that Origen had only sketched.

Berthold (1992); Crouzel (1996); Garijo (1964); Haykin (1982); Ziebritzki (1994), 192–259.

PETER MARTENS

Image-Making   In his comments on Exodus (*HomEx* 8.3), Origen explicates Exodus 20:4, "You shall not make for yourself an idol or any likeness," to mean that there is a difference between an "idol" and a "likeness." In support of this he quotes 1 Corinthians 8:4, "No idol in the world really exists," and thereby makes the point that Paul did not include a "likeness" in his definition. It is clear to Origen that making an "idol" and making a "likeness" are two separate things. He goes on to define the making of a likeness

as the reproduction of a subject in sculpture or painting and adds that it may even be adored. An idol, on the other hand, is a form that the "eye does not see," but the mind imagines. It is a form reproduced not from existing things but only from what the mind itself has invented. He gives as examples the placing of a dog's head on a human body (as with the Egyptian god Anubis) or the joining of a horse's body or the tail end of a fish to a human torso (like the Greek mythological creatures the centaur and siren).

A likeness, however, is fashioned after things that exist in heaven or on earth or in the waters. Origen points out that it is not possible to speak about heavenly likenesses in the same way that we speak about likenesses on earth or in the sea. He mentions representations of the sun, the moon, and the stars as found in the pagan tradition, but he does not mention images of spiritual beings such as angels, and the reason is clear from what he says at the end of his exegesis. Although he takes the trouble to distinguish an "idol" from a "likeness," in the final analysis he comes down firmly against the spiritual legitimacy (or utility) of any form of representation, however defined.

Origen's distinction and definition owes much to the discussion about types of images then extant in the philosophical schools. Plato himself adumbrates one such distinction in the *Sophist* (266D): " I mean two forms of the image-making art, the act of likeness-making (*eikastike*) and the act of semblance-making (*phantastike*)." This second type of image involves the use of special effects and perspective to create an illusion of reality in sculpture and painting. A further division of image-making into "imitation" (*mimesis*) and "imagination" (*phantasia*) is mentioned by Origen's contemporary Philostratus: "Imagination is a wiser and more subtle artist by far than imitation; for imitation can only create as its product what it has seen, but imagination can create even what it has not seen" (*Life of Apollonius of Tyana* 6.19). The passage goes on to compare and contrast the zoomorphic images of the Egyptian gods with the anthropomorphic images of the Greek gods. In a similar tradition, several centuries later, in *The Celestial Hierarchy* of Pseudo-Dionysius, scriptural descriptions of cherubim and seraphim are referred to as "unlike likenesses." Such "non-resembling images" are a means by which the mind is uplifted to those divine realities that lie beyond both representation and imagination (see *Image of God*).

In terms of the Christian theory of image-making, even though Origen is himself dismissive of the practice (and belongs to a period of the church's life when the practice of iconography was in its infancy), his ideas still had a remarkable and influential afterlife. We can follow the traces even through to the period of Byzantine iconoclasm. The iconophile patriarch of Constantinople, Nikephoros I, writes: "An idol is a work of fiction and the representation of a non-existent being, such things as the Greeks out of their lack of good sense and atheism made representations of; namely tritons, centaurs and other phantasms which do not exist. And in this respect icons and idols are to be distinguished from one another; those not accepting the distinction should rightly be called idolaters" (PG 100. 277B). Here composite images of tritons and centaurs are classified as idols, in contrast to images of existing beings that are classified as icons. Although Origen would have recognized this taxonomy, he would not have endorsed Nikephoros's defense of the legitimacy and utility of icons of Christ, Mary, and the saints. The difference between Origen's third-century perspective and the ninth-century iconodule patriarch illustrates the shift in attitude that had taken place regarding a Christian cult of images in the intervening period. It is of interest to note that in the fourth century, both the passionately pro-Origen Eusebius of Caesarea and the violently anti-Origen Epiphanius of Salamis were denouncing images that depicted Christ.

Celsus, in his book *On True Doctrine* (the work refuted by Origen in the *Contra Celsum*), seems to show awareness of Paul's statement that idols are "nothing in the world." He remarks, "So, if these idols are nothing, why is it so terrible to take part in the high festival?" (*CCels* 8.24). It suggests that by the end of the second century Paul's definition was being used as a standard Christian argument against the pagan cult of idols. Celsus has more things to say on the Christian repudiation of pagan images. For example: "Who but an utter infant imagines that these things are gods and not votive offerings and images of gods. But if they mean that we ought not to suppose that images are divine because God has a different shape . . . then they unwittingly refute themselves. For they themselves say that 'God made man in his own image' and that man's form is like his own" (*CCels* 7.62). Here Celsus turns the tables on the Christians for attacking the pagan cult of anthropomorphic images when they themselves affirm that humanity is made in the divine image. When he turns his attention to this charge, still Origen has no interest in defending any Christian cult of images (based on the theology of the *imago Dei*), and his reply to Celsus's argument turns strictly on the point of denying that the "bodily form" of man is in the divine image at all (*CCels* 7.66).

Origen is very emphatic on this point. In *HomGn* 1.13 he says: "We do not understand, however, this man indeed whom scripture says was made 'according to the image of God' to be corporeal. For the form of the body does not contain the image of God." And again in his *ComRm* 1.19.8 he writes: "Obviously the passage in which the Apostle says, 'they exchanged the glory of the incorruptible God for the likeness of the image of man,' must not be left out of consideration. This text must be understood as exposing not merely those who worship idols, but also as refuting the anthropomorphites who are in the Church, and who claim that the image of God is the bodily form of man." For Origen, the true image of God lies within the soul, just as Christ's physical appearance is not implied by his words, "Whoever sees me, sees the Father" (John 14:9). According to Origen, Christ did not even appear the same to all those who saw him, but changed his appearance according to the individual's power of perception (*CCels* 2.64).

The reference by Origen to anthropomorphites is of particular interest in relation to the **Origenist crisis** of the late fourth century, when the question of images, both mental and material, was keenly debated among Christian intellectuals. This controversy centered on the locus of the divine image in humanity and divided the Eastern monastic communities between those who wanted to contemplate an image of God in human form (the anthropomorphites) and those who wanted no image of God at all. Those of the latter type were dubbed "Origenists" by their opponents, and one of the most prominent of these Origenists was Evagrius Ponticus. The Evagrian view of the *imago Dei* conceded nothing to the bodily form of humanity, while simultaneously advocating the goal of the complete suppression of images from the mind during prayer. This state of "imageless prayer" became a prerequisite in the Byzantine ascetical tradition in preparing the hesychast for the experience of the uncreated light. It was one of the propositions that brought down condemnations on the head of Evagrius, and through him on Origen, at the Second Council of Constantinople in 553.

In his *Exhortation to Martyrdom* 33 Origen remarks that Christians under persecution might be forced to perform acts of worship before idols or the statue of the emperor. Here he writes: "Let us endure, because among the noble deeds of Job it is said: 'If I put my hand to my mouth and kissed it, this would be reckoned the greatest iniquity for me' (Job 31:27–28). And it is likely that they will order us to put our hand to our mouth

and kiss it." This is a reference to the gesture of blowing a kiss to a statue of a god in acknowledgment, and it was associated in the Greek world with the act of *proskynesis*. It became an issue for Alexander the Great when his Persian subjects made this gesture to him as an act of obeisance and his Macedonian generals thought he was setting himself up as a god.

Similarly, in the *Exhortation to Martyrdom* 6, Origen distinguishes between "bowing down" and "worshiping" and suggests that the Israelites "bowed down before" but did not "worship" the golden calf. In the *Contra Celsum* 8.66 he attacks the non-Christian who "does not really believe in the gods, but pretends to worship through cowardice, which he calls an accommodating temper, so that he may seem to be religious like most other people." Such a person, Origen remarks, "does not worship idols but only bows down to them." The distinction is used here to make two different points; first, to safeguard the Israelites from accusations of idol worship, and, second, to criticize pagans who merely pay lip service to the cult of idols. For Origen what is at stake here is the inner disposition and intention of the believer in relation to the veneration of images. While he was clearly not thinking of a Christian image cult per se, his opinion found an echo in the similar distinction later adopted by Byzantine iconophiles, who distinguished between the absolute worship offered to God alone (*latreia*) and the relative honor (*timetike proskynesis*) offered to the image of Christ and the saints.

In the *CCels* 3.76, Origen suggests that the pagans are stupid to imagine that the fashioning of images by craftspersons bestows honor upon beings that are truly divine, and he further suggests that the complete absence of painters and image-makers among the Jews demonstrates the superiority of Jewish to pagan worship (*CCels* 4.31). It is ironic that Origen should write this at a time when the Jews at Dura Europos on the Syrian border with Persia were decorating their synagogue with an extensive icono-graphic program. One panel in the Dura program even illustrates the fallen idol of Dagon as related in 1 Samuel 5. The fact is that by the mid-third century both Christians and Jews were decorating their burial places and sacred spaces with images, and these were not thought in any way to compromise the second commandment. We first hear of images of Christ among the gnostic Carpocra-tians in the second century, and there is no reason to suppose that other images of him were not being made.

In response to Celsus's criticism that Christians do not erect altars and images, Origen points to the interior life of the Christian to find where true altars and images are made. Christians do not set up lifeless images of wood and stone but living images of virtue that are imbued with the Holy Spirit (*CCels* 8.18). There are two parts to the "lifeless" argu-ment (deriving from the castigation of idols in the text of Isaiah) in the context of the early Christian polemic against idols. On the one hand, images are life-less because they are products of human craftsmanship, and on the other, they are lifeless because the rituals for animating them are ineffectual. They remain deaf and dumb, in contrast to the one living God. Origen's idea that Christians embody the divine virtues and so become living images was taken up by the Byzantine iconoclasts, who argued that in earlier tradition there was more authority for this aniconic interpretation than for setting up icons of the saints.

It can be observed from the passages cited above that a Christian cult of images was impossible for Origen. Georges Florovsky was the first scholar to suggest a possible link between Origen's opposi-tion to images and the theory of the Byzantine iconoclasts, but we have seen that his influence may not have been con-fined to the iconoclasts. Given his contro-versial reputation, and even his imperial condemnation in the sixth century, nei-ther side in the iconoclastic controversy would have dared to quote Origen by

name. But from an iconophile perspec-tive an essential element was missing from Origen's thought, and that was an affirmative theology of the body. It was not in fact until the eighth-century con-troversy over icons that Christian theolo-gians finally developed such a theology. The incarnational theology worked out by John of Damascus made a major advance in resolving the body-soul dichotomy that had so long troubled Christian theorists. In the context of Ori-gen's dualistic Christian view of the world such a theology was a long way from being realized. Even so, because of his long residual influence over most of the intellectual activity of the Eastern church, it is not surprising that several of his "image-related" ideas, or notes, as it were, reappear even in the hands of the iconodules who set him to work in a new and alien context.

Clark (1992); Florovsky (1950); Ginzburg (1992); McGuckin (1986); Schönborn (1994).

KEN PARRY

Image of God   The biblical idea of the image of God is important to Origen in two related domains. The first is rooted in the creation accounts. Origen reads the different narratives in Genesis 1 not as variants of the same event but as records of two distinct creations: that of the preexistent soul, and latterly that of the embodied soul, which is the human condition after the fall. The Genesis nar-rative suggests first that Man (*anthropos*) is in the "image and likeness" of God (Gen. 1:26) and then that Man is "in the image" of God (Gen. 1:27). Origen's sec-ond fundamental source is the Pauline texts (and christological hymns of the New Testament) that attribute to Christ the role and function of "image of the unseen God" (2 Cor. 4:4; Col. 1:15; Heb. 1:3; see 1 Cor. 11:7).

These two concepts, anthropological and christological, are already intimately related in Christian thought before

Origen, insofar as writers such as Irenaeus followed Paul's lead in identifying Christ as the "New Adam" (the archetypal restoration of *anthropos*, or the human race, within his own incarnate person). Origen, however, takes the correlation of the ideas to a new pitch in his exegetical work and leaves the ideas of the "likeness" and "image of God" (however "slight" they may have been in the prior biblical record) now poised to become one of the central poles of subsequent Christian theological thought on *Christology*, soteriology, pneumatology, and *anthropology* (see also *Cosmology, Holy Spirit, Souls*).

The notion of the likeness-image of God, was particularly appealing to Origen, as it seemed to him an ideal point of synthesis between the biblical tradition of revealed truth, to which he was axiomatically committed as a Christian, and the equally pressing philosophical axiom he had inherited from his Alexandrian environment that laid immense stress on the ubiquitous truth of the hierarchy of being, where lesser apprehensions of life, or truth, were derived as direct participations from higher realities. Such a hierarchically graded "patternism," or theory of successive derivations of ontology, is a Platonist intellectual superstructure that Origen reads directly into the biblical concept of the image, thus transforming it dramatically. The developed theory of hierarchy of being was itself a distinct modification of the early Platonic theory that the sensible world is "the image" of the world of ideas; just as the soul is "akin" to God (*syngeneia*) and can come to knowledge of the divine, since "only like knows like." Platonism, however, never placed more emphasis on the idea of image than this, for the simple reason that it was a notion indissolubly bound up with the world of the sensible and, as such, part of the fabric of the illusory (see *Image-Making*). One celebrated passage of Plato, however, did seem to have affected Origen considerably, which was

where "likeness" (*homoiosis*) to God was attributed as the highest goal of humanity (*Theaetetus* 176–77).

In considering how Man could be conceived as the image of God, Origen draws out the principal conclusion that image is a biblical cipher for that ontological mimesis of the divine, which affords to the human being the capacity to ascend back to communion with God. He returns to the notion at the very end of the *Peri archon*, when he is thinking about the "consummation" of the final end of things (see *Universalism*). The return to communion with God is, in a real sense, the reinstitution (see *Apokatastasis*) of the original destiny of souls who before the fall had derived their existence and beatitude directly from contemplative communion with the Logos of God, who personally mediated to them their participation in the unapproachable Father. This mediated hierarchy of being provided the ontological stability (*stasis*) of the souls; and now in the consummation, Origen muses, such ontological stability may be restored through the same means, what he describes as an ontic mimesis. He himself puts it in this fashion:

Moses points to this when recording the first creation of man he says, "And God said—Let us make man in our own image and likeness" (Gen. 1.26). And then he adds afterwards, "And so God made man: In the image of God he made him, male and female he made them, and he blessed them" (Gen. 1. 27–28). The fact that Moses said, "He made him in the image of God," and was then silent about the earlier issue of "likeness," points to nothing else but this, that man received the honour of God's image in his first creation, whereas the perfection of God's likeness was reserved for him at the consummation. The purpose for this was that Man should acquire it for himself, by his own earnest efforts to imitate God. In this way, while the possibility of attaining perfection was given to Man in the beginning, through the honour of "the image," even so he should, in the end, obtain for himself the "perfect likeness" by the accomplishment of these works. (*PArch* 3.6.1)

For Origen, it is important that the careful reader of Scripture notes the fundamental distinction made there between "image" and "likeness." The image is less perfect, as far as he is concerned, than the idea of likeness. The latter carries more of the concept of moral and voluntary assimilation (*mimesis*) to the archetype; and thus, while he allows that God had so fashioned humanity in the potentiality of communion (as a potential "image" of the divine), his overarching presupposition is that this earthly format is itself not "the beginning," or archetype of humanity's being (for the true origin of souls was as a perfect communion with God through the Logos) but merely "the beginning of the return" from the *fall*, through disciplined paideia. Therefore, as the soul becomes more faithful and illumined it becomes more and more transfigured into the "likeness" of God, by virtue of its mimesis (see **Divinization**). It moves into communion with the Logos (the only true Likeness of God), and from being an image in potency (that is, "made according to the image") it progresses to being imagelike in actuality, through its moral and mystical fidelity. For Origen, the body is never to be understood as "in the image," only the moral qualities of humankind (*PArch* 4.4.10). In the end result of this ascent, the final state (the consummation) will be like that of the actual beginning, when the Logos first made souls, a perfect harmony of beings, related to the Father by their mimesis of the divine Logos. In playing out this distinction between image and likeness, Origen took the similar theories of Irenaeus (*Haer* 5.6) and Clement of Alexandria (*Stromateis* 2.38.5) to a new pitch of extension. It is a concept to which he often returns (*CCels* 4.30; *ComRm* 4.5).

The apparent simplicity of this scheme of hierarchical progress—to the invisible God, through the mediation of the divine Logos, by the contemplative mimesis of the purified soul—is hindered by only one flaw: the attribution in Colossians 1:15 of the title "image" directly to Christ. Origen disposes of the difficulty carefully. The text, he says, confesses Christ as "Image of the Unseen God," and necessarily implies that it is in his divinity alone that he stands as a true "Image of the Unseen," which must (to be an accurate image) be itself unseen. This paradox of the invisible image, therefore (a "difficulty" by which the text points out a mystery to the attentive reader) is really a strong confirmation of Origen's teaching that only the Logos is the veritable "Likeness of God," and only the Logos is the true "Image of God." Human souls are caught up into the mimesis of this mystery, of course, and are rightly called "in the Image," "after the Image" (*kat' eikona*), or even "Image of the Image," but they are never themselves properly understood as the divine image per se. Origen insists that this precision is necessary in order to clarify the process of hierarchically mediated ascent, which is the path to divinization. Being the creature that is "In the Image" is, Origen insists, the "principal substance" of our human ontological state (*ComJn* 20. 22.[20].182). Souls are, then, "in the image of the Image (Logos) of God" insofar as they were created by the Logos, who remains their only mediator to the presence of the unapproachable Godhead.

While Origen himself does not envisage the Holy Spirit in terms of "image" (either of God, or of the Son), it was a step that his disciples took; beginning with Gregory Thaumaturgus (his own pupil in Caesarea) and through him to the Cappadocians of the fourth century who had such a monumental impact on the development of Christian Trinitarian theology. The theme of the image of God becomes in Origen's hands an extraordinary testimony to the vital imagination of the man, his energetic capacity in weaving together biblical and philosophical metaphysics, and his constant sensitivity to the nature of the theologian's task as a mystical symphonist.

Balas (1973); Crouzel (1956, 1989), 92–98; Rowe (1987).

JOHN A. McGUCKIN

Inspiration   See **Scripture, Holy Spirit.**

John the Theologian   According to Origen, John the son of Zebedee was a fisherman and in "earthly" terms an uneducated man. Like Paul and the other apostles, before knowing Jesus, John "bore the likeness more to the image of the devil" (*HomGn* 1.13). But by following the image of God, in Christ, John was transformed as a disciple "in the image" of divine wisdom. For Origen, John is the "High Priest" of the religion of the Logos. He had greatness of spiritual vision and charisms of healing, qualities that earthly possessions cannot give (*HomGn* 16.5). His close relationship with Jesus made John heir to the priestly "first fruits" of Jesus' teachings (*ComJn* 1.6). At the Last Supper John rested his head on Jesus' breast, which Origen interprets figuratively to mean that John lay on the Word, that is, had intimate communion with the Logos: "He lay back on the bosom of the Word, just as the Lord himself is called the 'Only Begotten' Word 'in the bosom of the Father'" (*ComLc* 16.23). John's close relation to Jesus results in his elevated teaching authority as a supreme apostolic witness (see **Apostles**) and in his masterly capacity to instruct the church in what Origen calls "the more mystical things" (*ComLc* 16.23).

Origen attributes the authorship of the Johannine New Testament writings (the Fourth Gospel, the letters of John, and the book of Revelation) to the apostle John, the son of Zebedee (*ComJn* 1.1,

6; 5.3; *HomGn* 7.4). He underscores the spiritual quality of the author and his words. His Gospel transcends the other three in the degree to which they themselves transcend the **Old Testament.** It is the "first fruits" of all Scripture, a veritable priestly offering (*ComJn* 1.23). John's presence on the mountain during Jesus' transfiguration signifies John's unique "spiritual capacity" (*ComLc* 5.1). Unlike the other disciples, who were left on the plain below, or even those who still wandered even lower ("in the valleys"), John had ascended with Jesus to be able to see beyond the things of the world (*ComMt* 12.36). Of all the Gospel writers, it is John, therefore, who relates most concerning the spiritual nature of Jesus and "plainly declares his Godhead" (*ComJn* 1.6). In his Gospel, Revelation, and letters, he teaches respectively that Jesus is the Light of the world, the Alpha and the Omega, and the Lord of a pure church that resists heresy. His Gospel (according to Origen, the last of the four Gospels to be written) represents the "greatest and most complete discourse about Jesus" (*ComJn* 1.6), a view that was to have determinative influence on Greek and Latin Christian theologians after him.

Origen lays stress on the idea that John's writings relate the existence of one single and creative **God** manifest in what Origen interprets to be the old and new ages. Origen thus elevates him as an authority who opposes the gnostic idea of separate deities (*ComJn* 1.14). It is thus no coincidence that he uses his *Commentary on John* to attack gnostic theologians (particularly **Heracleon**). Similarly, John's Gospel is a "type" (see **Typology**) of the Old Testament, representing the termination of the old era and the beginning of the new. The exalted and flying angel of the Apocalypse (Rev. 14:6–7) is taken by Origen as the symbol of the final end and the approach of the time of judgment (*ComJn* 1.14).

For Origen John is also a symbol of ascetic fruitfulness, an idea possibly dear to his heart as someone who had also adopted a celibate life of philosophical *sophrosyne*. In Origen's estimate John is often paired with the other prince of apostolic wisdom, Paul, since the one reclined on the bosom of the Logos (John 13:23) and the other was initiated in the third heaven (2 Cor. 12:2–4). Both of them are the highest possible mystical initiates of Jesus. Accordingly, Origen notes that although John the apostle never married and never had physical offspring, he yet left behind "spiritual seed and spiritual sons . . . and each had wisdom as their wife, since Paul also begot sons through the Gospel" (*HomGn* 11). It is clear from the immensely high regard Origen holds for John and Paul that in some real sense he saw his own ministry as teacher and initiate, a continuation of their own apostolic charism in the later ages of the church.

McGuckin (1985, 1995); Trigg (1981); Widdicombe (1997); Wiles (1960).

JEFFREY PETTIS

Judaism None of the Fathers knew and appreciated Judaism as well as Origen. His capacious theology resolved all apparent contradictions to affirm the unity of the Old and New Testaments, the old and new people of God, thus sealing the defeat of Marcionism. Christ's teaching cannot come from human wit but only from "the epiphany of God, with manifold wisdom and manifold powers first establishing Judaism (*Ioudaismos*), and after it Christianity (*Christianismos*)" (*CCels* 3.14). Origen's attention to the historical and theological bond between the two religions ensured that Christians would treasure their roots in ancient Israel and their spiritual unity with the patriarchs and prophets, who participate in their struggle and aid them with their prayers (*HomLev* 7.2; *HomNum* 26.6; *HomJos* 3.1; 16.5; 26.2). His study of Judaism, which gave Jewish learning a crucial place in Christian theology, has many facets: the pervasive influence of Philo, his major precursor as exegete and allegorist,

whose works he probably saved for posterity; his study of Hebrew (which may well have gone beyond a rudimentary level); his labor on the **Hexapla**, in consultation with Jewish scholars (*ComJn* 6. 212; *ComPs* 3:8); his use of tips from Jewish exegetical lore (*PArch* 4.3.14; *ComMt* 11.9; *HomGn* 2.2; *HomNum* 14.1; 27.12; *HomEz* 10.3), some acquired from personal contact (*HomNum* 13.5; *HomIs* 9), notably with Hillel the younger, son of the Patriarch Gamaliel III (*ComPs* Praef. [PG 12.1056]), and with a converted Jewish immigrant in Alexandria (*EpistAfr* 7; *HomJr* 20.2), who is probably the person cited at the start of his first public scriptural commentary (*ComPs* Praef. [PG 12.1080]); his occasional attention to Judeo-Christian traditions (*PArch* 1.3.4). The great halakhists of the academy of Rabbi Hoshaya were his contemporaries in Caesarea. His public debates with learned Jews were challenging and instructive (*ComJn* 10.163), though he presents himself as emerging victorious (*CCels* 1.45; 55–56) or as finding confirmation of Christian claims (*CCels* 2.31).

All this study served also to bolster Origen's theological claim that only in Christianity does Jewish tradition attain its proper fulfillment. Jews who fail to convert to Christ are in a tragic dead end, abandoned by God (though with a prospect of eschatological restoration). Thus, while Origen can correct the crude anti-Judaism of earlier and later theologians, the negative impact of his own account proved all the more dangerous for the future, in that it is so thoroughly argued, on a broad textual basis. A catena of his remarks seems to form an oppressive anti-Jewish vision, though it is questionable, perhaps, to take these out of their specific exegetical contexts so as to combine them in a system. Indeed, efforts to critique them can scarcely avoid tackling key New Testamental sources themselves, such as Matthew 21:43: "The kingdom of God will be taken away from you and given to a people that produces the fruits of the kingdom," which Origen sees as referring to a central purpose of the coming of Christ (*CCels* 4.3; 42; 5.58) and which provides the salvation-historical framework for comments on Judaism in the *ComMt* (especially *ComMt* 17.6–11). Paul often turns out to be a primary source of his anti-Judaistic apologetic. All of this is increasingly disturbing to his contemporary readers, who with the hindsight of the traumatic events of the twentieth century are less and less able to share the serenity of those Christian scholars who have reported Origen's anti-Judaistic apologia without criticism, or even accentuated it, treating those views even as intrinsic to Christian orthodoxy.

Sometimes Origen gives rationalistic accounts of the election of the Jews, seeing it as merited by their virtues. The Jews did not sin at the time of the tower of Babel and so kept the language of Adam and remained under immediate divine protection, while the other nations were consigned to the guidance of angels (*CCels* 5.31–32; *HomNum* 11.4). To be born in Israel, it is hinted, could be the reward of merit in a prior life. As in Philo, the excellence of the Jews is described in terms of Platonic ideals: "Even the last of the Jews fixes his eyes on the one God above all." For Origen, the privileges of Jews have been transferred to Christians for a corresponding reason, the moral falling away of the Jews. The same logic applies to Gentiles: we must learn from Israel's mistakes (*HomJr* 4.5; *HomEz* 7.1; *HomLev* 13.2; *HomPs* 36.3.10) and avoid the same fate of rejection, one that Origen fears for the tepid and overpopulous church of a time without persecutions (*HomJr* 4.3).

The transferal of true religion (*translatio religionis*) from Jews to Christians is evoked in Platonic terms, the Jews remaining trapped in the fleshly world of shadows and images, while Christians have broken through to the spiritual level: "The whole of religion has been transferred from Jews to Gentiles, from circumcision to faith, from letter to spirit, from shadow to truth, from carnal to spiritual observance" (*ComRm* 9.1). The obsolescence of Mosaic revelation in

light of Christ's surpassing glory (2 Cor. 3:7–11; *ComJn* 32.336–37; *ComRm* 3.11) is thought of as the obsolescence of Platonic "images" when the true reality appears. The earthly Jerusalem was destroyed when the heavenly appeared; one doesn't keep the clay model of a statue when the statue has been formed. Retention of the old cult, despite or because of its splendor (*HomNum* 23.1), would cause confusion and scandal (*HomLev* 10.1; *HomJos* 17.1), though the scriptural record of the old system retains a pedagogic and inspirational value (*ComCt* 2 [PG 13.136]). Origen insists that there is no function for a symbolic priesthood and temple when the true high priest has come (*ComMt* 16.3), yet Jews cling to the "sketch and shadow" (Heb. 8:5) and reject the reality itself (cf. Heb. 10:1) as a lie (*HomLev* 12.1). They boast in their birth, he says (echoing the apologetic sketched out in John 8:32f.), fascinated by the shifty world of becoming, like the daughter of Herodias who celebrated a birthday with a sinuous dance (*ComMt* 10.22). Here, in painful irony, a polemic of Philo against the Egyptians, accusing them of chameleonic inconstancy (Philo, *Ebr.* 36; 208), is transferred to the Jews. Jews cling to ancestral tradition, just as the Egyptians do to their custom of worshiping beasts, and so cannot open themselves to the higher doctrines taught by Jesus (*CCels* 1.52). Origen even develops an entire pathology of Jewish stubbornness, bad faith, and self-blinding (*ComMt* 11.13–14; *SerMt* 27; *HomIs* 6.5–6).

His vision of Jewish sinfulness culminates in the slaying of the prophets and of Christ. In punishment, their filial adoption and special divine protection have been withdrawn and are now transferred to Christians (*HomLev* 12.5). The New Testament signifies Christ's "bill of divorce" to the synagogue, which now consorts with the devil and has been replaced by a new Gentile spouse (*ComMt* 14.19). The contrast between Jewish defeat and shame and the triumphant worldwide progress of Christianity proves that "their father has spit in their face" (Num 12:14; *HomNum* 7.4). "The descendents of Israel are no longer Israel" (*ComJn* 28.94), and Christians are the "true Israel" (cf. Justin, *Dial.* 130.3; 135.3), "who with pure mind and sincere heart sees God" (*ComRm* 8.7). All this language is perhaps less offensive if we note that for Origen it is Christ in the first place who is the "true Israel" (*ComRm* 8.11), and that the true Israel is fully realized only in the heavenly community, which embraces Jews and Gentiles, humans and angels (*HomNum* 1.3; *HomJos* 9.4).

The increasingly hostile tone of the remarks in his later writings may also be contextualized in terms of attempted, and failed, exercises in interreligious dialogue at Caesarea. The late text, *Contra Celsum,* written shortly after the more polemical *Commentary on Matthew,* is invoked by those who see Origen as friendly to the Jews of his day. In reality, although the work defends the faith shared by Jews and Christians alike and magnifies the Old Testament saints and prophets, Origen still signals that the old economy is surpassed in the new (*CCels* 5.42–51) and formulates a negative judgment on the Jews of his time, who are, he says, "entirely abandoned, having nothing of what they formerly held sacred, not even a sign that there is anything divine among them" and are "punished more than others" (*CCels* 2.8) for their failure to recognize the one their prophets had foretold. The just punishment of the Jews is an important plank in Origen's apologetic argument (*CCels* 1.47; 2.13, 78; 4.32, 73; 5.43; 7.26; 8.47; 69). It might be argued that his vision of the Jewish people, the elder brother of the church (*ComCt* 2 [PG 13.142]), is tinged with pity and respect; except that here again the reference is not to contemporary Jews.

For Origen, all Jewish parties to the death of Jesus are punished; the scribes' punishment is that they are now blind to the intent of the Scriptures (*ComMt* 16.3). Christians, through allegorical interpretation of the *Old Testament,* can recuperate the entirety of Jewish experience. Origen thus saves the Hebrew Scriptures

for Christian use, but only by interpreting them in terms that few Jews would recognize as having any basis. With 2 Corinthians 3:12–16 as his warrant, he seeks Christ in the Scriptures under the veil of the letter. Jews, imprisoned in the letter, and missing the grace of a pneumatic reading of Scripture, are condemned to an infinite exile in their interpretative efforts (see *Allegory, Anagogical Interpretation, Typology*). For Christians the Torah is no longer a troubling foreign document; rather it is the Jews who understand the Law poorly and so do not accept Christ. The literal sense rarely satisfies Origen's need for a pneumatic, christological understanding of Scripture. Unless taken in a spiritual sense, the words of Leviticus signify impediment and ruination to the Christian religion (*HomLev* 5.1). Not to follow the Pauline method of spiritual interpretation would be to become a disciple of the Jews and an accomplice of the enemies of Christ (*HomEx* 5.1).

The letter of the Law is bitter and consigns the Jews to a bitter lot, but it is changed to sweetness by spiritual understanding (*HomEx* 7.1–2). For Origen, the Jews are always learning but never arrive at knowledge of the truth (*ComRm* 2.14) and are afflicted with stupidity, their minds befogged (*HomNum* 6.4; *ComMt* 11.11), unable to grasp the sense of their own laws. Their development has been aborted (*HomNum* 7.3). They have the scriptural books, yet the Scriptures are taken away from them, since they do not understand them (*HomJr* 14.12). They are victims of a blind Torah positivism; if asked the reason for their laws, they reply: "Such is the good pleasure of the Legislator; no one argues with the Lord" (*HomLev* 4.7). Christians honor the Law more, "by showing what depth of wise and mysterious teachings are found in those letters which the Jews have not well contemplated in their superficial reading that remains attached to fables" (*CCels* 2.4). "What the Jews have now is all fable and futility, for they lack the light of the knowledge of the Scriptures" (*CCels* 2.5). We have fled "the mythologies of the Jews" for "mystical contemplation of the Law and the prophets" (*CCels* 2.6).

The mystery of Jewish blindness can be understood only by God. Reading prophetic addresses to the kingdoms of Israel and Judah as referring to the present situation of Israel and the Gentiles, Origen rejoices in the Pauline idea that the stumbling of Israel was providential, allowing the Gentiles access to salvation (*HomJr* 4.2). Israel's present stony hardening is only a temporary condition (*HomEx* 6.9). Christ will take back his unfaithful spouse at the end (*ComMt* 14.20). Israel is a barren fig tree only until the fullness of the Gentiles has been gathered in (*ComMt* 16.26). Like Miriam, the synagogue is in a leprous condition, but her expulsion is temporary; at the end of time she will come back to the camp (*HomNum* 6.4). The Jews' meditation of the Law (albeit fruitless) and their zeal for God are both admirable even if misguided (*HomPs* 36.1.1; 5.3), and they are a pledge of the final restoration, when Jews, converted to Christ (*per fidem*), will fill up the number of the elect (*ComRm* 8.9; 12; *ComMt* 17.5). Just as Origen's idiosyncratic theory of preexistence lurks in the background of what he says about the election of Israel, so his idiosyncratic theory of postexistence may underlie his statements about Israel's ultimate destiny. "All Israel will be saved" (Rom. 11:26) seems to have a partial fulfillment at the end of this world, but complete fulfillment only in the final *apokatastasis* (*HomJr* 5.4). In this sense, his retrieval of Paul's positive ideas about Israel's final destiny (not to mention Matt. 5:17—see *Law*) is something that distinguishes Origen from most of the Fathers and even makes him a precursor of contemporary Christian-Jewish dialogue.

Blowers (1988); Heither (1990); De Lange (1976); McGuckin (1992); Philippou (1970); Sgherri (1982).

JOSEPH S. O'LEARY

Law
The Law of Moses

Origen presupposes that the religion of Israel was revealed by God and that the writings of the **Old Testament** were divinely inspired (*PArch* 1.3.1; 4.1.1; *ComJn* 6.48.29). The church rightly receives Moses and reads his writings, believing that he is a prophet who wrote down the future mysteries that God revealed to him in symbols, figures, and allegorical forms, which were fulfilled in their proper time (*HomLev* 10.1). Origen's assessment of Moses' role in salvation history is extremely high. Moses was the divinely commissioned lawgiver who imbued his nation with zeal for God's laws (*PArch* 4.1.1). Through Moses' ministry a certain part of humankind began to be liberated from the devil's kingdom of sin and death, and the cleansing of sins began to be ushered in (*ComRm* 5.1). He calls Moses' law a spiritual law and a life-giving Spirit for those who understand it spiritually (*ComRm* 6.9). But even if the laws of Moses are observed only literally, they do not generate sin. On the contrary, this is the effect of the law of the members (Rom. 7:23), which Origen sharply distinguishes from the law of Moses (*ComMt* 12.4; *ComRm* 6.7).

In spite of Origen's positive assessment of Israel's legislator and institutions, for Origen the true meaning of the laws of Moses is found not in the shadows or in the literal observance of these precepts, which is impossible, but in the reality of the spiritual understanding. The coming of Christ has removed the veil that had concealed the spiritual nature of these laws (*PArch* 4.1.6; *HomLev* 4.7). Origen constantly stresses that a carnal understanding of the law is not pleasing to God, whereas a spiritual understanding is (*HomGn* 7; *HomEx* 7).

Law and Gospel

Protestant scholars have rightly noted how drastically Origen's understanding of law differs from that of the magisterial

Reformers (who indeed generally detested Origen). They attribute this to Origen's "taming" (fundamentally misunderstanding) Paul. It is true that Origen is extremely averse to admitting any relation between the law of Moses and sin, other than a prohibitive one. He constantly defends the law from ultimate blame and views it as beneficial. Origen conceives the difference between law and gospel to be that of the difference between imperfect and perfect religion, between shadow and reality (Heb. 10:1), in terms of salvation history and the transformation of the individual. His hermeneutical principle derives robustly from Matthew 5:17: "I have not come to abolish [the law] but to fulfill [it]" (*ComMt* 10.12). He interprets Romans 10:4 as a restatement of the same idea: Christ is the "End" of the law (*telos nomou*) means that Christ is the perfection of the law, that is, the one who enables the believer to fulfill the righteousness that the law demands (*ComRm* 2.13; 3.11; 8.2). Such an interpretation is clearly at odds with the views of Marcion and Luther, for whom the contradiction between law and gospel was that of judgment and mercy; the role of law being to convince humankind of sin and bring all under God's judgment, whereas redemption comes by God's grace and forgiveness.

The Cultic Law and the Fall of the Temple

Unique to Origen among the Christian Fathers is the emphasis that the impossibility of the literal observance of the law of Moses is linked to the historical destruction of Jerusalem (*HomLev* 10.1; *HomJos* 2; *ComGa* 2; *ComRm* 6.7.12). This calamity confirms the inauguration of the spiritual observation of the law, which took place through the incarnation and was divinely superintended in order to remove what could have been a potent obstacle to conversion to Christianity: namely, that admiration for the splendors of true worship in the Jerusalem temple might have hindered spiritual souls from realizing that truth that has now replaced the type. Origen's interpretation, of course, implies a very positive assessment of the original temple cult (*HomNum* 23.1; *CCels* 5.44).

In *ComRm* 2.13 Origen discusses the arguments of Judaizing Christians who think that the law of Moses should still be followed. Origen distinguishes between the transitional period, during and shortly after the lifetime of Jesus, and the subsequent termination of the temple worship. He admits that Peter and Paul did observe the law in some cases: food laws, circumcision, and sacrifices of purification (as attested in Acts). In doing so, Origen says, they exemplified the principle of "becoming a Jew to win Jews" (1 Cor. 9:20–22), for they knew that certain excessively devoted Jews were not going to come to Christ if these observances were denied them. Therefore Paul grants that literal circumcision still has value for them if they keep the law. But that value does not apply to Gentiles or to any who think that some justification is to be obtained from this literal observance. Moreover, after the destruction of the temple, the transitional period has come to an end, since it is no longer possible to offer sacrifices or to celebrate the Passover, which was permitted in only one place. Therefore, arguing about circumcision has become pointless (*CCels* 2.1–2; *HomJr* 14.13).

The Abiding Relevance of the Law

Following Philo and Clement, Origen identifies the essence of the law of Moses with natural law, which he calls the law of God (*CCels* 1.4–5; 5.37) (see **Law of Nature**). Paul repudiates only the ceremonial law, in which the Jews boast, and not its moral content (*ComRm* 8.7). Interestingly, Origen thinks Paul is usually referring to natural law in his arguments throughout Romans, and not to the law of Moses (*ComRm* 3.6). Origen's stress on natural law in his *Commentary on Romans* actualizes the principle that God is not the God of the Jews only, but also of the Gentiles, for all the texts that speak of natural law apply also to Gentiles. This means that all of humanity is included in God's plan of salvation, not merely those from the circumcision (*ComRm* 6.7) (see *Judaism*). All will be judged (that is saved or condemned) through the law that one is under: angels through natural law, Gentiles through natural and civil laws, Jews through the law of Moses, and Christians through the law of Christ (*HomEz* 4.1; *ComRm* 2.8; 3.6). The law of nature is not found in humanity at all times, nor from birth, but is engrafted within us when reason arrives and teaches us to turn away from evil (*ComJn* 2.15). Thus little children alone are exempt from its precepts, and possibly the mentally incompetent (*ComRm* 3.6; 6.8).

Bammel (1991); Roukema (1988).
THOMAS P. SCHECK

Law of Nature   The origin of the concept of the law of nature (or natural law) can be found mainly in Stoic philosophy. In two of Origen's works, the *Commentary on Romans* and the *Contra Celsum*, it plays an important role. Through his influence (more so than that of the many Latin Fathers who endorsed it) the theory came to leave an abiding mark on Eastern Christian ascetical and soteriological theory.

First, in his *Commentary on Romans* Origen often refers to the law of nature in its moral sense, in order to explain the relationship between Jews and Gentiles, and to solve some exegetical problems. He quotes with approval the Stoic definition that the law is that which says what one ought to do and forbids what one ought not to do (*ComRm* 3.6.4; 3.6.9; 6.8.3; 6.9.9; *Philoc* 9.1). Rarely Origen refers to the law of nature in its physical sense, according to which, for example, a human being is bound to die (*ComRm* 4.10.1).

In his interpretation of Romans 2:14–15 Origen explains that the natural law teaches the Gentiles not to commit murder or adultery, not to steal, not to bear false witness, to honor father and mother, and perhaps even that God is one and the Creator of all things. In Origen's view these commandments agree with the laws of the Gospel, according to which one should not do to others what one does not want done to oneself (thus some manuscripts of Acts 15:20); moreover, the natural law may agree with the spiritual sense of the law of Moses, but not with its literal sense (*ComRm* 2.9.1). Origen identifies the law of nature with the "law of my mind" of Romans 7:23 (*ComRm* 5.6.3). As for the assertion of its synonymity with the essence of the Mosaic law, Origen is preceded in his assertion by Philo and **Clement of Alexandria.**

By means of his emphasis on the law of nature, Origen affirms that God revealed his law not only to the Jews but also to the Gentiles, so that, thanks to the law of nature, the latter have an inborn righteousness. Just as a Jew will be rewarded for his virtuous life on the ground on the Mosaic law, the same is true for a Gentile who was inspired by the natural law (cf. Rom. 2:10; *ComRm* 2.7.5–6; 7.19.6). However, the law of nature neither testifies to God's righteousness that is revealed in Christ (Rom. 3:21–22), nor does it incline humanity to believe that Jesus is the Christ of God (*ComRm* 3.7.8–10). In other words, Origen would not equate the law of nature with the "law of faith" that Paul spoke of in Romans 3:27, which leads to salvation (*ComRm* 3.9.8; 4.3). He rather upholds Paul's charge that both Jews and Greeks are under sin (Rom. 3:9) because of God's revelation of both the Mosaic and the natural law (*ComRm* 3.2.7–9) (see *Law*).

Furthermore, the concept of the law of nature enables Origen to interpret several Pauline texts that seem critical of the Mosaic law and could therefore be exploited by the Marcionites and gnostics to prove the defectiveness of the Old Testament. Paul's verdict that the whole world can be held accountable to God because of the law, "for through the law comes the knowledge of sin" (Rom. 3:19–20), applies, for Origen, to the natural law, since the law of Moses does not apply to the whole world (*ComRm* 3.6). Similarly, Paul's affirmation that "the law brings wrath" (Rom. 4:15) should be applied not just to the law of Moses, but rather to the "law in my members," which provokes sin (Rom. 7:23) and possibly also to the law of nature (*ComRm* 4.4). Likewise, Origen deems it impossible to interpret Romans 5:20 ("The law came in, with the result that the trespass multiplied"), with relation to the Mosaic law, since sin clearly existed (even abounded) long before Moses. In Origen's view Paul is here dealing once more with the "law in the members," which enters each human being "under the cover of the natural law" (*ComRm* 5.6.1–4). A key text in Origen's *Commentary on Romans* is Romans 7:9, where Paul says that he was once alive without the law, whereas the commandment provoked sin and death. Origen explains that Paul speaks about childhood, in which sins are not yet imputed to a human being, but that as soon as a child comes to know the commandments of the natural law, sins are imputed, so that spiritually one is said "to die" (*ComRm* 3.2.7–8; 5.1.23–26; 6.8.3–4). The advantage of this interpretation is twofold: it avoids the heretical disparagement of the law of Moses, and it is true for all people, not only for the Jews.

The second place in his corpus where the idea of natural law rises as significant is in his apology *Against Celsus*, where he deals with Celsus's criticism that the Christians withdraw from society by forming secret associations and do not respect the traditional laws. Celsus's attack betrays the rising anxiety that the growth of Christianity in the second century would destabilize the unity of the Roman Empire and deliver it to lawless barbarians (*CCels* 1.1; 8.68). In his reply Origen makes use of the Stoic distinction between the written codes of the cities and the law of nature. According to Stoic philosophy the written laws have been laid down by humans, but do not necessarily agree with the natural law, which is divine. Origen admits that Christians cannot always respect the written codes, as far as these laws prescribe things opposed to the divine law (for example, to sacrifice to demons and to worship pagan gods or to swear by the fortune of the Roman emperor). He argues, however, that Christians do live according to the law of nature that God has written in the hearts of people (Rom. 2:15) and which corresponds with the Stoic concept of "universal ideas" about morality (*CCels* 1.1; 1.4–5; 5.37; 5.40; 8.26; 8.52; 8.65; *ComRm* 5.2; 5.6). In contradistinction to Celsus's nationalism, Origen hopes and expects that humanity will be united under this one and divine law and will be united to the supreme God through his Son (*CCels* 8.72–75). This implies that Origen considers the law of nature as a tool for the Christianization and salvation of the whole world, a point of common discourse on higher realities among Hellenism, Judaism, and Christianity.

Banner (1954); Roukema (1988).
RIEMER ROUKEMA

Light In his *Commentary on John*, developing on an idea of Plato, Origen distinguishes between what he calls the "sensible," and the "true" light. Only Christ is the "true light" (following John 1:9). He is the "Sun" who shines on all creatures having reason and intellect. Through enlightenment of the mind he brings souls to salvation. Christ is the most determining and distinguished part of the material world, "the sun who makes the great day of the Lord" (*ComJn* 1.24; *HomEx* 7.8). The "solar beams" of the true light enable humans to discern things of the mind (noetic realities) that are otherwise indiscernible.

Sensible light exists as part of the nonspiritual world. It has various qualities of intensity, the sun having the highest quality, followed respectively by the moon and the stars (*ComJn* 1.24; *HomGn* 1.7). Having come into existence on the fourth day of creation, these lights "shed light on the things of the earth" (*ComJn* 1.24). As such, they are not the "true" light. Origen likens the moon and stars to the church and the disciples, which and who take on qualities of Christ's true light and provide a lesser illumination: "Thus we see the Church, the bride, to present an analogy to the moon and stars, and the disciples have a light, which is their own or borrowed from the true sun, so that they are able to illuminate those who have any spring of light in themselves" (*ComJn* 1.24).

Christ represents the true light, but this does not mean that the sensible light is false. Origen reads 1 Corinthians 4:9 ("We have become a spectacle to the world, to angels and to mortals") as Pauline testimony to a mortal world interacting with the immortal world and "being delivered from the bondage of corruption" (*ComJn* 1.24). One who receives even the sensible light and "shares in its beams will do the work of light and know of the higher sense, being illuminated by the light of the higher knowledge" (*ComJn* 1.20).

The firmament causes separation between night and day. Similarly, a spiritual division occurs within souls eager to ascend to the light. Those who come into the light are those who are "zealous that they should be called, and be made a heaven" (*HomGn* 1.5). Drawing from the Johannine writings, Origen sets out a strong dualism between light and dark. The latter can never overcome the former (John 1.5), one of the reasons Origen continued to advocate *Apokatastasis.* Those in darkness are without knowledge (*ComJn* 1.24). The evil deeds of human beings create "many darknesses" (*ComJn* 2.20). To walk in darkness is synonymous with evil. Even so, the last word of God's universal call of souls to life and salvation means that their essential natures can never wholly forget the call for them to ascend once more into the light (see *Anthropology*).

None of these many varieties of darknesses appears in God. Because Jesus was in the "likeness of the flesh of sin," he had darkness in him (*ComJn* 2.21). However, this darkness "fails to overtake" the light of Christ. Origen also refers to darkness in a good sense, in which the divine mysteries are cloaked in darkness (Ps. 18:11; Exod. 19:9,16). Such mysteries become revealed in the light of Christ to those who gain illumination (*ComJn* 2.23). This theme of the darkened veil of mysterious revelation was something his later disciple, Gregory of Nyssa, would underscore to high effect in the subsequent history of Christian mystical thought. Another disciple of the same era, Gregory Nazianzen, placed even greater stress, however, on Origen's correlation of God's revealed mysteries as a brilliant "illumination" of the soul. Between them, the two Gregories, each relying on Origen as an important source, established twin patterns of later Christian mysticism, using the images of radiant light and veiled darkness as analogies of God's self-revelation.

Bertrand (1951); McKenzie (1951); Pizziolato (2001).

JEFFREY PETTIS

Logos   The notion of Logos was predestined to play a central role in Origen's thought. The word has a wide range of meanings connected with rational thought and its expression in speech. In Hellenistic philosophy, Logos, elevated to a stable cosmic principle (*arche*), was the central mediating instance between the empirical world and the realm of ultimate reality, and at the same time the unifying bond of the cosmos and of human society. In the Hebrew Scriptures the creative divine Word, or Logos, had a semiautonomous existence (Isa. 55:11; Wis. 18:15) and became identified with Wisdom (Sir. 24:3), a personal or personified entity, whose mediating role in creation and salvation was assigned, in the Johannine prologue and the christological hymns of

Colossians and Ephesians, to Christ, the Logos made flesh. Logos had already assumed a central place among the titles of Christ in the Apologists. Irenaeus uses the term sparingly and seeks to reground it in the biblical economy, resisting speculative accounts of the divine.

Origen also resists the christological monopoly of the term *Logos* and reconnects it to some fifty other biblical titles of the Son, most of which name his saving roles toward humanity, but a few of which, such as Logos, Life, Wisdom, Truth, name his divine identity. The latter names too can have, or perhaps always have, a saving significance for us (*ComJn* 2.125–28). They name both the Son's being in his turning to God and the relation to us that springs from this. "Logos," for example, signifies God's own Word before it signifies the agent of revelation (*ComJn* 1.111; *PArch* 1.2.3). These names are called the aspects (see *Epinoiai*), since each corresponds to a particular human perspective on Christ (*HomJr* 8.2). Refusing to take the title "Logos" as a transparent, literal description of the Son, which Origen thought would entail christological modalism (*ComJn* 1.125; 151–54), he sought to grasp its intelligibility by defining its place within the ordered set of *epinoiai*. All of them name the same indivisible personal entity, thus overcoming the pullulation of syzygies and emanations erected by the Valentinian system of gnostic theory, while satisfying both the spiritual need for mediators and the speculative and exegetical curiosity that, of course, made gnosis appealing (see *Gnostics*).

Origen disciplines and revitalizes Logos theology by reanchoring it within Scripture and also by shaping a Platonistic hierarchization of mutually inherent aspects. He reconciles the biblical concerns of Irenaeus with the philosophical leanings of the Apologists, combining a phenomenology of Logos in terms of its function of revelation with a dynamic speculative grasp of its divine origin: the Logos is "God" by reason of his being "towards God" (John 1:1; *ComJn* 2.10),

though it is divine "not by participation but in essence" (*ComPs* 135:2). Because it is thus constituted, the Logos can enable creatures to become "gods" by participation (*ComJn* 2.17–20) (see *Divinization*).

Compared with Clement and even with Philo, Origen's discourse on Logos is thus more tightly organized, though still multifaceted. He carries over from them ambiguities about the ontological status of the Logos, which as mediator between God and creation exhibits both a transcendent and an immanent aspect. Though the primary role of Logos is to reveal the Father, this does not mean the Logos is a diminished and approachable form of God (as Celsus suspects and censures), for the Logos of the supreme God also shares in the "difficult" and "unapproachable" character of the very God it reveals (*CCels* 6.69). Seen from below, the Logos is one with God, above all things (*ComRm* 7.13 [PG 14.1140–41]), yet seen "from above" (in more theoretical reflection), its subordinate status in respect to the Father is stressed. Origen leaves open whether God is himself being or whether God lies beyond being and dignity and power (Plato, *Rep.* 509B) and is content to say that the Logos participates in being. He suggests, but does not strongly assert, that the Logos should be called the "essence of essences" (Origen's own coinage) and the "idea of ideas" (cf. Philo, *Opif.* 25; *Migr.* 103), or "the Beginning" (*arche*), while God the Father is beyond all these (*CCels* 6.64; *ComJn* 13.123; 19.37). He refrains from deciding an issue left unresolved in Philonic and Middle Platonist thinking and on which the Christian tradition itself had not much speculated as yet.

God is pure unity, but the Logos is a communion of plurality, the idea of ideas, the virtue of virtues (*ComJn* 1.119; *CCels* 5.39). The Logos is constituted from many ideas (*theoremata*), each of which is part of it, and embraces the principles (*logoi*) of the universe (*ComJn* 1.244; 5.5). As is usual in Middle Platonism, the Stoic terms in operation here are equivalent to the Platonic "ideas" (*PArch* 1.2.2–3). The ideas or reasons are produced by God in generating the Son (eternally). This production is imaged by Origen as the exhalation of a word from the depths of the divine mind (Ps. 45:1; *ComJn* 1.280–83), an echo of the Stoic understanding of the immanent and expressed Word (*logos endiathetos* and *prophorikos*), something that we can also see in Theophilus (*Autol.* 2.10, which also cites Ps. 45:1). Since the ideas or *logoi* are the basis of creation, one can say that the Creator is never without creatures. Origen sounds at times as if, like Philo, he is identifying the Logos with the Platonic notion of the noetic world (*kosmos noetos*) (*ComJn* 19.146–47), but elsewhere he contrasts the heavenly world with the Platonic figment (*PArch* 2.3.6). The Logos is seen as the founding dynamism of cosmic and spiritual harmony (*koinonia* or *symphonia*), as in Philo's *De confusione linguarum* (*CCels* 8.69; 72). The metaphysical theme of the communion (*koinonia*) of all rational beings in the Logos is conspicuously absent from the Johannine prologue but is certainly prominent in Origen's exegesis of it.

As in Philo, one of the functions of the Logos is to cushion God against naked contact with the debased material world. The Logos creates the world at God's behest (*ComJn* 1.110; *CCels* 2.9); he is its immediate creator while the Father is the creator-in-chief (*CCels* 6.60); he can even be seen as an instrument used by God in creation (*ComJn* 2.70–2). The "words" (*logoi*) of Christ that will not pass away (Matt. 24:35) are associated by Origen with the permanent seminal principles (*logoi*) of created things (*CCels* 5.22), which Origen even identifies with the Logos (*ComPs* Praef. [PG 12.1097]). The variations in Origen's accounts of the status of the Logos both in respect to God and in respect to creation occur within the subordinationist context that was that of mainstream ante-Nicene theology. In the later third century, Logos speculation would flounder amid incertitudes, until the Arian crisis precipitated the orthodox position enshrined in the Nicene Creed, which more or less spelled the end of "Logos" as a vibrant theological notion.

Another tension Origen inherits from his predecessors is that between the Logos as synthesis of the ideas and powers of God and the Logos as a personal being, what he calls the "second God" (*deuteros theos*) (*CCels* 5.39; *ComJn* 6.202; Philo, *QG* 2.63; Justin, *Dial.* 56.4). This tension is negotiated in Origen's original thesis of the eternal generation of the Logos (*PArch* 1.2.4; *HomJr* 9.4; *ComJn* 1.204), which is correlated with the Logos's eternal contemplation of the Father (*ComJn* 2.18; cf. Plotinus, *Enn.* 5.1.6). The name of Son is the principal name of Christ, the one identifying him as a person in relation to the Father. The other names nest within this, as it were. In the chain of *epinoiai* the title Wisdom precedes that of Logos. Their relation again suggests the Stoic concept of immanent and expressed Logos. Origen notes that God creates all things *in* Wisdom but *through* the Son (*ComJn* 2.90). Wisdom is the principle (*arche*) in which the ultimate patterns of things are contained. It is a hypostasis, a personal, wise, and living being (*animal quoddam sapiens*) (*PArch* 1.2.2), a phrase perhaps suggested by Plato's account of the cosmos as an "intelligible animal" embracing all other intellective life-forms (*noeta zoa*) (Plato, *Timaeus* 30C–D; cf. Clement of Alexandria, *Stromateis* 5.94.2), as well as by the words "the word is a living being" (*verbum animal vivens*), which he quotes from an apocryphon (*PArch* 1.2.3).

Logos, or Wisdom as communicated to the world, is a more personal name than Wisdom, especially when Origen deploys the image of the Logos as messenger (*ComJn* 1.277–78). The distinction that Wisdom has its subsistence in the Father, whence it is born (*PArch* 1.2.5), whereas Logos has its subsistence in Wisdom (*ComJn* 1.292), is not a reflection that can be pursued very far. All it means is that the Son receives his being from the Father, and that though each of the predicates of the Son names the Son when used as a subject, there is a logical subordination of one predicate to another. "Logos" presupposes "Wisdom," for example, and "Way" presupposes both titles, so that the subordinate predicate may be said to subsist in the predicate that logically mediates its subsistence in (or as) the hypostasis of the Son.

Biblical texts are given a double reading, as referring to an impersonal universal Logos (reason) and to the personal Logos. While the Logos is personalized as the sower of all good *logoi* in the soul (*ComMt* 10.2), and thus the source of all good acts (*CCels* 6.78), this image is demythologized by reduction to the idea that all *logikoi* participate in Logos (*PArch* 1.3.6); or one could say, conversely, that the metaphysical cliché is given new dynamism in Origen by the more personal and dynamic biblical image that he invokes. The personal coming of the Logos to the soul in the history of salvation (see **Atonement, Christology**) is conflated (as Justin had much earlier done with his identification of Logos and Nomos) with the universal metaphysical presence of the Logos within us as the natural law that speaks to the adult conscience (see **Law, Law of Nature**). The reference of John 15:22 shifts from one to the other (*PArch* 1.3.6; *ComJn* 1.270; *ComRm* 3.2; and cf. John 12:48 as it appears in *ComJn* 2.109–11). Universal values of truth and justice are treated as *epinoiai* of Christ in a similar to-and-fro between metaphysical and biblical registers (*PArch* 1.2.4; *HomJr* 14.3; 17.4; *HomPs* 36.2.1; *ComMt* 12.11; 24–25). A lurking ambivalence attends this treatment of the eternal Son as immanent principle of the ethical and physical cosmos; it is one that was ready to burst forth (and did so with great impact) in the later Arian and **Origenist crises**.

Letelier (1991); Pazzini (1992); Wolinski (1995).

JOSEPH S. O'LEARY

Love

Love Origen's understanding of the nature and expression of love and the vocabulary used to delineate it have been the subjects of intense study in recent years by scholars who have largely focused on Origen's reappropriation of Platonic teachings about eros, and Plotinus's later developments of Plato. Predominant in scholarly discussion have been the questions whether Origen sees the Greek terms for love (*agape* and *eros*) as synonymous; how Origen's concept of divine love differs from a Platonic conception of love as the desire to unite with beauty; and whether God, as a complete and perfect entity, experiences love in the sense of feeling bereft without, or needing to receive, love. Philo, and perhaps Ammonius Saccas (as Rist argues) helped to shape Origen's attempted synthesis of Christian and Hellenist-philosophical ideas about divine love. The uneasy marriage thus produced was subsequently to be visited by Gregory of Nyssa and Augustine. Gregory's *Homilies on the Song of Songs* greatly developed Origen's image of love as an existential "arrow" by which humanity is wounded (*ComJn* 1.32.229) and had a great resonance in later Christian tradition, as did Augustine's rhapsodic writings on love.

In studying Origen's understanding of the concept of love, one faces several semantic problems. First, the one English word "love" translates not only *eros* (which hardly ever appears in Origen's corpus) but the key theological terms *agape* (the preferred New Testament word for love) and *philanthropia* (the critical notion of the divine loving-kindness that motivates the **atonement**). Second, Origen's *Commentary* and *Homilies* on Canticle of Canticles, key primary sources for the idea, are extant only in Latin translation, which complicates the issue by adding Latin terms for love (*amor, caritas*, and *dilectio*) to the mix. In the prologue to the *Commentary,* Origen shows that he too was aware of the semantic issues: "It makes no difference, therefore, whether the Sacred Scriptures speak of love, or of charity, or of affection; except that the word 'charity' is so highly exalted that even God Himself is called Charity, as John says." *Philanthropia* is Origen's preferred term, denoting in most instances the loving-kindness of God toward humanity, regardless of humanity's response. Origen writes of love not in the standard "philosophical manner" as a basic "grasping desire" (*epithymia*), nor in the moralistic tradition, approaching it as an emotion rooted in fear or cupidity, but rather defines Christian love as an impulse that is other-oriented, disregards merit, and seeks wholeness and well-being for its object, and as such is a form of mimesis of the divine. Origen stresses that God loves equally and without merit: he loved the Egyptians as well as the Israelites.

Origen writes equally about the creation's love of God and God's love for the creation. His chosen genre shapes his treatment of the ideas. In commentary (*ComCt* 3), he presents the aspect of humanity's love for God. Here he argues that souls can never love God too much, though human loves must generally be ordered and measured to preserve their righteousness (*ComCt* 2). Origen follows the Jewish midrashic tradition in wanting to deter readers from accessing this text until they are sufficiently advanced as to understand it has no reference to "base or carnal" loves (*ComCt* Prologue 1.3). Here, as can be expected, Origen's standard use of **allegory** is heavily in evidence. The Bride's longing for the kisses of the Lover's mouth is explained as the soul's desire for the "solid and unadulterated doctrine of the Word of God Himself" (*ComCt* 1.1.5). Origen employs the Pauline image of spiritual maturity as solid food, affirming that as the nascent Christian develops, he or she is able to accommodate and digest different sorts of love (*ComCt* 1.5.8). The love of God reaches the interior of each person, through the outward senses (*ComCt* 1.4.13). Once spiritually mature, the Christian is enabled to love God with "one's whole soul, and one's whole strength, and with all one's heart" (*ComCt* 2.4.11). Thus one understanding of divine love in Origen is that of a human soul that is hungry for God's

truth: "this love with which the blessed soul is kindled and inflamed towards the Word of God" (*ComCt* Prologue 2.25).

Origen's understanding of love is that it has a "downward" as well as an ascentive force, and accordingly he speaks much of the self-emptying (*kenosis*) of divine love, demonstrated supremely by the incarnation, which makes visible an invisible love. This biblical sense he possesses of the God who "stoops down in loving kindness" is a factor that radically distinguishes Origen's approach to love from the Stoic and Platonic traditions. The kenotic act of incarnation is God's effusive *philanthropia* (*CCels* 4.17.18; 4.18.33; 1.64.17; 1.64.24). In the *Contra Celsum*, Origen is clearly exercised to refute Hellenistic philosophical presuppositions about the exclusivity and inaccessibility of divine love, and affirms instead the *philanthropia* of a universally acceptable and accepting God. He attacks the elitism of Celsus's vision of God (*CCels* 6.1.11) and states that it was

> because of his exceeding love towards man that God was able to give the educated a conception of the divine which could raise their soul from earthly things; and even so still came down to the level of the more defective capacities of ordinary men and simple women and slaves and, in general, of people who have been helped by none but by Jesus alone to live a better life, so far as they can, and to accept doctrines about God such as they had the capacity to receive. (*CCels* 7.41.26)

The kenotic nature of love incarnate is also a dominant motif in his approach to love in the *Commentary on John* (*ComJn* 6.57.294.2), where *philanthropia* is his term of choice (*ComJn* 1.20.121; 2.18.125; 2.66.166; 2.31.187). Origen's commentary on the Fourth Gospel, however, ceases before the occurrence of those radiant passages in the final discourse of Jesus in which the evangelist articulates the divine command to "love one another."

Nygren (1953); Osborne (1992, 1994); Rist (1964).

HANNAH HUNT

Marcion   See **Old Testament.**

Martyrdom   In his own life, as well
as in his thought and teachings, Origen
was immersed in the phenomenon of
martyrdom. According to Eusebius's
account, the experience of persecution
and martyrdom (of his friends, his students, his family, and eventually his own
torture) marks all the salient points of his
life. Origen's father, Leonides, was one
of "God's athletes" about whom Eusebius writes (*H.E.* 6), describing the persecution that occurred during the reign
of Septimius Severus (regnant 193–211).
There is ample evidence in Christian
writings of the period to indicate some
level of persecution of the church in several cities around the Mediterranean
during his reign. That Alexandria was
no exception is attested by Origen's
teacher Clement (*Stromateis* 2.20.125).
According to Eusebius, Origen as a child
was seized by a desire "eagerly to rush
into the struggle" of martyrdom. As the
story is told, it is only by "a heavenly
providence," acting through Origen's
mother, that he is held back, for she "hid
all of his clothes and thus brought about
the necessity that he remain home." The
wit of Eusebius or some earlier story-
teller may be evident here in using the
term "necessity" (*ananke*), which was
often used in the literature to denote the
would-be martyr's acceptance of the
divinely ordained "necessity" of immi-
nent death (and was also the common
Greek for "private parts"). In any event,
the story closes with yet another indication of childhood "eagerness" as Origen
goes on to draft, for his imprisoned
father, "a letter concerning martyrdom,"
which urges fortitude and single-mind-
edness (Eusebius, *H.E.* 6.2.3–6).

Such a letter foreshadows the fuller
composition of his *Exhortation to Martyrdom*, which was to come later. This,
famous *Exhortation* was written shortly
after the ascent of Maximin to the throne
(235–38), when Origen was resident in
Caesarea. It opens with a dedication to
"the most God-fearing Ambrose and the

most pious Protoctetus"; in the opening
Origen dwells on metaphors from Isaiah
and Paul about the development
expected in life, from breast milk to solid
food, thereby denoting that he intends his
work for "mature believers," those who
would embrace "the entire citizenship of
the Gospel" (*ExhMart* 12) and "the whole
time of our testing and temptation" (*Exh-
Mart* 11), even in "the presence of the tri-
bunals and of the naked swords drawn
against our necks" (*ExhMart* 4). Throughout his work, the familiar Platonist,
themes of the superiority of the noetic
over the corporal are present (*ExhMart* 2;
13), as are many and notable instances of
scriptural quotation, allusion, and proof-
texting. Perhaps some insight into the latter is indicated in a phrase in section
ExhMart 17: "Moreover, in the agree-
ments about religion long ago, you gave
your catechist this answer," which is followed by a biblical quotation. Even in old
age, the voice of the catechetical instructor is alive and resonant. Origen, it may
well be, in encouraging his friends to
stand up to the possibility of their own
executions, had not forgotten his own
students long before in Alexandria, who
had been delivered up to death on
account of the faith in which he had so
recently instructed them.

A sustained discussion of what scripture means by "the cup," marks the middle sections of *ExhMart* 28–30. Beginning
with the theme of reciprocity ("a saint . . .
wishes to respond to the benefits that
have overtaken him from God and . . .
searches out what he can do for the Lord
in return"), Origen quotes Psalm 116:12:
"What shall I return to the LORD for all his
bounty to me?" The next verse in that
psalm, and the next sentence from Origen's pen, includes this reply: "I will lift
up the cup of salvation and call on the
name of the LORD." Having set up this
proem, Origen then states: "Martyrdom
is customarily called the cup of salvation,
as we find in the Gospels." After a consideration of the Synoptic accounts of
Jesus' reply to the sons of Zebedee ("Are
you able to drink of the cup?" Matt.

20:22; Mark 10:38) and of Jesus' request that, if possible, the cup be removed from him (Matt. 26:39; Mark 14:36; Luke 22:42), as well as a quotation from Psalm 116:15 ("Precious in the sight of the LORD is the death of his faithful ones"), Origen concludes: "Therefore, death comes to us as precious if we are God's saints and worthy of dying not the common death, if I may call it that, but a special kind of death; Christian, religious, and holy." Such is the exalted lot of the martyr.

Those familiar with these Synoptic accounts of the cup of suffering that had been passed to Jesus will know that the Markan text includes the words, "Or be baptized with the baptism with which I am baptized." That citation leads to Origen's definition of martyrdom as a heightened form of baptism and to this statement: "Consider also whether baptism by martyrdom (just as the Savior's brought cleansing to the world), may not also serve to cleanse many" (*ExhMart* 31). That such a statement may potentially be seen to weaken the unique mediation of Jesus is not lost on Origen (*ExhMart* 35). Nonetheless he pursues the thought to its logical end and, somewhat tentatively, adopts it: "And perhaps just as we have been redeemed by the precious blood of Jesus . . . so some will be redeemed by the precious blood of the martyrs" (*ExhMart* 50). Earlier, he states as much regarding the efficacy of the martyrs' supreme act of witness for themselves: martyrdom can be a "baptism of blood" that washes away all prior sins (*ExhMart* 39). In these remarks Origen shows a lively consciousness of the common Christian attitude to the martyrs as the saints par excellence, whose blood pleads before God for the suffering saints on earth.

Throughout his *Exhortation*, references to "endurance" are found in abundance (*ExhMart* 23, 37, 44), something that is characteristic of much early Christian discourse from Paul and the earliest Gospels onward. Something that is more particular to Origen, however, is the new rhetorical tone of "eagerness" for martyrdom (*ExhMart* 39) and the confident absolutism ("Jesus will make those who are tested either martyrs or idolaters" [*ExhMart* 32]) with which he approaches the subject. Origen's great predecessor, **Clement of Alexandria**, had many reservations regarding such tendencies: "Now we too blame those who have leapt on death for they do not really belong to us. These 'athletes of dying' . . . give themselves up to a vain death" (Clement, *Stromateis* 4.4.17.1). The problem of the overzealous martyr is, however, not something Origen really wishes to encourage. He too has many assertions that Jesus himself advocated flight rather than the necessity of martyrdom (Matt. 10:23), and he warns how the would-be martyr must not rush forward in an overwhelming desire for the status of martyrdom, since "perhaps none, or only a few, will attain some special and greater flood of blessings" (*ExhMart* 14). Elsewhere he is careful to distance the church from accusations (from the likes of Celsus) that it encourages an intemperate death wish. "We [Christians] have not gone mad. We do not rush forward on our own to raise the ire of an emperor or governor, bringing on ourselves beatings, tortures and even death" (*CCels* 8.65). He knows, however, in his deeper Christian sentiment, that persecution and martyrdom are not far from the path of discipleship in a world that has lost its apprehension of justice, and he is well aware of the prevalence of this theme in the Gospels (Matt. 5:11; Luke 11:49; John 15:20).

When he himself had reached old age, Origen was imprisoned in Caesarea toward the end of the reign of Decius (249–51), and exposed to torture and other ill-treatment (Eusebius, *H.E.* 6.39.5). But his was not to be lot of the martyr "in a great theatre filled with spectators" (*ExhMart* 18). After being released from prison, the great theologian died in 254, much weakened by his treatment while incarcerated. If he had died a martyr's death, it is interesting to speculate whether his reputation and the impact of his works would have reached even greater heights than they subsequently did.

Hartmann (1958); McGuckin (1993); Weidmann (1999).

FREDERICK W. WEIDMANN

Mary In Origen's theology, Mary, the mother of Jesus, occupies an important place. Origen, indeed, can be considered as one of the most influential thinkers about Mary and her role in the history of human salvation, in the development of the Christian tradition. This emphasis Origen gives to Mary's role in God's redemptive plan follows the same generic form of reflection as we find in other Christian writers of the first four centuries who speak of Mary. Yet here, as in so many areas, Origen's insights are more profound than any of the other theologians.

Origen speaks of Mary as the virgin mother of Jesus in order to affirm the humanity and the divinity of Jesus and his salvific role in human history. This christological setting is determinative for all of Origen's comments about Mary. Thus, as did earlier writers, Origen underscores the parallel between Eve and Mary (*HomLc* 8.1; *FragmLc* 12). The fact that Jesus was born truly of a woman (*ex Maria*) and not through a woman (*per Mariam*) is critical for Origen (*HomLc* 17.4; *ComRm*, 3.10). This fact allows Origen to argue against Docetists, the followers of Marcion, and **gnostics** who wished to deny that Jesus participated in any way in corporeality. In contrast to all such views, Origen insists that the body of Christ is real and like that of all other human beings (*PArch* Praef. 4; *HomEz* 7.8; 12.4; *HomLc* 1.1). Origen presents such conclusions in the context of his teaching of the preexistence of human **souls**. At a precise moment determined by God the Father, the human soul of Christ, because of its love for its fallen spouse, the preexistent church, takes on human flesh in the womb of Mary and thus adopts the form of a slave (*HomJr*

10.7; *ComMt* 14.17; *ComJn* 20.19) (see **Christology**). The purpose of such action is to save the church and to restore it within the heavenly Jerusalem. The soul of the Son of God, mixed with his divinity, is thus far older than his birth from Mary (*ComJn* 1.32).

For Origen it is important that Mary has been overshadowed by the power of God himself and so conceived in this "divine manner." This overshadowing by the Most High that comes upon Mary is nothing other than the overshadowing of the Word, overseeing the enfleshment of the preexistent soul of Jesus (*PArch* 2.6.7; *HomCt* 2.6). Here Origen develops one of his significant themes: the birth and the growth of the Word in the soul of the individual believer. Mary can be an exemplar to the worthy believer of this indwelling and growth (*HomGn* 3.7).

Jesus' birth from the Virgin Mary also provides Origen with resources to combat those who, unlike the gnostics or Marcionites, wish to reject the divinity of Jesus. Within the environments of Hellenistic and Jewish thought were those, such as the Ebionites or Origen's Jewish opponents, who wanted to stress Jesus' humanity and refute attributions of divinity. For them, Jesus was merely a human person, at most prophetically inspired, with a singular divine mission. This Jesus was adopted by God at the time of his baptism at the Jordan. Against such views Origen emphasizes the full divinity of Jesus, and he does this especially in regard to his virgin birth from Mary. This birth discloses the uniqueness of Christ's nativity and the absolute priority of God's initiative and intervention in the process of the incarnation. Origen wishes to refute the view that Jesus is the natural son of Joseph and thus through him secures his descent from David (*HomLc* 12.1–4; *ComMt* 16.12; *ComRm* 1.5). In view of the Jewish report (preserved in the Talmud) that Jesus' birth was the result of an adulterous relation that Mary had with a certain Pantheras, a Roman soldier, Origen stressed the miraculous nature of his birth by a virgin (*CCels* 1.28–35; *ComJn* 20.16; *Fragm HomLc* 45). For Origen, only God was able to be born from a virgin, and only a virgin was able to submit to this act of placing God in the world. Origen regularly ties the virginity of Mary directly to the proof of the divinity of Jesus (*CCels* 6.73). Mary presents her body to the Lord as a living host. Jesus' origin in the flesh comes from Mary (*ComRm* 3.10; 9.1).

Closely connected with these thoughts is Origen's teaching of the perpetual virginity of Mary (*HomLc* 7.4; *ComJn* 1.4). As a perpetual virgin, Mary is the "first fruits" and the very model for Christian life (*ComMt* 10.17). Using the paradigm of the wedding of Christ with the church, Origen shows that the union of the soul with the Word is accomplished in the context of virginity (*ComCt* 2). This virginity, which Mary models, has value as it is inspired by the love of God and frees human beings for divine service. For Origen only a virgin could play this role of entire dedication to God's service, to the full.

It is not clear whether for Origen this perpetual virginity entails for Mary a virginity *in partu* (in the process of birth) (*HomLev* 8.2; *HomLc* 14.3). Yet Origen teaches without any doubt that Mary, like all believers, stands in need of redemption for her sins (*HomLc* 17). The perpetual virginity of Mary raises for Origen the question of Jesus' brothers. Origen does not hesitate to use the **apocryphal** books of the *Gospel of Peter* and the *Proto-Evangelium of James* to answer this question. The "brothers and sisters" of Jesus mentioned in the New Testament text are sons of a previous marriage of Joseph, whose first wife has died (*ComMt* 10.17). Origen probably described Mary as *theotokos*. The later historian Socrates (*H.E.* 7.32) makes this explicit claim, and it is one that is quite likely, both in terms of his background and high esteem of her. The title Theotokos is now found only in some Origenian fragments whose authenticity is open to question (*SelDt* 22 and 23;

FragmHomLc 41 and 80). The application of this title, one of the panoply of the titles of Isis, was a bold and innovative step for Origen. He is hostile to any suspicion that flesh and divinity merge in the case of the incarnation, so his adoption of this title for Mary needs to be seen in the missionary context of reapplying older pagan terms in the service of Christian proclamation.

An important aspect of Mary, as Origen understands it, is her role as an example for the Christian faithful. Mary's holiness is a result of the descent on her of the Holy Spirit and the divine Word (*HomLc* 7.2–4; *ComMt* 10.17). Origen lists Mary in the ranks of the prophets because of the presence of the Holy Spirit in her (*HomLc* 8.1). Although counted among the poor of this world (*HomLev* 8.4), Mary reveals two of the significant characteristics of Origen's spirituality: she is continually studying and meditating on Holy Scripture (*HomLc* 6.7; *HomJr* 5.13), and she exercises the apostolic function as at the time of the visitation, when filled with the Holy Spirit she announces John the Baptist's mission to him, still in his mother's womb, and conveys to him the grace of the Holy Spirit (*ComJn* 6.49; *HomLc* 7.1–3). Origen's rich and suggestive Marian theology set the terms for much of what would be developed in later patristic thought, both in the Eastern and Western churches.

Crouzel (1998); Grillmeier (1975); McGuckin (2001); Vagaggini (1942).

WILLIAM G. RUSCH

Miracles

The miracles discussed in Origen's writings are mainly those narrated in the Scriptures. Origen's interpretation of these miracles must be seen against the wider background of his view on God's continuing providence for humanity, administered through the Logos, and the role of the incarnated Logos. In the incarnation the divine power of God, the Logos, descends to reside in the earthly Jesus, manifesting itself in his life, words, deeds, his resurrection, and his miracles. Thus, his miracles must be interpreted as taking place at the intersection of the timeless with time.

Origen observes that the *Old Testament,* especially the Pentateuch and the historical books, are full of miracles. This is particularly the case with the book of Exodus, which Origen reads as a story of liberation, metaphorically prefiguring the story of salvation through Christ. The "plagues" of Egypt, representing the aberrations and vices of paganism, are defeated by Moses' stick (that is, God's law) and by the cross (*HomEx* 4.5–8). Likewise, the death of the Egyptian firstborn signifies Christ's triumph over the authors and inventors of false religion (*HomEx* 4.7). The manna is a prefiguration of Christ, bread from heaven (*HomEx* 7.4–8). The bitter water of Marah that could be drunk only after Moses had sweetened it by throwing a log into it, is compared to the bitter Jewish law that was only made sweet thanks to Christ, his teachings, and the Christian interpretation of the law (*HomEx* 7.1). Both exoduses, that of Moses through the Red Sea and that of Joshua (Jesus in the LXX) through the River Jordan, represent Christian *baptism* (*HomEx* 5.1; *HomJos* 1.4.2). And the walls of the city of Jericho that collapsed signify the "present age" that is collapsing because of the stirring sound of the proclamation of the Gospel (*HomJos* 7.1).

Miracles, especially those narrated in the New Testament, were an important issue in the debate between *Celsus* and Origen. The pagan philosopher Celsus denied the historicity of the miracles as narrated in the Christian sources. And in Jesus' life, one in obscure and inglorious circumstances (not to mention his miserable end on the cross), Celsus claimed that it was impossible to recognize the power that ought to be expected from a divine man (*CCels* 2.26.33.35; 3.24–34). In his reply to Celsus, Origen strongly defends the historicity of the New Testament miracle stories. Comparing them to the ones of the Old Testament, he asks, rhetorically, why the historicity of the ancient miracle stories is easily accepted whereas doubt is cast on those of the New Testament (*CCels* 2.54–55; 3.23–27). Moreover, Origen goes on, it would be inconceivable that so many people followed Jesus, unless he had convinced them with indisputable miracles (*CCels* 2.29.43.46). Miracles, indeed, were part of the message of Christ's life. It was not his purpose to judge but to give an inspiring example. "He intended to sow the seed of his word by miracles and by a certain divine power among the whole human race" (*CCels* 2.38). Origen also argued in defense of the historicity of particular miraculous events; such as the virgin birth (*CCels* 1.32–37), the star that appeared to the magi (*CCels* 1.58–60), the healings and other miracles of the ministry (*CCels* 1.48), and, the greatest of all, the resurrection itself (*CCels* 2.56–58; 61–64).

Christ's signs and miracles described in the New Testament, are taken by Origen as primary demonstrations of his divine power (*ComJn* 10.148) and his philanthropy (see *Love*) toward humankind (*ComMt* 10.1.23). They carry a spiritual meaning that must be discovered by reading the story against the background of the Old Testament, as well as by interpreting the event in its higher allegorical meaning. Thus the Lord's two visits to Cana (where, incidentally, he performs his first miracle) for Origen largely represent the Savior's double coming (the incarnation and the parousia of the end times) (*ComJn* 13.391–92; 13.441). Christ's healing many people suffering from physical sicknesses is interpreted by Origen as really significant of the healing of the inner sicknesses affecting the human soul (*ComMt* 13.3; *HomJr* 17.4). With regard to the healing of the nobleman's son, Origen proposes a double interpretation: a "historical" one (God's dealings with the world) and a "psychological" one (God's dealings with the individual soul). The healing of the nobleman's son is thus pictured either as the second coming of the Savior to the world for Israel's final redemption, or else it is explained as the Logos's second visitation of the soul to purge it of the residual traces of sin (*ComJn* 13.394–434). Christ's walking on the waters and his calming of the storm both prefigure his victory over death, as well as over all that threatens the church or individual souls, such as persecutions, heresy, temptations, or passions (*HomLc* 31. 4–5; *ComMt* 11.4–7; *ComJn* 6.8–10).

But Origen also senses that miracles are not limited to the period of the Old and the New Testaments. Even in the church of the second and the third centuries (and beyond), the divine Logos was and is at work. That so many people converted to Christianity in his own time and that Christianity won the day despite all oppositions it encountered are vital signs for Origen of the continuing influence exercised by the Logos (*CCels* 1.3.27; 1.26–27). Christ's *apostles* even performed greater miracles than the Lord. Whereas he did physical healings, they performed spiritual healings: "The eyes of people blind in soul are being opened, and the ears of those who were deaf to any talk about virtue eagerly hear about God and the blessed life with Him, and many too who were lame in the feet of their inner man . . . do not just leap, but now leap like a deer" (*CCels* 2. 48). So, for subsequent generations, the most important miracles worked by the Logos within the church were these spiritual healings of individual human beings. Thus Origen gives these miracles, taking place in his own time, a place within his framework of salvation-history of near cosmic proportions. Through the ongoing miracle of the life of the church Origen sees the salvific effects of the incarnation as increasingly spreading out to the entire creation through the history of humankind.

Mosetto (1986); Wiles (1960).

JOHAN LEEMANS

Moses   See **Law.**

Mysteries   Origen refers to the existence of "the mysteries" or "the mystery" (*mysterion*) in a large variety of different contexts. Etymologically the word signified that which (especially because of its sacred associations) could not properly be spoken in common speech or uttered aloud (the root *myein* means "to keep silence"). The primary signification of the term *mystery* as it is used by Origen is that of a secret or hidden wisdom, and a knowledge of a higher reality, namely, the celestial or spiritual realms. The term is used by him in reference to the pagan mystery religions and Christian rites (sacraments), as well as to aspects of Scripture, particularly the gospel, to Jesus and the many mysterious aspects (see *Epinoiai*) of his manifestation, and to the revelations given to the prophets and the apostles.

Since Christianity was sometimes associated with a secret religious formation, as suggested by *Celsus*, it was classified with other mystery religions, which were often viewed with suspicion by the Roman authorities as a danger to the social status quo. Origen emphatically denies any overt similarity between Christianity and the mystery religions. The latter he associates with sorcery, the proclamation of myths rather than the truth, and with mistaken worship of images instead of the one god (*CCels* 3.36–81). Nonetheless, he places a positive emphasis on the religious notion of mystery, not only with regard to Christian rites, but also in reference to Scripture and the gospel proclamation.

Origen understands the scriptural writings to be concerned primarily with the exposition and propagation of divine mysteries, which need to be discerned and properly understood. He believes that the mysteries, or as he often terms them "the hidden wisdom and truth," are the most important dimension of Scripture, namely, the spiritual meaning of the text (*HomLev* 5.5) (see *Allegory, Anagogical Interpretation, Typology*). Furthermore, he thinks that many of the mysteries revealed to the apostles were never recorded by them for fear of inappropriateness, as these mysteries were unutterable or perhaps had potentially harmful effects if given to the inexperienced too soon (*ComJn* 13.28). He asserts this on the basis of the Johannine and Pauline testimonies (John 21:25; 2 Cor. 12:4) that there were many "additional revelations" that they chose not to record (*ComJn* 13.27). It is noteworthy that Origen interprets these apostolic assertions, in quasi-*gnostic* fashion, to mean that they were forbidden to report certain mysteries not meant for a general readership. Similarly Origen argues that there were teachings imparted to the disciples of Jesus that were meant only "for the few," not for promulgation to the multitude of people (*ComMt* 11.4; *ComJn* 2.28). Accordingly, Origen asserts that the knowledge of some divine mysteries is a special privilege granted to the elect, the more spiritually advanced, rather than the mass of believers. This particular interpretation of the biblical texts leads Origen to conclude that the Scriptures contain only the rudiments of the religious mysteries rather than the entire profundity, and thus serve as an introductory *pro-paideusis* to these (*ComJn* 13.26–34).

Even so, despite his various speculations on the hiddenness of religious mysteries, Origen considers the divulging of divine mysteries to be the central focus of his exegetical enterprise, as well as the essence of the Christian religion. In this he follows the lead of Paul, who developed the terminology of mystery extensively (Rom. 11:25; 16:25; 1 Cor. 2:7; 1 Cor. 4:1; 1 Cor. 13:2; 14:2; 15:51; Eph. 1:9; 3:3–4) but also played on the explicit paradox of "uttering the mystery" or speaking the unspeakable (Eph. 5:32; 6:19; Col. 1:26f.). It is not the plain and the purely historical meaning of Scripture that Origen considers to be of central importance but rather the uncovering and deciphering of the deeper layers of meaning that are hidden and point to a higher order of reality. In accordance with Origen's understanding of Scrip-

ture, which he divides into various parts or levels (such as soul, body, and spirit), the divine mysteries pertain to the highest level of meaning and interpretation of the Bible: the spiritual and noetic level of insight. The main objective of every believer is to the best of his or her intellectual abilities to seek to understand the highest order of meaning of the scriptural text, which thus allows perfection.

Origen considers the gospel to be the image of the divine mysteries and a pointer to them (*ComJn* 1.7.39). Even though some of the prophets and the patriarchs were given the chance to perceive partially divine mysteries, it is the *apostles* and the disciples of Jesus who were instructed in these mysteries and were charged with their proclamation (*ComJn* 6.4). The revelation and the proclamation of the divine mysteries are not only the essence of Scripture but are also the purpose of Jesus, who is a teacher par excellence (*CCels* 3.61). Although the **Old Testament** contains symbols of higher truths (for example, the temple sacrifices are symbols of celestial mysteries [*ComJn* 6.51]), they were rarely understood as such until the advent of Jesus, who came to explain the true meaning of the Jewish *law* and render the religious mysteries comprehensible (*ComJn* 1.6) (see **Christology**). The mystery of the gospel is accordingly revealed by Jesus Christ in strictly hierarchal order: first to his elect and illumined disciples and then to all believers. So it continues to be in the process of the church's ongoing life.

Origen expounds on the fact that Jesus is not only the revealer of the divine mysteries, but he himself represents many mysteries that are not understood by all. The profound mysteries of his divinity, incarnation, passion, death, and resurrection are fully understood only by elect and illuminated believers, who comprehend the significance and true meaning of these most elevated truths (*ComJn* 6.5; 6.56; 10.35). For Origen, therefore, Jesus is not only the teacher of hidden mysteries; he is also the embodiment and pedagogical representation of many of them.

Berchman (1984); Hanson (2002); Kennedy (1913).

STAMENKA ANTONOVA

Mystical Thought

Describing the mysticism of Origen is somewhat complicated, first, by the fact that the postmedieval concept of "mysticism " is somewhat anachronistic and, second, by the fact that he does not present his mystical, or rather spiritual, theology of communion with God in any systematic form. What we can legitimately call his "mystical" insights (for Origen is certainly the "father" of Christian mystical theology) tend to emerge singly, as part of his exegesis of scriptural passages, and the overall structure of his thought becomes more apparent only from prolonged study of the commentaries and homilies. This is perhaps appropriate, since for Origen access to the divine *mysteries* themselves has been placed within *Scripture*, and it is only after assiduous and faithful *prayer*, ascetic self-discipline, and prolonged study that the *Logos* who is incarnate in Scripture begins to speak to us and begins to initiate us into those mysteries (see *Christology, Priesthood, Worship*).

It is not only *scriptural interpretation* that forms the basis for Origen's mystical thought, however. Origen was also deeply influenced by the thought of Plato in the variegated forms in which it reached him. To a Christian theologian with philosophical training, Plato's *cosmology* and *anthropology* could be seen as "sufficiently" similar to those of the Bible to allow some sort of intellectual-spiritual synthesis and reappropriation according to Christian norms. In terms of the basic dynamic of the movement of the soul to God, Origen appreciated that any such synthesis was necessarily limited by the fact that, whereas Plato sought an ascent to and participation in an indistinct "Divine," Origen's God was one who had acted personally in history, made covenants with human beings, and embraced physical existence in the life of Jesus Christ, the Word made flesh.

In Platonic cosmology, the intelligible world, the realm of ideal forms, is contrasted with the sensible world, the realm of materiality, multiplicity, passions, and concrete sense objects, which are only a pale and inferior reflection of their corresponding ideal forms. Origen developed on that to posit a constant doctrine that embodied *souls* have "no lasting city" here (Heb. 13:14) but must use their earthly experience to pierce through to the ultimate truth about earthly existence, that it is a training school for the soul's purified return to the lost contemplation of God (see *Preexistence, Fall*). But Origen is a Christian, not a Platonist who sees the world of material forms as irrelevant (see *Asceticism*), and so places an important stress on the nature of the soul's earthly experience for an authentic communion with God. Although a vast distance separates this world from heaven, Origen teaches, God has nevertheless filled it with a sort of beauty and wonder that are shadows and signs of the true wonders of heaven: "He who made all things in wisdom so created all the species of visible things upon earth that He placed in them some teaching and knowledge of things invisible and heavenly whereby the human mind might mount to spiritual understanding and seek the grounds of things in heaven" (*ComCt* 3.12). Thus the physical creation serves as an object of initial contemplation and a signpost toward the mystical ascent.

The idea of the soul's mystical ascent to a restored communion with the Logos is central to Origen's spiritual theology and can be seen to be based on his foundational *anthropology*, where he teaches the double creation of humanity. His idea is, of course, influenced by that of Plato, as it is expounded primarily in the *Phaedrus*. For Origen, the fall of preexistent souls into sensible existence was caused by their lack of attentiveness and perseverance in divine contemplation (*theoria*). This makes mystical contemplation, in Origen's understanding, a fundamentally ontological dynamism in humanity. The spiritual communion with God is nothing other than the apprehension of a creature's principle of existential stability, and thus prayer is life, as well as true vision, and ultimate communion with God.

For Origen, any possibility of regaining the presence of God can occur only through the restoration of God's image within the soul. Yet this soul, by nature created pure and meant to mirror the glory of God, cannot fulfill its function. Weighted down and enveloped by the physical mass of the human body, the mirror of the soul is pitted and darkened by the impurity of sin. Thus a turning back to God, the cleansing of his image, the reversal of the fall from his presence, must occur. The initial impulse for this does not come from human beings, however, but solely from the mercy of God. Origen's doctrine in this instance had a deep effect on Athanasius of Alexandria (*De incarnatione*) and through him into the mainstream of Alexandrian patristic theology.

Origen sees the cosmic ascent of the soul, perfectly mirrored in an individual believer's spiritual progress (which ultimately becomes a disciple's mystical ascent). First, through the grace of God the believer hears the proclamation of the gospel truth and comes to know "Christ, and him crucified." The response to this message leads to *baptism*, which is the first step in the mystical ascent. Baptism not only incorporates the individual into the body of believers, it also plants the Word in the heart of the individual and begins the process of *divinization*. In following Christ and fulfilling the moral demands of baptism, Origen teaches that the disciple begins to be more and more Christlike, even begins to share in his life and qualities (see *Epinoiai*) through a gradual process of their interiorization within the soul, as

the soul orientates itself more and more toward its God and grows in communion (*koinonia*) with him. Origen makes it clear that this is only the beginning of a long and arduous path to "perfect participation" (*methexis*) in God. Most persons, either from lack of intellectual and spiritual ability or from spiritual laziness, he complains, do not choose to undertake this journey, and remain at the level of spiritual children (*simpliciores*). They focus on the earthly Jesus of healings and miracles, and not on the eternal Word. They are passive, while for Origen the spiritual life is entirely a dynamic process of activity and growth. Their understanding of the Bible, if they choose to study it at all, is literal, while for Origen it is only the *allegorical interpretation* of Scripture that unlocks the divine mysteries hidden within it, which are only for the more spiritually acute. Thus, there is, within his overarching distinction of the simple and the more spiritual members of the church, an implicit concept of "judgment" within the idea of mystical ascent; for Origen also insists that the soul's ascent to or descent from God within its earthly life is ultimately a matter of free choice, since all have been established by God with sufficient *grace* (see *Virtue*).

The Bible not only contains hidden mysteries within its text, but its very structure models the process of spiritual growth and mystical ascent. Some books outshine others, just as the Gospels and the Pauline revelations outshine all other Scriptures so as to become the keys of their interpretation. The Song of Songs is one of the books Origen regards as integral to the revelation of the soul's path to communion with God. In the preface to the *Commentary on Song of Songs* Origen describes the Song as the culmination of a progression of canticles in the Old Testament designed by God to lead to growth in spiritual knowledge. The three books attributed to Solomon—Proverbs, Ecclesiastes, and the Song of Songs—taken together furnish a blueprint for the three stages of the mystical life. Origen calls these stages ethical (*ethike*), natural (*physike*), and intuitive (*optike*).

The first stage pertains to the purification of life and the ascetic discipline of prayer and study necessary for anyone seeking to grow in spiritual knowledge. The second stage deals with the nature of physical creation. Here a person strives to understand God's purpose in the creation of every thing, what higher reality each thing points to as an image, and the ultimate transience and inadequacy of all sensible things. The third stage, that of intuition, represents the contemplation of the highest spiritual realities: God, the Trinity, angels, things heavenly, and all other mysteries. At this stage the human soul becomes one with the divine Word, this unification being symbolized by the marital eros of the bride and bridegroom in the Song of Songs. It is significant that Origen interprets this symbolism variously as both the marriage of Christ with his church and the joining of the Word with the individual soul. Earlier theologians never applied the notion of the bridal chamber in an individual sense, but referred the "mystical marriage" only to the whole body of believers. In several aspects of his teaching he thus had a powerful impact on subsequent Christian tradition. Very soon his tripartite schema of the mystical ascent was renamed (by Evagrius) practical (*praxis*), theoretical (*theoria*), and gnostic (*gnosis*), more or less to convey exactly what Origen had meant about the soul's necessary apprenticeship from prayer to fulfill our ethical obligations, to prayer that lifts up the eyes of the soul to the greater realities that surround it, and finally to prayer that merges into the ineffable communion of love and transcends this earthly limit (literally, as the soul ascends back to God).

Origen's mysticism is christocentric, though it is more related to the Logos than to the human Jesus. But Origen, unlike the gnostics, does not devalue the humanity of Christ: "Even if we attain the most sublime and highest contemplation of the Word and of the truth, we shall not forget completely that we were introduced to him by his coming in our body" (*ComJn* 2.61). Yet focus upon the fleshly Christ he sees as belonging primarily to the earlier stages of mystical contemplation, where he "is known according to the flesh by those who do not go up to the lofty mountain of wisdom; but by the perfect he is known no longer according to the flesh, but rather is known in his divinity" (*ComMt* 12.37). Relying extensively on the image of the radiantly transfigured Jesus (Matt. 17), Origen teaches that it is on this "lofty mountain of wisdom" that the Word also transfigures those who are faithful in following him and patterning their lives after him. Through the increasing attainment of spiritual knowledge the Word, the true light, the sun of righteousness, fills believers with light and makes them capable of beholding the light of God face to face, no longer "through a mirror darkly": "For if the light of the mind that is in a disciple, and the purity of his heart shall be bright and shining, he will have this noon time within himself; and, being set as it were in the midday light through this purity of heart, he will see God" (*ComCt* 2.4). Following in the line of biblical theophanies of light, Origen here set the tone for a long-standing Christian mystical tradition that has often been called a "mysticism of light." Therein, the central imagery of the soul's ultimate communion with God is instinctively drawn in terms redolent of illumined transfiguration. Most of the leading Christian mystics of later generations (not least, his immediate successors in mystical theory, Gregory of Nazianzus and Maximus Confessor) owed him an immense debt in this regard. Even Gregory of Nyssa (also an ardent Origenian), who often conceived the ultimate communion with God in terms of obscure darkness (*gnophos*) was still dependent on Origen in much of what he had to say on the mystical life, for Origen himself is no less insistent that as the soul finds deeper and deeper union with God, it enters into a "cloud of unknowing" as it touches the very limits and incapacities of its own being, in the face of the transcendent Logos.

The Word grants illumination to the soul that follows the spiritual path but gives spiritual nourishment as well. Again Origen complains the simple believer contents himself too often with the milk of children, but to the one who has progressed in knowledge, the Word gives the flesh of the Lamb, and the bread of heaven, both through the words of Scripture and through the eucharistic meal. The Word becomes a spring of living water welling up within the soul. To this is added the wine that produces "an intoxication which is not irrational but divine," provided by the "True Vine" (*ComJn* 1.205.206). The Word transforms its substance into that which nourishes the believer, and is literally incorporated in him or her. In this way, paradoxically, the Word both gives birth to spiritual knowledge and is himself born within the believer: "And every soul, virgin and uncorrupted, which conceives by the Holy Spirit, so as to give birth to the will of the Father, is the mother of Jesus" (*FragMt* 281). This procreative imitation (*mimesis*) of the Word demands a total commitment on the part of the disciple, an identification so complete that "there is even marked upon the soul the impress of the wounds, and this is the Christ in each individual, derived from Christ the Word" (*CCels* 6.9). The sense of participation in the divine becomes so complete that the soul "yearns for the Word by day and night, and can speak of nothing else but Him, and would hear of nothing else but Him, and can think of nothing else but Him. It is pleasing to God to strike souls with such a wound as this, to pierce them with such spears and darts, and mark them with such healthgiving wounds that, since God is Love (1 Jn. 4.8), they may say of themselves: 'I too have been wounded by Love'" (*ComCt* 3.8). Thus in Origen began that long Christian association of mystical ascent with the theme of the "wounds of love"

that would so characteristically mark it through long succeeding centuries.

At the culmination of the spiritual experience, contact with the sensible world is replaced almost entirely by participation in the intelligible realm. Origen symbolizes this by the supercession of the physical senses through spiritual senses. He is the first Christian thinker to advance a doctrine of the "five spiritual senses." These spiritual senses, which are granted by the grace of God, allow the Word to be perceived directly, without intermediary, by mystical vision. He presumes the common philosophical axiom that only like understands like. So, when participation is advanced, the soul will use its intellective (noetic) senses in freedom, no longer relying on the body's five material senses to dominate its conceptions and movements. These noetic senses, in any case, are far more reliable than physical senses in apprehending divine things. For Origen the image is pressed heavily: spiritual organs consume the spiritual Bread of Life, just as pure hearts can see God in a spiritual and intellective way. In the advanced state of communion, distance between the bride and bridegroom has vanished, and so there is no longer need for speech in order to communicate intimately and completely. As Rahner has pointed out (Rahner [1979], 88), the gift of the "spiritual senses" allows to the soul, as Origen understands it then, an almost intuitive sense of the will of God, an anticipation of the feelings and desires of the Beloved.

Although Origen wavers somewhat on the point, he does not seem to believe that complete spiritual perfection is possible in this life. A faithful and purified soul can achieve a large measure of participation in the Word while it is yet enfleshed, and because the Word eternally contemplates the Father, the soul in union with the Logos can sometimes catch glimpses of the Father through its participation. Even so, it is after this life, freed from the hindrances of flesh and physical senses that the soul's contemplation will be perfected and its mystical vision made clear: "And so the rational being, growing at each successive stage, not as it grew in this life in the flesh, but increasing in mind and intelligence, advances as a mind already perfect into perfect knowledge, no longer hindered by its formal carnal senses, but developing in intellectual power, ever approaching the pure and now even gazing face to face, if I may so speak, on the causes of things. In this way it attains perfection" (*PArch* 2.11.7).

Bertrand (1951); Crouzel (1961, 1977, 1989), 121–33; Louth (1981), 52–74; Rahner (1979).

ALAN G. PADDLE

Nature   See **Law of Nature.**

Number Symbolism   The most extensive treatment of number symbolism in Origen occurs in his *Homilies on the Book of Numbers*. Origen sets out the symbolic meaning of the "stations" (the various encampments mentioned in the exodus story) of Israel's journey in the wilderness (*HomNum* 33.5–48). He likens the forty-two stations (he carefully counts them all) to the many rooms of the Father's house spoken of by Jesus (John 14:2). Each station has been prepared and leads to the Father through Christ, who is the gate. The progressive movement through the stages of the wilderness journey symbolizes the soul's liberation from the old body and a "putting on of a new body" (*HomNum.* 27.2). The rising and descending numerical order of the stations symbolizes Christ's movements in the world. Each of the forty-two stations symbolizes the step-by-step progression of one's spiritual development by "each degree of virtue" toward the perfection of the steadfast believer.

Origen gives each station a particular symbolic meaning. The first stage involves the agitation and errant life of the sojourner. Successive stages involve themes such as temptation (*HomNum* 8,

18, 29, 33, 40), Law (*HomNum* 12), vision and ecstasy (*HomNum* 15, 24, 37], travail (*HomNum* 3, 10), mastery (*HomNum* 19, 20), patience (*HomNum* 23, 26), and passage (*HomNum* 5, 31). With the last station the soul has "passed through all of the virtues and attained the very summit of perfection" (*HomNum* 27.12).

In his *Commentary on John* Origen writes specifically about the church and its numerical symbolism. The gathering of the 142,000 people of Christ spoken of in the book of Revelation have what he calls a "mystical" connection with the twelve tribes of Israel. As Gentiles, they have an "inner Jewishness" and "have not defiled themselves with women." On their foreheads are written the name of "the Lamb and his Father." Whereas the "old order" had a Levite priestly system of leadership, the new order has a rule that includes those given solely to the study of Scripture (*ComJn* 1.1–2).

In the course of his writings, Origen also speaks to the symbolism of a range of selected individual numbers (as well as personal names that carried numerical significance by virtue of their etymologies). In his discourse on Jesus' transfiguration, for example, he identifies six as the perfect number, which symbolizes the God's creation of the material world and the point in time that stands in the face of the eternal world (*ComJn* 1.3.6). Similarly, the number one hundred symbolizes fullness and perfection, and contains "the mystery of the whole rational creation" (*HomGn* 2.5). The number three symbolizes the mystery of the Trinity (*HomLev* 8.10); while number eight relates to the "mystery of the future age," the eighth day of the eschaton (*ComRm* 2.13.21; 2.12.2). Number five symbolizes the five spiritual senses of the "inner" human being that find expression in "holy deeds and religious ministries" (*HomLev* 3.7.2). The number fifty symbolizes forgiveness and remission, according to the law of remission of property and bondage spoken of in the Old Testament as given on the fiftieth year (*HomGn* 2.5). The single number, one, is what Origen calls the "total construction," there being one God of all things (*HomGn* 2.5). Number seven symbolizes the many mysteries of the law, while the number ten is a "sacred" number of perfection that symbolizes the Decalogue. By the "ten" *mysteries* are revealed, such as the truly illumined disciples who discover and follow Jesus the Messiah on the tenth hour of the day (*HomEx* 9.3; *ComJn* 1.29).

Speculation about the mystical significance of numbers and of the hidden numerical ciphers lodged in the etymological values of words in the Bible (for letters also carried numerical status) was a common part of life both in the Alexandrian schools of philosophy (it had seeped into much Middle Platonism from its Pythagorean origins) and in the rabbinic academies of Origen's day. He is, therefore, not unusual in his mysticism of numbers, but it is certainly a theme that Origen takes to heart and often develops when he is seeking, or expounding a "higher mystery" of the text. In this, his influence was pervasive and enduring in subsequent Christian exegesis, enduring through the high Middle Ages before it fell into disfavor in the Reformation era.

Berchman (1984); Cocchini (1994); Copleston (1993).

JEFFREY PETTIS

Old Testament

To appreciate Origen's view of the OT, one must understand the problem posed by the OT for Christians and the prior history of the struggle over it. According to the NT accounts, Jesus had appeared to criticize parts of the OT, suggesting that they were provisional or of human derivation (Matt. 5:31–34; 19:8; Mark 7:19; 10:4; Luke 16:16–18) and, in any case, asserting a personal authority over the Scriptures. Paul had also suggested that the *law* had only a temporary role as a pedagogue (Gal. 3:17–25). *Gnostic* interpreters (such as Ptolemy in the *Letter to Flora*) had taken this approach further and offered rules for distinguishing the divine and the human in the OT. The most radical position was that of Marcion, who had rejected the OT altogether and attributed it to the creator god (the demiurge), rather than to the Father of Jesus Christ. The prophetic and allegorical interpretation of OT texts already found in the NT (especially by Paul, as in Gal. 4:21–26; 1 Cor. 9:8–10; 10:1–11) rendered the position of Marcion impossible except through a radical editing and excision of NT texts, a project that Marcion himself carried out consistently. Origen inherited from the extensive second-century Christian polemic against the radical solutions proposed by Marcion and gnostic writers (particularly as exemplified by Irenaeus) and contributed much of his own (*PArch* 2.7.1; *ComJn* 2.171.199; *HomLev* 5.1; 13.4; *HomNum* 7.1).

The result was a Christian position that canonized the entire Old Testament (the Septuagintal version) and viewed all of it as literally inspired. Thus the "selective approach" tentatively suggested by Jesus and Paul was forgotten and the totalistic approach (as adumbrated in Matt. 5.17–19; 2 Tim. 3:16) was adopted (and through Origen widely accepted in the Christian church). This necessitated, however, extensive reinterpretation of many passages that, for various reasons, could not be accepted at face value or were in plain conflict with NT teachings. The principal instrument for such reinterpretation was the extensive application of *allegory* and *anagogical interpretation*, which were already widely employed in the interpretation of the Homeric canon of literature in non-Christian circles and were also extensively developed by *Philo of Alexandria*, a major influence on Origen. Such forms of symbolic interpretation had been explicitly rejected by Marcion.

Although Origen thought that his way of interpreting the Scriptures was a continuation of the example and rules that Paul himself had given, saying that he "taught the church which he gathered from the Gentiles how it ought to interpret the books of the Law" (*HomEx* 5.1), his attitude toward the OT was actually very different. After his conversion, Paul saw Christ as the key to interpreting the Scriptures correctly, but as a practicing Jew he had been attached to these Scriptures as an integral part of his identity, even though his culture was rooted in Hellenistic Judaism. One hundred and fifty years later Origen's situation was quite different. Fully at home in the culture of the Hellenistic world, Origen evaluated somewhat negatively the OT text on the literal level. He went so far as to say that the "divine character" of the prophetic writings and the spiritual meaning of the law of Moses were revealed only with the coming of Christ. Previously, it was not possible to bring forth convincing arguments for the inspiration of the Old Testament. For Origen, the light contained in the law of Moses, covered by a veil, was now shown forth at the coming of Christ, when the veil was removed and it became possible to have "knowledge of the goods of which the literal expression contained the shadow" (*PArch* 4.1.6). With reference to those who insist that the letter of the law is its "real" meaning, he says: "I am ashamed to say and to profess that God should have given such laws. In that case, the laws of men, for example of the Romans or of the Athenians or of the Spartans, will seem more refined and reasonable" (*HomLev* 7.5). In fact, Origen's evaluation of the text on the literal level was not far from that of Marcion.

According to Origen, Paul was aware of the possibility that the books of the Law might be incorrectly interpreted by the Gentile converts because of their lack of familiarity with this literature. "For that reason," says Origen, "[Paul] gives some examples of interpretation that we also might note similar things in other passages, lest we believe that by imitation of the text and document of the Jews we be made disciples." Disciples of

Christ are distinguished "by understanding the Law spiritually" (*HomEx* 5.1). First, we should analyze these examples and imitate the principles and procedures that Paul used in order to continue the work of interpreting the Scriptures. Second, this program of interpretation can be described as "understanding the Law spiritually." The two ideas are united in a similar phrase later in the same homily, where Origen speaks of the "seeds of spiritual understanding received from the blessed apostle Paul." When this program is carried out, then the Scriptures appear in their true light as "given for the instruction of the Church." This means, of course, that the Scriptures are, in fact, not a Jewish, but a Christian sacred book, since the Scriptures have been given "for us." This latter principle governs the whole process of spiritual interpretation for Origen (see *Scripture*).

Paul's "examples of interpretation" that Origen cites most frequently are 1 Corinthians 10:1–11; 2 Corinthians 3:6–18; Galatians 4:21–24; Hebrews 8:5; 10:1. He frequently cites the text about "removing the veil from the face of Moses" (2 Cor. 3:7–18) not only as an example of Pauline exegesis, but as virtually a program of interpretation. In commenting on Exodus 34:33–34, where the veil over the glorified face of Moses is mentioned, Origen describes Paul's interpretation as "magnificent" (*HomEx* 12.1). Then he proceeds to dwell especially on the significance of the "veil" and the question of how it can be removed. Only if one leads a life superior to the common person can one contemplate the glory on the face of Moses. Moses still speaks with glorified face, but we cannot see it because we lack sufficient zeal. The veil remains over the letter of the OT (2 Cor. 3:14). Only if one is converted to the Lord will the veil be removed (2 Cor. 3:16). Origen then explains that this veil can be interpreted to mean preoccupation with the affairs of this world, with money, the attraction of riches. To be converted to the Lord means to turn our back on all these things and dedicate our-selves to the word of God, meditating on his law day and night (Ps. 1:2). He notes that parents who want their children to receive a liberal education spare no expense to achieve this goal. The same must be done in pursuit of the under-standing of the Scriptures. As for those who do not even bother to listen to the proclamation of the Scriptures, but engage in idle conversation in the cor-ners of the church while they are being read, not only a veil but a "wall" is placed over their hearts (*HomEx* 12.1).

When the veil is taken away, how-ever, Christ is revealed as already pres-ent in the entire OT. For example, commenting on the verse of the Song of Songs in which the bridegroom is pic-tured "leaping upon the mountains, bounding over the hills" (Song 2:8), he observes that "when the veil is removed for the Bride, that is, for the Church that has turned to God, she suddenly sees Him leaping upon those mountains, that is, the books of the Law; and on the hills of the prophetical writings. . . . Turning the pages of the prophets one by one, for instance, she finds Christ springing forth from them" (*ComCt* 3.[2:8]). The "veil" as interpreted by Origen is often simply the literal historical account or the "letter." (For other examples of the use of this text, see *HomGn* 2.3; 7.1; 12.1; *HomLev* 1.1; *HomNum* 26.3.) In order to remove this veil, however, the coming of Christ was indispensable.

"Understanding the law spiritually" (Rom. 7:14) also serves as a program of interpretation for Origen. In attempting to explain the scandalous story in Gene-sis 20 in which Abraham gives his wife to Abimelech, saying that she is his sis-ter, Origen tells his listeners, somewhat polemically, that if anyone wants to understand these words literally, he should gather with the Jews rather than with the Christians. The passage that fol-lows is worth citing at length for the jux-taposition of texts and the insight that it gives into Origen's understanding of the task of biblical interpretation:

But if the hearer wishes to be a Chris-tian and a disciple of Paul, let him hear Paul saying that "the Law is spir-itual" (Rom 7.14), declaring that these words are "allegorical" (Gal 4.22–24) when the law speaks of Abraham and his wife and sons. And although no one of us can easily discover what kind of allegories these words should contain, nevertheless one ought to pray that "the veil might be removed" from his heart, "if there is anyone who tries to turn to the Lord" (2 Cor 3.16)—"for the Lord is the Spirit" (2 Cor 3.17)—that the Lord might remove the veil of the letter and uncover the light of the Spirit and we might be able to say that "beholding the glory of the Lord with open face we are transformed into the same image from glory to glory, as by the Spirit of the Lord" (2 Cor 3.18; *HomGn* 6.1)

This passage is of particular interest because it gives us in condensed form almost the entire exegetical program of Origen.

For him "spiritual" understanding of the law, or of the Scriptures in general, is equivalent to allegorical understanding. Origen uses the term *allegory* in the same sense as Paul, to denote a text in which one thing is said but another is intended. The text taken literally does have meaning, but there is also another meaning, which is generally the more important one. This discovery of the alle-gorical meaning can also be described as "removing the veil," for which interior conversion and possession of the Spirit of the Lord are required. In this case, by means of an etymology that ascribes the meaning of "virtue" to the name Sarah, Origen is able to transpose the whole story onto the moral plane and to explain away the scandalous aspects of the story (*HomGn* 6.1–2).

In a similar situation in his *Homilies on Numbers*, Origen remarks that passages from Leviticus or Numbers, read with-out an adequate explanation, can make the hearers critical of Moses. Christians begin to ask why such passages on the Jewish ritual, the observance of the

Sabbath, and suchlike are read in church, since they have nothing to do with the hearers. To avoid such scandals, says Origen, it is necessary to explain that "the Law is spiritual" (*HomNum* 7.2). Here again Origen cites 2 Corinthians 3:16 as an exhortation to be converted to the Lord so that he will take away the veil and Moses will appear to us, not as deformed but glorious and splendid.

The actual content of the "spiritual" meaning that Origen discovers hidden beneath the letter of the text generally refers both to Christ (the Logos) and to the spiritual life (the individual soul). This content is often discovered through "interpreting the Scriptures by means of the Scriptures" (see *Scripture*). Thus Origen can proclaim that "the Gospel agrees with the law" (*HomEx* 5.3). The result is that the OT text becomes a vehicle for teaching NT doctrine and a theory of the spiritual life that owes much to Hellenistic philosophy and to Philo of Alexandria. A prime example in which the two threads are skillfully woven together is Origen's *HomNum* 27.

Origen was the first Christian writer to produce commentaries on the OT on a grand scale. He saw this as cultivating the "seeds of spiritual understanding" received from Paul (*HomEx* 5.1). These were of two types: "tomes" or scholarly commentaries, and homilies. We know that he wrote commentaries on the books of the Pentateuch, Isaiah, Ezekiel, the minor prophets, Psalms, Proverbs, Ecclesiastes, Song of Songs, and Lamentations, although many of these are now lost or attested only in fragments or quotations from the Catenae. He also composed homilies (delivered in Caesarea following the continuous reading of the texts in the liturgy) on the books of the Pentateuch, Joshua, Judges, 1 Kings (1 Sam), Isaiah, Jeremiah, Ezekiel, Psalms, Job, Proverbs, Ecclesiastes, and the Song of Songs. Origen regarded some books as suitable only for those who had made progress spiritually (which was particularly true of reading the Song); it was an idea related to his concept of Scripture as

having body, soul, and spirit (see *Scripture, Mysteries*).

Dawson (1992); Heine (1997); Lienhard (2000); Torjesen (1986).
                                        MARK SHERIDAN

Origenism   See **Origenist Crises.**

Origenist Crises   Origen's precisely nuanced utterances, his careful categorizations of evidence, and his generally sophisticated method of theological inquiry left his works vulnerable to misinterpretation, oversimplification, and often wild exaggeration in misapplied contexts by his successors. Multiple factors led to increasingly complex disputes concerning Origen and orthodoxy between later parties within the church. The boundaries along which pro- and anti-Origenists situated themselves were defined by relations of political power, social connection, and interpretive training and inclination, as much as they were by a commitment to any set of coherent theological stances, let alone to "orthodoxy" in a wider conception. The contentions surrounding hermeneutical, doctrinal, and political implications of Origen and his later legacy in the church evolved out of the theological climate and issues of their own day read backward.

As was the mode in antiquity, Origen and his writings were critiqued according to the doctrinal standards of the contemporary era, rather than those of Origen's own day. Since he was so often a pioneer of foundational Christian positions, his statements on Christology, Trinity, souls, and suchlike often seemed unacceptably "divergent" in relation to the standards of later orthodoxy; and he was judged for it, not commended for his original insights.

There were two major crises regarding the heritage of his thought and its abiding significance for wider Christianity. Both have come to be known (and thus frequently merged in an unhelpful synthesis) as Origenism. One took place at the waning of the fifth century, the second during the sixth. There had been other, earlier periods of controversy over Origen and his legacy (beginning in his own lifetime) that caused expressions of hostility to break out in several places. Methodius of Olympus was an early critic, and so too were Peter of Alexandria and Eustathius of Antioch; and the work of Gregory of Nazianzus in the mid-fourth century on the *Philocalia* project (a positively motivated gathering of the "unobjectionable" passages of Origen on hermeneutics) also suggests a conscious effort on the part of his admirers to offset the signs of a gathering climate of resistance to his undoubted (and extensive) fame. Palestine, from the time of Origen's death through the fourth century, had been a center of the defense of Origen's legacy, centered, of course, in the Schola of Caesarea, where his memory was most valued. Pamphilus and other guardians of the Palestinian Library, not least Eusebius, were among the leading defenders of the cause. The account of Origen's life and work in Eusebius's *H.E.* (6), itself partly based upon Pamphilus's *Apology for Origen*, has to be understood as a carefully crafted *apologia* of defense, which thus renders many of its statements suspect. It was unarguable that the Arian crisis of the fourth century had damaged Origen's name, at least by association of many of his christological ideas with the leading members of the Homoian party. The later Origenist crises can be seen, to an extent, as continuing exercises of damage-limitation after the impact of the defeat of Arianism, even though many of the leading Nicene theologians (such as Athanasius, Gregory of Nazianzus, and Gregory of Nyssa) were themselves deeply indebted to the Alexandrian. The last Origenist crisis culminated in Emperor Justinian's two very damaging juridical and synodical condemnations of Origen, along with his major later interpreters, Evagrius Ponticus and Didymus the Blind. From that crushing blow, Origen's reputation took a long time to recover (in scholarly terms, not

until recent years), although his legacy had already been safely "digested" into the theological macrostructure of Christianity in general (through his biblical philosophy) and Byzantine religious thought in particular (through numerous "orthodox" translators of his intent, such as the Cappadocians, Maximus Confessor, and Dionysius the Areopagite (see *Disciples of Origen*).

If we turn our attention to the two major Origenist crises, that of the turn of the fifth century is by far the better documented. The major sources include the letters and other writings of Epiphanius of Salamis, Theophilus of Alexandria, Rufinus, and Jerome; the works of the fifth-century historians Sozomen, Socrates, and Palladius; and, to a lesser extent, the anonymous Coptic *Life of Apa Aphou*. The loci and events of the later sixth-century crisis are known largely from the writings of Cyril of Scythopolis, particularly his *Life of St. Sabas*, and from the synodical records associated with Justinian's administration.

The fourth-century Origenist crisis blew up at a significant period, concomitant with the first flourishing of Palestinian monasticism. The controversy reflected both uncertainty and dissent within monastic circles surrounding issues of literal biblical readings and asceticism, not least the relationship to the body and sexuality. The first stirrings of controversy began with the work of Epiphanius of Salamis, whose quest to root out and expose all heretical teachings produced the *Ancoratus* (375) and the *Panarion* (376). Epiphanius started to make a list of several of Origen's "heretical" claims, especially the subordination of the Son to the Father, and he launched a general attack on his "excessive" allegorical hermeneutic technique. Epiphanius was especially concerned with Origen's allegorizing in terms of his doctrines of creation and resurrection (see *Anthropology, Resurrection*). However, he also took issue with the Alexandrian thinker's speculations, which he had said were to be interpreted "speculatively, as exercises," rather than "dogmatically"; this included his speculation on whether Adam had ever "lost the image of God." Epiphanius sought a condemnation from John, bishop of Jerusalem, but was refused. John was not ready to begin making up posthumous retroactive condemnations, and in any case recognized Epiphanius as a troublemaker from a long way off.

In 393, a petition for Origen's censure circulated through the Palestinian monasteries, advanced by a monk named Atarbius. The petition was rejected outright by Rufinus when it was brought to him at his monastery on the Mount of Olives. At Bethlehem, Rufinus's longtime friend Jerome, who was a former student of Origen's writings (and who remained ever deeply indebted to him), saw that the wind was changing and moved to the opposite pole of opinion concerning Origen, accepting the petition to condemn him. Thus began a long and bitter resentment between the former friends, Jerome and Rufinus, grinding around the issue of Origen's legacy to the church.

In 394, Epiphanius wrote to John of Jerusalem to persuade the bishop that Origen's work denigrated human sexual reproduction, a damning accusation that cast him in the light of a heretical encratite. The contents of this letter mark an intersection between "Origenism" and the church's conflicted relationship to the ascetical movement during this era (see *Asceticism*). The scholarly John of Jerusalem, the senior bishop presiding over the Palestinian monasteries, was unmoved and continued to support Origen. By 395, Jerome had allied himself with Epiphanius against the defenders of Origen's teaching. Jerome undertook a plea to John of Jerusalem to have Origen condemned, but he too was met with rejection. Epiphanius, now adopting the role of itinerant witch-finder, accused John of being an Origenist deviant, and began to preach publicly against him (even in John's own churches), successfully persuading Jer-

ome to break communion with him. Epiphanius went so far as to ordain Jerome's brother Paulinianus in defiance of John's authority, in order to gain a species of ecclesiastical autonomy for his monastery. The conflict thus erupted into a fully fledged battle, with John, Rufinus, and several others defending Origen's legacy over against Jerome, Epiphanius, and their allies, who condemned it as heretical. Hopelessly intermingled in all of the arguments were the central "canonical" issues of episcopal jurisdiction over the ascetic communities of Palestine.

After leaving Bethlehem and returning to Rome, Rufinus published a Latin translation of Origen's *First Principles*, in which he made sarcastic reference to Jerome's former studies on Origen. Jerome had been trained at one stage at the feet of the Origenist ascetic Didymus the Blind. Angered by Rufinus' publication, and recognizing the threat posed to his own reputation by being associated with heresy, Jerome responded by putting forth his own translation of the *First Principles* in Latin. This translation was intended to be more literal and to highlight the potentially heretical and speculative aspects of Origen's texts (and incidentally to denounce Rufinus as a poor scholar).

By 399, the controversy had reached Egypt. Bishop Theophilus of Alexandria had been drawn in to act in a reconciliatory capacity, negotiating a truce between Rufinus and John, on the one hand, and Jerome, on the other. Theophilus himself was well disposed toward Origen, having studied his writings. He was himself working to overcome the theological and political problem posed by a segment of the Egyptian monastic population to whom he referred as the "simple ones" or illiterates, who were possessed of an understanding of God that was too literal and "anthropomorphizing" to be orthodox. Theophilus had an initial sympathy with John; at the same time, however, he was struggling to gain control over the monks of the communities in Nitria, who were recalcitrant and resisted the power of the Alexandrian see. These Nitrian monks were largely Origenists. In his *Festal Letter* of 399, Theophilus addressed the incorporeality of God and denounced "anthropomorphic" prayer. In response to the *Letter*, a large gathering of "simple" monks rioted in the city, protesting the condemnation of their tradition of prayer. Theophilus made an abrupt volte-face and chimed in against Origen and those teachings associated with him. In 400, he convoked a synod at Alexandria to demand the condemnation of Origen (and Origenists by implication). He persuaded Pope Anastasius I to sign the letter of the Council, in which the list of offenses targeted primarily those teachings associated with Evagrius Ponticus, the spiritual hero of the Nitrian monks (whom Theophilus has always treated with respect while he lived), rather than the writings of Origen himself. So began an association of Origen, Origenism, and monastic traditions derived from Evagrius, which would run on into the sixth-century Origenistic crisis.

In 402, Theophilus expelled Origenist monks from the monasteries of Egypt and exiled the most influential disciples of Evagrius, the so-called "Tall Brothers" who then fled to Constantinople to seek asylum under John Chrysostom. Theophilus made use of the fact that Chrysostom harbored the Origenist monks to orchestrate his downfall at the scandalous Synod of the Oak, and thus removed a rival to the preeminence of his own see. Having secured his power over Nitria and cowed the international episcopate by the manner in which he had orchestrated Chrysostom's downfall at the capital, Theophilus pacified the "anthropomorphite" monks and resumed his scholarly persona by reestablishing contact with some of the leading Origenist ascetics in Egypt. Thus the first Origenistic crisis faded away, though with the issues largely unresolved, as is evinced by the eruption of many of them again in the sixth century.

The second major Origenist crisis also started in Palestine, this time during the sixth century, when the monastic communities of Byzantine Palestine were at their height. It was a furor that was first located in the regions of Gaza and the desert regions between Jerusalem and the Dead Sea. For this controversy we do not have access to so many historical accounts. However, careful study of the available texts (primarily that of Cyril of Scythopolis) has led to the opinion that, at heart, it was a conflict over intellectual freedom and its place within monastic life (and monasticism's relation to ecclesiastical authority), rather than a real battle over specific doctrinal issues. Most of the Origenist ideas that were in question at this time were actually rooted in the teachings of Evagrius Ponticus. His ascetical theories of prayer were being read and argued over, it would seem, rather than the text of Origen himself.

There was a broad fault line in the sixth-century monastic communities between those who prioritized the ascetical endeavor (fasting, labors, vigils) and those who sought "imageless prayer" (Evagrian speculations, the life of the mind, the freedom of noetic prayer). Among Origen's ascetic admirers were certain Palestinian monks who extrapolated Origen's speculations concerning the preexistence of souls to conclude that the human spiritual intellect (*nous*), both at the beginning of its existence and again at the end of its spiritual ascent to God, was and would be equal to Christ. These were dubbed by their opponents the Isochristoi (those who would assume equality with Christ). An opposing monastic circle of Origenists laid stress on the Origenian theory of the soul of Jesus (see *Christology, Preexistence, Souls*), as the firstborn of the whole choir of souls destined to ascend to God, and the supreme Nous. These were called (again by their opponents) the Protoktistoi (the "First-Createds"). The Protoktistoi were the more "moderate" group of Origenians, who wished merely to assert Christ's role as "leader of many brethren." Tension mounted between the two groups, both of which accused one another, and were accused by others, of questionable orthodoxy or outright heresy. The Protoktistoi were accused of affirming and elevating a "created soul" (of Jesus) into the Trinity as a fourth person of the Godhead. The Isocharistoi were largely seen as scandalously reducing Christ to the ranks of the created souls. Christologically, the Protoktistoi fell more or less within the traditions of the Antiochene school, whereas the Isochristoi were sympathetic to the Alexandrian tradition.

The Protoktistoi appealed to the emperor against the Isochristoi, through the agency of the papal Apocrisarius, Pelagius, and in 543 the latter presented a compilation of documents for the attention of the Emperor Justinian, including the *Letter to Menas* (or *Liber adversus Origenem*) with an appendix comprised of selections from Origen's *PArch* and several anathemata attached. The domestic synod, the patriarch's standing synod at the capital, agreed that there was a case against the teachings, and the petition for censure was passed on for signature to the pope and the Eastern patriarchs. This, the first act in what would be revisited at the Council of 553, was aimed at the person and teaching of Origen himself, seen as the culprit of the present disturbances caused by the Isochristoi in the monasteries. The estimate of Origen here is often far from accurate.

The problem was not resolved by the time the Fifth Ecumenical Council assembled at Constantinople in 553. In the early days of that council, when Pope Vigilius was still refusing to take part, even though held as a hostage by the emperor, it has been thought (Diekamp) that the imperial bureau reissued an open letter denouncing Origen and the Isochristoi to the gathered bishops. This letter set an agenda, insofar as it was the first draft of the fifteen anathemata that appeared later in the acts of the council,

but it was not part of the official conciliar acts themselves. It more or less repeated the point of the edict of 543: Origen is condemned because he is the leader of the Isochristoi. Objectionable texts are cited; these turn out to be those of Evagrius Ponticus.

After opening the Council of 553, without Vigilius's cooperation, Justinian presented to the bishops the central issue of the *Three Chapters* (a general attack on Antiochene Christology, which had been resisting the Cyrilline christological standard that had been in the ascendancy since the Council of Ephesus in 431). There were additional anathemata drawn up to condemn the christological deviancy of the *Three Chapters*, and here in the eleventh anathema one again finds the name of Origen listed (quite anachronistically) as a christological heretic. However, the same list of heretics that appears in the conciliar anathemata forms the content of Justinian's edict (the *Homonoia*) which had been issued from the imperial chancery as the first draft of those anathemata. In the *Homonoia* (the prior text) Origen's name does not appear at all, making it at least possible that the name of the third-century theologian had been inserted into the conciliar acts retrospectively. When Vigilius, considerably later, reluctantly agreed to sign the conciliar condemnations that he had refused to attend in person, it is again noticeable that the name of Origen does not explicitly figure in his version of the anathemata texts. It is clear enough, from all this confusion, that Origen was condemned at the council mainly as a figure who synopsized the sixth-century Isochristoi, who themselves were predominantly following Evagrian themes and speculations. The conciliar "condemnation," however ill targeted, nevertheless had the immediate effect of devastating Origen's text tradition and its reception for later Christian ages.

The influence of Origenist (or rather Evagrian) epistemology and mysticism in the Palestinian desert primarily was manifested as a struggle for influence and intellectual autonomy within monastic circles, but it assumed a newer and harder definition when called onto the conciliar floor as a matter of "heresy." It is difficult to discover the real beliefs and practices of these monks, because all our sources (including Cyril of Scythopolis) were very hostile to them and present them anachronistically, in the light of the Nestorian and Neo-Chalcedonian christological controversies of a much later date. The story of this struggle is chiefly recounted from the perspective of the anti-Origenists in Cyril's *Life of St. Sabas*, in which the hero-saint confronts the rise within his community of a group of "crypto-Origenists" who break with his founder's authority and set up the New Lavra in opposition to him.

Di Berardino (1992), 623–24 (article "Origenism," by Crouzel); Clark (1992); Crouzel (1999); Daley (1995); Diekamp (1899); Hombergen (2001); Ledegang (1999); Prinzivalli (1999).

E. M. HARDING

Paul the Apostle Origen's theology, preaching, and teaching are deeply influenced by Pauline terminology and theology. This influence increased during the last twenty years of Origen's life (which can be seen easily in *CCels*), probably because of a longer time of engaged scientific and spiritual work on the Pauline letters, especially through the composition of his commentaries on Philemon, Ephesians, Philippians, and Colossians (sometime after 233), his *Homilies on 1 Corinthians* (around 240), his *Commentary on Romans* (244), and a greater number of lost homilies and commentaries (e.g., *ComGa* and *ComTt*). In *HomJos* 7.1, "14 of his epistles" are listed as commented on by Origen, although it is unclear whether the translator (in this case Rufinus) has altered the numbering (cf. Eusebius, *H.E.* 6.25.11–14 and *EpistAfr* 14).

Origen thus had a special relation to Paul, whom he called "a holy, apostolic and blessed man" (*Fragm1Co* 13), "the greatest apostle" (*HomNum* 3.3), a "divine man" (*theios aner: PArch* 4.2.6), the "perfect witness" (*idoneus testis: HomNum* 36.6), or "a marvellous witness, confident of the heavenly mysteries" (*ComCt* 2). He is not only an admired apostle and interpreter of Scripture, but also a model for Origen himself, an example for the best way to perfection. Paul in his letters offers a model for the soul's ascent (*anagoge*) from the visible to the invisible things (*PArch* 4.4.10; *HomGn* 1.2). With his ascent he is a shining example, "a spectacle" for Christians (1 Cor. 4:9; *Fragm1Co* 20). Therefore he also is a help for Origen personally, who says: "I would not ascend there, if not Paul had gone ahead" (*HomNum* 3.3). Origen's "Paulinism" is expressed not so much through a number of dogmatic sentences, but rather through a chain of relations: first, the relation that Paul proclaims between Christ and himself; second, the relation that Origen perceives between Paul and himself; and third, the relation that Origen would like to establish between Christ, Paul, and his readers. In his letters Paul is not only a perfect teacher but also a sensible therapist of the human soul (*Fragm1Co* 31; "steward of God's mysteries," 1 Cor. 4:1). He restricts his preaching according to the mental and spiritual capacity of his hearers (*CCels* 2.66; *ComRm* 8.6; *Fragm1Co* 12; *ComJn* 1.7.43). Nevertheless Origen takes note of the great difficulties involved in the interpretation of Paul's letters, largely he thinks because of the multiple sense of terms often used within them, and because of the very simple style of the apostle (*CCels* 3.20; *ComRm* 5.20; *ComJn* 5; Eusebius, *H.E.* 6.25.7; *Philoc* 9.3).

A sign of Origen's deep familiarity with the Pauline epistles is his concept of a development that takes place in Paul's thought, and that Origen first drew attention to, long in advance of modern scientific theories of literary development (but with slight chronological differences from modern interpreters). In the prologue to his *Commentary on Romans,* Origen explains that there was a development during Paul's life, which can be seen because of its traces in his letters. Origen thinks that during his writing of 1 Corinthians Paul was making great progress in regard to his own perfection (*ComRm* Praef.), while in his letter to the Philippians he was indicating "that I . . . have [not] already reached the goal" (Phil. 3:12). Through the intermediate stage of 2 Corinthians Paul reached that fuller standard of perfection which is manifested in his Epistle to the Romans, which Origen supports by the citation of Romans 8:38 (*ComRm* Praef.). Origen ranked Ephesians as the pinnacle of the maturity witnessed in the Pauline epistles (*CCels* 3.19–20). Origen understands Paul's perfection to be rooted in the unity of the apostle with Christ, based on his mimesis of the Lord (*Fragm1Co* 17; cf. 1 Cor. 11:1). Because of this union, Paul was able to comprehend the mystery of God, to achieve the ultimate goal of all theological teachers, which is the "deeper sense" of the Scriptures. This is also the main reason for his apostolic dignity (*ComRm* 6.9), which Origen defends against the anti-Pauline currents in some areas of the early church (e.g., in some Jewish-Christian groups: *CCels* 5.65 and *HomJr* 19.12). To be a Christian, therefore, means to be a disciple of Paul and to hear Paul's sayings (*HomGn* 6.1).

In Paul's letters Origen found the principles of his own exegesis, as well as concrete interpretations, which he adopted in his commentaries and homilies. In his passages on hermeneutics in *On First Principles,* Origen uses Paul as his primary basis for his model of a threefold sense of Holy Scripture (*PArch* 4.2.6). Christians have "received from the blessed apostle Paul" "the seeds of spiritual understanding of scripture" (*HomEx* 5.1), he says. In his teaching the apostle delivered the rules of interpretation of the law, the differentiation

between literal and spiritual meaning of the text, and offered options to understand the text's mystical sense. In the homilies Paul therefore is the chief witness, which Origen uses to testify to his own policy for the interpretation of Scripture. Or as he puts it: "The issue of the unleavened bread is already explained by the apostle. What I offer is not my own interpretation" (*HomJr* 14.16).

Origen endeavored to understand Paul in the framework of the whole Bible (especially of the Old Testament) in an inclusively "Canonical reading." There is for him a narrow relation between Paul's teaching and the "treasure of law and prophets" in the Old Testament (*ComRm* 3.8). Against Marcion (cf. also *HomLc* 25.5) Origen emphasized the continuity between Israel and the church: "In the whole text of the epistle Paul has expressed how the pinnacle of religious insight was translated from Jews to Gentiles, from the circumcision to the faith, from the letter to the spirit, from the shadow to the truth" (*ComRm* 9.1). But there is another dimension of translation for Origen, and that concerns the translation of faith to contemporary Christians, through careful reading and interpretation of the Scriptures and through the guiding of the Holy Spirit.

Origen is convinced that Paul is "a teacher of the Church" and that to differ from Paul is to "aid the enemies of Christ" (*HomEx* 5.1). There has been an ongoing debate in Western Europe since the time of the Reformation as to whether Origen really understood the main theological point of Paul's letter to the Romans, which many interpreters have tended to locate in the doctrine of justification and the theology of the cross. But such a critique has often too summarily dismissed Origen's profound immersion in the Pauline texts and the holistically Pauline character of his preaching and teaching. Far from being an irrelevant anachronism, his special perspective on Paul could well serve as a stimulation to deepen the traditional Western understandings of what "Paulinism" actually amounts to.

Bammel (1995); Cocchini (1992a, 1992b); Dassmann (1986); Heine (2002); Heither (1990); Layton (1996); Wiles (1967).

CHRISTOPH MARKSCHIES

Philo of Alexandria   Origen had extensive contact with *Judaism* during his lifetime, especially after he moved from Alexandria to Caesarea, but an earlier period of Judaism was also important for him. In Alexandria and other Greek-speaking centers, from the third century B.C. onward, a form of Judaism developed that read the Bible in the Greek version of the Septuagint and basically wrote and thought in the Greek language. Modern scholars have named it Hellenistic Judaism. Its most important representative is the exegete and philosopher Philo, who lived in Alexandria from 15 B.C. to A.D. 50.

Philo was a member of a wealthy and influential Jewish Alexandrian family. At an early age he was attracted to the achievements of Hellenic culture, as well as to the religious tradition of his ancestors. He received a thorough training in Greek philosophy, which he decided to use in service of the cause of his people. His numerous writings, most of which are extant, are devoted mainly to the exposition of Scripture and the Jewish law. Philo is a fervent defender of the allegorical interpretation of the Bible (see *Allegory, Anagogical Interpretation, Old Testament*), which allows him to locate philosophical themes in the heart of the scriptural text. Other Hellenistic-Jewish writers were less sophisticated than Philo, but they all stand in a tradition that is influenced by the dominant Greek culture.

In the Origenian corpus as we have it today, there are three direct references to Philo and his writings. At *CCels* 4.51 he cites Celsus's attack on allegorical interpretations of the Scriptures and responds,

He appears by this to mean the works of Philo or even of writers still earlier such as the writings of Aristoboulus [a second-cent. B.C. Hellenistic-Jewish writer from Alexandria]. But I hazard the guess that Celsus has not read the books, for I think that in many places they are so successful that even Greek philosophers would have been won over by what they say. Not only do they have an attractive style, but they also discuss ideas and doctrines, making use of the myths (as Celsus regards them) in the scriptures.

Further on in the same work (*CCels* 6.21) Origen refers to Jacob's dream of angels ascending and descending on a ladder reaching to heaven. Perhaps, he argues, Moses was hinting at the truths of the Platonic doctrine of the spheres of the planets or at yet more profound doctrines. He then adds, "Philo also composed a book about this ladder, which is worthy of intelligent study by those who wish to find the truth." This is a reference to Philo's treatise *On Dreams*, in which he commented extensively upon the story of Jacob's ladder. A third direct reference to Philo is found in Origen's exegesis of Matthew 19:12 in *ComMt* 15.3, where Origen remarks, "And Philo, who enjoys a high reputation among intelligent people for many subjects discussed in his treatises on the Law of Moses, remarks (in his book entitled *On that the worse is accustomed to attack the better*) that it would be better to be eunuchized than to rage after sexual intercourse." Here Origen makes a general reference to Philo's commentaries and then goes on to name one and cite a brief section from it (*Quod deterius* 176). The contents of the passage are striking, not least because it refers to the act of castration that, at least according to Eusebius (*H.E.* 6.8), Origen perpetrated on himself in his younger years.

Although Origen names Philo only three times, it is certain that he knew and had studied his works very carefully.

Recent research has shown that on at least twenty occasions he refers to Philo when he speaks of earlier exegetes by means of anonymous phrases such as "one of our predecessors" or "some (exegetes) before us." For example, when commenting on Herod's birthday as mentioned in Matthew 14:6, Origen castigates those who revel in their birthdays and recalls a Philonic text that he had once read (*De ebrietate* 208): "Indeed one of our predecessors has observed that the birthday of Pharaoh is recorded in Genesis and recounts that it is the wicked man who, being in love with the affairs of birth and becoming, celebrates his birthday. But we, taking our cue from that interpreter, discover that nowhere in the scriptures is a birthday celebrated by a righteous person." Most likely Origen does not feel the need to name Philo explicitly, because he regards him as standing in a long line of inspired exegesis, which he can draw on when writing his own commentaries.

These "cited" passages, however, are only the tip of the iceberg when we consider all those texts of Origen in which influence of Philo's writings and thought can be discerned. Editors have identified more than four hundred such passages, of which about one hundred involve repetition. Some involve certain dependency, similar to those passages cited above. Others reveal shared themes that make Philonic influence very probable, but not certain beyond doubt. Yet others reveal similarities that make a relationship possible but no more than that. In some cases, however, Origen may be drawing on a more general tradition that is shared by him and Philo. This is the case for a large number of etymologies of Hebrew names found in both authors. Jerome (CCL 72.1.59) informs us of a statement by Origen that Philo had published a book of Hebrew names that he himself used. The assertion on the Philonic authorship of the work was almost certainly mistaken, but shows us Origen's recognition that the etymological interpretation of scriptural names stands in an Alexandrian tradition.

What, then, did Origen learn from his extensive reading of Philo? The Philonic legacy in his work can be divided into two major areas. The first is the practice of biblical exposition. When Origen expounds Scripture, and especially the books of Moses in the Pentateuch, he habitually takes over themes that are found in Philo. This starts with the interpretation of the creation of the world and of humankind, and the fall of the first humans into sin (see *Cosmology, Fall, Anthropology*). Unfortunately most of the *Commentary on Genesis* is lost, but the remaining fragments suggest heavy use of Philonic themes. Other Pentateuchal themes interpreted in a Philonic manner are the paradise of virtues, Noah and the flood, the story of Isaac, Moses and the exodus of Israel from the realm of the corporeal (Egypt). In his reading of the story of Hagar and Sarah, Origen opts for Philo's interpretation even in preference to that of Paul in Galatians. For his method of allegorical exegesis, Origen is strongly indebted to Philo. The basic technique of reading philosophical, psychological, and spiritual ideas into biblical stories and names derives from the Alexandrian tradition, which in turn has taken it over from Greek interpretations of Homer and the myths. Origen doubtless applies it more broadly than Philo because his Bible is wider in scope. As noted above in the case of Pharaoh's birthday, Origen can use allegorical themes to establish links between the New Testament and its *Old Testament* background.

The second major area in which Origen draws on Philo is for philosophical and theological themes. Origen agrees with Philo that Platonism is the philosophical system most conducive to the exposition of scriptural thought. Just like Philo, he is convinced that its basic tenets of the divisions between the intelligible realm and the corporeal realm and between true being and derivative being are found in the Bible itself. Origen follows Philo in emphasizing that God is "not like a man" (cf. Num. 23:19). This means he is not subject to change or to any form of passion or feeling. All talk of God's joy or sorrow is meant figuratively. Origen's anticorporeal stance seems even stronger than Philo's. There are, however, a few texts in which Origen speaks of God's "sympathy" with humankind in sending his Son. In one of these he cites Deuteronomy 1:31, which is parallel to the text of Deuteronomy 8:5, used by Philo to show that in some respects God can indeed be "like a human being." Just as Philo did, Origen attaches great importance to the biblical doctrine that human beings are created "according to the Logos," which means they are not the direct *image of God*, but first, images of his Logos. For Origen, however, the Logos is identified with both the preexistent Christ and the historical person of Jesus, a doctrine that Philo would not have understood (see *Christology*).

It is plain that a strict division between exegetical and philosophical—theological indebtedness to Philo cannot be maintained, because allegorical interpretations often include philosophical components, frequently with ethical connotations. An important example is the antithesis between the evil and the good person, the latter moving through practice to perfection. These are derived from the nexus of Stoic ethics and its notion of moral progress. At the same time philosophical and theological themes are most often related to biblical themes. Just like that of Philo, Origen's thought is seldom purely systematic. A marked exception is his great and controversial work *First Principles*. Although Philo enunciates five "greatest doctrines" at the end of his work on creation (*De opificio mundi* 170–72), he never wrote a systematic theology. It should also be noted that a significant number of themes that Origen takes over from Philo are more spiritual than theological in nature, such as the importance of thanksgiving and the role of sacrifice, the nature of sin and repentance, and the remarkable conception of "sober drunk-

enness," which describes the joy felt by the pious soul in experiencing of the presence of the divine.

Detailed analysis of Origen's specific debts to Philo has proved that he was acquainted with at least half of the writings of Philo that are extant. These works belong exclusively to the exegetical part of Philo's oeuvre, especially the *Allegorical Commentary* and the *Questions on Genesis and Exodus*. Philo's philosophical and apologetic treatises are not directly used by Origen. Later exegetes in the Antiochene tradition, such as Theodore of Mopsuestia and the Syriac fathers, recognized this acquaintance and evaluated it negatively. They sharply criticized Origen for taking over the method of allegorical exegesis from Philo and adopting an insufficiently critical stance toward his Platonism. From another perspective, however, there is every reason to be grateful for this development. Study of the textual transmission of the Philonic corpus suggests that it was the presence of these works in the library of the Schola of Caesarea that enabled them to be preserved for posterity. It is almost certain that they found their way into the library because Origen had taken a complete set of them from Alexandria when he moved to Caesarea in mid-career. It must be concluded, therefore, that Origen is directly and personally responsible for the fact that we can still read Philo's writings today. Were it not for his interest in Hellenistic Judaism, we would know very little about this fascinating form of Jewish thought.

Van den Hoek (2000, 2002); Runia (1993), 157–83; Runia (1996), 476–95.

DAVID T. RUNIA

Philosophy Philosophy, invented and developed by the Greeks, was a dominant intellectual force in the Greco-Roman world in which early Christianity originated and into which Origen was born. The only mention of philosophy in the New Testament is negative. In

Colossians 2:8 we read: "See to it that no one takes you captive through philosophy and empty deceit, according to human tradition, according to the elemental spirits of the universe, and not according to Christ." In the *Contra Celsum* (see *Celsus*) Origen cites this text explicitly (*CCels* Praef. 5), and his comments on it are illuminating. He introduces it by stating that "Paul perceived that there are impressive doctrines which are convincing to most people, but which present as truth what is untrue." The text of Colossians is then cited, and Origen continues: "Seeing that there was some greatness apparent in the theories of the wisdom of the cosmos, he said that the theories of the philosophers were 'according to the elements of the cosmos.' But no intelligent person would say that this was the case for Celsus." The context is polemical, doubtless, but gives us valuable insight into Origen's view of Greek philosophy. He is not enthusiastic about it. It cannot compete with the truth of Scripture and the gospel. And yet Origen recognizes that it has some value, and indeed even "some greatness."

Origen came into contact with philosophy early in his life, as he grew up in the metropolis of Alexandria. Eusebius (*H.E.* 6.1) cites a controversial passage from the philosopher Porphyry that states that he studied with Ammonius, who later also became the teacher of Plotinus. There is no need to be skeptical about this information, but the Christian Origen probably cannot be identified with the fellow student with whom Plotinus made a pact not to divulge the doctrines of their teacher (Porphyry, *Vita Plotini* 3). Porphyry also tells us that Origen "was always consorting with Plato" and was also familiar with Platonist and Stoic authors. Even without this information it is plain from Origen's writings that he had undergone a thorough immersion in Greek philosophy. His writings are a valuable source of information about the philosophical tradi-

tion. He had studied the writings of Plato and Chrysippus carefully and also knew well the handbook literature derived from them. He stands in the Alexandrian tradition of **Philo** and **Clement of Alexandria,** both of whom knew Greek philosophy very well. In two respects he stands closer to Philo than to Clement. He was not converted from Platonism but grew up in a Christian home (just as Philo was always a Jew); and like Philo his writings are mainly commentaries, in which he uses philosophy for exegetical purposes. Origen does not flaunt his knowledge in the way that Clement does in his *Stromateis.* The great exception is the *Contra Celsum,* in which he refutes the second-century writer's work *The True Doctrine* section by section, revealing his impressive knowledge of Greek philosophy in the process.

For Origen, philosophy is the exercise of the reason that is inherent in all human beings. The ancient doctrine (*logos*) going back to the beginnings of humankind was developed by the Greeks in an impressive way. But Origen cannot agree that Greek philosophy furnishes the "true doctrine" (Gk. "logos of truth"), as Celsus claimed. There are certainly true doctrines to be found in Plato, but only because Plato saw something of the truth. Philosophy is by no means indispensable for the acceptance of the Christian faith. Otherwise Jesus would certainly not have chosen simple fishermen to be his apostles (*CCels* 1.62). Origen is aware that philosophy is an elitist enterprise. The appeal of the Christian faith is much broader. The most important consequence of the Christian faith is the regenerated life that it fosters. Philosophers, especially the Stoics, advocate a noble life, free from passion and petty-mindedness (*sophrosyne*). Christianity has reached a much wider audience with a similar message, successfully advocating the ethical life.

The great value of philosophy for the Christian, as Origen sees it, is as an instrument when studying the Scriptures. Philosophy can be used to gain a deeper understanding of the underlying meaning of the revealed sacred texts and the creed that the apostles left to the church. Logic and dialectic can be used to test theological arguments but also have their use in defending the faith against unwarranted attacks. Natural philosophy (see *Law of Nature*) can help the Christian understand the world of creation (see *Cosmology*). Ethics can illuminate issues that arise when people choose their way of life and interact socially. Origen's own command of philosophical issues relevant to a theological context emerges most clearly in his treatise *On First Principles*, that unique work in his oeuvre where he attempts to develop a rational theology from the starting point of the articles of the Christian faith. The value that Origen attached to philosophy can also be gauged from his own practice in the school he established in Caesarea. His pupil Gregory Thaumaturgus records how

he praised the lovers of philosophy with many great and suitable laudations, declaring that the only people who lead a life truly worthy of reasonable creatures are those who aim at living an upright life, and who seek to know first of all themselves, what kind of persons they are, and then the things that are truly good, which one should strive after, and then the things that are really evil, from which one ought to flee. . . . He further asserted that there no genuine piety towards the Lord of all could be found in the person who despised this gift of philosophy, a gift which human beings alone of all the creatures on earth have been deemed honorable and worthy enough to possess. (*Gregory's Letter of Thanksgiving to Origen* [*Panegyric*] 6)

The Socratic theme of "knowing oneself" and the Platonic theme of philosophy as a divine gift to humankind can be clearly recognized. Philosophy is described here above all as an ideal, but the instruction in the school also

involved reading the Greek philosophers themselves. Gregory continues: "Origen considered it right for us to study philosophy in such a way that we read with utmost diligence all that has been written, both by the philosophers and the poets of old, rejecting nothing and repudiating nothing, except only what had been written by the atheists . . . who deny the existence of God or providence" (*Panegyric* 13).

The allegorical interpretations that Origen gives of *Old Testament* passages also yield insight into his views on the role of philosophy. Like other church fathers he cites Exodus 12:36, in which the children of Israel on leaving Egypt despoil the Egyptians of their treasures, taking the text to mean that Christians can make use of the valuable parts of pagan culture, and especially philosophy, in order to construct the new tabernacle of God, that is, to develop the true philosophy of Christianity (*Philoc* 13). Deuteronomy 21:10–21, the text in which a warrior who captures a beautiful woman is instructed to shave her head and cut her nails, is taken to mean that if the Christian should find anything among his enemies that is wisely or eruditely said, all that is dead or useless should be purified and trimmed away before use (*HomLev* 7.6). The text of the Song of Songs 6:8–9: "There are sixty queens and eighty concubines, and maidens without number, but my dove, my perfect one, is one alone" was not fulfilled in the person of Solomon. The works of the philosophers, Origen argues, present a confusing multiplicity, not to be compared with the unique teaching of Christian truth (*HomNum* 20.3). The relations between Abimelech, king of the Philistines, and Isaac in Genesis 26 are sometimes cordial and sometimes hostile. For Origen, Abimelech represents the philosophers and sages of the world, who through the study of philosophy have managed to comprehend much of the truth. Isaac, however, symbolizes the Logos of God contained in the law. Philosophy is neither wholly contrary to the law nor in full agreement with it. Origen expands this point at some length:

> Many philosophers write that there is one God, who created all things. In this they agree with the divine Law. Some have also added that God both made and rules all things through his Logos. In this they write what is in agreement not only with the Law, but also with the Gospel. In both Ethics and almost the whole of Natural philosophy their views are the same as ours. But the latter disagrees with us when it maintains that matter is coeternal with God. It also disagrees when it denies that God takes heed of mortal affairs and limits providence to the realm above the moon. They disagree with us when they make the lives of those who are born depend on the movements of the stars. They disagree when they say that this world is eternal and will never have an end. (*HomGn* 14.3)

This text coheres well with Origen's own attitude to the various philosophical schools. The hedonism and nonteleological atomism of Epicurus place his philosophy entirely beyond the pale, as far as Origen is concerned. He agrees with the teleology of Stoic physics but attacks their materialism, this pantheism, and the determinism of their cyclical cosmo-biology. He fully accepts their conception of natural law and "common notions" of God and good and evil. The austere Stoic ethic emphasizing rational choice and freedom from passion is also deeply appealing to Origen. But ultimately human action must be based on love of God and divine grace. Origen is also attracted to arguments used in the Stoic theodicy. His attitude toward Aristotelianism is fairly distant. He knows Aristotelian logic well but recognizes the dangers of dialectical hairsplitting. Both the limitations on the action of providence and the doctrines of the eternity of the world and the fifth element are roundly rejected.

Like other early Christians, Origen regards Plato as the greatest of the Greek philosophers, even though he condemns him for not fully abandoning polytheism. Much of the Platonic worldview Origen takes for granted, most notably the division of reality into an intelligible or spiritual realm and a physical realm. Origen's conception of God as a divine mind, unchangeable and impassible, not subject to time or space, fully transcending the world of physical reality that he created, is strongly influenced by contemporary Platonist interpretations of the Platonic dialogues. His thought is more theocentric, however, and influenced by the way that Philo and Clement before him wedded Platonism to biblical conceptions. For this reason one reads little about the Platonic "Ideas" in Origen, but much more about the *Logos* and the *Holy Spirit.* There are also Platonic doctrines that Origen firmly rejects, such as the view the cosmos was made out of preexistent matter and will never come to an end. For Origen souls are not ungenerated and eternal, but created by God from the beginning. He disagrees strongly with Plato's doctrine of the transmigration of souls. Yet his own doctrine of the *fall* of the *souls* by free choice and their possible ultimate return to God (see *Apokatastasis*) shows structural similarities to the metaphysics of conversion and return as it was developed in Neoplatonism through the philosophy of Plotinus.

Origen's attitude to Greek philosophy is complex and perhaps not wholly coherent. He knows philosophy very well and is indebted to both its methods and some of its doctrines. He agrees that it can be useful but is wary of its charms. Yet in the eyes of later church leaders Origen was not critical enough in his attitude. They may be accused of too narrow a view of orthodoxy and a failure to recognize the strength of his devotion to Scripture and Christian learning. Nevertheless it seems true that he himself did not realize the extent to which Platonism had entered the very marrow of his thought. As Henry Chadwick has eloquently argued, Origen's fate is a classic illustration of "the perennial issue" of the relation between Christian thought and classical culture.

Chadwick (1984), 95–123; Crouzel (1989), 156–63; Dorival (1992); Van Winden (1997), 257–68.

DAVID T. RUNIA

Prayer   Although in Origen's writings there is but one short treatise dedicated specifically to prayer (*De oratione*, or *Peri Euches*), numerous remarks about the subject, and indeed texts of his own composed prayers, are scattered throughout most of his other works. His treatises often begin and conclude with invocation-like formulae centering upon the names of *God, Logos,* or Christ (*PArch* 1.1; *CCels* 8.1; *PEuch* 2.1; *HomGn* 15; *ComJn* 20.1.1). The idea of prayer was clearly important to him and is closely and organically related to his other major theological ideas, such as *Christology, Trinity* and *scriptural interpretation.* In the last, for example, the divine sense of the Scriptures is attainable for an interpreter-theologian only, as Origen sees it, as a result of assiduous personal prayer. He recommends this truth to his pupil Gregory: "But you sir, my son, first and foremost attend to the reading of the Holy Scriptures. Attend to them carefully. Seek rightly, and with unwavering faith in God, for the mind of the divine letters, that is hidden from the majority. Do not be content simply with knowing and seeking; for most essential is prayer for the understanding of divine things" (*EpistGreg*).

His general approach in the *PEuch* is dictated by philosophical and scriptural premises. While other Christian theologians had already written on prayer (e.g., Tertullian, *De oratione*, which Origen may have consulted) no others before him had ever composed a formal commentary on the Lord's Prayer. Therein he proved immensely influential and was the originator of a distinguished Christian literary and spiritual tradition, counting among its exponents such as Gregory of Nyssa,

Ambrose of Milan, Cyril of Jerusalem, John Chrysostom, and Maximus Confessor. His commentary on the Lord's Prayer probably emanates from his exercise of priestly office in Caesarea, where the instruction of catechumens in the central forms and rites of Christianity was a basic part of the Lenten catechetical instructions. The general thrust of Origen's thought about prayer is that it is a means of obtaining God's *grace* and favor, and as such is conducive to the soul's spiritual perfection and the attainment of the goal of human life, which is "to become like God" (*CCels.* 8.17).

In the beginning of the *PEuch* (chap. 5) Origen is concerned to address the issue of how prayer for particular things can be reconciled with the sense that all reality is under God's providential and stable guidance. Just as it would be foolish, he says, to pray for the sun to rise each morning (since this is governed by fixed *providence*), so would it also be foolish to ask God for specific things, since God may have already fixed his will in regard to each soul's earthly life and condition? Origen here wishes to attack those who are of the opinion that prayer effects nothing, identifying the group that holds such views as those who "do away with all sense perception and practise neither Baptism nor the Eucharist" (*PEuch* 5.1). This is, most likely, a reference to certain *gnostic* factions who, adhering to a strictly determinist position, condemned Christian acts of asceticism and worship and denied the efficacy of sacraments.

Origen defends the importance of prayer, distinguishing God's providence from his foresight, and allowing that the overarching providence of God can actually be influenced by human prayer, since God can foresee the prayer of individuals from ages before and takes it into consideration in establishing his economy of spiritual care. Origen's chief motive in all this, to rebut fatalistic determinism, underscores his recurrent and fundamental belief in the importance of the freedom of will as a coagentive force (not a contrary dynamic) in the all-embracing providence of God; and Origen thus makes an important theological step forward by suggesting the idea of human synergy with God in the shaping of human destiny through prayer. Origen asserts that "our wills are free and consequently subject to commendation or condemnation" (*PEuch* 6.2). It is the basic human freedom to pray or not to pray that gives sense to the phrase "Lead us not into temptation" within the Lord's Prayer (*PEuch* 29.5ff.). While the purpose of temptations is to make manifest "what was in your heart" (Deut. 8:2), it is nonetheless fitting and necessary for a person to pray that God does not finally abandon one: "to the desires of his heart unto uncleanness" (*PEuch* 29.16; cf. Rom. 1:24–26).

Origen spends a considerable amount of time in the treatise considering "how one ought to pray." For him it matters a great deal that a disciple should pray correctly. There is, then, a need for purification before coming to stand before God. The preeminence of the spiritual over the physical in Origen's thought is manifested in his insistence here that purification ought to be essentially a spiritual phenomenon: the putting off of anger and the forgiving of those that have offended against us (*PEuch* 8.1). *Peri Euches* 9.3 mentions forgiveness as the "greatest of perfections" and a prerequisite for prayer. Origen also insists on the importance for prayer of the place, and the time, and the posture of the body. The body is the very expression of the soul's attitude to prayer and far from insignificant in the matter of the rising of the soul back to spiritual perfection (see *Asceticism*). Following Paul in 1 Thessalonians 5:17, Origen insists upon praying "without ceasing," stressing that the life of the saint ought to be one continuous prayer (*PEuch* 12.2). He understands this injunction in the sense of joining prayer to good works, for "virtuous works form part of prayer" (*PEuch* 12.2). He is also much concerned with the question, "To whom should one pray?" In the *Peri Euches* Origen states categorically that we "must never pray to anything generated, not even to Christ" (*PEuch* 15.1) and that it is a "sin of ignorance" to pray to Christ (*idiotiken hamartian*) (*PEuch* 16.1). In his later works, however, Origen seems to have changed this view and certainly allows prayer to be addressed directly to Christ (*CCels* 8.26; *HomEx* 13.3). In fact, he often addresses invocations of his own to the divine Christ. In the treatise he points out, however, that Christ himself is the one who teaches us to pray to the Father and not to himself, because, as the high priest and mediator between God and man, Christ prays "with man and on behalf of man" (*PEuch* 10.2). This theology of Christ's high **priesthood** is fully scriptural and enables Origen to assert that the Father-Son relationship between God and humanity has become definitive and unalterable with the advent of the Savior (*PEuch* 22.1). In the age of the later Arian crisis, this aspect of Origen's **Christology** raised the ire of many Nicenes against him, seeming as it did to emphasize his view of the subordination of the Son of God, and to separate him from the Deity. In its original context, however, Origen's Christology is here revolving around biblical ideas (especially from Hebrews) about the mediating high priesthood of the Son. Origen thus comprehends "prayer to the Father alone" not as a reduction of the status of the Logos of God, but rather as an affirmation of his divine status, since no created being can approach the unapproachable Godhead in prayer, except through the mediation of that Logos who created the cosmos on behalf of his Father. Origen's theology of prayer, in short, grew out of the twin stimuli of his antignostic agenda, and his position as a priest in the ongoing liturgical life of the church. It was a seminally important aspect of his work and laid the basis for a close connection between mystical and ascetical themes in the later monastic movement.

Bertrand (1992); Perrone (1993); Quasten (1975), 69; Sheerin (1988).

JULIA KONSTANTINOVSKY

Preaching A major part of Origen's activity as a Christian presbyter-theologian was preaching, a responsibility he took with the utmost seriousness. Often Origen is considered primarily as a biblical scholar or a systematic theologian, but he was clearly also an effective preacher, and many aspects of his exegetical theology can be best understood in the light of a preacher's pedagogical mind-set. Expounding Scripture as the word of God before a congregation was one of Origen's major tasks as he saw it. This is certainly true in the later part of his life. This activity fitted very closely with his view of the Bible as the center of Christian life and faith. His passion to study, mediate, and analyze the scriptural text, which was for him one of the characteristics of his spirituality (*HomLc* 6.7; *HomJr* 5.13), flowed over into his preaching. Origen's preaching is also important for church historians since so very little evidence of Christian homilies exists before his time. In various states of completion, 279 homilies of Origen survive today. Most of them are available only in Latin translations, although some complete Greek texts and fragments do exist (see p. 28, "The Scholarly Works of Origen: Homilies"). Apart from his biblical preaching, it is known that Origen also delivered sermons on Pascha, and on peace, fasting, and monogamy.

The dating of these sermons is open to some question. Some authorities believe that the homilies on Luke date from 233 or 234 and all the other texts are from after 245. This view would agree with the witness of Eusebius of Caesarea (*H.E.* 6.36). Others reject this opinion and believe that all the sermons fall within the years 239 and 242. In either case, all the sermons are to be placed in the period of Origen's residence in Caesarea after his departure from Alexandria, and when he exercised the role and office of a presbyter in the liturgical life of the church.

Origen's sermons on the Old Testament appear usually to be based on a section of text, or pericope, some two or three chapters in length. His Lukan homilies, however, discuss only about ten verses of the Gospel at a time. This may well reflect the practice of the Caesarean church to read the Old Testament and the Gospels in a single cycle of three years.

The range of subjects in his sermons is considerable. Origen deals with the theme of providence and the problem of evil (*HomJr* 6.2; 12.11). He has several sermons "against the Jews" (*HomJr* 4.3; 12.30), following an unfortunate apologetic tradition that was already well established in his own day (see *Judaism*). He also warned of certain heretics such as Marcion, Valentinus, and Basilides (*HomJr* 1.16; 9.1; 10.5; 5.8) (see *Gnostics*). Origen addresses certain topics of Christian doctrine such as the Trinity (*HomJr* 15.6; 9.4) and the incarnation (*HomLc* 7.7) (see **Holy Spirit, Christology, Trinitarianism**). He gives attention to various aspects of *eschatology* (*HomJr* 20.3; *HomLev* 8.3–4; *HomLc* 14.3). He describes the Christian life (*HomLev* 9.7; *HomNum* 27.1). In his general portrayal of Christian conduct, Origen the preacher avoids moralism. Rather, he stresses that his audience should flee from all kinds of sins and nourish their Christian life in the Holy Scriptures (*HomJr* 20.3; *HomLev* 9.7).

As a preacher, Origen understood his role to be that of a teacher, a Didaskalos. Yet this role was more than that of simply teaching. The teacher was meant to convert disciples, to move them, to provoke repentance and the change of conduct (*HomJr* 5.13; 20.6). Origen's view of a preacher reflects certain parallels with the understanding of the role of the philosopher in his day.

Within Origen's homilies there are numerous hints about his audience and himself. He complains about the lack of attention given to his preaching (*HomGn* 10.1; 11.3). Members of the congregation leave before the sermon (*HomEx* 12.2). His congregation is composed of simple believers, including catechumens, and those of higher education and more advanced in the faith (*HomJos* 4.1; *HomLev* 1.4). Often the people are inattentive

(*HomEx* 13.3). He complains about Christians who attend church services only on festival days (*HomGn* 10.3). Origen was humble about himself as a preacher (*HomEx* 9.2). He could be spontaneous, preaching on a specific text or subject at a moment's notice (*Hom1Sam* 28.1). References to his own personal thoughts or feelings can be detected (*HomJr* 4.3; 20.8).

Origen's preaching was shaped by Hebraic and Hellenic influences. Both had given to him a profound knowledge of biblical texts and a deep appreciation for every word in a text. No word is placed in a text accidentally. Every specific word has a particular meaning, and the preacher must struggle with that word to discover its significance (*HomGn* 16.3; *HomLev* 6.6) (see **Old Testament, Scriptural Interpretation**). This meaning may indeed be manifold, for Origen the preacher is consistent with Origen the biblical commentator, who sees various dimensions within the biblical text. On various occasions Origen spoke of the body, soul, and spirit of Scripture (*PArch* 4.2.4) or of the historical, mystical, and allegorical meanings of Scripture (*HomGn* 2.1) or even the letter, spirit, and moral point in Scripture (*HomGn* 11.3). Such insights informed Origen as he struggled with the whole of the Bible, and not just favorite texts. Such a hermeneutic method was not always well received by his audience when he preached (*HomGn* 12.4; *HomLev* 1. 1).

Unlike his biblical commentaries, Origen's sermons were determined by the structure of the liturgy, his congregation's span of attention, and their ability to comprehend his message. He strove to make his message direct, simple, and often spontaneous, while trying to be deeply rooted in the biblical text. For such efforts he must certainly be regarded as one of the most impressive homilists in the history of the church.

Brilioth (1965); Lienhard (1989); Nautin (1977).

WILLIAM G. RUSCH

Preexistence   Origen refers to the preexistence of intelligences (*noes*) or rational minds, which were not coeternal with God but existed before the material, bodily world. Initially, each intelligence contemplated God through individual free choice and as part of a unified group, without differentiation in rank before God (*PArch* 1–2; *ComJn* 1.92). As intelligences turned from their contemplation (which he explains in terms of "satiety"), they "cooled down" (*PArch* 2.8.3.) and became souls (*psychai*) that could enter into the material, bodily world and fall varying distances from God (see **Anthropology, Cosmology, Fall, Souls**).

Origen stresses that intelligences were "creatures," not coeternal with God. Because the divinity is always active, Origen argues, it has eternally generated the pattern that creation models. Thus, a Platonic world of ideas or forms of creation may be coeternal with God (*PArch* 1.4.3–5; 2.3.6), but all creatures, including intelligences, are images of it and, far from being an eternal cosmos (as Plato had envisaged), actually came into being (*PArch* 2.1.4 and 4.4.6–7).

Intelligences contemplated God by free choice, because that faculty is innate to the divine image imprinted upon them at creation (*ExhMart* 12; *HomGn* 1.13). Still, they did not enjoy full likeness with God, which was the *proprium* of the Logos (see **Image of God, Logos**). Defining love as the desire for what one does not fully possess (as in Plato's *Symposium*), Origen stresses that God established perfect likeness to God as the goal that all intelligences must obtain for themselves through contemplating and perfectly imitating God through the mediation of the divine Logos (*PArch* 2.11; 3.6.1; 4.4). The preexistent state, then, was not the *telos*, or fulfillment, of intelligences, but a framework within which they could progress toward fullness of love and perfect knowledge of and union with God. This notion of eventual progress toward perfect enjoyment of God recalls Irenaeus's theology (see **Apokatastasis, Atonement**).

Intelligences

Intelligences, however, exercised free choice to cease contemplating God and thus entered into the less exalted ontological condition of being souls. Scholars often refer to the dominant notion of "the preexistence of souls" in Origen's thought, but, technically, preexistent "intelligences" became souls only upon falling from their contemplation of God. Intelligences, then, effectively experienced two creation processes: first, God created them after eternal divine forms, and, second, when they cooled and became souls, God created the material bodies and sensible world into which they fell (*HomGn* 1.13; *ComJn* 1.95).

Bostock (1987); Daley (1991); Harl (1966).
ELIZABETH A. DIVELY LAURO

Priesthood Origen of Alexandria was ordained priest in Caesarea by Bishop Theoctistus in the early 230s. According to Eusebius, Origen's ordination provoked a final crisis in his relationship with his bishop, Demetrius of Alexandria, and the Alexandrian theologian moved permanently to Caesarea, reestablishing an extensive ministry of commenting and preaching on the Scriptures in this lively imperial city on the eastern seaboard of the Mediterranean. Given these circumstances, one might hope for richer insights than we find into the concept of Christian priesthood understood as an institutional office, that is, its spiritual and theological significance in the life of the third-century church. Origen gives us little to go on in this area.

On the other hand, Origen's reflections on priesthood are inextricably linked with central concerns in his *Christology*, ecclesiology, and ascetic theology (see *Church, Asceticism, Anthropology*). His focus on Christology and the wider notion of the elect church does not imply any negativity toward the clerical structures of the third-century church (see *Bishops*). Rather, it illumines the nature and bias of Origen's thought. Framing

Origen's theology of the priesthood is the spiritual world of the cosmic drama of salvation, in which Christ the high priest stands before the Father on behalf of all. The unique high priest, "according to the order of Melchizedek" (Ps. 110:4) stands alone as victim and priest in the garments of his blood (the "bloodied vesture" is taken by Origen as a symbol of the incarnation), while the priestly congregation of the church waits outside of the Holy of Holies in prayerful attentiveness and penance.

Origen's theological reflections on the priesthood can be found in scattered comments throughout his writings, notably in his commentaries on the Gospels, but these reflections occur with special density in the sixteen *Homilies on Leviticus* preached around 240 in Caesarea. The New Testament texts that are foundational for his theological reflections on priesthood are Hebrews, in which he explores the relationship between the Levitical priesthood and the priesthood of Christ, and 1 Peter, where Origen is constantly drawn to comment on the priestly nature of the community of faith (referring especially to 1 Pet. 2:5; 2:9a): "Like living stones, let yourselves be built into a spiritual house, to be a holy priesthood, to offer spiritual sacrifices acceptable to God through Jesus Christ. . . . you are a chosen race, a royal priesthood, a holy nation." Origen's *Commentary on Hebrews* has been lost, but there remain more than a thousand citations of the letter in his extant works, numerous instances of which can be found in the *Homilies on Leviticus*.

There are six distinct but interrelated categories of Origen's considerations of priesthood: the priesthood of the Logos; the Levitical priesthood; the priesthood of Christ; the priesthood of the baptized; the heavenly priesthood of the saints; and lastly, the spiritual levels of the exercise of priestly ministry in the body of Christ. In all of these categories, Origen emphasizes the centrality of reconciliation and restoration as the distinctive marks of the priesthood. Let us consider them separately.

The Logos exercises priesthood in the cosmic arena of the noetic world, the world of the rational spirits. This is the world quintessentially real, and here the Logos of God is eternal reconciler between the world of spirit and the unapproachable Godhead. As early as the first *Homilies on Leviticus* we read that the Logos is offerer and offering, and that angels are priests in the heavens (*HomLev* 1.3). In the *ComJn* 1.4 we read, "He is the great High Priest not for the sake of mankind alone but for every rational being, offering himself as a sacrificial offering once and for all."

The Levitical priesthood exercised its reconciliatory role in the "fleshly" worship of ancient Israel, as a shadow of reality, and pointed to the eternal priesthood of the Logos and the priesthood of the Christ within the economy of salvation. Origen argues (*ComMt* 16.3): "For it is my opinion that the types and shadows of heavenly things celebrated in the ancient cult are brought to a final fulfillment by those heavenly realities themselves; for when the true High Priest comes the symbolic high priesthood ceases."

The priesthood of Christ is linked with the incarnation and the passion of the redeemer, at once priest and victim. It is the high priesthood "according to Melchizedech" and, as a spiritual priesthood, it is a perfect image of reality. Origen notes (*HomLev* 9.2): "If anyone examines the entire epistle written to the Hebrews and especially this place where he compares the high priest of the Law with the high priest of the promise about whom it is written, 'You are a priest forever after the order of Melchizedech,' he will find how this entire passage of the Apostle shows those things which were written in the Law are 'copies' and 'forms' of living and new things." In the same *Homily* (*HomLev* 9.9) Origen sees the entry of the high priest into the Holy of Holies at Yom Kippur as a type of Christ's passing through the veil of death. He writes, "The high priest, dressed in the sanctified garments, proceeds and enters into the interior of the veil . . . and so Jesus entered not into a sanctuary made by hands, but into heaven itself, and he appears for us before the face of God" (see Heb. 9:24). Origen insists that the unique priestly office of Christ is not repeated in the yearly festival but is expressed definitively, once and for all, in the priestly robes of the incarnation and of his salvific death. In the bloodied garment of the flesh Christ stands as high priest for the sake of humanity, in the heavenly "interior sanctuary" before the throne of God.

Origen understands the priesthood of the body of Christ as the ministry of reconciliation exercised by the baptized as a "priestly people," participating in the image of the perfect priesthood of Christ the high priest. As "priestly people" the community of the faithful inherits the Levitical (Aaronic) priesthood of ancient Israel. Thus they have an authentic priesthood, but it is differentiated by Origen from the Melchizedech high priesthood, which belongs to the Logos alone. In the fourth homily on Leviticus, commenting on Leviticus 6:1–6, he urges his listeners to keep the fire of faith and the lamp of knowledge alight like the priests of old, "For it is said: You are an elect race, a royal priesthood, an acquired people. If, therefore, you want to exercise the priesthood of your souls, let the fire never depart from your altar" (*HomLev* 4:6). It was to be a concept that when related to prayer, had a vivid impact on the Syro-Byzantine tradition of Christian mysticism.

Beyond the ministry of the community of the baptized, or the "priesthood of the faithful," there is another priestly ministry that Origen considers, the ministry of the heavenly priesthood of the saints, who enjoy full participation in the priesthood of Christ. This refers to what the creedal statements later called the "communion of saints." It comprised the Christian sense of the ongoing efficacy of prayer and supplication of the martyrs and saints who had left the earthly struggle. This doctrine is a significant element in the teaching of Origen, especially with regard to the "combat with the demons." There is a priestly office of prayer exercised by the saints, on behalf of those who are still on earth and battling temptations. This too was one of the most immediate legacies Origen bequeathed to the young monastic movement of the fourth century.

In his ascetic theology Origen never tired of exhortations for deepening the spiritual life. Within the priesthood of the faithful, according to Origen, there are different levels of exercising the role of priestly mediation and reconciliation. In the *HomJos* 17.2, Origen explores the distinction between "Levite" and "Priest" as respective types of "the many who believe in simplicity and in the fear of God," on the one hand, and of the "few, extremely rare, souls who devote themselves to knowledge and wisdom. These light up the path for the more simple brethren." The Levites are believers; the priests are the rare souls who have been able to assume the role of spiritual teacher and illumined guide to the Scriptures. Even more audaciously in the *ComJn* 1.3, Origen suggests that there are those in the community who may even be at the highest level of priesthood: "It may even be the case that those who stand out as preeminent in their own age could be called High Priest according to the order of Aaron, but never according to the order of Melchizedech." In this vein of thought he calls Paul a high priest, in reference to the teaching office in the church. He calls Paul "the wisest of high priests, the most knowledgeable of priests," changing "robes" in the style of his address (*HomLev* 4.6). There is one robe of teaching in the Holy of Holies, and another robe of teaching for "children" (cf. Heb. 5:13f.), once again in recognition of different levels of spiritual growth and commitment within the community of faith. It is clear enough that Origen sees himself, in terms of his office as teacher and exegete, as a "priest" (perhaps even a high priest in

the line of Aaron). This spiritual capacity validates the real Christian priesthood for him, not an institutional ordination (which he presumes, of course, but never mentions). All in all, Origen's reflections on priesthood form a rich and varied tapestry of thought but are always clearly integrated within the christological and ecclesial structures of his theology, underscoring his views on salvation as a pedagogical experience.

<hr>

Bright (1988, 1995); Daly (1982); Hermas (1996); Lecuyer (1970); McGuckin (1985, 1993); Schaeffer (1977); Vilela (1971).

PAMELA BRIGHT

Providence

Providence   Origen considers the question of providence to be of central importance, not only in his intellectual assault of various philosophical and of *gnostic* teachings, but also in his understanding of Christian theology and soteriology (*CCels* 4.68–84) (see *Atonement*). His understanding of providence lies at the foundation of his understanding of God and of creation (see *Cosmology*), as well as the ultimate destiny of humanity (see *Anthropology*). First, Origen considers God to be present in creation not in a physical manner, after the fashion of the Stoics, but rather in a spiritual manner, namely, in the form of all-embracing providence that pervades the entirety of creation and manifests the divine care in every aspect of the physical world (*CCels* 6.71.10).

In the *PEuch* 5–6, Origen has an extensive discussion, distinguishing the providence of God from the divine "foresight and fore-knowledge," and explaining how God will both directly care for the believer (thus the point of praying for assistance) yet also establish laws of providential care that will operate for the care of the world (thus there would be no point in praying for the sun to rise each morning). The apparent conflict between the domain of free will, on the one hand (God choosing to respond to an individual's prayer, and the individual soul choosing to embrace or reject the divine plan), and, on the other, the ordained providence of God is reconciled by the overarching foreknowledge of the divinity, who, foreseeing all things, is able to weave all into the universal plan of salvation (even as the apparent hardening of Pharaoh's heart did not become an obstacle to the Exodus, which was given a wide circulation among the church by its inclusion in *Philoc* 21–27).

In spite of Origen's vision of the pervasiveness of divine providence (thus contradicting, as a Christian, many Hellenistic schemes of divine providence that affirmed the divinity really exercised oversight only over the superlunar dimensions of the cosmos), he nevertheless concedes that not all the "signs" of the hand of an active providence can be read and comprehended by human beings, on account of their limited spiritual capacity. The fact that providence cannot always be understood and discerned, however, does not mean that its existence is negated (*PArch* 4.1.7.7). Even so, he expresses the confidence that providence governs the entirety of God's creation and is especially designed to serve humanity, the rational part of it (*CCels* 4.81). In this scheme of things, every element of the physical world points to an eternal reality.

In the event that one can recognize and understand a manifestation of God's providence, one can choose either to cooperate and act according to God's plan and desire (the spiritual ascent that is the destiny of all fallen souls) or not to (embracing further dissolution and chaos through evil) (see *Cosmology, Demonology, Fall*). Origen thus assigns great power to the human agent, who possesses both the ability to understand and the freedom to act, either in unison with the divine purpose revealed by providence or in opposition to it (*PEuch* 6.2–4; *PArch* 3.17). In his system, human free will helps to explain the enduring existence of evil and sin in spite of the pervasiveness and ultimate irresistibility of divine providence (*CCels* 7.68; *Philoc*. 21–27) (see *Apokatastasis, Grace, Virtue*).

The prime significance of providence for Origen lies in its pedagogical value and its soteriological end. The care of the creator for his creation, and for humankind in particular, is revealed in the fact that providence becomes a pedagogical tool that leads embodied *souls* back to the realization and actualization of their salvation in communion with the divine *Logos* (see *Christology*). Providence, therefore, can lead to the punishment of the individual believer or to the communal body (the latter as demonstrated for Origen by the destruction of the Jerusalem temple "on account of the transgressions of the Jews" [*CCels* 2.78]), or alternatively it can provide a reward for virtuous deeds (*PEuch* 31.6). Notwithstanding the particular form or manifestation of providence, it always and necessarily leads to the ultimate goal of enlightenment and perfection of the individual or the collection of individuals. As a result, the image of *God* that Origen presents is that of the teacher and the parent who acts through the aid of his providence in this world and thus both shows the way for perfection and for salvation, and punishes and rewards, so that embodied souls may be corrected and encouraged to achieve the end of their salvation (*HomJr* 6.2). Origen's doctrine of providence is a strongly argued synthesis of his biblical theology and his antignostic (antifatalistic) agenda and marks him out as one of the most powerful minds among the early Christian thinkers.

Koch (1932); Reardon (1973); Roselli (1992).

STAMENKA ANTONOVA

Repentance   To fully understand Origen's teaching on repentance, we must go further than isolating his simple etymological use of *metanoia* (145 instances in the corpus). In Origen, repentance is a tripartite process, beginning with conversion from sin (*HomLc* 17 [3], *CCels* 3.71.114; *PEuch* 25.1), followed by turning to God (*PArch* 3.1.6.35), and finally the external evidence, the manifested fruits of repentance (*HomLc* 22.5 and 8) by which "you will be said to have made a propitiation for transgression" (*HomLev* 5.4 [4]). For Origen, then, repentance includes both the soul's realization of its fallen state (see *Fall*) and the active engagement in the dynamic process of a fruitfully penitent life thereafter (*HomLev* 14, 4 [6]), which is synonymous with a progressive ascent to illumination (see *Atonement*).

Many of Origen's explicit considerations of the concept of metanoia occur within the *Commentary on John* (*ComJn* 6.22.122.116; 6.26.136.5; 6.31.159.4; 6.32.162.6ff.; 6.33.165.3) and mostly comprise a straightforward gloss on the biblical texts relating to *baptism* into repentance. The purifying nature of baptism is found also in *HomLc* 21.128.6, where Origen preaches on repentance: "The descending river of God, one running with a vigorous force, is the Lord our Saviour. Into Him we are baptized with true water, saving water. Baptism is also preached 'for the remission of sins.' Come, catechumens! Do penance, so that Baptism for the remission of sins will follow. He who stops sinning receives Baptism for the remission of sins." The *Homilies on Leviticus* provide more complex evidence of Origen's understanding of the nature, purpose, and expression of repentance. Origen suggests that both baptism and the Trinity (see *Trinitarianism*) are essential for purification (*HomLev* 8.11). However, he lists (*HomLev* 2.4 [5]) six types of remission of sin in addition to baptism: martyrdom, almsgiving, forgiving others' sins, conversion of another, receiving God's love, and "weeping penance" (see also *HomLev* 15.2 [4], and *ComJn* 28.4.26.5). Public confession of sin is necessary in order to receive the sacrifice which is "recapitulated" in Christ (*HomLev* 3.5).

The authority granted to nonpriestly agents of remission suggests that Origen shared a charismatic understanding, visible in many successive Christian generations, that binding and loosing of sins was effected, not so much by the institutional authority of priestly orders (see *Priesthood*), but rather through *grace*. He is not unaware of the significance of the church's public rites of repentance, noting here that even the efficacy of ritual metanoia relied on the holiness and purity of both confessor and sincere penitent (*HomLev* 13 [6]). Origen thus contributes to an established and enduring debate about ecclesial authority with regard to repentance (*PEuch* 25.1; 29.17).

In common with Cyprian (Cyprian, *Ep.* 67.6; *Ep.* 72.2) and Peter of Alexandria (Peter Alex, *Ep. Canon 10*), Origen asserts that those who repented but fell again could, if truly penitent, be restored to the church, but never to positions of authority within it (*HomLev* 11.2; *HomJos* 5.6; *ComMt* 17.24). Such penitents might receive a covering of their postbaptismal sins but never again the remission (*aphesin*) that was given in baptism. Origen criticizes those "priests" who have taken it on themselves to assure forgiveness of these orders of sins, thus showing an incidental witness to the rise of the church's system of reconciliation, and the controversial passage it had.

Crouzel (1989), 229–33; Rahner (1950); Trigg (1983), 196–200.

HANNAH HUNT

Resurrection One of the most controversial aspects of Origen's theology, in antiquity and in modern scholarship, has been his understanding of the Christian hope for a bodily resurrection. In the preface to *On First Principles* Origen affirms, as part of apostolic tradition, that the soul, "possessing its own substance and life," will meet the reward or punishment of its deeds after death, but also that "there will be a time for the resurrection of the dead," when our present corruptible body will "rise in incorruption" (*PArch* Praef. 5, alluding to 1 Cor.

15:42). In answer to the philosopher Celsus's scornful criticism of Christian hope for a simple reconstitution of our present material bodies, on the other hand, Origen insists that Christians look for resurrection "in a way that is worthy of God": the raising of what Paul, in 1 Corinthians 15, refers to as a "spiritual body," related causally to the present one, but incorruptible and wholly new in qualities and appearance (*CCels* 5. 18–23).

Origen was strongly criticized, during his own lifetime and in the centuries that followed, for conceiving the risen body in such a spiritualized fashion that it would be, in effect, no body at all. Epiphanius of Salamis, at the end of the fourth century, considered his approach to the resurrection to be little different from that of the gnostic sects, who tended to understand resurrection in terms of enlightenment and the escape from all materiality (Epiphanius, *Panarion* 64.71.14; cf. the second-century Valentinian *Epistle to Rheginus, on the Resurrection*). Jerome also assembled a dossier of texts from Origen to prove that his conception of the resurrection denied its real corporeality (see especially *To Pammachius, against John of Jerusalem* 23–36).

Origen was concerned to establish a more nuanced view of the resurrection than his opponents recognized—so concerned that he wrote no less than two early treatises and two dialogues on the subject, which are now lost, apart from a few fragments. He assumed that every living creature, even an intellectual one, needs a body of some kind in order to be situated in a place, to live, and to move: bodiliness was for him a part of limitation, and only God is incorporeal (*asomatos*), because only God is without limit (*PArch* Praef. 9; 1.6.4; 2.2.1–2; 3.6.1; 4.3.15; 4.8–10; *CCels* 7.32; *FragmPs* 15 [PG 12.1093–96]). So the church's faith in a future resurrection unquestionably implied, for Origen, that some form of our own present body will be "our clothing" (*indumentum*) in the age to come and will be recognizable by its "shape" (*habitus*) (*PArch* 2.10.1–2) as that which is ours.

One of Origen's most famous discussions of the characteristics of the risen body comes from a long, if summarized, fragment of his commentary on Psalm 1, quoted by Methodius of Olympus in his own work *On the Resurrection* and preserved in Greek by Epiphanius of Salamis (*Panarion* 64). Commenting on the verse: "There the impious will not rise in the judgment" (Ps 1:5 LXX), Origen rejects as naive literalism the idea that all humans will rise in a body that will simply be reconstructed from the scattered elements of the present one. The matter of the present body, he argues, is constantly in flux, as its components are assimilated and discharged; it is the soul that gives the body substantial continuity, and that imposes on it the unique perceptible "form" (*eidos*) by which features remain identifiable despite the changes of age, growth, and illness. At the resurrection, the soul will produce this characteristic form anew, and through it will shape whatever matter then exists into a new, "sparkling" or luminous body, reminiscent of the body's original form before sin caused its "descent" into its present coarseness (see *PArch* 2.2.2; 3.6.4–6; also Fragm. in Procopius of Gaza, *Catena on Genesis* 321 [PG 87.221]). Just as we would need fins and gills to survive in our environment if we lived in the sea, he suggests, so this transformed body will enable us to live and move in the spiritual world of heaven. In this passage and others (e.g., *PArch* 2.10.3), Origen attributes this transformation to the presence in our bodies of an "inherent structure" (*insita ratio*) that functions like the "seminal rational principles" (*logoi spermatikoi*) of living things posited by Stoic cosmology (*CCels* 7.32): like the transformation of the "bare seed, perhaps of wheat" into a full ear, to which Paul refers in 1 Corinthians 15:37, 42–44, the resurrection of the body will reveal the unknown future form of glory lurking within our present material limitations.

The ultimate principle of continuity, however, between the present body and that of the resurrection is, for Origen, the soul, which he holds to be naturally immortal because of its kinship with God (*PArch* 4.4.9–10; cf. *ComJn* 13.61). Although his teaching seems to disturb some of his listeners, perhaps because of its Platonic overtones, he insists in his *Dialogue with Heracleides* that the soul or "inner person"—the part of us originally made in God's image—shares in eternal life with Christ even before the final resurrection (*DialHer* 154, 166–68). It is the soul, in its purified final state, that will eventually "clothe" its body or limited form, presently coarse material, with its own immortality and incorruptibility (*PArch* 2.3.2; 3.6.4; *ComJn* 13.61; *CCels* 7.32). Origen was less clear, however, about just how he imagined this final bodily form. While his later critics suggested he really supposed that in the end all matter will simply pass away (e.g., Jerome in *Epist.* 92.2; 96.9,13,15; 124.5, 9–10), Origen suggests rather that while the total spiritualization of matter is hypothetically tenable, his own resurrection hope is for a state of such refined materiality that bodily corruption and change for the worse will no longer be possible (*PArch* 2.3.7). In that stable condition, which will reach beyond human bodies to include a transfigured cosmos, the just will find their abiding peace with God and with each other.

Le Boulluec (1975); Rius-Camps (1976); Chadwick (1948); Crouzel (1973); Daley (1991); Hennessey (1991).

BRIAN E. DALEY, S.J.

Roman Empire   State-sponsored persecution frames Origen's life, but is almost peripheral to his extant works. His father had been martyred (Eusebius, *H.E.* 6.1–2), and as a young teacher he himself outfaced hostile crowds, attending disciples to their execution (Eusebius, *H.E.* 6.3); but by his maturity this had become a half-forgotten past (*HomJr* 4.3). Although he would die from injuries sustained in the mid-third-cen-

tury persecution of Decius (Eusebius, *H.E.* 6.39.5), his surviving writings are all pre-Decian. Unlike subsequent Christian authors, he confidently reduces the prospect of state repression to a localized and spasmodic phenomenon, its swift "failure" briskly packaged in biblical precedent (*HomJos* 9.10). The responsibilities conferred by his own pedigree, as far as he saw it, concerned moral life, not noble death (*HomEz* 4.8).

Origen never encountered a persecuting emperor at close quarters. The *Exhortation to Martyrdom*, his fullest response to a specific government persecution, treats this as a cosmic event rather than a particular policy enacted by Maximinus Thrax; only incidentally does he reveal that the martyrdom to which he exhorted his addressees would require them to be shipped from Alexandria to imperial headquarters in Germany, an improbably sustained effort by the government (*ExhMart* 41). His perspectives have caused difficulties for interpreters both ancient and modern. The controversy over the "no small war across Alexandria" that first drove him from Egypt (whether it refers metaphorically to an ecclesiastical conflict, or literally to the slaughter ordered by Caracalla) reflects the uncertainty of Eusebius, who seems to cite Origen's *Apology* verbatim (Eusebius, *H.E.* 6.19.16). Eusebius himself, of course, had experienced a real "war" against the Christians (*H.E.* 8.4.2; 8.13.9): his inability to penetrate Origen's intended meaning here suggests the gap that separated the experience of their two generations on this matter.

In his experience of the actuality of empire Origen more resembles contemporary intellectuals than his fellow Christians: witness his successive invitations abroad, to Arabia from the provincial governor, and to Antioch from the empress mother (*H.E.* 16.19.15; 6.21.3). His assurance that compulsion was in both cases involved (a formal summons via the civic authorities, and the ambiguous honor of a military escort) indicates his need to justify such journeys to a Christian readership. And despite obtaining a level of access unrivaled by other Christian apologists, Origen produced no formal *Apology* of his own during these encounters. The suggestion by Nautin that he wrote a volume of his *Commentary on John* at Antioch might imply that he instead made a point of continuing his exegetical routine at court, much as contemporary philosophers demonstrated their detached *sophrosyne* in the manner they refused to be put off their stride by imperial attentions. But the principal significance of the visit seems to concern Origen's definitive departure from Alexandria, which belongs to the same period; it is unclear whether the visit came first (which would suggest either that his enhanced prestige had proved intolerable to the local establishment or that an imperial honorarium provided him with financial independence) or whether it came later, as an experiment, perhaps, in staking out an intellectual position independent of any church (see *Bishops*).

No further contacts at this level are recorded until the two letters addressed to the emperor Philip and his wife (Eusebius, *H.E.* 6.36.3). Despite modern attempts to relate these to ecclesiastical controversy, the silence of Eusebius (who knew the correspondence) concerning the contents suggests a bland and at most exploratory salutation; in any case, the initial approach seems not to have been followed up. So while Origen came into contact with the highest levels of imperial government, these encounters were isolated and occasional; he never formally represented the church before the state.

His exegesis shows a similar confident detachment. For example, where earlier commentators on Matthew 22:21 ("Render unto Caesar,") had applied this literally to the relationships between individuals and the state (Justin to demonstrate Christians' reliability as taxpayers, or Tertullian to denounce the

decoration of doorposts on state festivals), Origen notes that "some people" admit such "straightforward interpretations," but he finds them boringly obvious and discusses instead the different images imprinted upon the human soul (*HomLuc* 39). Elsewhere he again concentrates on the deeper equation of Caesar with "the body," while allowing in passing a "traditional" Christian identification with the devil (*ComMt* 17.25), an almost casual demonization of imperial rule that denotes considerable distance on his part. Similarly, with Paul's command concerning submission to authorities (Rom. 13:1), both the offhand claim that "spiritual" Christians like himself were exempt from Caesar's jurisdiction (*ComRm* 9.25) and the apparent shrugging off of government responsibility for persecution (*ComRm* 9.26), suggest how successfully Origen had managed to depoliticize Christian commitment.

At the beginning of the *Contra Celsum*, Origen likewise brushes aside the issue of the illegality of Christianity as merely a detail, and when he condones the assassination of tyrants who make evil laws, he evidently does not imagine that this could include Roman emperors who kept anti-Christian legislation on the statute book (*CCels* 1.1). He returns to politics in the final book of the *Contra Celsum*, magisterially rebutting the charge that refusal to swear by the imperial genius implied disloyalty (*CCels* 8.63–65). Less successful, no doubt because of his instinctive adherence to Christian pacifist traditions, is his reply to the subsequent point that empire-wide conversion to Christianity would leave the emperor helpless against the barbarians (*CCels* 8.68–70). To Celsus's charge that if successive emperors were themselves converted they would simply be taken prisoner, until finally this record of failure provoked a backlash, Origen can only deny indignantly that the Christians intended any such systematic campaign to evangelize their rulers (*CCels* 8.71). Sixty years before

Constantine's victory at the Milvian Bridge, Origen is still clearly finding it more than difficult to imagine a Christian emperor. He finds the idea that a Christian emperor might lead an army into battle a contradiction in terms. Origen's Christian empire requires two parallel states, so that Christians can keep their hands clean (*CCels* 8.73).

Although Eusebius would construct, from Origen's corpus, a Christian political philosophy capable of accommodating Constantine, Origen himself had neutralized the Roman state largely by ignoring it. Even the Augustan *Pax Romana* inspired not so much the "providential" enthusiasm of such as Melito of Sardis or Hippolytus or the other earlier Christian writers who had seen it as God's device for the spreading of the church. On Origen's part, we find a reference to the idea that then dwindles off into simply a learned note concerning citizen conscription during the Peloponnesian War (*CCels* 2.30). Once again, his books block out any lived experience of empire.

For twenty years at Caesarea he worked in a center of Roman administration, the seat of the provincial government, yet the soldiers and officials who operated there leave no trace in his voluminous output; Origen's hinterland is not the Roman province of Palaestina, but a biblically defined Holy Land.

Caspary (1979); Frede (1999), 131–55; Nautin (1977), 367–68; Rizzi (1998).

NEIL McLYNN

Rule of Faith   The rule of faith (*regula fidei*), or as Irenaeus of Lyons also called it, the "canon of truth" (*kanon tes aetheias*), appears in certain writers of the second and third centuries as an authoritative digest or summary of Christian belief, a more or less presupposed standard of confessional solidarity with the church catholic and apostolic. The rule was neither a theological statement per se nor the hard copy of a baptismal creed, but its precise character and context have been heavily debated. Some historians have seen the rule as a principle of *tradition* signaling the church's original possession of, and unanimity in, the orthodox faith. Others have viewed it as a doctrinal standard inherent in Scripture, basic to the emerging scriptural canon itself, and capable of being extracted as a guide to theological interpretation of the Bible. Still others have understood the rule as a principle of theological reasoning and argumentation independent of, yet critically applicable to, both ecclesiastical tradition and Scripture.

In actual appearance the rule reads as an epitome of the Christian faith narrative, typically in a Trinitarian (sometimes binitarian) format, accentuating the oneness of God and his priority as Creator, as well as recounting the central kerygma of the incarnation, death, resurrection, and second coming of Christ. The variable renditions of the rule (even within individual writers) indicate not only that it was not a terminologically fixed creed but that it was most likely expounded in more than one communal setting: for example, in catechetical contexts as a kind of teaching syllabus, in liturgical contexts as rehearsing the salvation story central to worship and sacraments, or in polemical contexts as a means to "inoculate" churches against heterodox threats.

Prior to Origen, the most substantial versions of the rule of faith appear in Irenaeus and Tertullian, both of whom invoke the rule against gnostic and Marcionite heresies, and both of whom emphasize its originality, universality, and irreformability (Irenaeus, *Haer.* 1.10.3; 1.22.1; 3.4.2; *Dem.* 3; 6; Tertullian, *Praescr.* 13.1–6; *Virg.* 1; *Prax.* 2.1–2). Yet while Irenaeus insists on the self-evident consistency of the rule as establishing the true *hypothesis* (the essential plot or argument) of the scriptural revelation (cf. Irenaeus, *Haer.* 1.9.4; 1.10.3), he also recognizes the brokenness of human knowledge (*Haer.*

2.28.2) and the need for disciplined interpretation. With some questions (for
example, why God shows patience
toward fallen angels and humans; why
he created some beings earthly and others heavenly; why the Logos became
incarnate; or how eschatological events
will unfold), that is, where Scripture is
not absolutely lucid, Irenaeus admits the
need for "bringing out more fully the
meaning of whatever was said in [scrip-
tural] parables and adapting it exactly
to the *hypothesis* of the truth" (*Haer.*
1.10.3). Irenaeus here elicits a principle
that Origen will exploit even more
aggressively: that the rule of faith is fixed
within the apostolic tradition but, when
applied as a criterion to interpret Scripture, still allows for the continued development and deepening of Christian
understanding.

In a number of passages in his works,
Origen indicates his confidence in an
original and apostolic rule of faith as
exclusively defining the way to salvation
and standing over against heretical (by
which he means *gnostic*) teaching. In
ComJn 32.15–16, for example, he declares
the following as normative beliefs: one
God, Creator and Perfecter of all things;
Jesus Christ, fully divine and human,
born of a virgin and crucified under Pon-
tius Pilate as the Savior of the world (see
Christology); the *Holy Spirit*; and the
freedom and moral responsibility of
human beings (see *Grace*). In a comment
on Matthew (*SerMt* 33) he also adds the
"*resurrection* from the dead" to this fundamental list. It is in the Preface to his
First Principles, however, that we find
Origen's most substantial (and controversial), rendition of the rule of faith. It is
preserved mainly in Rufinus's Latin
translation (thought by most scholars to
be faithful enough to the original). The
Preface straightforwardly expresses a
Trinitarian (see *Trinitarianism*) faith
handed down in unwavering succession
from the apostles: that the one God, Creator of all, sent his only begotten Son,
through whom he created the world, in
the flesh, born of a virgin; that Jesus

Christ, God and man, truly suffered and
died, and was raised and ascended; that
the Holy Spirit is united in dignity and
honor with the Father and the Son, and
that he inspired both prophets and apostles. In this Preface, Origen acknowledges that many alleged Christian
believers ("Greeks and barbarians")
have been led into conflicting views not
only on trivial questions but even on
issues of consequence. For Origen, the
fact stands that the *apostles* delivered
the "necessary" doctrines in the most
explicit terms, though still open to investigation by the spiritually gifted (see
Mysteries). Moreover, like Irenaeus, Origen recognizes that the biblical writers
were not so explicit on other matters,
leaving room for Christian sages to exercise their intellectual acuities. Indeed,
even with a doctrine as weighty as that of
the Holy Spirit, Origen submits that the
apostolic sources are not clear whether
the Spirit is unbegotten of God or (like
the Son) begotten. Such is a matter for
disciplined and diligent investigation, as
far as he is concerned.

Origen goes on in the Preface of *On
First Principles* to list numerous items not
included in earlier versions of the rule of
faith but still under the discipline of the
apostolic teaching: the soul, its destiny,
its freedom of will, and its relation to the
body; the devil and fallen spiritual powers; the temporal beginning and destruction of the world; and the nature of
Scripture as containing spiritual mysteries beneath the obvious (literal) meaning. Such are precisely the issues falling
under careful scrutiny in the rest of *On
First Principles*, where Origen, as a
Didaskalos committed to elucidating
what is obscure in Scripture and modu-
lating his explanations for a Christian
audience confronted with Gnosticism,
shows his skill as a heuristic theologian.

For him, while the rule of faith was
indeed a criterion of apostolic teaching
imposed on all Christian interpreters,
and while all interpretations demanded
ultimate conformity with the rule, nevertheless the rule of faith did not thwart

the careful investigator's attempts to propose reasonable explanations of theological "loose ends" that were hardly indifferent in an environment of radically competitive religious worldviews. The concept of Origen as a "research theologian" active in the *First Principles* and elsewhere is thus helpful in conveying his desire to be at once constrained by the church's discipline (its *regula fidei*), and yet simultaneously poised on the cutting edge of Christian reflection in his day.

Behr (2001); Blowers (1997); Van den Eynde (1933); Osborn (1989); Outler (1984); Williams (1989).

PAUL M. BLOWERS

Sacraments   In commenting on Origen's understanding of the Christian sacraments we perhaps need to define the term for our present considerations (for it has had a considerable development in the history of the church) as something akin to the conception of a visible form or mediation of God's invisible grace. In this sense, the church set out its sacramental rituals (particularly in relation to **baptism, Eucharist,** and **repentance**) as concrete channels of sanctification and *grace*. In relation to all of the above "sacraments," Origen appears much more interested in the spiritual significance of the inner reality of the mysterious events than the institutional aspects. Indeed he cautions on many occasions against thinking that any external form (even the sacramental life of the church) can signify anything if the inner spirit is not instructed and illumined by God (see *Priesthood*).

Over and above this specific approach to the various Christian sacraments, there is in Origen's work an overall sense of sacrament, or "mystery" (*mysterion*) as a concrete localization of the supreme "Mystery of salvation," which, as Origen understands it, is the dynamic of sanctification operative in the world, whereby the Logos calls back the fallen souls to communion with God

(see *Anthropology, Atonement, Christology, Fall, Souls*). The idea of mystery in this extended sense (see *Mysteries*), is both significant and common in Origen's work, connoting the ubiquitous life-giving and salvific energies of the Word of God. The idea of mystery is, for Origen, more a metaphorical evocation of an internal comprehension and sanctification than any "physical" representation of grace and sanctity, for he invariably sees the presence of the Holy in this material cosmos as first and foremost designed to make the soul ascend from its corporeal (fallen) condition.

The prime example of Origen's generic approach to sacramentality is manifested in his view of the Scripture as the chief "sacramental" revelation of the Logos within the material world. This is why he is concerned with the "ingestion and digestion" of Scripture, both by the individual who reads and absorbs Scripture and through the more sophisticated, informed interpretation of biblical texts. His choice of metaphors of eating shows clearly that he intends to draw an explicit connection (and perhaps point up some points of tension) to the more familiar sacramental process of the Eucharist. By "digesting the word," Origen argues, the Christian soul is fed as surely as through the sacrament of the eucharistic bread. Origen develops an exegesis of the "five loaves" (widely understood in Christian art and preaching to have been a eucharistic symbol) in order to demonstrate this point (*ComMt* 11.1–2). Origen expects that "even the more simple believers" will admit that "certain mysterious dispensations are disclosed by the holy Scriptures" (*PArch* 4.2.2). And similarly, commenting on Gen. 3:8 (in *PArch* 4.3.1), Origen underscores the need to approach exegesis sacramentally: "Surely, I think no one doubts that these statements are made by Scripture in the form of a type by which they point towards certain mysteries." Origen's confidence that the truth of the gospel message (its sacramental dynamic) should be available to all who seek it through true illumination (*ComJn* 2.28.174.3) forms a chief part of his polemic against the elitist views of **Celsus**, whom Origen sees as having misunderstood the "Christian mystery" as something comparable to Hellenistic mystery religions (*CCels* 3.81.16).

The Scripture is sacramental for Origen in that it represents the "corporeal form" of inner and sacred mysteries of grace. He argues the point at the very beginning of his systematic work in *On First Principles*: "The contents of scripture are the outward forms of certain mysteries and the images of divine things. On this point the entire Church is unanimous, that while the whole law is spiritual, the inspired meaning is not recognized by all, but only by those who are gifted with the Holy Spirit in the word of wisdom and knowledge" (*PArch* Praef. 8). The sacramentality of Scripture lies in its spiritual meaning, which is ever present, even when there is no "bodily meaning" (*PArch* 4.3.5). Origen finds the sense of Scripture as a sacrament primarily witnessed in 1 Corinthians 2:6–7, and much of *PArch* 4 develops on the idea. His other chief sources, to which he returns frequently, are Romans 16:25–27 and 2 Timothy 1:10, which he considers in the *CCels* 3.61.11.

Hanson (1959), (2002), 327–32; Shin (1999); Trigg (1983), 191–96.

HANNAH HUNT

Satan   See **Angels, Demonology, Anthropology, Apokatastasis.**

School of Alexandria   In book 6 of his *Ecclesiastical History*, Eusebius of Caesarea is at pains to present a picture of the second- and third-century church of Alexandria as the home of a noble "School," both in the sense of an institution and in the sense of an intellectual or theological tradition. At the center of this picture stands the figure of Origen, the child of Christian parents, who not long after the martyrdom of his father (ca.

202) took up, at around the age of eighteen, the work of a professional Grammatikos. During a new period of persecution, which opened in 206 and of course stifled the normal teaching activities of the church, he boldly took in certain youthful Christians and Christian fellow travelers who wanted instruction in the faith. With them he studied the Scriptures; and when certain of them were arrested and condemned, he stood by them and helped them as much as he could during their imprisonment. In recognition of this work, Eusebius tells us, Demetrius, the bishop of Alexandria, when he had returned from exile, encouraged Origen to continue his work of catechesis. It was not long before Origen gave up the teaching of Greek literature entirely, adopted an ascetic mode of life, and dedicated himself wholly to the study and teaching of the Old and New Testaments (*H.E.* 6.3.8–9). Thus originated the episcopally sponsored "catechetical school" that is the centerpiece of Eusebius's portrayal of the Alexandrian teaching tradition.

Eusebius, however, wanted to do more than this and sought to push the origin of the "School" well back into the second century. He states that in the Alexandrian church it was a matter of "ancient custom" to maintain a "school (*didaskaleion*) of sacred letters," and that this institution had survived even to his own day (*H.E.* 5.10.1). The first name he associated with it was that of Pantaenus, whom he describes as its head. Pantaenus's successor in this role was, he tells us, **Clement of Alexandria**; to support this, Eusebius quotes Clement's expression of his determination to pass on the apostolic tradition transmitted to him by the teacher he had found "hidden away in Egypt" (and whom all reckon to have been Pantaenus) (*H.E.* 5.11.3–5). Origen was, in his turn, a pupil of Clement, Eusebius asserts (*H.E.* 6.6.1), and succeeded Clement as head of the *didaskaleion* when he was just eighteen (*H.E.* 6.3.3), that is, at roughly the time when Clement left Alexandria to avoid the persecution in which Origen's father was martyred. Thus, for Eusebius, there was a true "succession" of teachers in Alexandria, each perpetuating the tradition taught him by his predecessor; a continuity of doctrine buttressed by the continuity of an institution. And of course Eusebius traces the succession well beyond Origen, who, after transferring his activity to Caesarea Maritima, was himself succeeded by his pupils Heraclas and Dionysius, in that order (*H.E.* 6.29.4).

Recent scholarship has questioned this picture at a number of points. For one thing, while there is no reason to question the relationship Eusebius sees between Pantaenus and Clement, there is very good reason to doubt his assertion that these two were successive heads of an official catechetical school of the church of Alexandria or, indeed, that there ever was such an institution before Origen's day. No doubt Alexandria contained Christian teachers who conducted private schools (*didaskaleia*) and thus fulfilled the sort of role that Justin Martyr had in Rome; but these were most likely to have been informal and personal undertakings, more than one in number and, like contemporary philosophical "schools," to have represented differing outlooks. It is highly probable that *gnostic* teachers such as Valentinus and Basilides had earlier on presided over this type of *didaskaleion*.

In the second place, there is a question about the relationship of Origen to his "predecessor," Clement of Alexandria. There can be no question that Origen knew of Clement and his writings; but he does not mention Clement at any point, nor does his teaching repeat much of Clement, either in terms of style or in relation to its characteristic themes and emphases. In other words, the two do not seem to constitute a "school of thought," save insofar as both reflect the intellectual culture of the city of *Philo*, Alcinous, and Ammonius Saccas.

Then in the third place, the same appears to be true of Origen's successors as heads of the Alexandrian catechetical school. Both Heraclas and Dionysius were, by Eusebius's account, long-standing associates and pupils of Origen's; and Heraclas for his part was Origen's assistant for a time, having been put in charge of introductory studies in the school. On the other hand, as the gulf between Origen and Bishop Demetrius gradually widened, stimulated by Origen's absences from Alexandria and culminating in his ordination at the hands of the bishop of Caesarea Maritima (and in suspicions regarding his doctrinal correctness), Heraclas clearly sided with Demetrius and seems, in the end, when he himself quickly succeeded Demetrius as bishop, to have been the author of Origen's final condemnation by the Alexandrian church.

Eusebius's picture, then, is in large part a product of wishful thinking on the part of one who admired Origen and might himself have claimed to qualify as a sort of "successor" of Origen's, though in Caesarea Maritima, not Alexandria; for it was there that, in the end, Origen's "school" was established, not so much as a catechetical school but as a Christian version of, and alternative to, the customary higher education of his day, and therefore as a school whose crowning discipline was the exegesis of the Scriptures. This is not to say that Origen's memory and influence disappeared in Alexandria, indeed far from it; but it is to suggest that Palestine was and remained a second, and not merely secondary, home of his teaching (see *School of Caesarea*).

Bienert (1978); Van den Broek (1995); Van den Hoek (1997); Nautin (1977).

R. A. NORRIS

School of Caesarea

School of Caesarea   Caesarea Maritima on the Palestinian coast may not have originally enjoyed the prestige of Alexandria, but by Origen's time it was emerging as a major center of Greco-Roman culture in its own right, with a lively diversity of competing religious communities: Jewish, Christian, and Samaritan, as well as pagan. Gnosticism challenged Jewish and Christian constituencies alike, while Marcionism posed a viable threat to the Caesarean church. The need for a sophisticated, biblically literate Christian leadership and intellectual cadre was critical.

Before coming to Caesarea around 233 and opening a school there, Origen had already led a Christian academy (*didaskaleion*) in his native Alexandria. The nature of the **School of Alexandria** (in the sense of the catechetical school mentioned by Eusebius [*H.E.* 6.3.3, 8; 6.6.1]) has been much debated, with questions as to whether the teaching was mainly private and tutorial or public and episcopally supervised, and whether it entailed a theological curriculum as such or consisted simply of prebaptismal instruction for new converts. Most likely, the school evolved over time and entailed both lay instructors (Didaskaloi, like Origen himself) and the bishop's oversight. Critically important, however, is Eusebius's depiction of the school as ultimately taking the shape of other "philosophical" schools of the time. He specifically describes Origen as adopting a kind of Christian philosophical asceticism that eventually drew in even impressionable young pagans to become his disciples (*H.E.* 6.3.9–13).

Relocated in Caesarea by 233, Origen, though now an ordained presbyter with new duties in public preaching, opened a similar *didaskaleion*, a school for moral and spiritual formation. Adolf Knauber's thesis (that Origen developed in Caesarea essentially a "missionary" school to educate young pagan men out of secular Greek thought and into the true Christian *philosophia*) is quite compelling. The goal was not to repudiate all secular learning but to use that learning (viz., Middle Platonism) as a prolegomenon for the study of the higher truth (and indeed the superior way of life) as commended in the Christian revelation.

We have the distinct advantage of a firsthand insight into Origen's instructional style from one of his own pupils, Gregory Thaumaturgus, who as a young man perhaps still unbaptized, forsook the study of law and ended up in Caesarea under Origen's tutelage. Gregory's *Address of Thanksgiving,* or *Panegyric,* eulogizes Origen as an exemplar of the philosophical life, a spiritual friend, a physician of souls and guide to true virtue, who, sometimes gently and pastorally, sometimes through the fierce repartee of the Socratic method, formed his students in an ascetic diligence (*Panegyric* 4.40–7.108). Gregory even gives some hints of a curriculum. Origen willingly launched his students with sciences like physics, geometry, and astronomy to lay a groundwork for commanding worldly knowledge (*Panegyric* 8.109–14). Moreover, in the study of ethics, Gregory says that it was precisely Origen, a Christian teacher, who first introduced him to the moral teachings of the pagan philosophical schools; since these required careful consideration in the overall process of reestablishing the virtues on a Christian foundation (*Panegyric* 9.115–12.149). All this, however, was directed to the sublime study of divinity, namely, the exposition of Holy Scripture (see **Sacraments, Old Testament, Apostles**), for which, in Gregory's estimation, Origen had a genuinely prophetic giftedness (*Panegyric* 13.150–17.202).

If not an institute of higher learning in our modern sense, nevertheless Origen's school in Caesarea did entail strict disciplines, and an orderly training; but its true character, again, was the ancient philosophical model of the sage bonded with a close circle of disciples; and those disciples were doubtless at various levels of maturity and Christianization. Gregory Thaumaturgus, for one, went on to a distinguished career as a bishop in Neocaesarea (Pontus). He is often credited as the Gregory who received the *Letter* from Origen recommending the intellectual "despoiling of Egypt" and encouraging astute Christians continuously to knock on the door of Scripture (cf. Matt. 7:7) to seek its hidden mysteries.

Another from Origen's circle in Caesarea, however, took the master's teaching in a very different direction from Gregory. Porphyry of Tyre, destined to become an eminent Neoplatonist, may never have sympathized with Origen's faith, but he did listen to him lecture, enough so that he later criticized Origen as a "lapsed Platonist" (Eusebius, *H.E.* 6.19.1–9). It was probably from Origen that Porphyry learned how to approach the Hebrew Scriptures with a critical eye to the constraints of the texts at the literal level. The fruit of Porphyry's research was a sophisticated and hostile broadside on various discrepancies in the Bible in his treatise *Against the Christians*.

Though Origen's school thrived on the intimate interaction of teacher and disciples in a private or semiprivate tutorial context, it is unimaginable that, in this instruction, just as in his public preaching, Origen was not fully cognizant of the immediate challenges facing the Christian community in Caesarea, a city teeming with religious and philosophical missionaries. Origen was aware, for example, that rabbinic scholarship in Galilee was thriving, due in no small part to the influential academy of Rabbi Hoshaya, founded in Caesarea about the same time as Origen's own. The rabbis, moreover, were themselves thoroughly committed to forming their students in a philosophical asceticism and in the careful, graduated study of Scripture. Origen himself indicates that it was from the "Hebrews" that "we have received" the practice of withholding certain texts of Scripture, the so-called *deuteroseis* (including inter alia the Song of Songs), from the immature, until they were prepared to study them (*ComCt* Prologue). Origen had sufficient respect for rabbinic exegesis occasionally to dispute the rabbis' expositions both in public debate and in his homilies on Old Testament texts. We can reasonably assume that he prepared his own students in the *didaskaleion* to counter Jewish as well as pagan "philosophy."

In one other interesting sense, the school in Caesarea was a means for Origen, in an intimate setting, to put his own hermeneutical enterprise (the elevation of Christians to an ever more trenchant knowledge of Scripture) on its educational feet. He projected his students as modeling for the entire Christian community a discipline that, in principle, imposed itself on the church as a whole, and all the more so on himself. Perhaps Gregory Thaumaturgus's most telling comment is his indication that Origen did not simply set himself up as *the* paragon of this discipline, but as one aspiring to be such a paragon (*Panegyric* 11.135–36).

Blowers (1988); Crouzel (1970); Levine (1975); McGuckin (1992a, 1992b); Wilken (1984).

PAUL M. BLOWERS

Scriptural Interpretation   The subject of scriptural interpretation in Origen is vast and complicated. Origen was perhaps the most accomplished of all ancient interpreters of the Bible. Indeed, it would be impossible to understand any of Origen's theology without considering at the same time the central role biblical interpretation played in his life project (see **Old Testament, Scripture, Allegory, Typology, Mysteries, Sacraments**). Over the course of his career, Origen composed commentaries on nearly every book of the Bible. He also composed hundreds of homilies and letters containing exegetical content. Altogether he produced more than two thousand works, most of which have been lost. Fortunately, enough of his corpus does survive to provide us with a good understanding of his approach to biblical interpretation.

Origen's interpretive method rests upon the basic Pauline tension between the spirit and the letter. According to Origen, literal interpretation begins at the base meaning of the text or the "plain sense." While often obvious, meaning at this level is helpful to simple Christians or to those Christians just beginning to explore the spiritual life, but it is not sufficient for those who were seeking to grow spiritually. Since Scripture at the literal level often contained contradictions and errors, the text could actually be a stumbling block to intelligent readers. Scripture, then, has another, spiritual layer of meaning above the literal. This spiritual layer is much more important, because it actually teaches the reader about the hidden mysteries of God and Christ. In his famous work, *First Principles*, Origen develops this basic distinction between literal and spiritual reading into a large macrotheory of interpretation (*PArch* 4.2) The theory draws upon the classic Greek division of the human person into body, soul, and spirit. Origen transfers this anthropological distinction to the Bible: he suggests that that Scripture actually operates at three levels, the "bodily," the "soulish," and the "spiritual":

> One must therefore portray the meaning of the sacred writings in a threefold way upon his own soul, that is, so that the simple may be edified by what we may call the "flesh of the scripture," this name being the obvious interpretation; while the "man who has made some progress" may be edified by its soul . . . and the "man who is perfect" . . . may be edified by the spiritual law, which has "a shadow of the good things to come." For just as man consists of body, soul, and spirit, so in the same way does the scripture, which had been prepared by God to be given for man's salvation. (*PArch* 4.2.4)

Many scholars have been confused by the methodological discussions Origen advances in *First Principles* because Origen himself does not rigidly apply a tripartite system throughout his corpus. Nonetheless, the distinctions do capture the essence of what Origen hoped to achieve exegetically. According to some scholars, the best way to understand what Origen meant by positing a bodily, a "soulish," and spiritual meaning is to set it in the context of a pedagogy of ascent. As a Platonist, Origen naturally believed that spiritual reality was higher

than physical reality. This position made it difficult for him to find permanent value in the material creation (see **Cosmology**). Origen believed that the bodily or literal level of Scripture could be of benefit to simple folks, who were not advanced in the spiritual life. At the second, or psychic, level, Scripture delivered lessons to those who were moving toward perfection. Finally, at the spiritual level, Scripture deals with the mysteries of the Christian faith, such as the nature of the Son, his incarnation, the true nature of the world, and our place in it. Observers find it difficult to grasp what Origen meant by the psychic level. Some scholars suggest that this level had to do with extracting "moral" meaning from the text, but there appears to be little support for such a view in Origen's extant writings. One way to understand this level may be to see it as somewhere between the literal meaning and allegorical meanings that deal specifically with the mysteries of faith.

Origen's penchant for looking beyond the literal to the spiritual meaning of the text strikes many modern readers as arbitrary. **Allegory**, when viewed from the standards of modern historical criticism, appears to be nothing more than a creative fantasy, destructive of the integrity of the text. This perspective, though understandable, is not helpful, for no ancient biblical interpreter ever applied the principles of modern criticism, including Origen. It is also incorrect. Origen's desire to uncover spiritual meaning did not mean that he trivialized the literal text or was unconcerned with the actual words. In fact, Origen was one of the earliest and most careful "text critics" among the early Christian writers. More than any other ancient Christian exegete, Origen understood that the text of the Bible was not stable and was subject to human error. He devoted massive energy, for example, to creating the **Hexapla**. Origen's interest in the literal text can also be seen in his nearly obsessive attention to detail which he takes extremely seriously (see

Scripture). His discussion of the word *arche* (in *ComJn* 1.90–124) is a classic example of his style. No other ancient author was more aware of the Bible's many inconsistencies at the literal level, and no other ancient author worked harder to resolve them.

Still, despite Origen's considerable efforts to attend to the literal text, many modern commentators insist that Origen only feigned interest in the literal. Others accuse him of amateurism, noting, for example, that the *Hexapla* seriously corrupted the text of the Septuagint and did more damage than good to the textual tradition. Yet, as noted above, to evaluate Origen in this way is to apply modern historical critical bias anachronistically to one's assessment of his project. While it is true that Origen's understanding of the complexity of history is unsophisticated by modern standards, we should not, therefore, conclude that he had no interest in or appreciation for the words on the page or the details of the Bible.

Modern (and indeed ancient) criticism of Origen's exegesis, however, goes beyond concern with his limitations as a text critic. During the twentieth century, many readers of Origen worried that spiritual and allegorical reading of the Bible radically devalued history and causes Christianity to free float above the concrete and the particular. Some scholars saw in Origen's interpretive method clear evidence that in the end he was a Platonist—or worse, a gnostic—who had forgotten the incarnational principle of Christianity. Allegory or spiritual reading, in this view, does irreparable harm to the Christian message and is a contagion that must be eradicated from Christianity once and for all. This perspective contributed to a general tendency within the academies that largely practiced historical criticism to reject all ancient Christian interpretation out of hand, not just that of Origen. Other scholars, recognizing that Christianity could not hold on to the Old Testament as Scripture without allowing some form of "spiritual reading," attempted to distinguish between *typology* and *allegory*. Allegedly, the former respected historical particularity while the latter denied it. But even here, Origen emerged as a fringe figure whose exegetical antics had supposedly led him away from legitimate typology into illegitimate allegory.

In recent years, however, under the influence of postmodern literary theory, it has become possible to offer a more sympathetic reading of Origen the allegorist. From this perspective allegory and typology are not really very different; both are forms of figurative reading in which the literal text is read as meaning something other than it appears to mean. Typology is not any more respectful of history than allegory is. Reading figuratively, whether allegorically or typologically, is simply part of the way human beings appropriate texts and inscribe upon them enduring value. Without figurative reading, a text such as the Bible would cease to be a living text for the community and sink to the level of an artifact. One might, again from this perspective, disagree with the theology embedded in the reading or with some of the conclusions of the exegete, but the effort to bridge the distance between the experience of the reader and the text through the use of figure is by no means illegitimate. Students of Origen influenced by this approach to interpretation point out that historical critical inquiry, on its own, cannot preserve the Bible as a meaningful document for the Christian community. In a context of renewed sympathy for ancient exegesis in general, Origen emerges not as a dangerous subversive who destroys the letter but as the giant who helped the Christian church to preserve its mooring in the ancient text, and through that text to maintain its historical link to ancient Israel. For these reasons, study of Origen over the last fifty years has labored extensively to illuminate his extraordinary exegesis.

We now recognize that Origen understood the importance of such a connection. He did not, after all, develop his exegetical method simply as a thought experiment. Origen, like *Clement of Alexandria* before him, worried about the tendency of some Christians to dismiss the Old Testament as irrelevant or, worse, as the product of a malevolent god bent on the destruction of the children of the light (see *Gnostics*). This broad dualistic movement that we now call Gnosticism attracted many Christians and forced those who would resist to develop methods of interpretation that would preserve the church's connection to the text and the past, without falling into a kind of wooden literalism that was then, as it is now, essentially untenable. Scriptural interpretation in Origen must be understood as a broadly antignostic agenda (*ComJn* 13).

Resistance to gnostic reading, however, explains Origen's exegetical project only partially. A second powerful factor in the development of Origen's method was emerging rabbinic *Judaism*. More and more patristic scholars recognize that Christianity and rabbinic Judaism developed in tandem and, to some extent, in reaction to each other. During the first through third centuries, and perhaps into the fourth in some areas, the Christian and the Jewish communities existed in close proximity to each other. Christianity and Judaism had not yet so clearly defined themselves that they were always recognizable as separate religions. The ambiguity of these boundaries was most keenly felt in the early centuries of Christian and rabbinic Jewish history. We also know that Origen was more aware of Judaism and Jewish interpretation than perhaps any other ancient Christian author. We should not, therefore, underestimate the extent to which Origen's exegesis developed in response to his knowledge of the emerging rabbinic tradition. When Origen read the Bible figuratively, he was staking the Christian claim for the same text and the same history that the rabbis were claiming for themselves. It is worth noting that although rabbinic exegesis is not the same as Christian exegesis,

neither is it historical-critical. Rabbinic Judaism, via the Talmud, developed its own methods of preserving a connection to ancient Israel and its texts.

A final factor vital to understanding Origen's use of figurative reading is his attempt to understand biblical revelation in the light of Platonic metaphysics. The Platonic universe explodes from the pages of Origen's exegesis, especially the classic problems of the relationship between the one and the many, and between spirit and matter (*PArch* 2.1.4; 3.4.6). On the one hand, we can say that when Origen interpreted the Bible and Christianity Platonically, he was doing nothing more than what many contemporary theologians do when they attempt to understand the Bible and Christianity in the light of quantum physics. Origen believed in the unity of truth and knowledge; it was inconceivable to him that Plato and Moses would teach fundamentally opposing views of reality. On the other hand, from the point of view of the larger Christian tradition, some aspects of Platonism cannot be easily reconciled with Christianity, especially the Christian understanding of creation from nothing, the enduring value of bodily life, and even the particularity of the human sexual differentiation.

Many of Origen's ideas about these issues were expanded and modified by later generations of Christian theologians who traced their own path back to Origen with varying degrees of accuracy. These "Origenists," as well as Origen himself, were eventually condemned at the Second Council of Constantinople in 553, largely for their tendency to draw too close to Platonism in the areas noted above (see *Origenist Crises*). The condemnation of Origen and Origenism had a significant impact on the reception and transmission of Origen's exegetical project, even though by the time it happened his principles had been largely absorbed into the bloodstream of the church, as it were. The most obvious consequence of Origen's condemnation was the material loss of his work. Much has been lost, and much of what does survive does so only in Latin translation. A second, less obvious consequence of the condemnation, however, was the introduction of new exegetical terminology into Christian exegesis. Many of the opponents of Origen, while really objecting to certain theological positions, traced the Origenist problem to exegetical practices associated with the term *allegoria*. As a result, subsequent generations of interpreters, eager to avoid the charge of Origenism, preferred the more neutral term *theoria*. The actual exegetical practice, however, remained virtually unchanged. We see this especially in the work of the Cappadocians, but also in the writing of Cyril of Alexandria and even the Antiochene exegete Theodoret of Cyrrhus.

Readers who are unaware of the political problems surrounding the word *allegory* in the fourth and fifth centuries would be seriously mistaken to take the condemnation of the term *allegoria* as a condemnation of allegorical or figurative reading. Indeed, while the extremes of Origenist accommodation to Platonism were controlled by later theology, there is no evidence that Origen's approach to the Bible was abandoned. Scriptural interpretation in Origen was primarily a process by which the Christian community maintained its connection to historical Israel and its texts. It was not a tragic accommodation to Platonist antimaterialism, as many generalizing commentators have complained in the past. Moreover, the essentials of Origen's style continued to be practiced in both the Eastern and Western church until the advent of historical-critical inquiry. When judged in historical terms, Origen's method seems to be nothing more than pious fantasy. However, in recent years scholars have increasingly pointed out the limits of historical-critical method. If the trend continues, Origen's methods may yet be the subject of serious attention beyond the community of patristic scholars. No matter what, Origen certainly deserves

to be remembered as one of the greatest Christian interpreters of the Bible in the history of the Christian church.

Clark (1992); Dawson (2002); Torjesen (1985, 1986); Trigg (1983).
                                    JOHN J. O'KEEFE

Scripture   Origen's approach to the Scriptures depends on certain presuppositions about their nature, the first and most important of which is that the text of Scripture is "divine writing," not human. Through an examination of the fulfillment of the "oracles" of Christ (Matt. 24:14; 7:22) and of other prophetic utterances in the Scriptures (Gen. 49:10; Hos. 3:4), Origen demonstrates the divine nature of the Scriptures or, as he says, that they are "divine writings" (*theion grammaton*) (*PArch* 4.1.2–3). Origen accepts the common Christian doctrine that the **Holy Spirit** inspired all the authors of Scripture, whether Moses or the **apostles**, to such an extent that the Holy Spirit is to be considered the true author of the sacred texts (*PArch* 1. Praef. 4; 1.3.1; 4.2.7; 4.3.14; *CCels* 3.3; 5.60; *ComMt* 14.4; *HomGn* 7.1; *HomEx* 2.1; *HomNum* 1.1; 2.1; *HomJos* 8.6; *Hom 1R* (*1S*) 5.4). The corollary of this is that "the words which are believed by us to be from God are not the compositions of men (*anthropon syngrammata*)" (*PArch* 4.1.6), a conclusion that has important consequences for the concept of "Scripture" and its interpretation. The same idea is restated further on: "the sacred books are not the works of men . . . they were composed and have come down to us as a result of the inspiration of the Holy Spirit by the will of the Father of the universe through Jesus Christ" (*PArch* 4.2.2).

Building on the basic principle that Scripture contains an esoteric or cryptic sense (*PArch* 1. Praef. 8; 4.2.2), an assumption he shared with virtually all ancient interpreters, Origen cites Proverbs 22:20–21 to justify the idea of a threefold sense in the Scriptures, an idea supported also by comparison with the human composite of body, soul, and spirit (1 Thess. 5:23; *PArch* 4.2.4; *HomNum* 9.7; *HomLev* 5.1) (see **Allegory, Sacraments, Scriptural Interpretation**). This theoretical foundation allowed Origen to perceive at least two spiritual senses hidden beneath the veil of the letter, which also correspond to different degrees of spiritual initiation or progress: beginners, advanced and perfect (cf. 1 Cor 2:6), a progression found already in **Philo** (see also *HomJos* 6.1; *ComMt* 12.32). This progression can also be seen to correspond to the division of the law, the prophets, and the gospel (*HomLev* 1.4).

Another basic assumption Origen shared with other ancient interpreters was that of the actuality of the Scriptures. He often cites 1 Corinthians 10, especially verses 6 and 11, to emphasize that the Scriptures were written "for us" and reach their fulfillment in the present time (the time of the church), which is also understood as the "end of the ages." The text is often cited as an introduction to moral exhortation, which is indeed the original Pauline context of 1 Corinthians 10:1–11. Commenting on the expression "by mud and bricks" (Exod. 1:14), Origen states: "These words were not written to instruct us in history, nor must we think that the divine books narrate the acts of the Egyptians. What has been written has been written for our instruction and admonition," and in dealing with the command of the king of Egypt to the midwives to kill the male children of the Israelites, he observes that "we have learned that all things which are written are written not to relate ancient history, but for our discipline and our use" (*HomEx* 1.5; see also the other texts where Origen cites 1 Cor. 10:6,11, namely, *HomEx* 7.4; *HomJos* 5.2; *HomJd* 2.3; *HomJr* 12.3;19.15; *HomEz* 12.2). To this general idea of the actuality of the Scriptures Paul had added the concept of the two ages (1 Cor. 10:11), which considerably facilitates the possibility of allegorical comparisons between the two ages, then and now, such as is found in 1 Corinthians 10:1–11 and Galatians 4:21–24. Since the text is "for us," it must also have a meaning that is "useful" to us, a criterion of interpretation that had already been developed by Philo and was suggested also by affirmation that "all Scripture is useful" (2 Tim. 3:16; see *Hom 1R (1S)* 5.2; *PArch* 4.1.7; 4.2.6; *HomNum* 27.1). "Useful," for Origen generally means that which is helpful for moral or spiritual nourishment.

Another presupposition about the nature of the text, which also becomes a criterion of interpretation, is that its real meaning must be "worthy of the divine majesty" (*HomLev* 7.5). In this phrase we can perceive an ancient idea that goes back to the philosopher Xenophanes, an idea that had been used as a hermeneutical tool in the interpretation of Homer and then later by Philo in the interpretation of the law of Moses, where its most characteristic expression is found in the expression "fitting" or "appropriate" to God (*theoprepes*). The concept is formulated by Origen also in the context of the controversial principle of the missing literal sense (*defectus litterae*). He explains that certain stumbling blocks and impossibilities have been inserted in the biblical books of law and history "in order that we may not be completely drawn away by the sheer attractiveness of the language, and so either reject the true doctrines absolutely, on the ground that we learn from the scriptures nothing worthy of God, or else by never moving away from the letter fail to learn anything of the more divine element." The more skillful and inquiring readers may thus "gain a sound conviction of the necessity of seeking in such instances a meaning worthy of God" (*PArch* 4.2.9). This principle as well as the accompanying ideas of illogical (*alogon*) and impossible (*adunaton*) things inserted into the text by the divine author, in order to incite the reader to seek a suitable meaning, are features of interpretation that had been already used extensively by Philo of Alexandria.

These presuppositions produce a paradoxical situation: the text on the literal level may not be worthy of God, but when it is given a spiritual interpretation, it can be seen to be divine, and viewed as a divine composition, it is superior to all other human texts. Origen remarks: "And he who approaches the prophetic words with care and attention will feel from his very reading a trace of their divine inspiration (*to entheon*) and will be convinced by his own feelings that the words which are believed by us to be from God are not the compositions of men." The reader is able to perceive the inspired nature (*to entheon*) of the Scripture through a kind of mystical transport or "enthusiasm" (*enthusiasmos*). It may be possible to perceive this even on the level of the literal text, but certainly not in the literal level of many or most texts of the Old Testament, for Origen says explicitly that it was not possible before the advent of Christ. What is perceived then is not the literal text but the "spiritual nature" or the "light" contained within the law of Moses (*PArch* 4.1.6; *ComJn* 1.30.33; *CCels* 6.5).

Another consequence of the idea of the divine, not human, composition of Scripture is that God is the author of the text even in (what a modern writer might consider) its most insignificant details. Commenting on Genesis 22:1, where God calls out, "Abraham!" Origen exhorts his congregation: "Observe each detail which has been written. For, if one knows how to dig into the depth, he will find a treasure in the details, and perhaps also, the precious jewels of the mysteries lie hidden where they are not esteemed" (*HomGn* 8.1). The phrase "a treasure in the details" could be taken as emblematic for a certain understanding of the nature of the biblical text itself. In this particular case Origen goes on to explain that nowhere had God ever called Abraham by the name Abram, nor had he ever said "Abram, Abram." The reason God never called Abraham by the name Abram is that he could not call him by a name that was to be abolished, but

only by the name that he himself gave, the name that means "I have made you the ancestor of a multitude of nations" (Gen. 17:5). Similar details such as "the mountains" (Gen. 22:2 LXX), or "the third day" (Gen. 22:4), serve as a springboard for spiritual or christological interpretations (*HomGn* 8.3–4). Thus details are given a high significance that they did not have in the original context of the narrative of the sacrifice of Isaac. This procedure may even run counter to the normal rules of rhetoric, as in the case of Origen's interpretation of "the hand [NRSV, "the leadership"] of Moses and Aaron" (Num. 33:1 LXX) to represent two aspects of the spiritual life, the practical and the contemplative, inseparably united (as one hand) even though this is a clear case of common *synecdoche* (the rhetorical use of the singular for the plural), which (as Origen knew) was a very well-known figure of speech (*HomNum* 27.6). Such procedures are possible because of the basic conception of the text as an oracular, encoded text, with an esoteric meaning, even if the text itself is public and widely diffused.

A result of this conception of the text is the devaluation of the historical or narrative character of the text. In another example of attention to details, Origen observes that the expressions "to go up" and "to go down" (Gen. 13:1) are never employed in such a way that "anyone is ever said to have gone down to a holy place nor is anyone ever related to have gone up to a blameworthy place." This demonstrates that Scripture was composed with care (lit., "with attention to details") and not "in illiterate and uncultivated language," because Scripture is devoted not "so much to historical narratives as to things and ideas which are mystical" (*HomGn* 15.1). The contrast between history and mystery, found many times in Origen, is part of his inheritance from Philo (cf. Philo, *Somn.* 1.52–58; *Cher.* 42–49) and has its roots in the Greek view that neither history nor natural science can provide the "truth that is really useful." In philosophical terms, this is because what is really useful is perennially valid, whereas history is contingent and particular. Origen's twenty-seventh homily on Numbers is an excellent example where the narrative of Israel's movements in the desert is made to reveal mystical truths about the economy of salvation and the journey of the soul (see **Number Symbolism**). This means "seeking out the mysteries of the Scriptures with attentive exertions" (*HomNum* 27.8), that is, deciphering the letter in order to find the spiritual content. The term *mystery* had been employed extensively by Paul to indicate God's plan or dispensation revealed in Jesus Christ. Origen of course knows and cites these passages from Paul, but the idea of Scripture itself as containing or covering mysteries had already been developed extensively by Philo, to whom, as already noted, Origen is deeply indebted (see **Mysteries, Sacraments**).

In practice, the meaning that is useful for us and fitting to God is often achieved through recourse to the principle of "interpreting the Scriptures by means of the Scriptures," a principle of interpretation already developed in the Hellenistic exegesis of Homer and extensively employed by Philo of Alexandria. Origen uses the Pauline phrase "comparing spiritual things with spiritual things" (NRSV, "interpreting spiritual things to those who are spiritual") (1 Cor. 2:13) to legitimate the procedure (*HomGn* 2.6), but he also sees the practice as a response to Jesus' command to "search the scriptures" (John 5:39; *PArch* 4.3.5). He relates a simile that he heard from a rabbi, in which the Scriptures are compared to a house with a large number of locked rooms in which the keys have been mixed up and dispersed. We are able to understand obscure passages of Scripture when we take as a point of departure a similar passage from another portion of Scripture, because "the principle of interpretation has been dispersed among them" (*Philoc* 2.3). For example, to explain Song of Songs 2.9, in which the beloved is compared to a

gazelle or young stag, Origen assembles all references to these animals that he can find in other books of Scripture (*ComCt* 3). This procedure of explaining Scripture by Scripture is based on the fundamental premise that the Holy Spirit is the true author of the whole Bible, as we have already mentioned, and that all that is written in it are words of the same God (*HomEz* 1.4).

The question of the unity of the Scriptures was a major concern for Origen as a result of the **gnostic** and Marcionite challenge (see **Old Testament**). As a result he stresses that the entire Scriptures are the word of Christ, and Christ is the key to understanding all of them. By "words of Christ" he means not only those words that formed his teaching after the incarnation, but also Moses and the prophets, who were filled with the spirit of Christ. For it is the same Word of God that is found in the Scriptures before the incarnation as the Word Incarnate (*PArch* 1. Praef. 1; *HomIs* 1.5; *SerMt* 28.54.119; *FragmJn* 46). For Origen, the entirety of Scripture is the revelation of Christ, whether the Old Testament (the Law and the Prophets) or the New Testament (the gospel and the apostles). Christ himself, since he is the Logos, is the Word of God itself, and consequently Christ and the Scriptures are to be identified. Scripture is nothing other than the perennial incarnation of the **Logos** (see **Christology**). Thus Origen can identify the treasure hidden in the field (Matt. 13:44) with both Christ and Scripture (*ComMt* 10.6) and likewise compares the Word of God that is clothed with flesh through Mary with the Scripture that is covered with the veil of the literal sense (*HomLev* 1.1). Only through a searching study of the Scriptures can we know Christ. The same concern for knowing Christ in the Scriptures and for the significance of every detail is reflected in Origen's view that to preach the word of God is to preach Christ and is a process of revelation realized in the understanding created in the individual mind of the listener. The word preached and received in the heart and understanding of the individual constructs the tabernacle in which the Lord lives. The reception of the details of the word may be compared (even compared more favorably) to the reception of the body of the Lord in the Eucharist (*HomEx* 13.3).

Crouzel (1989), 61–84; Hanson (1959, 2002); Nardoni (1984); Shin (1999); Trigg (1984).

MARK SHERIDAN

Souls Although Paul's occasional distinction of the three aspects of the human being, "spirit, soul, and body" (1 Thess. 5:23), is referred to several times in Origen's works, this does not mean that, for him, humanity had originally been created as such (see *Anthropology, Cosmology*). In the beginning, as Origen saw it, God had created a certain number of rational creatures, that is spiritual (*noetic*) beings without material bodies, gifted with reason (*logos*), and destined to contemplate God (see *Preexistence*). In Rufinus's Latin translation of the *First Principles*, these rational, spiritual creatures are called *mens*, which is a translation of the Greek term *nous*, which means "mind," "intelligence," "spirit." Inspired by Plato and Philo, Origen supposes that Genesis 1 deals with an initial, immaterial creation, of which humanity, as *nous*, is said to be created in God's image and likeness (Gen. 1:26). But since rational creatures decided to fall away from God, who is fire, they lost their original state of *nous* and cooled down to become "souls." Thus Origen alludes to the then well-known interpretation of the Greek term *psyche* (soul), which was derived from *psychesthai*, "to grow cold" (*PArch* 2.8.3). Origen believes that Jesus referred to this fall of spirits to become souls in Matthew 24:12, "Because of the increase of lawlessness, the love of many will grow cold." To these souls, who chilled in quite different degrees, God gave bodies that corresponded to the gravity of their respective fall. Some souls received celestial bodies (stars and planets were considered as being animated); others became angels or demons (see *Demonology*); still other souls received human bodies (see *Fall*). Origen supposes that the second, material creation of humanity is described in Genesis 2:7, which says that God formed the man of the "dust of the ground" and made him "a living soul." By means of this interpretation Origen intends to explain that some people, such as Jacob and Esau, for example, are profoundly different because each one of them as preexistent spirits took a free and distinct decision to what extent one wanted to participate in this premundane fall. Thus Origen tries to refute the Marcionites and the *gnostics*, who held (at least as far as he understood them) that the *Old Testament* Creator was unjust (*PArch* 1.7; 1.8.4; 2.8.1; 2.8.3–4; 2.9.1–6; *DialHer* 15–16).

According to Origen, however, one soul, namely, the soul of Jesus, the one who would "love righteousness and hate wickedness" (Ps. 45:7), did not fall away from God and was therefore to be anointed, which means that this soul was elected (and itself elected) to be united with Christ (see *Christology*). It may seem problematic that Origen speaks of the soul of Christ as existing prior to the fall of the other rational creatures, who became souls precisely because of their fall. But since Christ clearly refers to his soul (John 10:18; 12:27; Matt. 26:38), and Origen clearly dismisses from consideration that his soul had taken any part in the fall, he was pressed to take account of this scriptural evidence. Since Scripture even speaks of God's soul (Isa. 1:14; 42:1; Ezek. 23:18), Origen presumes that God's soul may be his only begotten Son (*PArch* 2.6.3–5; 2.8.2; 2.8.4–5).

Origen considers that animals also have souls, at least as they answer to the traditional definition that the soul is an "imaginary and reacting substance"; however, he does not admit that animals (as less than rational) can ever receive human souls (*PArch* 2.8.1) (see

Transmigration of Souls, Universalism). As for human souls, Origen is critical about the Platonic tripartition of the soul into a reasonable, a desirous, and an irascible part, since it is not a scripturally validated doctrine; yet he occasionally refers to it positively (*PArch* 3.4.1; *HomEz* 1.16; *FragmHomLc* 187). He rejects the (probably gnostic) opinion that human beings have two souls, a good or celestial one, which is related to the spirit, and an inferior or earthly one, related to the flesh. Instead, Origen makes use of the binary Pauline distinction of the flesh and the spirit (Rom. 8:3–16; Gal. 5:16–26; also Matt. 26:41). He argues that during their earthly lives human souls are placed "in between" these two conditions. If a soul is inclined to follow the spirit (*pneuma*), she is related to the Spirit of God, but if she follows the vices of the flesh and the body, she is hostile to God (*PArch* 3.4.2–5). In contrast to the interpretation of Genesis 1:26 given above, Origen even suggests that the creation of humanity according to God's image as male and female (Gen. 1:26–27) may allegorically point to the existence of the "male spirit" and the "female soul," which implies that the spirit and the soul have to find an existential unity in order to be "fruitful" (*HomGn* 1.15).

Origen teaches that the soul should acquire self-knowledge regarding her origin, identity, and disposition. She has to learn that she was created in God's image and that she is destined to be restored to her original state, and not to transmigrate to another body under the conditions of the present life. Furthermore, the soul has to examine her acts, test her progress in the virtues, and review her faults. Basically, she has to know God and his creation and be united to the divine bridegroom, Christ (*ComCt* 2.5; cf. *HomNum* 27.5–13). A soul that is inclined to the flesh and to sin will undergo a harsh treatment when the body dies. Origen says that demons will claim the souls who are tainted with vices, whereas the Lord will save pure souls from the demons' claims (*HomPs*

36.5.7). He refers to Jesus' saying (according to the Greek text of Luke 12:46) that a bad servant will be "cut in twain" and that his part will be "put with the unfaithful." Origen explains that just so will the spirit be separated from the soul, the spirit in this case signifying either the *Holy Spirit* or the better part of the soul (that is, the *nous*), which is made "according to the *image of God*." When this spirit will be taken away from the soul, the latter will be "put with the unfaithful," that is, in *Hades* (*gehenna*). Thus it is true that "the spirit returns to God who gave it" (Eccl. 12:7; *PArch* 2.10.7; *SerMt* 57; 62). Yet Origen essentially holds that the soul's torments in hell are intended to purify and to restore her to her original state of *nous* (*PArch* 2.8.3; *CCels* 6.25).

Dupuis (1967); Ferwerda (1983); Hennessey (1991); Pierre (1984).

RIEMER ROUKEMA

Theoria   See **Allegory, Scriptural Interpretation.**

Three Senses of Scripture   See **Typology, Scriptural Interpretation.**

Tradition   The Bible, correctly interpreted, is the foundation upon which Origen's understanding of the Christian tradition stands (see *Scripture*). This scriptural tradition begins with Christ himself, who declares the truth about God to the disciples (even beginning with the ancient prophets in his role as *Logos* inspiring the *Old Testament* saints). They, in turn, write these teachings down and hand them down ultimately to the present generation, to illuminated Christian teachers (such as Origen considers himself as an inspired Didaskalos), who find the traces of these teachings in the written books and thus "possess the foundations of [their] own theology" (*CCels* 2.71). The tradition is further developed by "investigation of the logical consequences of the Scriptures and adherence to accuracy" (*PArch* Praef. 10). The illuminated Christian teacher interprets it faithfully, in agreement with the whole church, avoiding the private interpretations of gnostic sectarians, by fidelity to the *rule of faith*.

Even so, Origen's understanding of Christian tradition is inextricably bound up with his doctrine of a secret tradition of teaching and interpretation. Origen bases this doctrine on passages such as John 16:12 and 2 Corinthians 12:1–4, where secret wisdom and secret experience are described. *Paul*, in ascending to the third heaven, represents (along with *John the Theologian*) the paradigm of the Spirit-illumined interpreter of the *mysteries*. Origen also speculates that Christ imparted secret knowledge to certain of his followers, "whom he knew to be fit to receive unspeakable mysteries" (*HomJos* 23.4). The enlightened disciples are teachers par excellence, instructing and baptizing all nations. Because they are able to "discern the depths of God . . . they are called kings" (*HomNum* 12.2.4). Just as this secret tradition is imparted to only a few disciples, the gift of spiritual understanding of the mysteries is given to only an intellectual elite. There are "certain doctrines, as it were, taught in addition to the common level of teaching, which do not reach the majority of people" (*CCels* 1.7). These secret doctrines are not independent of the Bible but are derived from it only by those who have been given the gift of wisdom to "advance in discernment by the sanctification of the Holy Spirit" (*PArch* 1.3.4).

The secret tradition serves to amplify points of theology left unclear in Scripture, such as the salvation of souls, the nature of God and of the Son of God, the nature of angels, differences between souls, the nature of creation, and the origin and extent of evil (*PArch* Praef. 4–10), matters Origen knows the rule of faith has not yet settled. In contrast to "the most necessary doctrines," delivered in plain terms by the *apostles*, the deeper doctrines are intended to be explained by the spiritually gifted, (the immediate spiritual successors of the apostles) as "an exercise on which to prove the fruit of their ability" (*PArch* Praef. 4), through the application of allegorical interpretation. Intellectual ability is not enough. The true teacher must possess "a sincere and simple heart, and apply himself constantly and far into the night, to achieve a deep understanding of Scripture" (*ComRm* 7.17).

A major part of Christian tradition, as Origen understands it, and wishes to assimilate himself to it, is the rule of faith, which he describes variously as "the Church's principles," "the intention of sound teaching" (*HomJr* 5.14), and "the mind of the Church" (*ComMt* 17.35). He understands the rule of faith to be the whole content of Christian faith and teaching, as these are handed down in Scripture and made known in preaching and liturgy. The rule of faith is closely linked with Scripture and with preaching but is not identical with either. It is in part that which can be clearly affirmed from the apostolic preaching and teaching and is generally believed by the faithful in the church. It has in part, however, been deliberately left open for further investigation by charismatic teachers, through the study and allegorical interpretation of Scripture. The Alexandrian tradition as a whole considered allegorical interpretation, derived from the apostle Paul, to be itself part of the very rule of faith. Origen speaks often of the allegorization of Scripture as the church's special way of interpreting the Bible, handed down to her by the apostolic tradition (*HomLev* 5.8; 7.4; *HomEx* 5.1), for the interpretation of mysteries.

Although Scripture was central to Origen's understanding of tradition, he did not attempt to establish a canon of Scripture (see *Apostles, Gospels, Scripture*). He quoted often from apocryphal gospels and other noncanonical books, for the intrinsic theological value of a work and the tradition of its acceptance by the church seem to have been more important than authorship alone. Nevertheless,

Origen's primary use of the Septuagint, the four canonical Gospels, and the Pauline writings, certainly (and authoritatively) foreshadows the later Christian development of a canon of Scripture.

A part of Origen's understanding of tradition that may have contributed to his difficulties with the bishops of Alexandria is that leadership in the church is exercised on the basis of a charism of intellect, interpretation, and teaching, rather than on a hierarchical or organizational succession. As he argued it, "Grace is given to each of the saints . . . above all [to] teachers" (*ComEp* 9) (see *Bishops, Priesthood, Sacraments*). It is thus by the direct gift of the *Holy Spirit* that the charism of authority is passed on, not by any organizational claim. The apostles became the conduits for the tradition, not because they were officeholders, but because they were able "to discern the depths of God and pierce the mysteries [and thus] they are called kings" (*HomNum* 12.2). If they are kings, so the argument runs implicitly, then such illumined teachers as come after them (like Origen) are "princes" of the church. Such teachers are able to nourish other believers with the food of the Logos. They carry out quasi-sacramental functions: "Jesus, therefore, washed the feet of the disciples insofar as he was their teacher" (*ComJn* 32.115). For Origen it is always spiritual insight and holiness of life that evidence the true charisma of authority, rather than official position. The bearer of the church's tradition is the inspired exegete, the teacher who is responsible for mediating God's Word to believers at all levels of spiritual progress. For Origen, this implies that the true Christian tradition is passed down and advanced by charismatic individuals, not by organizations. It is a doctrine that many of the most influential Eastern fathers of the fourth century will emphasize, most particularly Gregory of Nazianzus. In the life and writings of Origen we see reflected the pivotal struggle to define the church's understanding of tradition and author-

ity. It was a struggle that cost Origen much in his own lifetime, and a point on which Christianity ever since has never quite come to rest.

Bardy (1919); Hanson (1954); Trigg (1981).
ALAN G. PADDLE

Transfiguration   Origen likes to distinguish between Jesus who appears as a servant to those in the Gospels (and symbolically also those represented under this figure in his own generation) who stand "below the mountain" (that is, hearing Jesus on the plains or in the valleys), and Jesus the Christ, who appears in the form of God to the disciples on the mountain (*ComMt* 12.37). In the elevated place, the mountain of his transfiguration (Matt. 17:1–9) (which denotes the spiritual acuity of those who see him more fully in his divinity), his face "shines as the sun," and he appears in *glory* (*HomEx*. 3.2; 12.3). For Origen, the transfiguration of Jesus involves a mystical event in which the Law and the Prophets, represented in the figures of Moses and Elijah, "become one with the Gospel of Jesus" (*ComMt* 12.38, 43) (see *Old Testament*). The "bright cloud" that appears during Jesus' transfiguration represents a "divine" tabernacle. It overshadows and therefore protects the "just" ones. Its appearance prefigures the forthcoming *resurrection* of Jesus (*ComMt* 12.42). The divine tabernacle contrasts with the three earthly tabernacles proposed by Peter, who "with evil intent," as Origen puts it, desires to separate out Jesus, Moses, and Elijah (*ComMt* 12.40). Origen's notice of the tone of censure of Peter that is recorded in the Gospel accounts of the transfiguration is thus transmuted into an antignostic motif, on the necessity of retaining a "seamless garment" of unity between the Old and New Testaments (see *Scripture*).

In the transfiguration Jesus' garments become the brightest and purest of all whites (*ComMt* 12.38). This metamorphosis of his clothing symbolizes the "letters of the Gospel with which he invested himself" (*ComMt* 12.38), and it is thus a directly christological aspect of Origen's generic teaching that the Scripture is the *sacrament* of Jesus' salvific presence. The illumination that is given to the eyes of the specially elected *apostles* results in their clear understanding of the Word and their special capacity to preach it. Even so, an illuminated disciple in the present age (an inspired interpreter of Scripture) can enter into the same experience of the metamorphosis. As Origen puts it, "When, therefore, you see any one not only with a thorough understanding of the theology concerning Jesus, but also making clear every expression of the Gospels, do not hesitate to say that for him the garments of Jesus have become as white as the light" (*ComMt* 12.38). Such illumination is far beyond any rhetorical brilliance that can be commanded by the "wise" of the world. They can never shine as bright as the glistening white of Jesus' transformed garments, when he is manifested as the divine Word (*ComMt* 12.39). Such eloquence can only aspire to the manner in which an "earthly fuller" can launder garments (cf. Mark 9:3).

It is significant for Origen that only those deemed to be "worthy" are elected to see Jesus transformed on the mountain. The chief apostles (Peter, James, and John) are given the divine grace of "spiritual vision" (*ComMt* 12.36). This enables them to see beyond the things of the world and the lusts of the body that "drag down the soul from the things which are better and more divine" (*ComMt* 12.36). Origen refers to the chosen disciples as the "children of light" who behold Jesus' face shine like the sun (*ComMt* 12.37).

Thus the brilliant light of the transfiguration of Jesus, as Origen sees it, has a hidden, intangible quality. Only an elected few have the spiritual experience of Jesus appearing "in the form of God" (cf. Phil. 2:6) (*ComMt* 12.37; *ComLc* 9.29). Only by divine intervention can one see

God, "even though our body and soul may make every effort to see" (*HomLc* 20). By contrast, Jesus in the Gospels is more easily seen "according to the flesh" by those who do not go the way of "the mountain" (*ComMt* 12.37; *HomLc.* 20.4). The "Beholding" of Jesus thus varies according to an individual's spiritual capacity to receive him (*ComMt* 12.36; *CCels* 2.64). Each sees according to his own "proper ability" (*HomGn* 1.7). Origen develops on this theme of the variability of Jesus, not merely through the concept of the spiritual *epinoiai* of the Logos, but even specifically to the point that Jesus, while on earth, actually appeared physically in a variety of forms to different characters in the Gospel story (and by implication to all embodied souls afterward) depending on their own spiritual state: appearing as noble, beautiful and persuasive, to those on the path to salvation; and as small, insignificant and a wicked teacher to those who were blinded by their sins. This, for Origen, is why the traitor Judas, knowing his master's capacity for confusing changes of appearance (and thus transcendence of a criminal "photofit"), when he prepared to hand him over in the garden, instructed the servants of the chief priest to lay hands only on the one he specifically identified by the act of kissing.

McGuckin (1986), (1987); Menard (1972).
JEFFREY PETTIS

Transmigration of Souls   Origen

has often been accused of teaching that after death human *souls* may transmigrate to animals, as a consequence of their wickedness. This accusation is mentioned in the early fourth century in Pamphilus's *Apology for Origen* 87 (PG 17.579B), in the early fifth century in Jerome's *Epistulae* 124.4, in the mid-sixth century in Justinian's *Letter to Mennas*, and in the ninth century in Photius's *Bibliotheca* 117. It has been repeated so many times that it has assumed the status of one of those things most people think they know about Origen. It is more or less a mistake. The allegation originates from Origen's investigation of the theme of metempsychosis (or the transmission of souls from one body to another) in *PArch* 1.8.4. The original Greek of this section is lost, meaning that we depend on Rufinus's abridged Latin translation, on Jerome's Latin version, and on Justinian's brief (and probably distorted) quotations in Greek. Transmigration of human souls to animals was debated by contemporary Pythagorean and Platonic philosophers, and Origen seems to know Christians who shared this opinion and referred to animals speaking with a human voice, such as Balaam's ass (Num. 22:28–30). According to Rufinus's version of *PArch* 1.8.4 Origen explicitly rejects this idea of transmigration as contrary to the Christian faith. Other texts in his corpus show that Rufinus's version of the story is correct. From *PArch* 2.9.3 and his earlier book *On the Resurrection* (see Pamphilus's *Apology* 134 [PG 17.596C]) it may be proved that Origen considers animals as dumb and secondary creatures and that he excludes the possibility that a sinner will ever receive an animal body. Even the hostile Jerome (*Epist.* 124.4) admits that Origen intended only to "investigate" the topic and not to establish a doctrine. In his later works Origen explicitly rejects the idea that the souls of humans were previously in beasts or birds or fish or will ever reincarnate in irrational animals (*ComRm* 6.6.8; *ComMt* 11.17; *CCels* 3.75; 4.83; 5.49; 8.30; cf. Ibid. 1.20).

It is the more unthinkable that Origen ever considered transmigration of human souls to animals as a serious possibility, as he also rejects the belief in transmigration of human souls to other human beings. Whenever he deals with the relationship between Elijah and John the Baptist, whom Jesus suggested were one and the same (Matt. 11:14; 17:10–13; John 1:21), he refutes the interpretation given by others (probably *gnostics*) who said that Elijah's soul had reincarnated

in John. One of Origen's opposing arguments is that Gabriel had announced that John would be endowed with Elijah's spirit and power, not with his soul (Luke 1:17). Furthermore he argues that, in case transmigration occurs because of sin, it would never end, since a soul would always have to dwell in a new body because of its former sins, so that it would be impossible that "heaven and earth will pass away" (Matt. 24:35). As a consequence, for Origen it is clear that "the doctrine of transmigration is foreign to the church of God" (*ComJn* 6.62–76; 6.85–86; *ComMt* 7; Pamphilus, *Apology* 178 [PG 17.608B–609A]; *ComMt* 13.1–2). The same refusal occurs time and again in his *Contra Celsum* (*CCels* 1.13; 4.17; 5.29; *ComCt* 2.5.24).

However, two reasons may be given why Origen was accused of teaching the transmigration of souls, in spite of his definite and repeated disapproval of this concept. First, the suspicion may sometimes have been inspired by a misunderstanding of his view of the *preexistence* of rational creatures and their subsequent incarnation as souls in human bodies. Yet Origen emphasizes that one should carefully distinguish between the incarnation of the soul and its transmigration (or reincarnation) (*ComJn* 6.85–86). This distinction is also underscored by the Neoplatonic philosopher Plotinus, who says that the first incarnation from an invisible body cannot be called transmigration (*Enn.* 4.3.9).

The second reason is weightier and shows that there is some truth in the ongoing suspicion that Origen taught the transmigration of souls. In his interpretation of Scripture, he often and extensively argues that God created all rational creatures with a free will (*PArch* 3.1; *Philoc* 23; 25–27). Thus he refutes his gnostic adversaries, who held (as Origen understands them) that God predestined human beings either for salvation or for perdition. In Origen's view, the free will of rational creatures brought about that they deliberately chose to fall away from their original and spiritual state of bliss (see *Fall, Demonology*). Subsequently, according to the gravity of their respective fall, God created for the descending souls the different bodies of *angels*, stars, planets, human beings, and demons (*PArch* 1.5.3; 1.7.2–5; 2.9.1–6). But since Origen is convinced that rational creatures will keep their free will when they will eventually be saved, and the age of this world will be restored to its original spiritual state, the theoretical possibility of a new fall will remain. For if a new fall were impossible, God's creatures would have lost their freedom. But Origen presumed that in case rational creatures would again fall away from God, God will create a new material world and new bodies for the falling souls. So, in some respect at least, he seems to accept the Greek, mainly Stoic, concept of a cycle of worlds (*CCels* 4.11–12; 4.67–68; 5.20–21). The implication of his argument is that souls that had fallen once and were saved and restored might fall again and receive another body, though not in the age of the present world (for Origen definitely excludes transmigration in this world order) but perhaps in the next age of a following world. There might even be a third and a fourth fall, and as many ages, but finally, Origen believes, God's love will overcome all inclination of his creatures to fall away from him and call all back in a universal *apokatastasis* (see *Universalism*) (*PArch* 1.3.8; 2.3.1–5; *PEuch* 27.15; 29.14; *ComRm* 5.10.13–16; 8.13.10; Jerome, *Epist.* 124.3–14; Jerome, *Ruf.* 2.12).

Although Origen presents this reasoning not as a doctrine but simply as a theoretical speculation, one may conclude that in an unusual way he let in the possibility of transmigration. In antiquity, however, the implications of an idea were just as often ascribed to a thinker as the explicit doctrine itself, and Origen's critical readers, such as Jerome, did not or would not understand the theoretical and experimental aspect of his arguments and indignantly accused him of teaching heresies, such as the

transmigration of souls. Whereas Origen in the third century was concerned with exploring the "boundaries" of the Christian faith with respect to contemporary Hellenistic metaphysics, most of his later readers could not appreciate his intentions and considered him as being led astray too often by pagan *philosophy*.

Albrecht (1983); Dorival (1980); Lies (1999); Roukema (1999).

RIEMER ROUKEMA

Trinitarianism

Origen's Trinitarian theology is one of the most influential elements of his thought. The so-called "Neo-Nicene" formula (*mia ousia, treis hypostaseis*; "one substance, three persons"), prepared by a council in Alexandria 362 (cf. PG 26.795–810) and dogmatized through the creed of the Council of Constantinople 381 (explicitly in a letter of the same synod in 382, as in Theodoret, *Historia ecclesiastica* 5.9.11), is a structure of thinking about the Trinity which is fundamentally based on Origen's thinking. It is equally true that anti-Nicene theologians of the fourth century, such as the church historian Eusebius of Caesarea and his confederate Eusebius of Nicomedia, relied on Origen for many of their arguments against the Nicene Creed. Insofar as the supporters, as well as the opponents, of subordinationist categories within Trinitarian theology all fought their cases with the help of Origen's doctrine, the whole argument (which can be more or less identified with the fourth-century Arian crisis) can be seen to be a struggle at international level over the authoritative interpretation of Origen's Trinitarian schema. The main reason for this double outcome (in pro- and anti-Nicene avenues) of his version of Trinitarianism is undoubtedly the unfinished and experimental character of the Trinitarian theology in his writings. One interesting sign of how these later debates profoundly affected issues of the reception of Origen is the way in which Rufinus corrected his translation of relevant passages in *First Principles* in order to make them conform more to Nicene standards (see, e.g., the polemic against any differentiation in the Trinity; *PArch* 1.3.7).

Origen calls faith in the Trinity "a threefold cord" (Eccl. 4:12), "from which the whole Church hangs and by which it is sustained" (*HomEx* 9.3). He uses the terms "venerable Trinity" (*he proskynete trias*; *ComJn* 6.33.166; *ComRm* 1.16), "eternal Trinity" (*he aionios trias*; *ComJn* 10.39.240), and "the primary" or "ruling Trinity" (*he archike trias*; *ComMt* 15.31; cf. *PArch* 1.4.3). Apart from introducing this terminology Origen also indicates the reason why he is not able to establish a fully developed system of the mystery of Trinity (*FragmJn* 20). In his homilies he carefully expounds allusions to the Trinity (e.g., *HomGn* 2.5; *HomNum* 21.2; *HomJr* 8.1; and *ComMt* 12.42; 17.4) but stresses that only Christ has brought fuller understanding in the latter times: "In these things, I see an indication, that those earlier figures who used to be led by the Law did indeed touch upon the knowledge of the Trinity, yet not entirely and perfectly but only 'in part'" (*HomJos* 3.2; for the Greek original, cf. PG 87.1: 997A). The notion of the Trinity as a "mystery adumbrated only in the last times" is also prevalent in Gregory of Nazianzus's exposition of the divinity of the Spirit, based very much on Origen's ideas, in his *Fifth Theological Oration* (*Orat.* 31), where he introduced a new technical term (procession) to describe and define Trinitarian process.

One of the most interesting and characteristic elements of Origen's doctrine of Trinity is its reception of the philosophic concept of *hypostasis* ("substance," in the sense of "actual existence" of a concrete being): "We, however, are persuaded that there are three hypostases, the Father, the Son, and the Holy Spirit, and we believe that only the Father is Unbegotten" (*ComJn* 2.10.75). Origen, therefore, uses the word in its earlier, more generic Middle Platonic

sense, not in the more specific connotation that would later be established by Porphyry in the Neoplatonic theory of principles. He calls it a "wrong faith" to reduce the Father and Son to one hypostasis (*ComMt* 17.14; *SelGn* PG 12.109D), thus attacking the old monarchian tradition. Elsewhere, again he deplores those who confuse the concepts (*ennoiai*) of Father and Son and make them out to be one in *hypostasis* (*ComMt* 17.14). From *ComJn* 1.24.151 and *FragmJn* 123 it becomes quite clear that (contrary to the later Neo-Nicene practice) *hypostasis* is for Origen the near equivalent to substance (*ousia*) and that the term implies that the Son and the Spirit have their own substance (*PEuch* 15.1: *heteros kat' ousian kai hypokeimenon*; cf. also *ComJn* 2.10.74; 2.37.246). This represents both his apologia against Monarchianism and his polemic against a "division of the divine unity" on one hand and against Jewish-Christian so-called "adoptionistic" tendencies on the other hand: "Many people who wish to be pious are troubled because they are afraid that they may proclaim two Gods and, for this reason, they fall into false and impious beliefs. They either deny that the individual nature of the Son is other than that of the Father . . . or they deny the divinity of the Son and make his individual nature and essence as an individual to be different from the Father" (*ComJn* 2.2.16). He would take up the issue again in his *Dialogue with Heracleides*.

Father and Son were designated by Origen as "two according to their nature, but one in like-mindedness, harmony, and identity of their will" (*CCels* 8.13; for the identity of their will, cf. also *PArch* 1.2.13 and *ComJn* 13.36.228f.). Therefore Origen rejected the term *homoousios* ("of one and the same substance") as a fitting description for the relation between Father and Son (the passage appearing to contradict this in *Commentary on Hebrews*, preserved in Pamphilus's *Apology* 1.99, was formulated by the translator Rufinus, who was anxious to distance his hero from Arian arguments of his own day against the Homoousion; cf. ibid. 1.94 and 100). For Origen, the term *homoousios* was probably too closely linked with gnostic and Platonic conceptions of emanation (*probole*, cf. *Corpus Hermeticum* 1.8). In contrast to such determinist views, Origen argues that the Son did not naturally derive or flow from the One but was created (*PArch* 4.4.1) by an eternal generation (*PArch* 1.2.9). This is why the Son, for Origen, is like "a secondary God" (*CCels* 5.39) (a term used in the manner of Philo and some other Middle Platonists), because he is not a coordinated member of a single class "God-head." It was this improper idea of a generic being shared by members of a class, that Origen probably thought was implied by the term *homoousios*. Eusebius of Caesarea had difficulties with the word, much later, for many of the same reasons.

In *PArch* 1.3.5 Origen differentiates between a common action of the whole Trinity and special actions of one of the three hypostases (*operatio specialis*) and introduces a hierarchy within the Trinity: The Son's sphere of activity is smaller than that of the Father, and the Spirit's sphere is smaller yet in comparison to both (*ComJn* 2.10.73–76). In some passages Origen adopts the Jewish and Jewish-Christian concept of two angels standing before God's throne (cf. Isa. 6:2f.: *PArch* 1.3.4; *HomIs* 4.1; *ComCt* 3.1) and applies it to the Son and the Spirit. In one sense, therefore, the three *hypostases* demonstrate a clearly subordinated taxonomy. In another sense, however, because their respective and specific nature is that of substantial goodness, they can be said to be "cosubstantive" (that is, consubstantial—*homoousios* in the broader sense of that term) and to this extent, as cosubstantively good, they are devoid of internal subordinate distinctions (*PArch* 1.8.3; cf. also 1.6.2 and *HomNum* 12.1). The point emerges from the Greek original of *PArch* 1.3.7, where he says: "It is not permissible to call anything in the Trinity major or minor." A similar idea comes

out in *Dialogue with Heracleides,* where he says: "To this extent our Saviour and Lord is, in his relation to the Father, one single God" (*heis theos: DialHer* 3; cf. John 10:30). Origen's aversion to the ambiguities of the word *homoousion* was to be an unfortunate focal point after the Arian crisis began to turn more and more around Nicaea and its advancement of that term to center stage. There can be no doubt that this cost Origen a great deal, in terms of reputation for orthodoxy. Even so, the development of Trinitarian theology in all parts of the church over the two centuries following him did little other than develop the schema he himself had first sketched out, by clarifying the loose ends of his concept. After the fourth century the whole body of Trinitarian doctrine was left alone, and to this day its architecture (as witnessed in the Neo-Nicene statements) shows the marks of the compromise (that sought-after balance of disparate emphases) we first find in Origen: a well-balanced mixture of Nicene Antisubordinationism (as in the coequality of the Persons) with legitimate subordinationism (e.g., the taxonomy observed in the Trinitarian aspects of prayer and liturgy and soteriological function).

Rius-Camps (1987); Hammerstaedt (1991); Hanson (1988); Markschies (2000); Schadel (1987); Ziebritzki (1994).
CHRISTOPH MARKSCHIES

Typology The word *typology* is of modern coinage. In one of its senses it has been employed to characterize a traditional form of Christian biblical exegesis that reads **Old Testament** reports of certain events, persons, or items as containing "types," that is, as bearing, in addition to their original contextual meaning, a reference forward to analogous events, persons, or practices in the New Testament or, to speak more broadly, to the work of Christ and to Christian believers' life "in Christ." This additional reference was understood to be discernible only in retrospect, by persons involved in the Christian dispensation and enlightened by the Spirit of Christ; it was not understood to function as prediction (see *Scripture, Scriptural Interpretation*).

Origen notoriously took it as a first principle that the Scriptures have a "hidden" sense in addition to their "obvious" sense and that they are therefore "forms of certain *mysteries*" and "images of divine things." This characterization of the Scriptures entailed, among other things, the view that the books of Moses have a "spiritual" or "mystical" as well as a "literal" meaning (*PArch 1*. Praef. 8). Hence it was natural for Origen to be interested in "types," not least because, in accord with previous Christian practice, he thought that when read or interpreted "spiritually," the *Law* and the Prophets anticipate the advent of the Christ. *Paul*, after all, had spoken of Adam as a "type of the one who is to come" (Rom. 5:14) and had further referred to the rock from which the Israelites had drunk in the wilderness (Num. 20:11) as "spiritual" and therefore as a manifestation of Christ. Indeed the apostle seems to have thought that the whole account of the experience of the Israelites in the wilderness was written "typically" (*typikos*), that is, to provide types that illuminate the present situation of Christians (1 Cor. 10:4,6). Moreover, this perception of the relationship between the Old and the New Covenants was basic to the early Christian polemic against both Marcion and the Christian *gnostics*, who chose to see the Old Testament, or most of it, as the revelation of a Deity distinct from, and morally inferior to, the God whom Jesus had manifested in his life and teaching. The typological reading of the Scriptures that Origen had inherited then, not merely from Paul but from what by his day was an established tradition of exegesis, seemed an essential bulwark of the thesis that the history of God with God's people exhibits continuity as well as change and difference—difference, indeed, within continuity.

This perception of Origen's exegesis has had to contend, however, with the more established portrayal of him as an heir of the sort of ethical allegory practiced by *Philo of Alexandria* in his systematic interpretation of the books of Moses, as well as the "physical" (or metaphysical) allegory that certain Stoic and Platonist philosophers had applied to the poems of Homer and the myths of the gods generally. Origen without question belonged to this broad tradition; if nothing else, the influence of Philo on the content and the form of his exegesis makes that apparent. On the other hand, it may be doubted whether Origen (or for that matter any of his contemporaries) would have seen a gulf set between the practice of typology (for which, in their vocabulary, a precise name was lacking) and that of *allegory*. The word *allegory*, after all (which did not come into use to denote a hermeneutical practice until the first century B.C.) refers to language that says one thing and means either something more than what it says or something other than what it says, whether in content or in form; and the perception of recorded events as "types" fulfills this definition exactly. Paul had himself described the story of Sarah and Hagar and their sons, which he treats precisely as a set of "types," as "allegorical" (*allegoroumena*) (Gal. 4:24).

In Origen's world, then, allegory seems to have labeled a large class of varying strategies in literary composition and interpretation; and any argument over the relative importance of allegory and typology in Origen's exegesis might best be settled by insisting that for him what we call typology counted, in practice, as a species of allegory, which, like all its other species, worked on the basis of some perception of "likeness" between two items or situations or levels of reality. It is not surprising, then, that in the use of such strategies (which he by preference labeled simply "mystical" or, in the language of Paul, "spiritual" as opposed to "literal") he mingled what his more critical posterity has elected to separate, and did so cheerfully, without attempting to achieve a perfect and principled consistency in hermeneutical method.

Thus Origen in one place can formally define three "senses" of Scripture (*PArch* 4.2.4–5). There he acknowledges not only a literal sense, but also a "psychic" and a "spiritual" sense. Of these, the literal or obvious sense, he thinks, is not always present, since not all biblical texts make sense if taken literally. The psychic or "moral" sense, meant for those who are making progress, turns out to be reminiscent of Philo's "ethical allegory"; while the spiritual sense has as its content the hidden "wisdom in a mystery" that the apostle had intended for the "perfect"; (cf. 1 Cor. 2:6–7). Having outlined this scheme with care, however, Origen himself neither follows it strictly nor repudiates it. He has no great interest in finding all three of these senses in every text, or even to find both of the "mystical" senses in texts that had no "literal" sense as such. Thus in one place he interprets Matthew 22:21 ("Render to Caesar what is Caesar's" [NRSV, "Give to the emperor . . ."]) simply according to the moral sense, suggesting that what belongs to Caesar is the image of the "Ruler of this present darkness" (cf. Eph. 6:12), which human disobedience takes to itself and which is to be returned to its owner; while what belongs to God is the *image of God* according to which humanity was originally created, and which is to be treasured (*HomLc* 39.5). But this tactic implies no denial of his theory of the threefold sense. On the other hand, he has a different procedure, which appears frequently in his exegetical practice, and which seems to have grown precisely out of a typological treatment of the Old Testament. It moves from the "type" to its fulfillment in the mystery of "Christ-and-the-Church"; and from this again to the interior actualization of that same mystery in the individual *soul*. One illustration of this procedure can be seen in Origen's treatment of the story of the

fall of Jericho. This is portrayed in the first instance as the triumph of Christ (as represented by his "type," Jesus the son of Nave) over the rulers of the present age, a triumph that is to be continued in the individual soul and fulfilled finally in second advent of the Redeemer (*HomJos* 1.2). This is yet another threefold scheme, but one that moves to a somewhat different logic: the three "senses" mark not stages in the individual believer's progress but stages in the world's conformation to the reign of God. This scheme, moreover, appears to be the one that governs the whole of Origen's interpretation of the Song of Songs, where in each section the bride is treated successively as church and as individual soul, and where the fundamental "types" are Solomon, the peaceable one who anticipates the divine bringer of peace, and one or another of his brides. For Origen, then, typology shapes a particular mode of allegorical interpretation, as one modality of hermeneutical style among several others in a deeply coherent, but not necessarily fully consistent, pattern of approach.

Daniélou (1960); Hanson (1959, 2002); Lampe and Woollcombe (1957); De Lubac (1998).

R. A. NORRIS

Universalism Universalism within Origen's thought derives from his understanding of the end (*telos*), when fallen intelligences (*noes*), or *souls* (*psychai*), will be restored to their initial contemplation of God (see *Apokatastasis, Fall, Preexistence*). While sometimes Origen suggests that some souls (for example, Satan) will not be restored to God (*PArch* 1.6.3), he more frequently asserts the final restoration of *all* souls to God (*PArch* 3.6.5) (see *Demonology*). In addition, different aspects of his theory of salvation logically support the universality of the end: namely, God is good and will give the individualized attention that is necessary to bring every soul back to himself, and also God designed rational creation so that as a whole it will accomplish its natural ontological fulfillment, which is eternal enjoyment of God.

On occasion, Origen expresses cautious uncertainty about the end's universality. In places, he suggests that salvation is not universal (*PArch* 2.9.8; *HomJr* 18; *ComJn* 19.88). For example, he states that he does not know if hell is final (see **Hades**) (*ComJn* 28.63–66) and that it may indeed be final for some (*HomJr* 12.5; 19.15; *HomLev* 3.4; 14.4), especially demons and Satan (*HomJos* 8.5; *ComJn* 20.174; *ComRm* 8.9; *HomJr* 18 and 19), who have become "non-beings" by falling so far from God (*ComJn* 2.93–98) that they cannot return (*PArch* 1.6.3). Also, he suggests that the power of the cross will destroy death and, likely, its author, Satan (*ComRm* 5.10.12). Influential persons may have pressured Origen to refrain from teaching the end's universality. For example, when responding in an apologetic letter to Alexandrians who voted to expel him under Bishop Demetrius in 231, Origen denied teaching Satan's sure salvation, which suggests he was aware that his preferred tendency to envisage a universally affirmed salvation was at conflict with the received ecclesial tradition of his day.

Even so, Origen frequently describes the End in universalist terms. For example, he often refers to the end as the consummation of *all* creation, when everyone, even Satan, will have paid the penalties for falling from God (*PArch* 1.6.1; 3.6.6 ; 3.6.9). The kingdom of God will be realized when the *entire* creation has been restored to God (*PArch* 2.1; 3.5.7).

In addition to explicitly universalist descriptions of the end, Origen's whole theory of salvation stresses universalism. Origen suggests that because God is good, kind, and just and a wise ruler and orderer (*PArch* 1.6; 1.8; 2.1; 2.5), God will not allow any soul to perish (*PArch* 4.4). Instead, God impartially cares for all souls, ensuring every soul's improvement by offering individual assistance

suitable to each (*PArch* 2.9.8; 3.1; 3.6.5). Restraining the full force of divine power (*PArch* 2.9; *HomJr* 18.6.7), God slowly applies divine **providence** in cooperation with the free will of souls, providing wise and sovereign guidance so that each soul may return freely to God at its own pace (*PArch* 2.1; 2.3 ; 3.1).

God's instruction and healing includes as many worlds and ages as each soul requires in order to choose to return to God permanently (*PArch* 2.3). Along the way, God allows additional falls as are necessary for the individual soul, such that each life may be a freely chosen advancement toward (or further fall away from) God. God bases the difficulties that each soul faces in one life on the merits or blame accumulated in the prior existence as a spirit (*HomJr* 1.11). In addition, further stages of growth will follow the **resurrection**, when souls will no longer experience bodily encasement (*HomNum* 27.2–9; 2.11.6–7). Despite backward steps along the way, a soul once committed by God to repentance in a human body will never fall back (in another life for example) into an irrational body (see **Transmigration of Souls**), since reason and choice are integral to learning, and God's goodness and wisdom will unfailingly provide each soul with every opportunity to rise again (*PArch* 1.8.4 ; *CCels* 8.30).

To teach and heal all souls, God uses the diverse aspects of the material world and the passions (*PArch* 1.6; *HomJr* 12), allowing the degree and duration of instructive suffering and punishment to vary based on individual guilt or merit (*HomJr* 19.15). God mercifully makes all punishments for sin beneficial to each soul (*PArch* 2.9.8; 3.1) and transforms temptation into medicine by allowing souls to be satiated with vice (*PArch* 2.9) so that they will learn to hate sin (*CCels* 5.32). As a result, they will root out *all* sin from themselves (*PArch* 2.10 and *HomJr* 28) and flee from evil and return to God (*PEuch* 13 and 17). For Origen, all suffering and experience purify souls of sin and vice and deepen their understanding of God's truth and love (*PArch* 2.3; 3.5.7), making the idea of any repeated fall unattractive.

God also appoints specific angels and demons to fight over individual human souls (*PArch* 3.2.4; *HomNum* 11 and 27; *CCels* 7.68–70) (see *Angels*). The demons will try to pull them into vice and away from God, while angels will try to facilitate their growth in virtue and return to God. As human souls learn from God's instruction, they will resist the demons and follow the angels. In addition, angels facilitate their own return to God by aiding humans (*PEuch* 10–11), as do demons, arguably, by mitigating their negative influences on humans.

In addition, God provides more direct intervention to aid souls. For example, God offers the instructions of Moses' *Law* and Christ's precepts in Scripture (*HomNum* 27; *HomGn* 2 and 11). God also makes available the redemption of Christ's death and resurrection (*HomLc* 14.1–6), which benefits those in heaven and those on earth (*HomLev* 1). God also provides the continued guidance of Christ and the Holy Spirit to lead souls to full spiritual knowledge (*PArch* 2.6–2.7; *ComJn* 19.24). In fact, the entire Trinity, as three sources of nourishing water (*HomJr* 18.9.1), constantly teaches and heals souls (see *Trinitarianism*).

The final return of all souls to God will be permanent and thus more stable than the initial, prefallen state of the spirits (*noi*). Origen envisions that through the pedagogical salvation process all members of rational creation move from immature innocence before God at the beginning to educated experience of God at the end. The end, though a restoration to the initial state of contemplating God (*PArch* 1.6; 2.1), will display all souls in an eternal hierarchy before God. The hierarchy will reflect the different degrees by which each soul fell and the experiences by which each learned to return to God (*PArch* 1.6; 1.8; 3.5.7; 3.6.1; 3.6.3; *HomNum* 28.3). This final state may include certain bodies in

which souls gained their experience (see *Resurrection*). More importantly, though, Origen suggests that the end will display Christ's resurrected body (*ComJn* 10.232–38), with each soul representing a different part of it.

This final state will mark the *telos*, or perfection, of creation as a whole (*PArch* 2.1), when *all* souls will reach the singular goal for which they were created: fullness of virtues (*HomNum* 27.5) and perfect imitation of and likeness to God (*PArch* 2.11; 3.6; 4.4). Origen develops Irenaeus's idea that God created all with the ability to progress toward a fullness of love for God, and he anticipates his later disciple, Gregory of Nyssa, by a sense of eternal advancement (*prokope*), acknowledging that it may be a qualified fulfillment, since God never can be grasped fully by a created mind (*PArch* 4.4.8; *HomNum* 17). Thus, in the end, *all* creatures will eternally approach God (*PArch* 2.11), who will both elude them and establish an ever-deeper intimacy with them.

In support of this final fulfillment of creation, Origen speculates that hell may be temporal. Origen makes a detailed gloss on the Gospel word for eternity (*aiones*), which may mean a long period of time but connotes in this case the eschatological sense of an "age" under God's dominion (see *Hades*). The "Eternal" hellfire, then, may represent not everlasting rejection from God's presence but a self-condemning conscience (*PArch* 2.10.4) that cleanses (*PEuch* 29.15) to the degree and duration relevant to each soul's guilt or merit, causing all to grow in knowledge and wisdom (*PArch* 3.6.9). Applying this reasoning, Origen stresses that God's assistance extends not only to human souls but to all rational creatures, including angels, astronomical bodies, and demons. God allows them also to rise and fall as needed in response to his instructive guidance, until they too eventually make an informed choice to return to God and never fall again (*PArch* 1.7; 1.8; *HomNum* 11). His vision is that what God has made for permanent existence surely cannot suffer destruction of substance (*PArch* 3.6.5), and no soul can perish, since it is made in the image of God (*PArch* 4.4.9). Since even Satan can never fully enter nonbeing but always possesses some degree of existence as a creature of God (*ComJn* 2.97–98), Satan and his demons also will benefit from Christ's final, fully effective triumph on the cross over the last enemy, which (apart from in his *ComRm*) he states is death, not Satan (*PArch* 1.6.2 ; 3.6.5; *CCels* 8.72; *ComJn* 6.295–96; *ExhMart* 13, citing Rom. 8:21). Logically, then, *every* soul eventually will achieve a healthy discernment of heavenly visions (*HomNum* 27.12) and permanent return to God (*PArch* 2.3), and *all* creation will bow down to Christ once and for all, making God once again "All in all" (*PArch* 3.5.7; *ComJn* 19.141–42). A modified universalism was clearly Origen's fundamental soteriological belief, and though he manifested several internal doubts and qualifications in his exposition, probably because the common opinion of the church of his day was against him on many aspects of the idea, he nevertheless presents a coherent theological narrative, though one that was not wholly consistent at every instance, and that gave his friends and critics in later ages room for further controversy on the subject (see **Origenist Crises**).

Babcock (1983); Crouzel (1989), 235–66; Daley (1991).

ELIZABETH A. DIVELY LAURO

Utility See **Scripture**.

Valentinus See **Gnostics**.

Virtue Origen's teaching on virtue is perhaps most clearly grasped through the eyes of his disciple and student Gregory Thaumaturgus. In his *Panegyric on Origen*, Gregory describes not only the process by which Origen taught his students about virtue but also the concrete

and practical expression that Origen's life lent to his teaching. At the close of five years of study under Origen's tutelage, Gregory portrays his teacher as the living example of the principles he sought to inculcate. By his own virtue, "this admirable man, this friend and advocate of the virtues," had done for his students "perhaps all that it lay in his power to do"(*Panegyric* 12). Like a "spark lighting upon their inmost soul" (*Panegyric* 6), he had made them "lovers of virtue, who should love it with the most ardent affection" (*Panegyric* 12).

Origen's instruction took as its starting point the premise that humankind had been put on earth (see **Anthropology, Fall, Soul**) to learn the necessity of spiritual ascent to communion with God through the **Logos**. Virtue was the process whereby the embodied soul learned to order its condition, cease its wandering, and voluntarily direct its ascent. Training in virtue began with learning to be at home with oneself and endeavoring, in the Socratic manner "to know oneself." No other activity "could be supposed to be so proper to the soul," for while the soul was "exercised in beholding itself . . . it reflected the divine mind in itself" (*Panegyric* 11). Gazing outward, or "busying oneself with alien matters" (*Panegyric* 11) stood in the way of achieving this goal. To this end, Origen persuaded his students to the *asceticism* of study, drawing them off from "the officious anxieties of life, and from the turbulence of the forum," and raising them to "the nobler vocation of looking into (themselves) and dealing with the things that [concerned themselves] in truth" (*Panegyric* 12).

Origen devotes his commentary on Song of Songs 1:8—"Unless you know yourself [NRSV, "If you do not know"], O fair one among women"—to elucidating this inward journey. He suggests that the bridegroom speaks with a certain sternness here to "turn the thoughts of the bride to the care for self-knowledge" in a manner clearly applicable to Christ and the church. "In addressing these words to His Bride, that is to the souls of believers, Christ makes the height of spiritual health and blessedness to consist in the knowledge and understanding of oneself" (*ComCt* 1.8). Drawing out these parallels, Origen frames a prescriptive concretization for the soul's journey as a series of questions. Does the soul have the good as its goal? Is it seeking after the various virtues? Is it making progress? Has it completely suppressed the passions of anger, sadness, fear, and love of glory? What is its manner of giving and receiving, or of judging the truth? (*ComCt* 1.8).

Origen's emphasis on self-scrutiny as the path of virtue is firmly rooted in the philosophical preoccupations of his day. Devoid of any explicitly Christian feature, similar queries are found in the writings of Pythagoras and later echoed by the Epicureans and the Stoics, thus contributing to the rich blend that was Middle Platonism in his day. All the various schools took as their starting point the premise that any who are "reasonable creatures" must aim at living uprightly and seeking "to know first of all themselves, what manner of persons they are, and then the things that are truly good, which man ought to strive for, and . . . the things that are evil, from which man ought to flee" (*Panegyric* 6). *Clement of Alexandria* had already sketched out how productive the Christianized exegesis of this tradition of moral sobriety (*sophrosyne*) could be as part of a pedagogical program. Origen takes this widespread philosophical practice, and energetically shaped it to his own ends. To the four cardinal virtues of temperance, justice, courage, and prudence he adds the two explicitly Christian virtues of endurance and holiness. More importantly, he proffers Christ as the exemplar and leader of the soul's journey. The prospect of attaining to the *image of God* and receiving a heavenly inheritance are its final end. These Christianized philosophical themes perhaps find their most explicit articulation in an allegorical treatment of

the Israelites' desert wanderings in *Hom-Num* 27 (see **Number Symbolism**). Here Origen posits two journeys of the soul. "One is the means of training the soul in virtues through the Law of God when it is placed in flesh; and by ascending through certain steps it makes progress as we have said, from virtue to virtue, and uses these progressions as stages." The other is a journey by which the soul gradually ascends to the heavens after the resurrection. It does not reach the highest point "unseasonably, but . . . is led through many stations. In them it is enlightened . . . illumined at each stage by the light of Wisdom, until it arrives at the Father of lights Himself."

It is in the "intelligence of the soul" that the seeds of virtue reside. In God, these same virtues exist in a static and complete form. They "can never enter or leave" (*PArch* 4.4.10). While these "traces of the divine image," the soul's "righteousness, temperance, courage, wisdom, discipline, and . . . the entire chorus of virtues . . . are present in God by substance," they "can be in man through effort and imitation (*mimesis*)," as "they are acquired little by little and one by one" (*PArch* 4.4.10). In their attainment, Christ leads as an example to all believers. Just as he always "chose good" even before "he knew evil" and "loved righteousness and hated wickedness (Ps. 45:6), so also each embodied soul after the *fall*, and after successive errors, must cleanse itself from stains by the example set forth; and since the soul has a leader for the journey, it is encouraged to enter upon the difficult road of virtue. The goal for which we hope is that, so far as this is possible, we may be made participants in the divine nature by imitating him" (*PArch* 4.4.4) (see **Divinization**).

With Christ as model, Origen conceived of the attainment of virtue as a cooperative effort between divinity and humanity (see **Christology, Grace**). To the end of becoming like God, divine assistance in this inward journey was understood as commensurate with an individual's own efforts. Exegeting the creation narrative of Genesis, Origen suggests:

> By saying "to the image of God He created him" and omitting the mention of "the likeness," he indicates nothing else but that man received the dignity of "the image" at his creation, but the perfection of "the likeness" was reserved for his consummation, that is, that he should acquire it by his personal efforts through the imitation of God; so that, while the possibility of reaching perfection was given him in the beginning by the dignity of "the image," he might by performing works himself achieve the perfect "likeness" in the end. (*PArch* 3.6.1)

Origen's Christianized understanding of moral progress in virtue, as an inward journey of coming to know God through attuning oneself to the rhythms of one's own soul and its innate "spiritual" tendency to ascentive union with the Logos, found a deep and popular resonance in the Christian ascetic communities of the generation after him and was one of the reasons he had such an impact on the burgeoning forms of monastic *asceticism*. Athanasius, for example, records Antony of Egypt as recommending to his disciples. "Note and record the actions and the stirrings of your souls as though you had to give an account of them to each other" (Athanasius, *Vita Antonii* 55.12). The extant letters of Antony and Ammonas also exhort their disciples to seek the higher reaches of virtue through an inwardly calibrated journey and ascent of the soul, worked out as the love of one's neighbor in concrete manifestation. In later generations, the practice of self-scrutiny came to be a formal and regular component of monastic life, where the ancient patterns of late antique moral philosophy, reformulated in the light of christological and soteriological imperatives, perhaps found their final home and most expansive propagation.

Dillon (1983); Hadot (1995); Jaeger (1961); Wilken (1984).

LILLIAN LARSEN

Wisdom   See **Logos**.

Worship   Origen's ideas on worship are governed by two leading contexts: how the church's practices are to be distinguished from their **Old Testament** antecedents and how Christian worship contrasts with the cultic practices witnessed in the Roman state. Origen's twin critique of **Judaism** and Hellenism develops along similar lines, arguing for the "external" and "material" nature of their cults, as opposed to the spiritual interiority of Christian worship. His concept of worship also involves him in an early and important consideration of the idea of Christian **sacrament**.

For Origen, Hellenistic cult is so evidently materialistic and sensual that it is sufficient witness to the material and earthly limitation of the whole religious system. It is the haunt of demons who use Roman cult to seduce and lead souls away from their destiny of spiritual ascent and liberation. On the other hand, the "inner" worship of Christ's revelation, which is the "worship . . . in spirit and truth" (John 4:23), has "cast aside the illusions of demons" (namely, denounced Hellenistic cult as demonic; see **Demonology**) and simultaneously replaced the "external" worship of the Old Testament that foreshadowed it (*ComJn*.10. 91; *HomLev* 6.3; 7.4; *HomNum* 23.5). Origen regards the "fading away" of the temple liturgy as something of a blessing, since the latter was so spectacular and impressive a worship of God that many would have been tempted to prolong it in the service of God (if the temple had not been destroyed), rather than following the ordained path toward the spiritual religion of Christ (*HomLev* 10.1). Despite his generic insistence that Christian cult is "spiritual," Origen is not unaware that it also has a definite external and material side to it. How does this kind of materiality combine with the spiritual nature of Christianity?

In the *CCels* 8, Origen sets out his views on the differences between Christian and Hellenistic worship. Celsus had accused the Christians of impiety on the grounds that they took no part in the worship prescribed by the state. He was shocked that they had neither altars, statues, nor dedicated temple buildings, the basic things that would allow the Christians to take part in worship as he understood it. Here is Origen's reply:

> The soul of every just man . . . is an altar and . . . sweet smelling offering, that is, the prayers put forth by a good conscience are offered on it in spirit and truth. The incense is the prayers of the saints. The right sort of statues and offerings to give to God are not the kind made by craftsmen. No, they are carved in our souls and given shape by the divine Logos; they are the virtues, likenesses of the Firstborn of every creature (Col. 1:15), who has patterns of all the virtues in Himself, patterns of justice, prudence, fortitude, wisdom and all the others. . . . Thus in every just man who strives to become as much like the Saviour as he can . . . there is a statue which is an Image of God. The man carves it himself, keeping his eyes fixed on God, keeping his heart pure and trying to become like God. All Christians, in short, strive to build altars and statues like these, things not devoid of life and feeling but capable of receiving God's spirit. (CCels 8.17–18) (See *Image of God, Image-Making*.)

External worship performed with the help of material objects here is sharply contrasted with his central Johannine notion of "worship in spirit and truth." The true cultic offering to God, as Origen sees it, is the offering up of the immaterial virtues of the soul. The models of these virtues are divine realities within the *Logos* (see *Virtue*). The divine Logos is both the model and the craftsperson that molds the soul into a divine likeness, which is a likeness of himself. To worship "in spirit and in truth" is to cooperate with the Logos in the laborious process of conforming the virtues of one's soul inasmuch as possible to their prototypes in the Logos. Thus, to worship in spirit and in truth is "to carve one's statue" and thereby become the

image of the Logos. Here are an echo of Plato's view on cult (*Phaedrus* 25.2.d) and resonances also with Plotinus (*Ennead* 1.6.9.1ff.). However, Daniélou's claim that Origen here relies upon Plotinus is not borne out by the evidence, since in Plotinus the image of the soul "never ceasing to work upon its own statue" is a solipsistic process in which the soul is supposed to realize its own beauty. In Plotinus's model, there is no objective divine reality for the soul to conform itself to; and this is something that contrasts markedly with Origen's (distinctively Christian) idea of direct assimilation to the image of God that is the Logos.

When Origen considers the system of Jewish worship (so prevalent in the scriptural texts he commented on, especially Leviticus), he uses the notion to stress the manner in which the incarnation of the Logos abolished the "figure" and brought about the "reality" (see *Typology*). For this reason, the need for the splendid Jerusalem temple was abolished when Christ, the "true Temple of God," came to live with humanity. Thus Christians no longer need to emulate pagan worshipers by building "temples made by hand," for their very bodies are temples of God. His key texts in this are clearly John 2:19f.; Acts 7:48; 1 Corinthians 3:16–17; and 1 Corinthians 6:19.

Origen, however, knew well enough that Christian worship had a visible and material side to it. How did he relate his contrast of spiritual and material practices with the fact that already by the third century Christian worship was organized around major liturgical structures, namely, the celebration of Sundays; the Lenten days of preparation, Pascha and Pentecost; and the developing praxis of the sacraments? Origen clearly considers the celebrations of the liturgical year, as well as the sacraments, as sacred and salvific, although he feels that their true and inner meaning has to be explained to the faithful. "There are things among the church's observances that everyone is obliged to do, and yet not everyone understands the reason for them" (*HomNum* 5.1). With regard to hearing the Word, and receiving the Eucharist, Origen asserts the need for the Christians to "communicate" in both more regularly: "Tell me, you who come to Church only on festal days, are the other days not festal days? Christians should eat the flesh of the Lamb every day, that is they should consume daily the flesh of the Logos." This is so because, following the psalmist (cf. Ps. 30:6), they live "in the evening of the world" and, until the time of "morning gladness" (Ps. 30:6), are in great need of the flesh of the Logos. In the inner heart, the Christian disciple who prays offers the sacrifice that is acceptable to God: "The man who does his duty, prays continuously, and continuously offers bloodless sacrifice to God in his prayers, celebrates the feast as it ought to be kept" (*CCels* 8.21) (see *Eucharist, Baptism, Prayer, Priesthood*).

This priority that Origen gives to "more spiritual" and true sacraments (comparable to the manner in which he regards Scripture as the sacrament par excellence and also sees *martyrdom* in sacramental terms) was something that became firmly rooted in later Eastern Christian, in particular, monastic, spirituality; and so for the ascetics Origen's theology of worship was a seminal factor. In short, there are in Origen's thought many dimensions to the central goal of "worship in spirit and in truth," just as there are many gradations of the spiritual acuity of souls, all of whom are called to the gradual ascent back toward the divine realities. On this road of ascent, the more physical and material aspect of worship, far from being disposable, serves as a "guarding vessel" for the more spiritual aspect.

Crouzel (1989), 223–33; Daniélou (1955), 36; Mazzucco (1996).

JULIA KONSTANTINOVSKY

Bibliography

M. C. Albrecht. "Reincarnation and the Early Church." U(NRM) 7. 2 (1983): 34–39.

C. Andresen. *Logos und Nomos. Die Polemik der Kelsos wider das Christentum.* Berlin, 1955.

H. E. Babcock. "Origen's Anti-Gnostic Polemic and the Doctrine of Universalism." *UUC* 38, no. 3–4 (1983): 53–59.

D. Balas. "The Idea of Participation in the Structure of Origen's Thought." In *Origenianum* (1), edited by H. Crouzel et al., 257–75. Bari, 1975.

C. P. Bammel. "Philocalia IX, Jerome, Epistle 121, and Origen's Exposition of Romans VII." *JTS* 32 (1981): 50–81.

———. "Adam in Origen." In *The Making of Orthodoxy: Essays in Honour of Henry Chadwick*, edited by R. Williams, 62–93. Cambridge, 1989.

———. "Law and Temple in Origen." In *Templum amicitiae: Essays on the Second Temple presented to Ernst Bammel*, edited by W. Horbury, 464–76. Sheffield, 1991.

———. "Augustine, Origen, and the Exegesis of St. Paul." *Augustinianum* 32 (1992): 341–68.

———. "Origen's Pauline Prefaces and the Chronology of His Pauline Commentaries." In *Origeniana Sexta*, edited by G. Dorival, A. Le Boulluec, et al., 495–513. Louvain: Peeters, 1995.

———. "Justification by Faith in Augustine and Origen." *JEH* 47 (1996): 223–35.

E. Bammel. "Die Zitate aus den Apokryphen bei Origenes." In *Origeniana Quinta*, edited by R. J. Daly, 131–36. Louvain, 1992.

W. A. Banner. "Origen and the Tradition of Natural Law Concepts." *DOP* 8 (1954): 49–82.

G. Bardy. "La règle de foi d'Origène." *RSR* 9 (1919): 162–96.

———. *La théologie de l'Église de saint Irénée au Concile de Nicée.* Paris, 1947.

A. Bastit-Kalinowska. "Conception du commentaire et tradition éxégetique dans le In Matthaeum d'Origène et de Hilaire de Poitiers." In *Origeniana Sexta*, edited by G. Dorival, A. Le Boulluec, et al., 675–92. Louvain: Peeters, 1995.

———. "L'interprétation de l'évangile comme récit dans le Commentaire sur Matthieu d'Origène." In *La Narrativa Cristiana Antica*, 267–82. Rome, 1995.

G. Beck. *Das Werk Christi bei Origenes.* Dissertation. Bonn, 1966.

J. Behr. *The Way to Nicaea.* New York: Crestwood, 2001.

A. Di Berardino, editor. *Encyclopedia of the Early Church.* Vols 1–2. New York, 1992.

R. Berchman. *From Philo to Origen: Middle Platonism in Tranistion.* Chico, Calif., 1984.

G. Berthold. "Origen and the Holy Spirit." In *Origeniana Quinta*, edited by R. J. Daly, 442–48. Louvain, 1992.

D. Bertrand. "Piété et sagesse dans le Peri Euches." In *Origeniana Quinta*, edited by R. J. Daly, 476–80. Louvain, 1992.

P. Bertrand. *Mystique de Jésus chez Origène.* Paris, 1951.

S. T. Bettencourt. *Doctrina ascetica Origenis: seu quid docuerit de ratione animae humanae cum daemonibus.* Rome, 1945.

H. Bianchi. *Arche e Telos: L'Antropologia di Origene e di Grigorio di Nissa.* Milan, 1981.

W. A. Bienert. *Dionysius von Alexandrien: zur Frage des Origenismus im dritten Jahrhundert.* Berlin, 1978.

C. Bigg. *The Christian Platonists of Alexandria.* Oxford, 1886. Reprint, New York, 1981.

C. Blanc. "Le baptême d'après Origène." StPatr 11 (TU 108): 113–24. Berlin, 1972.

———. "L'angélologie d'Origène." StPatr 14 (TU 117): 73–109. Berlin, 1976.

P. M. Blowers. "Origen, the Rabbis, and the Bible." In *Origen of Alexandria,* edited by C. Kannengiesser and W. L. Petersen, Notre Dame, Ind., 1988.

———. "The *Regula Fidei* and the Narrative Character of Early Christian Faith." *ProEccl* 6 (1997): 199–228.

M. Lot-Borodine. *La Deification de l'homme selon la doctrine des Pères grecs.* Paris, 1970.

M. Borret. "Celsus: A Pagan Perspective on Scripture." In *The Bible in Greek Christian Antiquity,* edited by P. Blowers, 259–88. Notre Dame, Ind., 1997.

G. Bostock. "The Sources of Origen's Doctrine of Pre-Existence." In *Origeniana Quarta,* edited by L. Lies, 259–64. Innsbruck-Wien, 1987.

A. Le Boulluec. "De la croissance selon les Stoïciens à la résurrection selon Origène." *REG* 88 (1975): 143–55.

———. *La notion d'hérésie dans la littérature grecque: IIe–IIIe siècles.* Études Augustiniennes. Paris, 1985.

———. "Vingt ans de recherches sur le Contre Celse. État des lieux." In *Discorsi di verità. Paganesimo, giudaismo, e cristianesimo a confronto nel Contro Celso di Origene,* edited by L. Perrone, 9–28. Rome, 1998.

A. De Boysson. "Avons nous un commentaire d'Origène sur l'Apocalypse?" *RBI* (N.S.) 10 (1913): 555–67.

P. Bright. "The Origenian Understanding of Martyrdom and Its Biblical Framework." In *Origen of Alexandria: His World and His Legacy,* edited by C. Kannengiesser and W. L. Petersen, 180–99. Notre Dame, Ind., 1988.

———. "The Epistle to the Hebrews in Origen's Christology." In *Origeniana Sexta,* edited by G. Dorival, A. Le Boulluec, et al., 559–65. Louvain: Peeters, 1995.

———. "The Combat with the Demons in Antony and Origen." In *Origeniana Septima,* edited by W. A. Bienert and U. Kühneweg, 339–45. Louvain, 1999.

Y. Brilioth. *A Brief History of Preaching.* Philadelphia, 1965.

R. Van den Broek. "The Christian School of Alexandria." In *Centres of Learning,* 39–47. Leiden, 1995.

G. Burke. "Des Origenes Lehre vom Urstand des Menschen." *ZKT* 72 (1950): 1–39.

R. Cadiou. *La Jeunesse d'Origène.Histoire de l'école d'Alexandrie au début du IIIe siècle.* Études de théologie historique. Paris, 1935.

P. T. Camelot. *Die Lehre von der Kirche: Väterzeit bis ausschliesslich Augustinus.* Freiburg, 1970.

J. Rius-Camps. *El Dinamismo trinitario en la divinización de los seres racionales según Origenes.* Pontificium Institutum Orientalium Studiorum. Rome, 1970.

———. "La suerte final de la naturaleza corpórea según el Peri Archon de Orígenes." StPatr 14 (TU 117): 167–79. Berlin, 1976.

———. "Subordinacianismo en Orígenes?" In *Origeniana Quarta,* edited by L. Lies, 154–86. Innsbruck-Wien, 1987.

B. Capelle. "L'Entretien d'Origène avec Héraclide." *JEH* 2 (1951): 143–57.

G. E. Caspary. *Politics and Exegesis: Origen and the "Two Swords" of Luke.* Berkeley, Calif., 1979.

A. Monaci Castagno. "L'idea della preesistenza delle anime e l'esegesi di Rom. 9.9–21. In *Origeniana Secunda,* edited by H. Crouzel and A. Quacquarelli, 69–78. Quaderni di Vetera Christianorum 15. Bari, 1980.

———. "Il diavolo e i suoi angeli. Testi e tradizioni (secoli I-III)." BP 28 (1996): 353–466.

A. Monaci Castagno, editor. *Origene: Dizionario. La cultura—il pensiero—le opere.* Rome, 2000.

H. Chadwick. "Origen, Celsus, and the Resurrection of the Body." *HTR* 14 (1948): 83–102.

———. "Enkrateia." *RAC* 5: 343–65. Stuttgart, 1962.

———. *Christianity and the Classical Tradition.* Oxford, 1966. Second edition, 1984.

J. H. Charlesworth with S. Patterson. "Apocrypha." In *Anchor Bible Dictionary,* edited by D. N. Freedman. New York, 1992.

J. Chenevert. *L'Église dans le Commentaire d'Origen sur le Cantique des Cantiques.* Paris, 1969.

E. Clark. *The Origenist Controversy: The Cultural Construction of an Early Christian Debate.* Princeton, 1992.

F. Cocchini. (a) *Il Paolo di Origene. Contributo alla storia della recezione delle epistole paoline nel III secolo.* Rome, 1992.

———. (b) "Paolo in Origene nel periodo allesandrino." In *Origeniana Quinta,* edited by R. J. Daly, 167–73. Louvain, 1992.

———. "Il progresso spirituale in Origene." In *Spiritual Progress,* edited by J. Driscoll and M. Sherdian, 29–45. Rome, 1994.

J. Coman. "La présence du Christ dans la nouvelle création." *RHPR* 48 (1968): 125–50.

F. C. Copleston. *A History of Philosophy.* Vol. 1. New York, 1993.

H. Cornélis. "Les fondements cosmologiques de l'eschatologie d'Origène." *RSPT* 43 (1959): 32–80, 201–47.

H. Crouzel. *Théologie de l'Image de Dieu chez Origène.* Paris, 1956.

———. *Origène et la connaissance mystique.* Bruges/ Paris, 1961.

———. "L'École d'Origène à Césarée." *BLE* 71 (1970): 15–27.

———. *Bibliographie critique d'Origène.* La Haye-Steenbrugge, 1971. Supplement to the same, up to 1980. LaHaye-Steenbrugge, 1982.

———. "La première et la seconde résurrection des hommes d'après Origène." *Didaskalia* 3 (1973): 3–19.

———. "Geist (Heiliger Geist)." *RAC* 9 (1976): 490–545.

———. "Thème du mariage mystique chez Origène et ses sources." *Studi Missionalia* 26 (1977): 37–57.

———. "Hades et la gehenne selon Origène." *Gregorianum* 59, no. 2 (1978): 291–331.

———. "La doctrine origénienne du corps ressuscité." *BLE* 81 (1980): 175–200.

———. "The Literature on Origen: 1970–1988." *TS* 49 (1988): 499–516.

———. *Origen,* translated by A. S. Worrall. Edinburgh, 1989.

———. *Les fins dernières selon Origène.* Aldershot, 1990.

———. "La théologie mariale d' Origène." In *Origène: Homélies sur s. Luc,* 11–64. SC 87. Paris, 1998.

———. "Les condemnations subies par Origène et sa doctrine." In *Origeniana Septima,* edited by W. A. Bienert and U. Kühneweg, 311–15. Louvain, 1999.

B. Daley. *The Hope of the Early Church: A Handbook of Patristic Eschatology.* Cambridge, 1991.

———. "What Did Origenism Mean in the Sixth Century?" In *Origeniana Sexta,* edited by G. Dorival, A. Le Boulluec, et al., 627–38. Louvain: Peeters, 1995.

R. J. Daly. "Sacrificial Soteriology in Origen's Homilies on Leviticus." *StPatr* 18, no. 2 (1982): 872–78.

J. Daniélou. *Les Anges et leurs mission d'après les Pères de l'Église.* Collection Irenikon. N.S. 5. Paris, 1952. English translation by D. Heimann. Westminster, Md., 1976.

———. *Origen,* translated by W. Mitchell. London, 1955.

———. *From Shadows to Reality.* London, 1960.

E. Dassmann. "Zum Paulusverständnis in der östlichen Kirche." JAC 29 (1986): 27–39.

D. Dawson. *Allegorical Readers and Cultural Revision in Ancient Alexandria.* Berkeley, Calif., 1992.

———. *Christian Figural Reading and the Fashioning of Identity.* Berkeley, Calif., 2002.

F. Diekamp. *Die origenistischen Streitigkeiten im sechsten Jahrhundert und das fünfte allgemeine Concil.* Münster, 1899.

J. Dillon. "Plotinus, Philo, and Origen on the Grades of Virtue." In *Platonismus und Christentum,* edited by H. D. Blume and F. Mann, 92–105. JAC 10. Münster, 1983.

G. Dorival. "L'apport des chaines exégétiques grecques à une réédition des Hexaples d'Origène." *RHT* 4 (1974): 39–74.

———. "Origène a-t-il enseigné la transmigration des âmes dans les corps d'animaux? (A propos de *PArch* 1.8.4)." In *Origeniana Secunda,* edited by H. Crouzel and A. Quacquarelli, 11–32. Bari, 1980.

———. "Versions anciennes de la Bible." In *Dictionnaire encyclopédique de la Bible,* 1304–11. Turnhout, 1987.

———. "L'apport d'Origène pour la connaissance de la philosophie grecque." In *Origeniana Quinta,* edited by R. J. Daly, 198–216. Louvain, 1992.

B. Drewery. *Origen and the Doctrine of Grace.* London, 1960.

J. Dupuis. *L'esprit de l'homme. Etude sur l'anthropologie religieuse d'Origène.* Bruges, 1967.

M. Edwards. *Christ or Plato? Origen on Revelation and Anthropology.* London, 1998.

R. B. Eno. "Origen and the Church of Rome." *AER* 167 (1973): 41–50.

D. Van den Eynde. *Les normes de l'enseignement chrétien dans la littérature patristique des trois premiers siècles.* Paris, 1933.

E. De Faye. *Origène.* Paris, 1928.

E. Ferguson. "Origen and the Election of Bishops." *CH* 43 (1974): 26–33.

R. Ferwerda. "Two souls. Origen's and Augustine's attitude toward the two souls doctrine. Its place in Greek and Christian Philosophy." *VC* 37 (1983): 360–78.

G. Florovsky. "Origen, Eusebius, and the Iconoclastic Controversy." *CH* 19 (1950): 77–96.

W. Foerster. *Gnosis: A Selection of Gnostic Texts,* translated by R. McL. Wilson. Oxford, 1972.

K. S. Frank. "Vita apostolica als Lebensnorm in der Alten Kirche." *IKaZ* 8 (1979): 106–20.

M. Frede. "Origen's Treatise against Celsus." In *Apologetics in the Roman Empire,* edited by M. Edwards et al., 131–55. Oxford, 1999.

M. M. Garijo. "Vocabulario origeniano sobre el Espírito Divino." *Scriptorium Victoriense* 11 (1964): 320–58.

G. Sfameni-Gasparro. "Doppia creazione e peccato di Adamo nel Peri Archon. Fondamenti biblici e presupposti platonici dell' esegesi origeniana." In *Origeniana Secunda*, edited by H. Crouzel and A. Quacquarelli, 57–67. Quaderni di Vetera Christianorum 15. Bari, 1980.

C. Ginzburg. "Idols and Likenesses: Origen, Homilies on Exodus VIII.3. and Its Reception." In *Sight and Insight: Essays in Honour of E. H. Gombrich at 85*, edited by J. Onians, 55–72. London, 1992.

A. Godin. *Erasme: Lecteur d'Origène*. Geneva, 1982.

G. Gould. "The Influence of Origen on Fourth-century Monasticism: Some Further Remarks." In *Origeniana Sexta*, edited by G. Dorival, A. Le Boulluec, et al., 591–98. Louvain: Peeters, 1995.

R. A. Greer. *Origen*. New York, 1979.

C. W. Griggs. *Early Egyptian Christianity: From Its Origins to 451 C.E.* Leiden, 1990.

A. Grillmeier. *Christ in Christian Tradition*. Vol. 1. Second edition, London, 1971.

———. "Maria Prophetin: Eine Studie zu einer Messianisch-Patristischen Mariologie." In *Mit ihm und ihm: Christologische Forschungen und Perspectiven*, edited by A. Grillmeier, 198–216. Freiburg, 1975.

J. N. Guinot. "La fortune des Hexaples d'Origèneau IVè et Vè siècles en milieu anti-ochien." In *Origeniana Sexta*, edited by G. Dorival, A. Le Boulluec, et al., 215–25. Louvain: Peeters, 1995.

P. Hadot. *Philosophy as a Way of Life: Spiritual Exercises from Socrates to Foucault*. Oxford, 1995.

G. Hallstrom. *Fides Simpliciorum according to Origen of Alexandria*. Helsinki, 1984.

D. J. Halperin. "Origen, Ezekiel's Merkabah, and the Ascension of Moses." *CH* 50 (1981): 261–75.

T. Halton. "The New Origen: Peri Pascha." *GOTR* 28 (1983): 73–80.

J. Hammerstaedt. "Der trinitarische Gebrauch des Hypostasenbegriffs bei Origenes." *JAC* 34 (1991): 12–20.

C. P. Hammond-Bammel. "Origen's Pauline Prefaces and the Chronology of His Pauline Commentaries." In *Origeniana Sexta*, edited by G. Dorival, A. Le Boulluec, et al., 495–513. Louvain: Peeters, 1995.

R. P. C. Hanson. *Origen's Doctrine of Tradition*. London, 1954.

———. *The Search for the Christian Doctrine of God: The Arian Controversy 318–381*. Edinburgh: T. & T. Clark, 1988.

———. *Allegory and Event*. Richmond, Va., 1959. Reprint with new intro., by J. Trigg. Louisville, Ky.: Westminster John Knox Press, 2002.

M. Harl. *Origène et la fonction révélatrice du verbe incarné*. Paris, 1958.

———. "Recherches sur l'origénisme d'Origène: la satiété (koros) de la contemplation comme motif de la chute des âmes." StPatr 8 (TU 93) (1966): 374–405.

———. "Structure et cohérence du Peri Archon." In *Origeniana 1*, edited by H. Crouzel et al., 11–32. Bari, 1975.

———. "La préexistence des ames dans l'oeuvre d'Origène." In *Origeniana Quarta*, edited by L. Lies, 238–58. Innsbruck-Wien, 1987.

A. Von Harnack. *History of Dogma*, translated by N. Buchanan. Vols. 1–7. Boston, 1895–1903.

P. Hartmann. "Origène et la théologie du martyre d'après le Protreptikos de 235." *ETL* 34 (1958): 773–824.

M. A. G. Haykin. "The Spirit of God: The Exegesis of 1 Cor. 2.10–12 by Origen and Athanasius." *SJT* 35, no. 6 (1982): 513–28.

R. E. Heine. "Origen's Commentary on John Compared with the Introductions to the Ancient Philosophical Commentaries on Aristotle." In *Origeniana Sexta*, edited by G. Dorival, A. Le Boulluec, et al., 1–12. Louvain: Peeters, 1995.

———. "Reading the Bible with Origen." In *The Bible in Greek Christian Antiquity*, edited by P. Blowers, 131–48. Notre Dame, Ind., 1997.

———. *The Commentaries of Origen and Jerome on St. Paul's Epistle to the Ephesians*. Oxford, 2002.

T. Heither. *Translatio Religionis: Die Paulusdeutung des Origenes in seinem Kommentar zum Römerbrief*. Cologne, 1990.

———. "Glaube in der Theologie des Origenes." *EG* 67 (1991): 255–65.

L. R. Hennessey. "Origen of Alexandria: The Fate of the Soul and the Body after Death." *SecCent* 8 (1991): 163–78.

T. Hermas. *Origène: Théologie Sacificielle du Sacerdoce des Chrétiens*. Théologie Historique 102. Paris, 1996.

A. Van Den Hoek. "Clement and Origen as Sources on Noncanonical Scriptural Traditions during the Late Second and Earlier Third Centuries." In *Origeniana Sexta*, edited by G. Dorival, A. Le Boulluec, et al. Louvain: Peeters, 1995.

———. "The Catechetical School of Early Christian Alexandria and Its Philonic Heritage." *HTR* 90 (1997): 59–87.

————. "Philo and Origen: A Descriptive Catalogue of Their Relationship." *Studia Philonica Annual* 12 (2000): 44–121.

————. "Assessing Philo's Influence in Christian Alexandria: The Case of Origen." In *Shem in the Tents of Japheth: Essays on the Encounter of Judaism and Hellenism*, edited by J. L. Kugel, 223–39. Supplements to the Journal for the Study of Judaism 74. Leiden, 2002.

R. J. Hoffmann. *Celsus: On the True Doctrine*. Oxford, 1987.

T. Holdcroft. "The Parable of the Pounds and Origen's Doctrine of Grace." *JTS* 24 (1973): 503–4.

D. Hombergen. *The Second Origenist Controversy: A New Perspective on Cyril of Scythopolis' Monastic Biographies as Historical Sources for Sixth-Century Origenism*. Rome, 2001.

H. J. Horn. "Ignis Aeternus: une interprétation morale du feu éternel chez Origène." *REG* 82 (1969): 76–88.

B. D. Jackson. "Sources of Origen's Doctrine of Freedom." *CH* 35 (1966): 13–23.

W. Jaeger. *Early Christianity and Greek Paideia*. Cambridge, 1961.

S. Jellicoe. *Studies in the Septuagint*. New York, 1974.

H. Jonas. *The Gnostic Religion*. London, 1992.

E. Junod. "Que savons-nous des 'Scholies' d'Origène." In *Origeniana Sexta*, edited by G. Dorival, A. Le Boulluec, et al., 133–49. Louvain: Peeters, 1995.

————. "Controverses autour de l'héritage origénien aux deux extrémités du 4ième siècle: Pamphile et Rufin." In *Origeniana Septima*, edited by W. A. Bienert and U. Kühneweg, 215–3. Louvain, 1999.

C. Kannengiesser. "Origen—Systematician in the De Principiis." In *Origeniana Quinta*, edited by R. J. Daly, 395–405. Louvain, 1992.

C. Kannengiesser and W. L. Petersen, editors. *Origen of Alexandria: His World and His Legacy*. Notre Dame, Ind., 1988.

G. Keith. "Patristic Views on Hell. Part 1." *EvQ* 71, no. 3 (1999): 217–32.

D. M. Kelly. "Origen: Heretic or Victim? The Apokatastasis Revisited." *PBR* 18–19 (2000–2001): 273–86.

H. A. A. Kennedy. *St. Paul and the Mystery Religions*. London, 1913.

R. Kimelman. "Rabbi Yohanan and Origen on the Song of Songs." *HTR* 73 (1980): 567–95.

A. Knauber. "Das Anliegen der Schule des Origenes zu Cäsarea." *MTZ* 19 (1968): 182–203.

H. Koch. *Pronoia und Paideus.Studien über Origenes und sein Verhältnis zum Platonismus*. Berlin and Leipzig, 1932.

G. W. H. Lampe and K. J. Woollcombe. *Essays on Typology*. Naperville, Ill., 1957.

N. R. M. De Lange. *Origen and the Jews: Studies in Jewish-Christian Relations in Third-Century Palestine*. Cambridge, 1976.

E. A. Dively Lauro. "Reconsidering Origen's Two Higher Senses of Scriptural Meaning: Identifying the Psychic and Pneumatic Senses." StPatr 34 (2001): 306–17.

R. A. Layton. *Origen as Reader of Paul: A Study of the Commentary on Ephesians*. Ph.D. diss. University of Virginia, 1996.

J. Lécuyer. "Sacerdoce des fidèles et sacerdoce ministériel chez Origène." *VetC* 7 (1970): 254–59.

F. Ledegang. "Anthropomorphites and Origenists in Egypt at the End of the Fourth Century." In *Origeniana Septima*, edited by W. A. Bienert and U. Kühneweg, 375–79. Louvain, 1999.

————. *Mysterium Ecclesiae: Images of the Church and Its Members in Origen*. Leiden: Brill, 2001.

G. M. Lee. "Origen, Dialogue with Heracleides 5.23.4." *VC* 21 (1967): 164.

D. Munoz Léon. *Gloria de la shekina: en los targumim del pentateuco*. Madrid: Instituto F. Suarez, 1977.

J. Letelier. "Le Logos chez Origène." *RSPT* 75 (1991): 587–612.

L. Levine. *Caesarea under Roman Rule*. Leiden, 1975.

J. T. Lienhard. "*Origen as Homilist*." In *Preaching in the Patristic Age: Studies in Honor of Walter J. Burghardt, S.J.*, edited by D. Hunter, 36–52. New York, 1989.

————. "Origen and the Crisis of the Old Testament in the Early Church." *ProEccl* 9, no. 3 (2000): 355–66.

L. Lies. *Wort und Eucharistie bei Origenes. Zur Spiritualisierungstendenz des Eucharistieverständnisses*. Innsbruck, 1978.

————. "Origenes und Reinkarnation." *ZKT* 121 (1999): 139–58, 249–68.

H. Lietzmann. *A History of the Early Church*. Vol. 2: The Founding of the Church Universal. London, 1960.

S. R. C. Lilla. *Clement of Alexandria: A Study in Christian Platonism and Gnosticism*. Oxford, 1971.

R. Lim. *Public Disputation, Power, and Social Order in Late Antiquity*. Berkeley, Calif., 1995.

A. Louth. *The Origins of the Christian Mystical Tradition*. Oxford, 1981.

H. De Lubac. *Histoire et Esprit. L'Intelligence de l'Écriture d'après Origène*. Paris, 1950.

———. *Medieval Exegesis: The Four Senses of Scripture*, translated by M. Sebanc and E. M. Macierowski. Vols. 1–2. Grand Rapids, 1998, 2000.

R. Lyman. *Christology and Cosmology: Models of Divine Activity in Origen, Eusebius, and Athanasius*. Oxford, 1993.

———. "Origen as Ascetic Theologian: Orthodoxy and Authority in the Fourth Century Church." In *Origeniana Septima*, edited by W. A. Bienert and U. Kühneweg, 187–94. Louvain, 1999.

L. M. McDonald. *The Formation of the Christian Biblical Canon*. Nashville, 1988.

J. A. McGuckin. (a) "Christian Asceticism and the Early School of Alexandria." In *Studies in Church History*. Vol. 22, *Monks, Hermits, and the Ascetic Tradition*, 25–39. Oxford, 1985.

———. (b) "Origen's Doctrine of the Priesthood." *CR* 70, no. 8 (August 1985): 277–86; no. 9 (September 1985): 318–25. Synopsis in *TD* 33, no. 3 (1986).

———. "The Changing Forms of Jesus According to Origen." *Origeniana Quarta*. Innsbrucker Theologischen Studien, Board 19, 1986, 215–22.

———. *The Transfiguration of Christ in Scripture and Tradition*. New York, 1987.

———. "Origen on the Glory of God." StPatr 21 (1989): 316–24.

———. (a) "Caesarea Maritima as Origen Knew It." In *Origeniana Quinta*, edited by R. J. Daly, 3–25. Louvain, 1992.

———. (b) "Origen on the Jews." SCH. Vol. 29, *Christianity and Judaism*, 1–13. Oxford, 1992. Reprinted in *Recent Studies in Church History*, edited by E. Ferguson, vol. 2. Hamden, Conn.: Garland Publishing, 1999.

———. "Martyr Devotion in the Alexandrian School: Origen to Athanasius." In *Martyrs and Martyrologies*, edited by D. Wood, 35–46. Oxford, 1993.

———. "Structural Design and Apologetic Intent in Origen's Commentary on John." In *Origeniana Sexta*, edited by G. Dorival, A. Le Boulluec, et al., 441–57. BETL 118. Louvain: Peeters, 1995.

———. "Eschaton and Kerygma: The Future of the Past in the Present Kairos [The Concept of Living Tradition in Orthodox Theology]." *St. Vladimir's Theological Quarterly* 42, nos. 3–4 (Winter 1998): 225–71.

———. "The Paradox of the Virgin-Theotokos: Evangelism and Imperial Politics in the Fifth-Century Byzantine World." *Maria* 3 (Autumn 2001): 5–23.

———. "Origen as Literary Critic in the Alexandrian Tradition." In *Origenianum Octavum*, edited by L. Perrone. Louvain: Peeters, 2002.

J. L. McKenzie. "A Chapter in the History of Spiritual Exegesis." *TS* 12 (1951): 365–81.

J. C. McLelland. *God the Anonymous*. Patristic Monograph Series. 4. Cambridge, Mass., 1976.

C. Markschies. *Alta Trinità Beata. Gesammelte Studien zur altkirchlichen Trinitätstheologie*. Tübingen, 2000.

———. "New Research on Ptolemaeus Gnosticus." *ZAC* 4 (2000): 225–54.

———. *Gnosticism*. Edinburgh, 2003.

C. Mazzucco. "Il culto liturgico nel pensiero di Origene." In *Dizionario di Spiritualita Biblico-Patristica*, edited by S. Panimolle, 12: 203–20. Rome, 1996.

J. E. Ménard. "Transfiguration et polymorphie chez Origène." In *Epektasis. Mélanges patristiques offerts à J Daniélou*, edited by C. Kannengiesser and J. Fontaine, 367–74. Paris, 1972.

T. Merton. *The Collected Poems of Thomas Merton*. New York, 1977.

B. M. Metzger. *The Canon of the New Testament: Its Origin, Development, and Significance*. Oxford, 1987.

F. Mosetto. *I Miracoli evangelici nel dibattito tra Celso e Origene*. Rome, 1986.

G. Muller. "Origenes und die Apokatastasis." *Theologische Geitschrift* 14 (1958): 174–90.

O. Munnich. "Les Hexaples d'Origène à la lumière de la tradition manuscrite de la Bible grecque." In *Origeniana Sexta*, edited by G. Dorival, A. Le Boulluec, et al., 167–85. Louvain, 1995.

F. X. Murphy. *Rufinus of Aquileia: His Life and Works*. Washington, 1954.

E. Nardoni. "Origen's Concept of Biblical Inspiration." *JECS* 4, no. 1 (1984): 9–23.

P. Nautin. *Lettres et Écrivains Chrétiens*. Paris, 1961.

———. "Origène predicateur." In *Origène: Homélies sur Jérémie*, edited by P. Nautin. SC 232. Paris, 1976.

———. *Origène: Sa vie et son oeuvre*. Paris, 1977.

P. Nemeshegyi. *La paternité de Dieu chez Origène*. Paris, 1960.

F. W. Norris. "Universal Salvation in Origen and Maximus." In *Universalism and the Doctrine of Hell*, edited by N. M. de S. Cameron. Grand Rapids, 1992.

R. A. Norris. "Heresy and Orthodoxy in the Later Second Century." *USQR* 52, nos. 1–2 (1998): 43–59.

A. Nygren. *Agape and Eros*. Philadelphia, 1953.

A. Orbe. *La Epinoia.* Rome: Pontificia Universitas Gregoriana, 1955.

E. Osborn. *The Philosophy of Clement of Alexandria.* Cambridge, 1957.

———. "Reason and the Rule of Faith in the Second Century A.D." In *The Making of Orthodoxy: Essays in Honour of Henry Chadwick,* edited by R. Williams, 40–61. Cambridge, 1989.

C. Osborne. "Neoplatonism and the Love of God in Origen." In *Origeniana Quinta,* edited by R. J. Daly, 270–83. Louvain, 1992.

———. *Eros Unveiled: Plato and the God of Love.* Oxford, 1994.

A. Outler. "Origen and the Rule of Faith." *SecCent* 4 (1984): 133–41.

E. H. Pagels. *The Johannine Gospel in Gnostic Exegesis: Heracleon's Commentary on John.* New York, 1973.

D. Pazzini. "Cristo Logos e Cristo Dynamis." In *Origeniana Quinta,* edited by R. J. Daly, 424–29. Louvain, 1992.

L. Perrone. "I paradigmi biblici della preghiera nel Peri Euches di Origene." *Augustinianum* 33 (1993): 339–68.

A. J. Philippou. "Origen and the Early Jewish-Christian Debate." *GOTR* 15, no. 1 (1970): 140–52.

M. J. Pierre. "L'ame dans l'anthropologie d'Origène." *POC* 34, nos. 1–2 (1984): 21–65.

L. F. Pizzivalli and M. Rizzi, editors. *Origene: Maestro di vita spirituale.* SPM 22. Milan, 2001.

J. M. Poffet. *La méthode exégétique d'Héracléon et d'Origène commentateurs de Jn 4: Jésus, la Samaritaine et les Samaritains.* Fribourg, 1985.

E. Prinzivalli. "The controversy about Origen before Epiphanius." In *Origeniana Septima,* edited by W. A. Bienert and U. Kühneweg, 195–213. Louvain, 1999.

H. C. Puech. "Les nouveaux écrits d'Origène et de Didyme découverts à Toura." *RHPR* 31 (1951): 293–329.

J. Quasten. *Patrology.* Vol. 2, *The Ante-Nicene Literature After Irenaeus.* Utrecht, 1975.

G. Quispel. "Origen and the Valentinian Gnosis." *VC* 28, no. 1 (1974): 29–42.

C. E. Rabinowitz. "Personal and Cosmic Salvation in Origen." *VC* 38, no. 4 (1984): 319–29.

K. Rahner. "La doctrine d'Origène sur la pénitence." *RSR* 37 (1950): 47–97, 252–86, 422–56.

———. "The Spiritual Senses in Origen." In K. Rahner, *Theological Investigations.* Vol. 16, *Experience of the Spirit,* 83-103. New York, 1979.

P. H. Reardon. "Providence in Origen's *Contra Celsum.*" *EP* 55 (1973): 501–16.

J. M. Rist. *Eros and Psyche: Studies in Plato, Plotinus, and Origen.* Toronto, 1964.

M. Rizzi. "Problematiche politiche nel dibattito tra Celso e Origene." In *Discorsi di Verita. Paganesimo, giudaismo, e cristianesimo a confronto nel Contro Celso di Origene,* edited by L. Perrone, 171–206. Rome, 1998.

A. Roselli. "Ho Technites Theos: La practica terapeutica come paradigma dell'operare di Dio in Philoc. 27 e *PArch* 3.1." In *Il cuore indurito del Faraone. Origene e il problema del libero arbitrio,* edited by L. Perrone, 65–83. Genoa, 1992.

R. Roukema. *The Diversity of Laws in Origen's Commentary on Romans.* Amsterdam, 1988.

———. "Origenes visie op de rechtvaardiging volgens zijn Commentaar op Romeinen." *GTT* 89 (1989): 94–105.

———. "Die Liebe kommt nie zu Fall. (1 Cor 13.8a) als Argument des Origenes gegen einen neuen Abfall der Seelen von Gott." In *Origeniana Septima,* edited by W. A. Bienert and U. Kühneweg, 15–23. Louvain, 1999.

J. N. Rowe. *Origen's Doctrine of Subordination.* Bern, 1987.

S. Rubensen. "Origen in the Egyptian Monastic Tradition of the Fourth Century." In *Origeniana Septima,* edited by W. A. Bienert and U. Kühneweg, 319–37. Louvain, 1999.

D. T. Runia. *Philo in Early Christian Literature: A Survey.* Compendia Rerum Iudaicarum ad Novum Testamentum III 3. Assen and Minneapolis, 1993.

———. *Philo and the Church Fathers.* Leiden, 1995.

———. "Caesarea Maritima and the Survival of Hellenistic-Jewish Literature." In *Caesarea Maritima: A Retrospective after Two Millennia,* edited by A. Raban and K. G. Holum, 476–95. Documenta et Monumenta Orientis Antiqui 21. Leiden, 1996.

E. Schadel. "Zum Trinitätskonzept des Origenes." In *Origeniana Quarta,* edited by L. Lies, 203–14. Innsbruck-Wien, 1987.

T. Schaeffer. *Das Priester-Bild im Leben und Werk des Origenes.* Cologne and Vienna, 1977.

T. P. Scheck. "Justification by Faith Alone in Origen's Commentary on Romans and Its Reception during the Reformation Era." In *Origeniana Octava,* edited by L. Perrone. Louvain: Peeters, 2003.

C. Schönborn. *God's Human Face: The Christ-Icon.* San Francisco, 1994.

A. B. Scott. *Origen and the Life of the Stars: A History of an Idea.* Oxford, 1991.

———. "Opposition and Concession: Origen's Relationship to Valentinianism." In *Origeniana Quinta*, edited by R. J. Daly, 79–84. Louvain, 1992.

G. Sgherri. *Chiesa e Sinagoga nelle opere di Origene*. Milan, 1982.

———. "Pasqua." In *Origene: Dizionario: la cultura. il pensiero. le opere*, edited by A. Monaci Castagno, 341–44. Rome, 2000.

D. Sheerin. "The Role of Prayer in Origen's Homilies." In *Origen of Alexandria: His World and His Legacy*, edited by C. Kannengiesser and W. L. Petersen, 200–214. Notre Dame, Ind., 1988.

D. Shin. "Some Light from Origen: Scripture as Sacrament." *Worship* 73, no. 5 (1999): 399–425.

M. Simonetti. "Due note sull'angelologia origeniana." *RCCM* 4 (1962): 169–208.

———. "La morte di Gesu in Origene." In *Studi sulla cristologia del II e III secolo*, 145–82. IPA. Rome, 1993.

———. *Biblical Interpretation in the Early Church: An Historical Introduction to Patristic Exegesis*. Edinburgh, 1994.

A. J. Smith. "The Commentary of Pelagius on Romans, Compared with That of Origen-Rufinus." *JTS* 20 (1919): 127–77.

C. A. Spada. "Origene e gli apocrifi del Nuovo Testamento." In *Origeniana Quarta*, edited by L. Lies, 44–53. Innsbruck-Wien, 1987.

H. Strutwolf. *Gnosis als System. Zur Rezeption der valentinianischen Gnosis bei Origenes*. Göttingen, 1993.

R. B. Tollinton. *Selections from the Commentaries and Homilies of Origen*. London, 1929.

K. Torjesen. "Body, Soul, and Spirit, in Origen's Theory of Exegesis." *AThR* 67 (1985): 17–30.

———. *Hermeneutical Procedure and Theological Method in Origen's Exegesis*. New York, 1986.

———. "Influence of Rhetoric on Origen's Old Testament Homilies." In *Origeniana Sexta*, edited by G. Dorival, A. Le Boulluec, et al., 13–25. BETL 118. Louvain: Peeters, 1995.

J. W. Trigg. "The Charismatic Intellectual: Origen's Understanding of Religious Leadership," *CH* 50 (1981): 5–19.

———. *Origen: The Bible and Philosophy in the Third-Century Church*. London, 1983.

———. *Message of the Fathers of the Early Church: Biblical Interpretation*. Del., 1988.

———. "Origen, Man of the Church." In *Origeniana Quinta*, edited by R. J. Daly, 51–56. Louvain, 1992.

C. N. Tsirpanlis. "Origen on Free Will, Grace, Predestination, Apocatastasis, and Their Ecclesiological Implications." *PBR* 9 (1990): 95–121.

P. Tzamalikos. *The Concept of Time in Origen*. Bern, 1993.

E. E. Urbach. "Rabbinic Exegesis and Origen's Commentary on the Song of Songs, and Jewish-Christian Polemics." *Tarbiz* 30 (1960): 148–70.

C. Vagaggini. *Maria nelle opere di Origene*. Rome, 1942.

A. Vilela. *La condition collégiale des prêtres au IIIe siècle*. Paris, 1971.

H. J. Vogt. *Das Kirchenverständnis des Origens*. Cologne, 1974.

———. "Wie Origenes in seinem Matthäuskommentar Fragen offen lässt?" In *Origeniana Secunda*, edited by H. Crouzel and A. Quacquarelli, 191–98. Quaderni di Vetera Christanorum 15. Bari, 1980.

W. Volker. "Paulus bei Origenes." *TSK* 102 (1930): 258–79.

———. *Das Vollkommenheitsideal des Origenes*. Tübingen, 1931.

J. Waldram. "Illuminatio verbi divini. Confessio fidei. Gratia baptismi. Wort, Glaube und Sakrament in Katechumenat und Taufliturgie bei Origenes." In *Fides sacramenti, Sacramentum fidei. Studies in Honour of Pieter Smulders*, edited by H. J. Auf der Maur, 41–95. Assen, 1981.

F. W. Weidmann. "Rushing Judgment? Willfulness and Martyrdom in Early Christianity." *USQR* 53 (1999): 61–69.

P. Widdicombe. *The Fatherhood of God from Origen to Athanasius*. Oxford, 1994.

———. "Knowing God: Origen and the Example of the Beloved Disciple." StPatr 31: 554–58. Papers presented at the Twelfth International Conference on Patristic Studies, Oxford, 1995. Edited by E. A. Livingstone. Louvain, 1997.

M. F. Wiles. *The Spiritual Gospel: The Interpretation of the Fourth Gospel in the Early Church*. Cambridge, 1960.

———. "Origen as Biblical Scholar." In *The Cambridge History of the Bible*. Vol. 1. Cambridge, 1963.

———. *The Divine Apostle. The Interpretation of St. Paul's Epistles in the Early Church*. Cambridge, 1967.

R. Wilken. "Alexandria: A School for Training in Virtue." In *Schools of Thought in the Christian Tradition*, edited by P. Henry, 15–30. Philadelphia, 1984.

R. Williams. "Does It Make Sense to Speak of Pre-Nicene Orthodoxy?" In *The Making of Orthodoxy: Essays in Honour of Henry Chadwick*, edited by R. Williams, 1–23. Cambridge, 1989.

V. Wimbush and R. Valantasis, editors. *Asceticism*. Papers from the International Conference on the Ascetic Dimension in Religious Life, Union Theological Seminary, New York, August 1993. New York and Oxford, 1995.

J. C. M. Van Winden. "Le Christianisme et la philosophie. Le commencement du dialgue entre la foi et la raison." In *Kyriakon*, 205–13. Festschrint J. Quasten. Münster, 1970.

———. "Origen's Definition of Eucharistia in De Oratione 14.2." *VC* 28, no. 2 (1974): 139–40.

———. "Two Kinds of Logos." In *Arche: A Collection of Patristic Studies*, edited by J. den Boeft and D. T. Runia, 257–68. Leiden, 1997.

J. Wolinski. "Le recours aux *epinoiai* du Christ dans le *Commentaire sur Jean* d'Origène." In *Origeniana Sexta*, edited by G. Dorival, A. Le Boulluec, et al., 465–92. Louvain: Peeters, 1995.

A. H. Wratislav. "Exegesis of Romans 8.18–25." *JSL* Third Series, 12 (1860–61): 410–20. Translated sections of *Commentary on Romans*.

F. Young. "The Rhetorical Schools and Their Influence on Patristic Exegesis." In *The Making of Orthodoxy: Essays in Honour of Henry Chadwick*, edited by R. Williams. Cambridge, 1989.

———. *Biblical Exegesis and the Formation of Christian Culture*. Cambridge, 1997.

H. Ziebritzki. *Heiliger Geist und Weltseele: Das Problem der dritten Hypostase bei Origenes, Plotin und ihren Vorläufern*. Tübingen, 1994.

FURTHER STUDIES

The best starting points for a comprehensive study of Origen are Crouzel (1989) and Trigg (1983), supplemented by Torjesen (1986) and Hanson (1959, 2002), for the substrate of his biblical mind.

The detailed study bibliography prepared by Henri Crouzel (1971) will be the next important step for anyone wishing to make up a more detailed bibliographic list for future specific researches. The American Theological Libraries Association (ATLA) also sponsors a marvelously comprehensive computer database that is held by most good research libraries, which can return word searches and bibliographic listings for most scholarly articles written on Origen of Alexandria in Europe and North America over the past fifteen years, taking up where Crouzel's bibliography ends. Sections of the present volume, of course, will also be of help in orientating a book search on specific topics. The sections at the end of the A–Z entries have focused on accessible scholarly articles and monographs, largely in the English language. Bibliographies including a wider array of European sources are also available for the various subject entries related to Origen in Quasten (1975) and, more to date, in Monaci Castagno, editor (2000).

In the last decades an international group of Origenian scholars (many of whom are represented as authors in this present volume) have assembled at regular intervals for colloquia on different aspects of Origen's world and intellectual culture. The papers from these gatherings have been regularly issued as the *Origeniana* series. They contain a mass of the latest scholarly research on the Alexandrian theologian and are a primary resource for futher work. Some essays from the *Origeniana* series appear in the select list above, but the complete list of studies in English, French, German, and Italian is truly exhaustive, a fact which itself testifies to the remarkable resurgence of interest in Origen from the latter part of the twentieth century onward. Details of the series are below.

ORIGENIANA SERIES

Origeniana. (1). Premier Colloque International des Études origéniennes (Montserrat, 18–21 septembre 1973) dirigé par H. Crouzel, G. Lomiento, J. Rius-Camps. Quaderni di Vetera Christianorum 12. Bari, 1975.

Origeniana Secunda. Second Colloque International des Études origéniennes (Bari, 20–23 septembre 1977), texts rassemblés par H. Crouzel and A. Quacquarelli. Quaderni di Vetera Christianorum 15. Bari, 1980.

Origeniana Tertia. The Third International Colloque for Origen Studies (University of Manchester, September 7–11, 1981); papers edited by R. P. C. Hanson and H. J. Crouzel. Rome, 1985.

Origeniana Quarta. Die Referate des 4. Internationalen Origenes-kongresses (Innsbruck, 2–6 September 1984), hrsg. von L. Lies. Innsbrucker theologische Studien 19. Innsbruck-Wien, 1987.

Origeniana Quinta. Papers of the 5th International Origen Congress (Boston College, 14–18 August 1989), edited by R. J. Daly. Bibliotheca Ephemeridum Theologicarum Lovaniensium 105. Louvain, 1992.

Origeniana Sexta. Origène et la Bible. Actes du Colloquium Origenianum Sextum (Chantilly, 30 aout–3 septembre 1993), edited by G. Dorival, A. Le Boulluec, et al. Bibliotheca Ephemeridum Theologicarum Lovaniensium 118. Louvain: Peeters, 1995.

Origeniana Septima. Origenes in den Auseinandersetzungen des 4. Jahrhunderts, hrsg. von W. A. Bienert and U. Kuhnweg. Bibliotheca Ephemeridum Theologicarum Lovaniensium 137. Louvain, 1999.

Origeniana Octava. Acts of the Eighth International Origen Colloquium (held in Pisa. August 2001), edited by L. Perrone. Forthcoming, Louvain, 2003.